Building the Caliphate

Building the Caliphate

Construction, Destruction, and Sectarian Identity in Early Fatimid Architecture

Jennifer A. Pruitt

Yale University Press New Haven and London

Published with assistance from the University of Wisconsin–Madison Office of the Vice Chancellor for Research and Graduate Education with funding from the Wisconsin Alumni Research Foundation.

Published with support from the Fund established in memory of Oliver Baty Cunningham, a distinguished graduate of the Class of 1917, Yale College, Captain, 15th United States Field Artillery, born in Chicago September 17, 1894, and killed while on active duty near Thiaucourt, France, September 17, 1918, the twenty-fourth anniversary of his birth.

yalebooks.com/art

Designed by Leslie Fitch
Jacket designed by Jeff Wincapaw
Set in Crimson and Source Sans Pro type by Julie Allred, BW&A Books, Inc.
Printed in China by Regent Publishing Services Limited

Library of Congress Control Number: 2019940765

ISBN 978-0-300-24682-7

A catalogue record for this book is available from the British Library.

This paper meets the requirements of ANSI/NISO Z39.48-1992 (Permanence of Paper).

10 9 8 7 6 5 4 3 2 1

Jacket illustrations: (front) detail of fig. 5.9; (back) fig. 4.1
Frontispiece: detail of fig. 4.1

For Josie and Eve—the lights of my life

CONTENTS

Acknowledgments ix

Introduction 1

1 The City Illuminated 13

2 A Contested Peace for the Churches 47

3 Al-Hakim's Esoteric Urbanism 69

4 Construction, Destruction, and Concealment under the "Mad Caliph" 95

5 Rebuilding the Fatimid City 127

Conclusion 153

Notes 161

Bibliography 180

Photo Credits 198

Index 199

ACKNOWLEDGMENTS

I owe thanks to the many wonderful teachers, friends, family, and colleagues who have made contributions to this project over the years. My research into Fatimid architecture began as a doctoral dissertation at Harvard University, where I had the honor and privilege to work with not one but two brilliant scholars of Islamic art history—Gülru Necipoğlu and David Roxburgh. Their stimulating questions, critiques, and encouragement greatly informed the current project from beginning to end. I am indebted to them for the support, guidance, inspiration, and model of scholarship they have provided. I only hope I can live up to their example. I would also like to thank Nasser Rabbat for his contributions to this study. His deep knowledge of Egypt and brilliant insights encouraged me to constantly rethink my work and push it in exciting new directions.

I would also like to thank my professors at Smith College, in particular Brigitte Buettner, John Davis, Barbara Kellum, and Dana Leibsohn. Not only did they inspire my early interest in art history, they later gave me my first opportunity to teach my own courses, offering invaluable feedback on my research as I navigated the stormy waters of the academic job market.

I conducted research for this project in Egypt, Italy, Palestine, Spain, Syria, Tunisia, and the United Kingdom, with the support of grants from the Fulbright IIE, the American Research Center in Egypt, the Institute of Ismaili Studies, the Aga Khan Program for Islamic Architecture, Harvard University, Smith College, and the University of Wisconsin–Madison. For their assistance, I thank Matthew Adams, Farhad Daftary, Deanna Dalrymple, Noha el-Gindi, Amira Khattab, Bruce Lohof, Gerry Scott, and Cynthia Verba. While conducting my research, I benefited greatly from the guidance and assistance of scholars, curators, and fellow researchers. In particular, I thank Muhammad Abbas, Iman Abdulfattah, Jere Bacharach, Jonathan Bloom, Fatemah al-Buloshi, Simonetta Calderini, Sheila Canby, Stefano Carboni, Delia Cortese, Edmund de Unger, Bassem al-Halac, Gordon Harvey, Zahi Hawass, Abeer Heider, Ibrahim Jibril, Yael Lempert, Ayelet Lester, Ashraf Nageh, Bernard O'Kane, Ben Outhwaite, Seif el-Rashidi, Sobhi Sabir, George Scanlon, Ola Seif, Peter Sheehan, Tarek Swelim, Osama Talaat, and Nicholas Warner for their help and feedback. I am particularly grateful to Bernard O'Kane, for early previews of his database of Egyptian inscriptions, and for sharing images of the Mosque of al-Hakim for this publication. I also thank Paul Walker, who offered valuable, early feedback on this project and generously shared his unpublished research on the life of al-Hakim.

I have been delighted to complete this book in the supportive environs of the University of Wisconsin–Madison. While in Madison, I received a semester fellowship at the Institute for Research in the Humanities and a First Book award, which brought a group of scholars together to offer me feedback on my manuscript. In addition, support for this research was provided by the University of Wisconsin–Madison Office of the Vice Chancellor for Research and Graduate Education with funding from the Wisconsin Alumni Research Foundation. At UW, I would like to give particular thanks to Carolina Alarcon, Anna Andrzejewski, Diane Bollant-Peschl, Shira Brisman, Suzy Buenger, Nick Cahill, Jill Casid, Preeti Chopra, Tom Dale, Hendry Drewal, Sam England, Kelly Fox, Susan Friedman, Gail Geiger, Sara Guyer, Steve Hutchinson, Teddy Kaul, Yuhang Li, Nancy Rose Marshall, Ann Smart Martin, Steve Nadler, Névine el-Nossery, Gene Phillips, Mitra Sharafi, Anna Simon, and Chris Stricker. For their feedback during the First Book seminar, I offer my deepest gratitude to Dede Ruggles and Yasser Tabbaa. I also thank the students at UW–Madison for keeping me on my toes, inspiring me with their brilliance, and making this all worth doing. In particular, I thank Ahmed Abdelazim for his help chasing footnotes and drawing up plans for the final stages of this project.

My thoughts on interfaith relations in the medieval Mediterranean developed significantly during a month-long residence at the National Endowment for the Humanities Institute in Barcelona. Thank you, in particular, to Heather Badamo, Brian Catlos, Sarah Davis-Secord, Marie Kelleher, and Sharon Kinoshita for their insights during this wonderful month.

So many art historians have offered ideas during talks, feedback on this draft, or other help. For their insights, I thank Glaire Anderson, Abigail Balbale, Persis Berlekamp, Patricia Blessing, Walter Denny, Margaret Graves, Christiane Gruber, Eva Hoffman, Joseph Connors, Karen Leal, Stephennie Mulder, Andras Riedlmayer, Mariam Rosser-Owen, Ünver Rüstem, Matt Saba, Yasmine al-Saleh, Sharon Smith, and Heghnar Watenpaugh.

It has been a pleasure to work with Yale University Press, especially Katherine Boller, Seth Ditchik, Mary Mayer, Raychel Rapazza, and Kate Zanzucchi, as well as free-lance copyeditor Alison Hagge, proofreader Glenn Perkins, indexer Enid Zafran, and cartographer Bill Nelson. I thank them for their thoroughness and efficiency and for making this such a manageable process.

The greatest joy of my academic trajectory has been the wonderful friendships I have made. Many of these individuals went above and beyond the call of duty in not only offering intellectual sustenance but in being the best of friends. I thank Ladan Akbarnia, Chanchal Dadlani, Matt Ellis, Emine Fetvaci, Alicia Walker, and Suzan Yalman for always making me glad I went down this path. I offer the greatest thanks to my Skype writing buddies and Cairo besties, Carmen Gitre and Shana Minkin, who made this process a lot less lonely. I love you all.

Then there are the people who just keep me (relatively) sane. For their laughter, love, and help along the way, I thank Annaliese Beery, Lisa Cooper, Ozzie Ercan, Maddie Jansen, Valerie Maine, Makenna Peterson, Soyang Phunktsok, Sara Pruss, Claire Reed, Jordan Rosenblum, and the fierce ladies of the best book club in the world. For my family members, who put up with me, thank you to Nancy Collins, Kevin Collins, Cheryl Hammond, Craig Hammond, and Karen Kovacs.

As happens with any long journey, in the process of completing this book, I lost dear friends and family. I am grateful to the memory of my friends Ann Musser and Betty Reed; my grandmothers, Virginia Kovacs and Jody Pruitt; and my father, Thomas Pruitt. I am sorry I can't celebrate the completion of this project with you but thank you for making life brighter while you were here.

Most of all, I am so very grateful to Mark, Josie, and Evie Hammond. To quote a toddler I know: "You're my best friends. I love you too much." Mark, I am forever thankful for your unwavering support, friendship, humor, and flexibility. You encouraged me to pursue this path, traipsed around the world with me, reminded me of our great fortune, and always kept me laughing. But I'm dedicating this book to the kids, because I think they'll get a bigger kick out of it.

Introduction

Circa 1010 CE, the "mad" Egyptian caliph, al-Hakim bi-Amr Allah, engaged in one of the most enigmatic acts in the history of Islamic architecture. Seven years after sponsoring masterfully carved, illuminated minarets, replete with esoteric Ismaili Shiʿi symbolism, the caliph ordered the covering of his own towers by an austere, brick casing. The new minaret bastions obscured the visible signs of Shiʿism and the bombastic carving of the original towers in favor of a more generic architectural style and Qurʾanic inscription—one that would be familiar to Sunni and Shiʿi Muslims alike.

In the same year that he ordered this curious concealment, al-Hakim called for the destruction of the most important church in Christendom—the Church of the Holy Sepulcher in Jerusalem. This act would initiate a frenzy of church destructions by the ruler throughout his empire. Eventually, the destruction of the Holy Sepulcher would act as a rallying cry to Latin Crusaders to wrest the Holy Land from Muslim hands—a struggle that would define Muslim-Christian relations in the centuries to come. However, it was a Christian who wrote the letter containing al-Hakim's order to destroy the famous church. Traumatized by his role in the event, the scribe spent the remainder of his days beating his own offending hand against the ground, tearing to shreds the fingers that drafted the order and cursed the church.[1]

These two architectural moments illuminate the complex relationship between architectural space and religious identity in the medieval Islamic world. In the case of the Holy Sepulcher, the Christian scribe occupied a high position in the caliph's court in Cairo with intimate access to the Muslim ruler. At the same time, he felt a profound allegiance to a Christian space in distant Jerusalem—a space he had likely never seen. The change in the minarets' appearance and Qurʾanic content points to a different negotiation of religious identities—between the esoteric beliefs of the Ismaili Shiʿi Fatimids and those of their majority Sunni populations.

These acts of destruction and concealment serve as a fulcrum for this book, which investigates the architecture of the Fatimids, a medieval Ismaili Shiʿi dynasty that founded Cairo (al-Qahira) as a capital city and dominated the early medieval Mediterranean (fig. 0.1).[2] Generally considered a golden age of multicultural, interfaith tolerance, the Fatimid era was characterized by an efflorescence of art and architecture.[3]

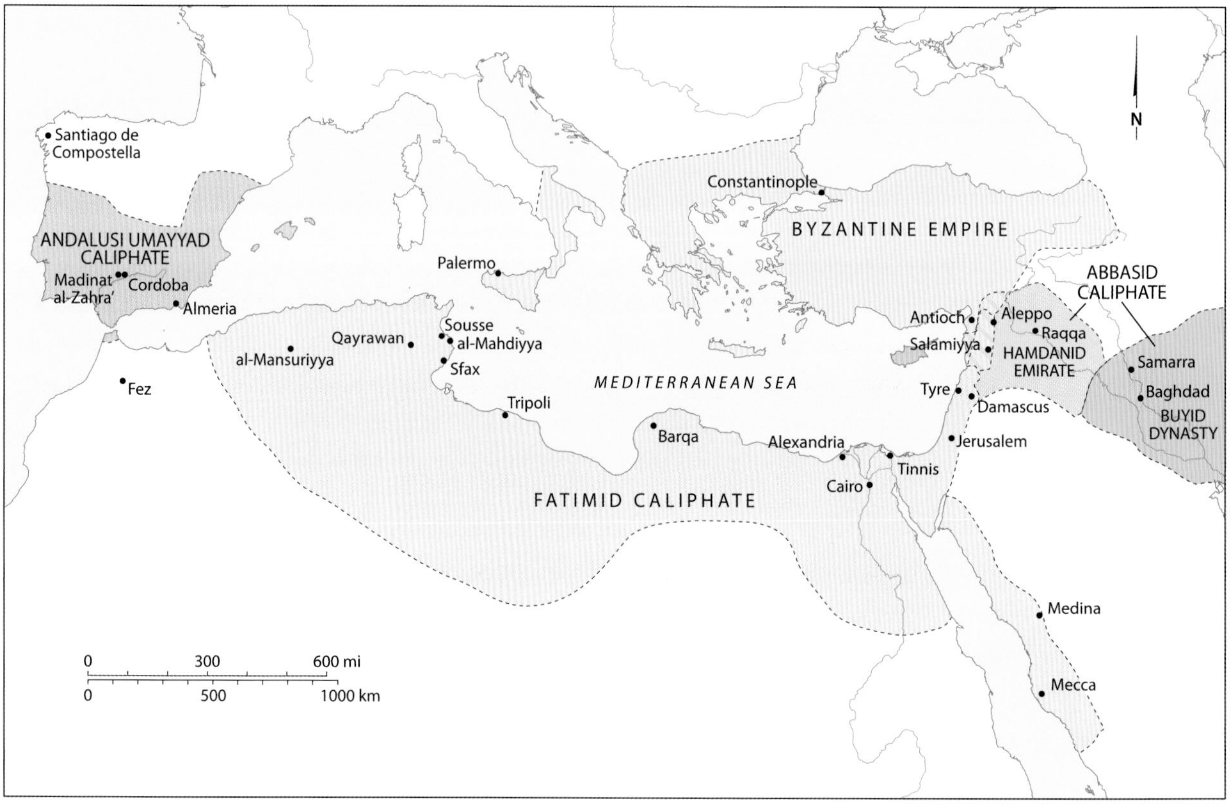

FIGURE 0.1

Map of the Mediterranean, ca. 1000

The single exception offered to this narrative is the reign of al-Hakim bi-Amr Allah (r. 996–1021). Notorious as a psychotic destroyer of churches and synagogues and as a cruel persecutor of Christians, Jews, and women, al-Hakim also sponsored significant architectural projects that would forever change the roles of Cairo and Jerusalem in the world. Rather than treating al-Hakim's reign as an exception, this study integrates his projects into a larger narrative about the negotiation of religious identity through architecture in the Fatimid realm. By considering Fatimid acts of destruction and construction as part of a unified building program, this book problematizes the simplistic notion of an age of artistic cooperation temporarily disrupted by a mad man.

It is often assumed that artistic efflorescence was a function of religious tolerance in the medieval Mediterranean. However, conflict, destruction, and difference played a crucial, productive role in the formation of medieval Islamic architecture, with interfaith contact and courtly exchange acting as places of both unity and rupture. Pervasive, reductive paradigms in scholarship often treat medieval Islamic culture as a locus of tolerance or as an example of a "clash of civilizations."[4] The prevailing narrative of Christians, Jews, Sunnis, and Shiʿa participating in a shared urban life and working in the same artistic mode is certainly a part of the story of medieval Islamic architecture. However, architecture could also act as a stage for competing claims of caliphal legitimacy and as a battleground for local and global sectarian conflicts.

This book analyzes the role of multivalent sectarian identities in the patronage of the early Fatimid rulers. Employing sources that have not been previously utilized in art historical studies of Fatimid buildings, it analyzes Arabic sources from Sunni, Shiʿi, and Christian traditions in order to contextualize early Fatimid architecture within the wider Mediterranean and Islamic world and demonstrate how rulers manipulated architectural form and urban topographies to express political legitimacy on a global stage. Fatimid architectural choices were geared not only toward the local interfaith populations of Sunni, Shiʿi, Christian, and Jewish populations. They were also made in conversation with the rival Sunni caliphates—the Iraqi Abbasids and Spanish Umayyads, demonstrating the competitive networks of architectural patronage in the declaration of caliphal legitimacy. In considering the Fatimids beyond the confines of Egypt, I argue that the architectural forms, patronage choices, and even patterns of destruction respond to and articulate these sectarian differences.[5]

THE HISTORICAL CONTEXT AND RELIGIOUS LANDSCAPE OF THE FATIMID EMPIRE

The Fatimids reigned over one of the most powerful, cohesive empires of the medieval Islamic world. From their new capital in Cairo, the Fatimids ruled over the Maghreb, Sicily, Egypt, the Yemen, and much of the Levant. Politically, they were the mightiest Islamic empire and Mediterranean power of the tenth and eleventh century. They also held the upper hand in Islamic religious legitimacy, as they controlled the holy cities of Mecca, Medina, and Jerusalem. However, the Fatimids' power was highly contested, as they were one of three dynasties that had declared themselves caliphs—successors to the Prophet Muhammad and commanders of all Muslims. Immediately following the death of the Prophet Muhammad in 631, individual successors, known as caliphs, followed in his footsteps as leaders of the entire Islamic community. For the next three centuries, the position of caliph was occupied by one man who ruled over the entire Muslim world.

This all began to change when the Fatimid ruler al-Mahdi (r. 909–34) directly opposed the Sunni Abbasid caliphate by declaring himself and his Ismaili Shiʿi dynasty a rival caliphate in 909. The Fatimid declaration of the caliphate provoked a third declaration—the Umayyads in Cordoba deemed themselves caliphs in 929 under ʿAbd al-Rahman III (r. 929–61). Thus, the nature of Islamic rule was forever changed. The monolithic power structure of the Umayyads and Abbasids splintered as these three dynasties fought for religious and political control over the Muslim world, each vying to be recognized as the rightful "Commander of the Faithful" (*amīr al-muʾminīn*) to all Muslims. All three caliphates relied on shared visual expressions of legitimacy.[6] Congregational mosques in the hypostyle form and luxurious palace-cities were shared by the three dynasties. In addition, caliphal prerogatives such as naming the ruler in the Friday sermon (*khuṭba*), minting coins (*sikka*) with the ruler's name, and producing official state textiles (*ṭirāz*) were used to declare the legitimacy of the respective caliphates and could be wielded as forms of competition.[7]

Along with the two other Muslim caliphates, the Fatimids vied for power with the Christian Byzantines, who ruled from Constantinople. The two dynasties were frequently engaged in territorial battles on the frontiers of Syria—battles that, in the period under consideration here, would increasingly be defined in terms of a holy war between Christianity and Islam. In addition to war, diplomatic missions, artistic exchange, and competition all characterized the dynamics between these superpowers.

Religious identity during the Fatimid period was kaleidoscopic in its complexity, defined as much by fracture as by unity. This complexity defined relations among diverse sects of Muslims, Christians, and Jews, in which fine-grained differences in religious doctrine formed the boundaries between communal identities. Among Muslims, the Fatimids were distinguished, both from the majority of their subjects and from the other caliphates, by their Ismaili Shiʿism. As Shiʿi Muslims, the Fatimids traced their lineage back to the Prophet Muhammad, through his son-in-law ʿAli, daughter Fatima, from whom they acquired their name, and grandson Husayn. According to the Shiʿa, during his lifetime, the Prophet resolutely selected ʿAli as his successor. Therefore, each subsequent caliph should be descended from this family line. To the Ismaili branch of Shiʿism, only the branch of descendants through Ismaʿil b. Jaʿfar al-Sadiq (d. 765) could rightfully lead the community.[8]

For the Fatimids, the ruler had a dual designation. As in the Umayyad and Abbasid context, the Fatimid ruler was a caliph—the commander of the faithful who followed in the footsteps of the Prophet in leading the Muslim community. However, to Ismailis, the Fatimid ruler held a special significance as the Imam—a divinely ordained, supreme, infallible figure who had final authority in both religious and social affairs. As such, the Fatimid Imam was the exclusive source of religious knowledge (*ʿilm*), a role not shared by the Sunni caliphs.

As the living embodiment and transmitter of the truth, the Imam was the final authority on matters of religious significance. He alone had access to the true meaning of the Qur'an and hadith, the meanings of which had been lost to or misinterpreted by ordinary humans. This was a drastically different practice from their Sunni counterparts, who strictly rejected the Shiʿi view of the Imam's divinity and omnipotence. Instead, Sunni Muslims were focused on recovering the traditions of the Prophet through legalistic analysis of the Qur'an, hadith, and precedent. These sources were interpreted and formed into Islamic law (*sharīʿa*) by the religious scholars (*ʿulamā'*), whose interpretations often conflicted with the ruler.[9]

A second fundamental difference between the Fatimids and their Sunni rivals was their espousal of the relationship between the esoteric (*bāṭin*) and exoteric (*ẓāhir*). In Ismailism, everything in existence consists of both a visible, *ẓāhir* aspect and a hidden, *bāṭin* essence.[10] To Ismailis, Islamic acts, such as daily prayer (*ṣalāt*), pilgrimage (*hajj*), and the performance of charity (*zakāt*), represented the *ẓāhir* aspect of Islam, which was to be practiced by all. However, the *bāṭin* significance of Islamic practice, along with the true meaning of the Qur'an and hadith, were known only to the Imam.[11] These truths were revealed gradually to the faithful through a system of allegorical interpretation (*ta'wīl*). Further distinguishing the Ismailis from their Sunni counterparts was their heterodox belief that cosmic and human history was cyclical and that the *bāṭin* truths were shared by all the Abrahamic faiths.

For Ismailis, the network of believers was called the mission (*daʿwa*), the fundamental operational unit of the medieval community. The *daʿwa* functioned as a clandestine missionary operation, composed of a hierarchically organized system of individual missionaries (*dāʿ*īs), who would secretly and gradually indoctrinate new believers into the Ismaili worldview and foment dissent against Sunni rivals. Ismaili *dāʿ*īs were dispersed throughout the Islamic world and were obligated to lead inconspicuous lives, blending in with the general urban population to avoid detection. Trade was a popular form of work for the *dāʿ*īs, bringing them into the medieval Mediterranean network of international exchange.[12]

Patricia Crone has evocatively characterized the relationship between the Imam and his *dāʿ*īs, noting that the Imam acted as "a conduit of supernatural knowledge that poured into the local missionary."[13] For the Ismailis, then, the Imam was the storehouse of divine knowledge while the *dāʿī* was the receptacle of this knowledge. However, this knowledge transfer was not instantaneous. Instead, it was poured drip by drip into stages of initiates. As a *dāʿī* was brought into the Ismaili fold, he would experience each level of the *bāṭin* truths over time as he became gradually initiated into the hierarchical levels of the *daʿwa*.

The Fatimid espousal of the relationship between the *bāṭin* and *ẓāhir* and their reliance on allegorical interpretation of the laws of Islam drew claims of heresy from rival Sunnis. According to Sunni critics, if the pillars of Islam, the Qur'an, and hadith could only be understood and revealed through allegory by the Imam, why should Muslims bother with the practice of Islam at all? These critiques of the Ismaili belief system led to the characterization of the Ismailis as *bāṭinīs*—a derogatory term used by Sunni Muslims to disparage the Ismailis. In contrast, the Ismailis called themselves "People of Truth" (*ahl al-ḥaqq*) and deemed their opponents "People of the *Ẓāhir*" (*ahl al-ẓāhir*).[14]

As the three caliphates vied for ideological legitimacy, the articulation of sectarian identity was a potent weapon in a war that was often waged through art and architecture. The belief in the sanctity of the Imam and the favoring of the *bāṭin* essence of Islamic teachings made the Fatimids radically different from their rival Sunni caliphs in Cordoba and Baghdad. North Africa became a particularly volatile sectarian battleground between the Fatimids and the Cordoban Umayyads, who ruled as a vehemently anti-Shiʿi, overtly *ẓāhirī* dynasty. After declaring himself a caliph, the Cordoban Umayyad ruler, ʿAbd al-Rahman III, sent letters to rulers in the Maghreb, trumpeting his revival of Islam, his orthodox fight against innovations, and his plans for expansion into the Islamic heartlands, even promising to claim Mecca for the Umayyad cause.[15] These declarations were made to situate the Cordoban Umayyads as the legitimate caliphs against the Fatimids. Along with his letters, the Sunni ruler sent robes of honor (*khilʿa*) and money to sway the loyalty of Maghrebi rulers.[16]

In the period under consideration here, the power of the Abbasid empire was in significant decline, as the starker, ever more complicated, contours of the Sunni-Shiʿi split threatened their legitimacy. The Buyids, a Shiʿi dynasty from the Iranian plateau, controlled Baghdad from 945 to 1055, further fracturing the sectarian identities of the Islamic world (*dār al-Islām*). Although they were Shiʿi, the Buyids differed significantly from the Ismaili Fatimids by adopting Twelver Shiʿism, rather than the Ismaili identity of the Fatimid sect.[17] As Twelvers (*ithnā ʿasharīa*), the Buyids believed that the eleventh Imam had mystically disappeared from the earth in 874. As a result, there was no living Imam who could legitimately rule on this earth, allowing the Buyids to accept the Abbasid caliph as the religious figurehead for the Islamic world, while they reigned as the de facto political leaders.[18] Further complicating the story of Islamic sectarianism in this period, several other powerful Shiʿi sects challenged the Abbasids, each of whom were also religiously distinct from the Fatimids. In particular, the Hamdanids controlled Aleppo in the tenth and early eleventh century; the Idrisids had a base in Morocco; the Uqaylids and Mazyadids operated in northern Syria and central Iran; and the Zaydis controlled the Yemen. Disputes over succession and doctrinal difference meant that these Shiʿi groups were often at odds with each other, in addition to their Sunni rivals.

Thus, the contours of sectarian identity in the tenth- and eleventh-century Islamic world were extraordinarily complex. Today, observers might view the maps delineating caliphal boundaries and imagine the relatively stable borders of the modern nation state. In fact, these borders were organic demarcations, constantly swelling and contracting through wars with competing imperial powers on the frontiers. Among the three caliphates, the boundaries of power were fought not only through military skirmishes but by promoting religious legitimacy through expressions of sectarian difference.

Further contributing to the kaleidoscope of religious identity in the Fatimid era were the complex identities and allegiances of their Christian and Jewish subjects. Like their Abbasid and Umayyad rivals, the Fatimids encountered a diverse community of religious identities. In all three caliphates, Christians and Jews were treated as "People of the Book" (*ahl al-kitāb*), as they shared the same prophetic tradition with Islam. As a result, Christians and Jews were considered to be living under Islamic protection (*dhimma*); their religious difference was tolerated in exchange for a special tax (*jizya*) paid to the caliphate as well as other provisions. The religious minorities living under the *dhimma* were known as *dhimmīs*.[19] The treatment of *dhimmī* monuments—particularly Christian churches—was a central aspect of the Fatimid architectural landscape and will be explored in detail in this study.

SOURCES FOR FATIMID ARCHITECTURE

This book is based on field research throughout the lands of the caliphs. While Fatimid patronage is often considered as a purely Egyptian phenomenon, my research brought me to the architectural sites and museum collections of Egypt, Tunisia, Spain, Syria, and Palestine. These travels form the basis of my architectural analysis. In order to consider the role of architecture in negotiating the complex religious identities of the empire, I incorporate sources that are rarely used in architectural history. For the facts and architectural description, the well-known compilations of al-Maqrizi (d. 1442) and the Persian, Ismaili traveler Nasir-i Khusraw (d. 1088) are used. These Islamic sources are considered alongside Christian sources on the status of churches under the Fatimids. Finally, I integrate newly available medieval Ismaili sources, which offer a valuable intellectual framework for understanding Fatimid patronage. Integrating a discussion of the era's best-known monuments with a consideration of buildings that no longer remain, demolition programs under each caliph, and changes to the urban fabric, this study elucidates the sophisticated architectural programs of the early Fatimid caliphs, contextualized through a close analysis of Sunni, Ismaili, and Christian textual sources.

While many medieval sources describe the Fatimid empire, scholars face several obstacles in constructing an accurate history of the empire. Although the Fatimids were famous for having one of the richest libraries in the medieval world, the library and many of its official documents were later destroyed. As a result, our knowledge of Fatimid history is based largely on Mamluk-era (fourteenth- to sixteenth-century) sources, which include eyewitness accounts from Fatimid-era historians. Mamluk historians, writing centuries after the fall of the Fatimids, often approach the dynasty with a Sunni bias, viewing the Fatimids as a heretical blight on the history of Egypt.[20] These large, sweeping, Mamluk histories tend to privilege information about courtly events and omit the nonimperial point of view. Likewise, their insight into the Ismaili teachings and activities of the *da'wa* is limited.

A prominent exception to the typical Sunni bias against the Fatimids can be found in the prolific and thorough writings of the fifteenth-century Mamluk historian Taqi al-Din Ahmad b. ʿAli al-Maqrizi. Although a Sunni writing in the Mamluk age, al-Maqrizi admired the Fatimids and accepted their genealogical claims, linking them to ʿAli.[21] Presumably, al-Maqrizi lacked exposure to Ismaili literature and, therefore, his accounts of the Fatimids omit key theological differences, such as the Ismaili concepts of *bāṭin*, *ẓāhir*, and cyclical history. Instead, al-Maqrizi treats the Fatimids' belief system simply as the Islamic legal school (*maddhab*) of ʿAli, not so distinct from his own Sunni beliefs.[22] Al-Maqrizi's desire to convey a less-biased consideration of Fatimids can also be seen in his privileging of contemporary, Egyptian sources over unfavorable sources from Syria and elsewhere. As a geographical, topographical, and historical tome on Egypt, al-Maqrizi's *Al-Mawāʿiẓ wa-l-iʿtibār bi dhikr al-khiṭaṭ wa-l-āthār* (Exhortations and instructions on the districts and antiquities; known in brief as *Al-Khiṭaṭ*) is an unrivaled source of information about Fatimid Egypt, particularly as a source on urban history and architecture in al-Qahira and Fustat-Misr. In addition, his *Ittiʿāẓ al-ḥunafāʾ bi-akhbār al-aʾimma al-Fāṭimiyyīn al-khulafāʾ* (Lessons for the seekers of the truth on the history of Fatimid Imams and caliphs; known in brief as *Ittiʿāẓ*) is an indispensable reference for historical events.[23]

While al-Maqrizi has long been utilized by scholars to understand the Fatimids, recent publications of primary sources by the Institute of Ismaili Studies shed new light on the previously mysterious aspects of the Ismaili sect. Since the early twentieth century, scholars have had greater access to hitherto unknown Ismaili sources. Previously, the secretive nature of the Ismaili mission and the destruction of the Fatimid library limited our knowledge of Ismaili sources.[24] However, medieval sources were copied and kept in Ismaili hands throughout the world. Since its foundation, the Institute has published dozens of Ismaili sources and studies. One of its stated missions is to rectify the anti-Ismaili bias in previous scholarship, which had been based on Sunni historiographers, Crusaders, and Abbasid propagandists who had labeled the Ismailis as a heretical sect.[25] In general, the primary sources published by the Institute of Ismaili Studies are concerned with theological and philosophical issues, rather than historical chronicles. However, many of these works offer valuable insight into the intellectual and religious history of the Fatimids, offering an invaluable contextualization of the era. This study, in particular, draws on the writing of a *dāʿī* from al-Hakim's era, al-Kirmani. A deep analysis of al-Kirmani's work forms the basis of chapter 4, allowing for a more fully contextualized historical understanding of the movement under this unusual ruler.

This study also draws on several important Christian sources from the period.[26] One of the most important of these is *Taʾrīkh baṭārikat al-kanīsa al-Miṣriyya* (*The History of the Patriarchs of the Egyptian Church*), written by several authors over a few centuries. The section of greatest interest to the Fatimid historian is the volume containing information on the period from the Arab conquest in 640 until 1046. This volume was written in Coptic by Michael, the Bishop of Tinnis, circa 1051. The text was later translated into Arabic.[27] The aim of its author was to record the biographies of the Coptic patriarchs and exalt the Coptic faith above all others. It also contains historical information about the Fatimid dynasty and recounts incidents relating to Egypt's Christian community. The historical details are blended seamlessly with hagiography and stories of miracles, awe-inspiring events, and anecdotes illustrating the superiority of Monophysite (Coptic) Christians over Muslims, Melkite Christians, and Jews. Because of this combination of fact and fantasy and the clear ideological bias of this text, it is difficult to rely on it for specific historical facts and chronologies. However, it is exceedingly rich in offering glimpses of the Coptic community's attitudes toward historical events and offers a unique view of urban-caliphal relations in the Fatimid period. Reconsidering the well-known Fatimid monuments in light of these sources allows for a syncretic model for understanding the early caliphate's architectural and urban agenda and a more nuanced method of examining the interactions between competing religions and caliphates in the medieval Islamic world.

CHAPTER OUTLINE

Chapter 1, "The City Illuminated," introduces the first Fatimid cities: al-Mahdiyya, al-Mansuriyya, and Cairo. Today, our understanding of Cairo is informed by its enduring role as a capital city and center of a millennium of Islamic history. However, it was likely intended to be the Fatimids' temporary capital on the road to conquering eastern Islamic lands. The early Fatimid architectural projects in Cairo are iconic—the Mosque of al-Azhar, the Mosque of al-Hakim (known in the Fatimid era as the Mosque of al-Anwar), and, most importantly, the Fatimid palace-city itself. However, the Fatimids continued a pattern that was established in the Maghreb, in which the city and its buildings were developed according to the esoteric elements of Ismaili Shiʿism. Fatimid architectural projects in this early period challenge our modern understanding of the parameters of sacred space; for the Ismailis, it was the palace rather than the mosque that was more religiously significant—whether it was in a temporary locale in Tunisia or the enduring capital of Cairo.

Chapter 2, "A Contested Peace for the Churches," complicates the notion of early Fatimid tolerance by exploring the status of Christian monuments beyond the palace-city's walls. Drawing on medieval Christian sources, it argues that although the early Fatimids were relatively tolerant of their Christian populations, this alliance was often fraught. Architecture played a crucial role in the articulation of this relationship, with Christian churches acting as proxies for the Christian community at large. In the medieval sources, Christian communities profoundly identified with their buildings. The physical condition of the churches—whether they were in good shape or had fallen into disrepair—acted as a barometer, indicating the status of the Christian community at any given time. The sources indicate that early Fatimid tolerance was highly contested, with mounting resentment from Cairo's Sunni Muslim majority toward the Imam-caliph's openness to the Christian population. Sources describe instances of mob violence against churches; controversies surrounding caliphal support of these monuments; and a famous miracle, in which the Christian community literally moved a mountain in order to rebuild a ruined church. Thus, even in this period of relative tolerance, the obstacles to church restoration and construction were substantial.

Chapter 3, "Al-Hakim's Esoteric Urbanism," considers the early years of the enigmatic caliph's patronage. Under al-Hakim, the first caliph born in the city, Cairo became an enduring capital of a great empire. Although al-Hakim's rule is generally known as a psychotic, destructive blip in the narrative of Fatimid coexistence, his reign was not merely destructive. On the contrary, al-Hakim patronized many important mosque projects and an observatory and established a major center of learning, drawings scholars from around the world, within the new capital city. Most notably, al-Hakim completed the mosque named for him, with a particular focus on its two famous minarets. Generally considered masterworks of Islamic stone carving, these minarets feature rich Ismaili symbolism, making them unique in the history of Islamic art. Al-Hakim departed from earlier Fatimid tradition by establishing mosque projects beyond the royal city and promoting more explicitly urban concerns. Indeed, his architectural commissions in the city suggest an investment in Cairo as a permanent capital that had not been seen under his predecessors. However, although the status of the city changed, al-Hakim's patronage continued the explicitly Ismaili idiom of his predecessors, building the city according to the esoteric aspects of the faith. His architectural priorities are mirrored in his treatment of his subjects and their monuments. In this early phase of al-Hakim's reign, there is evidence of increasing persecution of his subjects, but these are directed not only at Christians and Jews, but at Sunnis as well. However, in the treatment of Christian monuments, we see him following Fatimid precedent, allowing for the reconstruction and even construction of Christian buildings.

Chapter 4, "Construction, Destruction, and Concealment under the 'Mad Caliph,'" investigates al-Hakim's most notorious architectural destructions, integrating them with a discussion of his new architectural commissions. Focusing on the destruction of the Holy Sepulcher in Jerusalem and the concealment of the minarets at the Mosque of al-Hakim, the chapter argues that his projects in this period recast the ruler from the esoteric Imam of the Ismaili Shiʿi faith to an ideal Islamic ruler whose primary role was to "command the good and forbid the bad" to his Sunni and Shiʿi subjects. Considering architecture in light of contemporary religious tracts demonstrates that this claim was made in direct opposition to his caliphal rivals in Iraq and Spain. Uniting a consideration of construction and demolition, this chapter calls for a fundamental reevaluation of the nature of destruction under al-Hakim, removing it from the context of despotic whimsy to consider it as one component of the large-scale political and architectural reorientation of the empire.

Chapter 5, "Rebuilding the Fatimid City," investigates the aftermath of al-Hakim's reign, arguing for a productive outcome of his destruction. Al-Hakim's destructions irrevocably changed the architectural fabric of Cairo and Jerusalem and the roles occupied by each in Islamic thought. Focusing on the rise of the Druze movement in the late years of al-Hakim's reign and in the reconstruction of Jerusalem under his successor, al-Zahir, this chapter suggests that al-Zahir engaged in an unprecedented level of patronage in Jerusalem, investing in large-scale restorations of the Dome of the Rock and the Aqsa Mosque, thereby changing the status of the city in Islamic thought. Ultimately, al-Zahir's renovations emphasized a tradition of Islamic orthodoxy, aimed at undoing the excesses of al-Hakim's late reign. Thus, although the status of Jerusalem is rightfully seen as changing irrevocably with the coming of the Crusades, this chapter argues that its role in Islamic thought had already changed as a result of al-Hakim's destruction of the Holy Sepulcher, pointing to the ways that destruction was generative, acting as a catalyst for the invigoration of the Islamic city.

1 The City Illuminated

> After passing through many winding passages and devious ways, whose wonders might well detail even the busiest men in contemplation, they reached the palace itself. Here still larger groups of armed men and throngs of attending satellites testified by their appearance and numbers to the incomparable glory of their lord. The very aspect of the palace gave indisputable proof of the opulence and extraordinary riches of the monarch . . . curtains embroidered with pearls and gold, which hung down and hid the throne, were drawn aside with [the Imam-caliph's] face unveiled. Seated on a throne of gold, surrounded by some of his privy counsellors and eunuchs, he presented an appearance more than regal.
>
> —William of Tyre on the Fatimid palace in Cairo

> As the pilgrim kissed the [sacred] corner, we kiss the court of your palace.
>
> —Ibn ʿIdhari on the Fatimid palace in al-Mahdiyya

These two passages describe distinct modes of encountering the Fatimid city. For the Crusader author William of Tyre, the Fatimid palace is a site of material wealth and marvels.[1] Winding passages are filled with wonders and throngs of subjects, attesting to the riches of the ruler. The climactic unveiling of the caliph is understood primarily in terms of the rich materials that surround him—the pearls, the gold—and the spectacle of it all. For art historians, the tales of the material splendor of the Fatimid palace and the rich contents of its famous treasury are hallmarks of the dynasty.[2] Textual sources describe the Fatimid penchant for luxury in a palace-city with few material remains. However, Ibn ʿIdhari's poem evoking the Fatimid palace in al-Mahdiyya points to another mode of experiencing the space. Using an allegory of the sacred corner of the kaaba in Mecca, the author describes the Ismaili understanding of the Fatimid palace as a venerated space and sacred pilgrimage site.

Cairo, Mosque of al-Azhar, courtyard, begun 970 (see fig. 1.15)

The Fatimid establishment of Cairo is often considered as a break from Fatimid patronage in the Maghreb. The conquest of Egypt was certainly a turning point for the dynasty and would make Cairo a major Islamic capital for the first time in its history. It is through this lens of Cairo's permanence and legacy that we often view Fatimid architectural history. However, in considering the Fatimid establishment of Cairo along with their earlier Tunisian capitals—al-Mahdiyya and al-Mansuriyya—this chapter argues that architectural patronage in all three capitals followed similar patterns and embodied consistent meanings. Early Fatimid architectural projects in Tunisia and under the first two Imam-caliphs in Cairo embellished the Imam's walled cities according to the needs of the Ismaili community and were focused on the esoteric aspects of the faith. In all three cities, the Fatimid city and its architecture would have been received differently, depending on its viewer. For non-Ismailis, the Fatimid city and its architecture were impressive expressions of wealth, power, and shared Islamic practice. In other words, non-Ismailis encountered the exoteric (*ẓāhir*) aspects of the Fatimid city. For the Ismailis, however, the Fatimid cities contained a more precious, esoteric (*bāṭin*) meaning. To them, the Fatimid city was the dwelling place of the living Imam and was, consequently, the navel of the Ismaili spiritual universe.[3] Even when the capital was never envisioned to be permanent, as was the case for al-Mahdiyya and al-Mansuriyya, any place that contained the presence of the Imam held a special status and functioned as a pilgrimage destination for the faithful. Thus, the question of whether or not Cairo was intended to be a permanent capital is, in some ways, secondary to the fact that any place that housed the living Imam was precious and worthy of elaboration to the Ismaili devotees.

In all three cities, early Fatimid architecture and urban patronage was constructed in conversation and competition with rival caliphates in al-Andalus and Iraq. On the one hand, the Fatimid projects in this period participated in a shared courtly aesthetic, with a reliance on hypostyle mosque plans, elaborate palace-cities, and shared images of courtly life and artistic splendor. However, they were also expressions of a fierce caliphal competition for Islamic legitimacy. Thus, although Fatimid Cairo is often considered as a localized phenomenon, early Fatimid architecture was engaged in broader conversations with rival Islamic powers. In this larger Islamic conversation, architecture and its function expressed the particularities of sectarian identity.

FATIMID CITIES IN THE MAGHREB

The Fatimid conquest of the Maghreb was a watershed moment in the history of the dynasty. A generation after the Fatimid conquest of North Africa, the famed historian and jurist, al-Qadi al-Nuʿman, recorded a prophecy regarding their fate. The prophecy foretold that the "sun of God will rise in the west," indicating the predestined importance of their North African conquest.[4] Prior to their arrival in Tunisia, the Fatimids had operated in secrecy. Although the details of the dynasty's inception are unclear, its roots can be traced to the ninth century in the town of Salamiyya in Syria, which had been the center of the Ismaili mission (*daʿwa*).[5] From this base in the central Islamic lands, the Fatimid leader proclaimed himself as the Mahdi, a messianic figure who would usher in the final age of the world.[6] Al-Mahdi left Salamiyya, traveling across Palestine and through Egypt until he finally settled in Tunisia, near Qayrawan, circa 909. After his arrival, al-Mahdi directly opposed the Sunni Abbasids by declaring himself and his Ismaili Shiʿi dynasty a rival caliphate, forever changing the nature of the dynasty from a network of clandestine individual missionaries (*dāʿīs*), operating in the shadow of the historical record, to a publicly declared caliphate, with a flurry of new chronicles and architectural projects, demonstrating the Fatimid consciousness of their own historic importance.

Al-Mahdi's declaration cleaved the caliphate in two, with the Sunni Abbasids reigning from Baghdad and the Shiʿi Fatimids occupying the Maghreb. Islamic sermons (*khuṭbas*) spread the word of the new rulers to the Muslim community by announcing the new caliph's name and by introducing the new Ismaili prayer formula, calling on the blessings of the Prophet, ʿAli, Hasan, Husayn, and Fatima, thereby articulating the distinct genealogical claims and sectarian identity of the Fatimids clearly to all those gathered for the Friday prayer. Shortly after his conquest, al-Mahdi gave a *khuṭba* to his new subjects, imploring God to conquer "the easts of the lands and its wests" and to offer support "against the iniquitous rebels."[7] The text of this sermon demonstrates that, from the outset, the Fatimids were not content to remain in their North African domain, seeking instead to conquer the east and west, uniting the entire Islamic world under their rule, in direct opposition to the mighty Abbasids and their closer rivals, the Cordoban Umayyads.

The first years of al-Mahdi's North African administration were characterized by an adaptation of former Aghlabid administrative and architectural practices. As vassals to the Abbasids, the Aghlabids had ruled in Tunisia for a century before the Fatimid conquest.[8] Their reign was characterized by an adherence to strict, Maliki Sunnism, administered from their capital in Qayrawan. Upon his conquest of Aghlabid territory, the Fatimid caliph did not construct a new palace immediately but simply moved into the old Aghlabid residences.[9] However, Fatimid rule in Qayrawan was never secure, as its majority Maliki population did not recognize the legitimacy of the Fatimid rulers. To make matters worse, many of their Berber subjects were Seccessionists (Kharijites), who had seceded from ʿAli in the seventh century, declaring that the caliphate could not be inherited. As a result, the Kharijites violently opposed Fatimid rule and imperiled the fledgling dynasty for the next decades.[10]

After only three years of tumultuous rule in Qayrawan, the Fatimids moved once again, to a new capital on the eastern shores of Tunisia, named al-Mahdiyya after its founder.[11] In al-Mahdiyya we begin to see some of the characteristic forms of a walled Fatimid city. Al-Mahdiyya was a highly fortified defensive city, situated on the mile-long Hamma peninsula (fig. 1.1). It could only be approached via a road "narrow as a shoe lace,"[12] choked off by a long, fortified gate known today as "the Dark Vestibule" (*al-saqīfa*

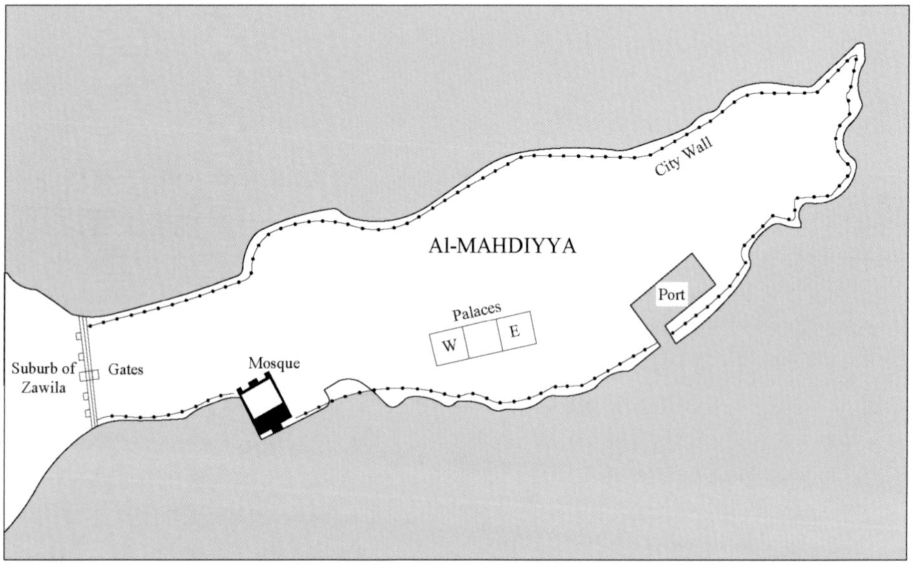

FIGURE 1.1
Plan of al-Mahdiyya, Tunisia, ca. 921

al-kaḥla).[13] On its other sides, al-Mahdiyya was bordered by fortified city walls, shielding the peninsula from sea invasions.

Within this highly protected domain sat the Fatimid palace, mosque, treasury, and mint.[14] Nothing of the Fatimid city remains today, and the scant archaeological evidence makes a detailed reconstruction difficult. However, we know that al-Mahdiyya's mosque was fortified and incorporated into the city walls. It has been renovated to resemble the Fatimid original, based on archaeological evidence.[15] In plan and execution, the mosque looks similar to what is still standing of the Great Mosque of Qayrawan (figs. 1.2–1.3), with the most striking difference being its omission of Qayrawan's distinctive minaret. In lieu of a minaret, the Great Mosque of al-Mahdiyya features a portal with two cistern towers on either side of the facade. In the tenth-century world of caliphal competition, the presence or absence of a minaret became an architectural expression of sectarian identity. For the Shiʿi Fatimids, minarets were not required to execute the call to prayer—in fact, they were discouraged in favor of calling the faithful to prayer from the doorway or roof of a mosque, in the tradition of ʿAli.[16] On the other hand, Sunni mosques in Abbasid realms prominently featured a single minaret, usually directly across from the mihrab, to mark their structural purpose. The Fatimids' replacement of this form with a monumental portal visually marked the Ismaili mosque as distinct from its Sunni rivals.[17]

Al-Mahdiyya established the Fatimid precedent of a walled, sacred royal city that was distinct from the urban areas beyond it. Within the tightly controlled peninsular palace-city, the Ismaili faithful encountered the pure dwelling place of the infallible Imam. While just beyond its boundaries resided the Sunni majority population—including the hostile and volatile Kharijites. The special religious significance the site

FIGURE 1.2
Great Mosque of al-Mahdiyya, Tunisia, completed 921

FIGURE 1.3
Great Mosque of Qayrawan, Tunisia, 9th century

would have had, as the dwelling place of the Imam, can be seen in a poem written at the time of al-Mahdiyya's foundation.

> My congratulations, O generous prince, for your arrival upon which our epoch smiles.
> You have established your camp in a noble land, prepared for you by glorious angels.
> The sanctuary and its environs, its lofty shrines are exalted
> And in the West is an exalted residence where prayer and fasting are accepted:
> It is al-Mahdiyya, sacred and protected, as the sacred city is in Tihama.
> Your footsteps make the ground wherever you tread like the Maqam Ibrahaim.
> Just as the pilgrim kissed the [sacred] corner, so do we kiss the walls of your palace.
> Through the course of time, an empire grows old, its foundations crumble under the
> test of time

But your empire, O Mahdi, will always be young, Time itself will serve it
The world belongs to you and your descendants wherever you may be; It will always find an Imam in you![18]

Ibn ʿIdhari's poem makes explicit a fundamental role of any Fatimid city. As the residence of the Imam, the Fatimid city was, by definition, a sacred space. The poem's reference to Tihama (western Arabia) and evocations of kissing the sacred corner allegorically equate the Fatimid city to Mecca itself, with the sacred corner of the kaaba duplicated in the corner of the Fatimid palace. Ismailis from across the world would gather in al-Mahdiyya to be in the proximity of the living Imam, much as Muslims throughout the world would descend on the kaaba. The poem further tells us that the world belongs to the Imam and his family "wherever you may be," meaning that the sacred function of the Fatimid city as a pilgrimage center was not tied to a specific location but moved with the body of the Imam. The Imam's city, wherever it may be, acted as an ever-changing epicenter of the world, a pilgrimage site equivalent to Mecca by virtue of his presence.

At the same time al-Mahdiyya operated as a sacred center for Ismailis, it also operated as a city fully engaged in a shared Mediterranean artistic culture. Although little remains of al-Mahdiyya's palace, a marble relief evokes the royal life of the time. In the center, a cross-legged ruler holds a cup; to the left, a musician blows a horn while looking toward the seated figure (fig. 1.4). It is a standard scene of the princely cycle, evoking the shared pleasures of the Islamic courts.[19] A similar scene of a seated, cross-legged, cup-bearing figure can be found in other caliphal contexts, including a luster bowl, likely from Abbasid Samarra (fig. 1.5). The seated, cross-legged royal, accompanied by a musician is also commonly found in the Cordoban Umayyad milieu, most beautifully depicted in the Pyxis of al-Mughira (fig. 1.6). Thus, the sculpture from al-Mahdiyya is

FIGURE 1.4
Marble relief with musician and seated ruler, holding a cup, al-Mahdiyya, 10th century, Bardo Museum, Tunis

FIGURE 1.5
Abbasid luster bowl, depicting a man holding a cup and a flowering branch, attributed to Iraq, 10th century, The Metropolitan Museum of Art, New York, 1977.126

FIGURE 1.6
The Pyxis of al-Mughira, detail with prince, his lutist, and fan-bearer, Musée du Louvre, Inv. 4068

part of a larger corpus of stock images of caliphal rulership, making it part of a shared culture of royal depictions. Further contributing to the common language of caliphal rule, in the example from al-Mahdiyya, a band of geometric carving encircles each of the ruler's arms, evoking the text that would have been found on the official state textiles (*ṭirāz*) of the period, one of the most potent representations of power and prestige among all three caliphates.[20] If we consider the relief sculpture from al-Mahdiyya along with Ibn ʿIdhari's poem, we see the two registers of Fatimid palace life evoked. To non-Ismailis, the Fatimid city was much like the relief sculpture—a luxurious site of a court fully engaged in the universal pursuits of Islamic royal life. To the Ismailis, Ibn ʿIdhari's poem points to the deeper meaning of the city as a unique, sacred center, resplendent in the presence of the living Imam.

Al-Mahdiyya remained the Fatimid capital under the reign of al-Mahdi's son al-Qaʾim (r. 935–46), but the capital would be relocated inland under the reign of the third Fatimid caliph, al-Mansur (r. 946–53), in 946. Named Sabra al-Mansuriyya after its founder, the new city adopted the round plan of Abbasid Baghdad, suggesting the Fatimid emulation of and competition with this distant, powerful center.[21] The tenth-century geographer al-Muqaddasi (d. 991) described the similarities between the two cities and noted that the names of many of the palace courts also referenced the splendor of the Islamic east, with one of these named Khawarnaq after the ancient Persian palace. He also recorded that at the center of the city stood the ruler's palace and a congregational mosque known as al-Azhar ("the Radiant")—an epithet that would later be applied to the Fatimids' famous Cairene mosque.[22] Two of the city gates would also set the precedent for those later established in Cairo, with the western gate called Bab al-Futuh and the eastern gate known as Bab Zuwayla.

A poem by Ibn Hani' (d. 973) expressed the inherent pilgrimage role of the Imam's domicile in al-Mansuriyya, writing about the Fatimid Imam-caliph al-Mu'izz:

> We are brought by noble camels in pilgrimage to the sanctuary (*ḥaram*) of the Imam,
> across vast expanses of desert
> Our dust-covered locks are anointed by our coming to kiss the corner (*rukn*) [of his
> palace] . . .
> Will Paradise be permitted to me, now that I have seen one of its open doors?[23]

Ibn Hani''s poem celebrates the arduous journey of the faithful across the desert, only to come close enough to kiss the Imam's palace. Using the phrase "coming to kiss the corner," the poet once again evokes the pilgrimage to Mecca itself, making an Ismaili visit to the Imam's city equivalent to visiting the most sacred city in Islam. In comparing the poetry of Ibn 'Idhari and Ibn Hani', we see that this function was consistent between al-Mahdiyya and al-Mansuriyya.

The establishment of al-Mansuriyya responded to a new dynamic in the Fatimid quest for the caliphate. In 929, the Cordoban Umayyads had joined the Fatimids in declaring themselves a caliphate, resulting in a triad of rival caliphs. Shortly after their declaration, the new Umayyad caliph, 'Abd al-Rahman III, constructed a lavish palace-city called Madinat al-Zahra', close to Cordoba (fig. 1.7).[24] This palace-city similarly adapted Abbasid-style palace forms, though in this case, it was modeled on Abbasid Samarra rather than Baghdad.[25] Both of the new caliphal cities were luxurious stages for ceremonial statecraft and featured elaborate gardens and waterworks. The competitive context of these projects can be seen in their naming conventions. Madinat al-Zahra' and the central mosque of al-Mansuriyya, al-Azhar, rely on the same root letters (z-h-r). Al-Azhar has often been interpreted to refer to the nickname of the dynasty's namesake, Fatima, who was called al-Zahra'. However, the root letters also refer to luminosity or brightness, adding an air of shimmering light to both of the competitive projects.[26]

With their close proximity and historical animosity, the Cordoban Umayyads and Fatimids waged ideological warfare against one another, using art and architecture as weapons in their disputes. This was carried out both in terms of competitive construction—as seen in Madinat al-Zahra' and al-Mansuriyya—and in material destruction. Soon after the Cordoban Umayyad declaration of the caliphate, the *khuṭba* was given in favor of the Fatimid ruler within the Umayyad realm. As punishment for this treachery, the Umayyad ruler 'Abd al-Rahman III destroyed the minbar of the mosque from which this declaration was made. This act was repeated in mosques throughout North Africa, in which Cordoban Umayyad loyalists destroyed minbars in Fatimid realms.[27] To these iconoclasts, the minbar from which the *khuṭba* offering the Fatimids'

FIGURE 1.7
Madinat al-Zahra', the Great Portico, 10th century

name stood as a proxy for the empire itself and its destruction was carried out as an anti-Fatimid sign of their fealty to the Cordoban Umayyads.

Mosques were also poignant sites of ideological battles. Following the Fatimid attack on Almeria in 955, ʿAbd al-Rahman III ordered that the sermons in all Andalusi mosques curse their Fatimid rivals, while the companions of the Prophet and Rashidun were cursed in Fatimid mosques. As a reward, ʿAbd al-Rahman III sent one-fifth of the rewards of his campaigns against Christians, which were used to expand the sanctuary and minaret of the Mosque of Qarawiyyin in Fez. In turn, the Cordoban Umayyads accused the Fatimids of being *bāṭinīs*, who only cared about their esoteric interpretations of Islam and made legal what was forbidden. They asserted that Holy War (jihad) against them was even better than jihad against Christians, an equation that legitimized their alliances with Byzantium against Fatimid forces.[28]

During this period of heated ideological contention, ʿAbd al-Rahman III added a new, monumental minaret to the Great Mosque of Cordoba, distinguishing it from the Fatimid mosques in North Africa, which lacked this form, thereby marking it as a resolutely Sunni structure (fig. 1.8).[29] Later, his son al-Hakam II transformed the mosque into one befitting the new caliphate, adding the famous *maqṣūra* (special enclosure in the mosque reserved for royalty), outfitting it with luxurious mosaic decorations that linked the monument to Syrian Umayyad prototypes (figs. 1.9–1.10) and adding a hierarchical axiality to the monument (fig. 1.11).[30] The *maqṣūra*'s mosaics were created by Byzantine mosaicists from Constantinople, made possible by a new alliance formed between the Cordoban Umayyads and the Byzantines—an alliance that directly threatened the Fatimid cause. The transformation of Cordoba's mosque was carried out in overtly sectarian terms. The tenth-century *maqṣūra* included an innovative tripartite mihrab, with

(CLOCKWISE FROM ABOVE)

FIGURE 1.8
ʿAbd al-Rahman III added a new minaret to the Great Mosque of Cordoba after declaring the caliphate in 929. This minaret was enclosed and transformed into a bell tower after the mosque was converted into a church in the 13th century.

FIGURE 1.9
Great Mosque of Cordoba, interior, 8th century, before the addition of the 10th-century *maqṣūra*

FIGURE 1.10
Great Mosque of Cordoba, 10th-century *maqṣūra* addition

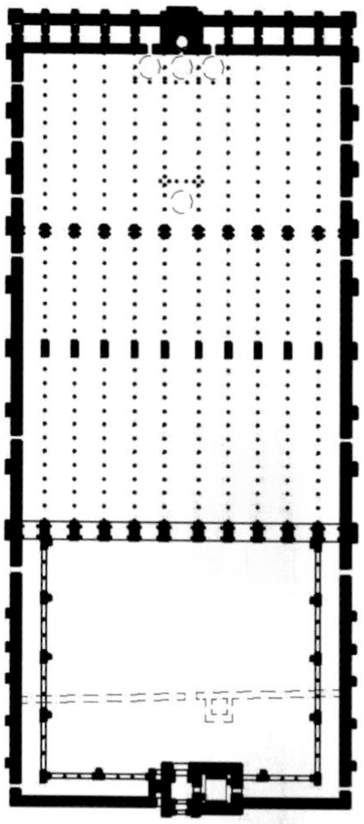

FIGURE 1.11
Cordoba, Great Mosque, plan, after the expansion under al-Hakam II, ca. 962

rooms behind each niche. These rooms housed a potent relic—the blood-splattered pages of ʿUthman's Qur'an, which had been stained during his assassination in Medina in 656. In this way, the luxury of the mosque's renovations declared imperial ambition and the Cordoban Umayyads' courtly refinement. At the same time, the relic housed within the mosque linked the new caliphate directly to the Medinese tradition of Maliki Sunnism, a bloody reminder of their staunch opposition to the Shiʿi Fatimids.[31]

The Maghrebi period of Fatimid rule was temporary, lasting only sixty years and always intended to be a stopping place on the path to ruling over the eastern Islamic heartland. However, despite its temporary status, we see that the development of some of the most important aspects of Fatimid architecture and politics developed there. In al-Mahdiyya and al-Mansuriyya, the most important function of each city was as the dwelling place of the living Imam; his presence made them sacred sites. At the same time, the surviving sculptural relief demonstrates that the Fatimids were fully versed in the shared courtly culture of the Mediterranean.[32]

Moreover, in this period, art and architecture were wielded as weapons in the expression of caliphal legitimacy. Both the Cordoban Umayyads and the Fatimids developed cities that, at their core, served the same functions as their rival Abbasid cities of Samarra and Baghdad, with a palace, mosque, and mint at their centers. They even based the plans of these cities on Abbasid prototypes, all while directly opposing Abbasid rule. Their cities were constructed in response to each other's projects, with naming conventions directly articulating this link. However, in the construction or omission of minarets and, in the case of Cordoba, the inclusion of an overtly sectarian relic, they pointedly distinguished their doctrinal beliefs from one another. The competitive discourse is seen most clearly in the competitive *khuṭbas* of mosques in the region and the subsequent destruction of associated minbars.

THE ESTABLISHMENT OF AL-QAHIRA

The Fatimid Imam-caliph, al-Mansur, would ultimately have a very short reign, dying in the year 953 at the age of forty. His son Maʿadd was given the regnal title al-Muʿizz li-Din Allah ("Mighty for the Religion of God") and was named his successor as the Fatimid Imam-caliph (r. 953–75). Under al-Muʿizz's leadership, the Fatimids finally conquered Egypt in 969—a crucial gain for their eastern ambitions. For generations, Fatimid rulers had attempted to conquer Egypt, launching dozens of unsuccessful campaigns into the country. Not until al-Muʿizz had subdued the Kharijite rebellions was the empire finally able to expand eastward into this strategic land. As had been the case in the Maghreb, Ismaili *dāʿīs* infiltrated the country prior to their conquest, working as merchants and helping to pave ideological inroads for Fatimid rule.[33] The Fatimid general Jawhar led the efforts to conquer the country while al-Muʿizz remained in al-Mansuriyya. This time, Jawhar encountered a land in a state of chaos, ravaged by famine and ruled ineffectually by the Ikhshidids.[34] As a result, the conquest of 969 came easily. After conquering the city, Jawhar spent three years preparing the new city for al-Muʿizz's arrival while the spiritual heart of the empire remained centered around the Imam in al-Mansuriyya.

Under Fatimid rule, Cairo became a capital city of a great empire for the first time in its long history.[35] However, as had been the case in al-Mahdiyya and al-Mansuriyya, the Fatimids encountered preexisting urban populations and architectural marvels. Indeed, the area had been a significant population center since before the seventh-century Arab conquest, with populations centered in the urban enclaves of Fustat, al-Qataʿiʾ, and al-ʿAskar—an area that I will refer to collectively as Fustat-Misr (fig. 1.12).[36] At the center of Fustat-Misr were the mosques of ʿAmr and Ibn Tulun, which continued to be used as significant congregational mosques throughout the Fatimid era.

From the time of Jawhar's arrival, the status of Fustat-Misr's mosques was a key term of surrender for the Muslim community in Egypt. Immediately after taking Cairo, Jawhar met with a delegation consisting of local Hasanid and Husaynid descendents and the supreme judge (*qāḍī*) of the city. With them, he drew up a letter of safety (*amān*), which was preserved in later Mamluk chronicles. This letter swore that the new Fatimid ruler would ensure the security and protection of Egypt, guarantee the safety of travelers and pilgrims, improve the quality of coins, and conduct inheritance laws according to the Qurʾan and the sunna. The status of mosques was a key feature of this letter, which guaranteed that new mosques would be built, old ones restored, and their staffs paid. Thus, the vibrancy of mosques was linked directly to the prosperity of Egypt's Muslim community. Overt sectarian difference was carefully omitted from this letter, which was written instead to assuage the fears and gain the loyalty of the Sunni-majority Egyptian power structure. Jawhar's letter concluded with a discussion of Fatimid religious policy, emphasizing what was common to all Muslims. It guaranteed that Islamic religious acts—including charity, the observance of the Ramadan fast and feast, pilgrimage, prayer, and jihad would continue according to the proscriptions of Islamic law, concluding with the pronouncement that Christians and Jews would be kept in their proper place.[37]

Jawhar's letter of *amān* demonstrates that at the time of the conquest, prior to the arrival of the Imam-caliph, universally Islamic laws were emphasized over a specifically Ismaili system of rule. Likewise, in this period, although the Abbasid caliph's name was replaced by that of al-Muʿizz in the *khuṭbas* of the mosques of ʿAmr and Ibn Tulun, the distinctive Ismaili formula for the call to prayer was not yet added. Instead, Jawhar emphasized the common practice of all Muslims.

In the three years after the Fatimid conquest, prior to al-Muʿizz's arrival in Egypt, Jawhar prepared the palace-city and secured the new administration. After conquering and marching through Fustat-Misr, Jawhar and his armies camped in an area to the north of the preexisting urban agglomerations. This area, which would become the space to the north of al-Qahira's walls, was sparsely populated, containing only the gardens of the former Ikhshidid ruler, Kafur, a Coptic Christian monastery,

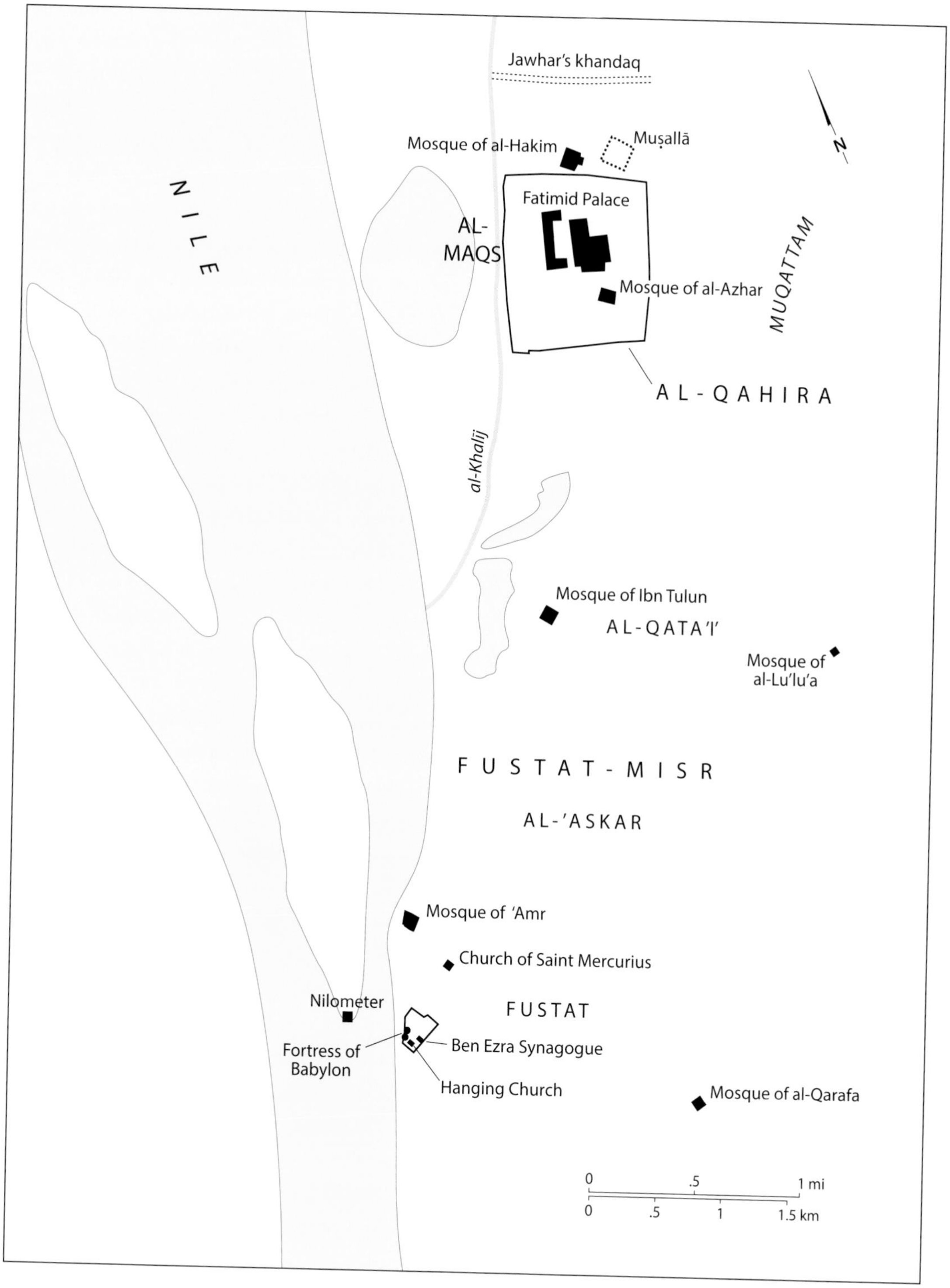

FIGURE 1.12

Map of Cairo, ca. 1000

and a small palace (*qaṣr*).[38] Soon after his arrival, Jawhar constructed a walled enclave on this site. In location, it followed the long-established Islamic Egyptian tradition of constructing an encampment to the north of the preexisting centers. However, in form it resembled the sanctified Ismaili cities of Tunisia. The new enclave—initially named al-Mansuriyya—would be surrounded by mud-brick walls, thereby physically separating the Imam and his retinue from the urban populations to the south. Further recalling the Imam's Maghrebi city, the new al-Mansuriyya adopted the names of two of the old city's gates: Bab al-Futuh and Bab Zuwayla, which stood at either end of the major thoroughfare of both cities.[39] The resonance between the new capital and the old evoked the presence of the Imam-caliph, even if he had not yet moved to his new city.

The new al-Mansuriyya's walls were punctuated by a limited number of entrances—Bab al-Futuh (Conquest Gate) and Bab al-Nasr (Victory Gate) to the north and Bab Zuwayla to the south. The Mamluk historian al-Maqrizi wrote that the city was fortified in order to prevent an attack by the Qarmatians, the Ismaili splinter group that had so violently opposed the early Fatimid rulers and that had just defeated the Fatimid army at Damascus.[40] Adding to the city's fortifications was the addition of a trench (*khandaq*), which ran from the city's canal (*khalīj*) in the west to the Muqattam Hills in the east.[41] As the Qarmatian threat subsided, five more gates were added to the city walls, bringing the total number to eight.[42]

The new Fatimid capital was located strategically for defense, trade, and travel. It was situated between the Muqattam Hills to the east and the ancient canal (*khalīj*), connecting the Nile River to the Red Sea, to the west.[43] Jawhar immediately ordered the construction of a bridge over the canal, connecting the Fatimid city to the port of al-Maqs, just to the west of the walled enclave, thereby integrating the new city into Egypt's rich trade network. Al-Muqaddasi commented on the city's position on the road to Syria, noting that no one could enter Fustat without first passing through al-Qahira.[44]

Soon after conquering Egypt, Jawhar gained a stunning ideological victory for the Ismaili dynasty by conquering Mecca and Medina for the Fatimid cause. As the keeper of the two holiest cities in Islam, al-Mu'izz strengthened his claim to be the "Commander of the Faithful" (*amīr al-mu'minīn*)—the true caliph of the Islamic world. For centuries, Mecca had been an unstable city with tenuous imperial control by the Abbasids. 'Alid groups regularly attacked caravans making the hajj and, at times, even plundered the treasures of the kaaba.[45] After the Fatimids secured the Maghreb, Mecca's precarious status continued, as the city was controlled by the Qarmatians, who blocked hajj caravans and, in 930, massacred thousands of residents of the city, absconding with the black stone of the kaaba, which they brought to their headquarters in Bahrain. By 950, the Qarmatian threat had subsided and Mecca was controlled by 'Alid representatives (*sharīfs*). Even after the Fatimids gained control of the holy cities, the *sharīfs* exerted their independence, going so far as to refuse to support the Fatimids in 976.[46] However, even though imperial control of the city remained elusive, every year the kiswa, the finely crafted textile covering the kaaba, was produced in Egypt and sent by special caravan to the holy city.

In Ramadan of 973, the center of the Ismaili world would once again shift, as al-Muʿizz, the living Imam, finally entered his new capital city. Al-Maqrizi later commented on the political significance of this event, writing that "Egypt, after having been the seat of an emirate, became the seat of the caliphate."[47] For the Sunni historian, the significance of the Fatimid arrival was seen in political terms; moving the capital to Cairo meant it was the center of a caliphate for the first time. What al-Maqrizi did not record was what this move must have meant to the Ismailis. The city now housed the Imam—the center of Ismaili knowledge and the storehouse of God's wisdom on earth.[48]

The Egyptian city became the center of the Ismaili world by virtue of the Imam's presence within it. The potency of the Imam's corporeal presence was made even more explicit as al-Muʿizz brought the bodies of his forbearers—al-Mahdi, al-Qaʾim, and al-Mansur—with him. Their remains were carried in coffins across the desert and reinterred in the Saffron Tombs (*turbat al-zaʿfarān*) constructed within the palace of his new city. The procession of the Imams' bodies would have made a dramatic impression on the medieval viewer, serving as a testament both to the significance of the dynasty's lineage and to the palace's crucial role in housing the bodies of the Imams. Transferring the physical chain of the Imamate to the new capital thereby strengthened its spiritual significance to Ismailis and decreased the sanctity of the old capital.

Upon al-Muʿizz's arrival, the new al-Mansuriyya was renamed al-Qahira al-Muʿizziya or simply, al-Qahira "the Victorious."[49] For Ismailis, the world had changed forever with the Imam's resettlement. However, administratively, little changed at first. Jawhar's Ikhshidid-inspired administration continued, as did collaborations with prominent civilian residents in Fustat, though now with Ismaili, Kutama Berber overseers. The new caliph's presence in his capital was short lived, as he died only two years after arriving in Egypt. His son al-ʿAziz Bi'llah (r. 975–96) is credited with fully establishing Fatimid sovereignty in the new land of Egypt. Al-ʿAziz's rule is generally considered the apogee of Fatimid rule, characterized by economic prosperity, military expansion, domestic stability, and administrative consolidation.[50] Militarily, al-ʿAziz devoted much of his reign to frontier wars with the Byzantine empire, in an effort to declare Syria and Palestine as Fatimid territories, efforts that were complicated by the involvement of the Qarmatians and local Bedouins. Following significant defeat by the Byzantines in 975, al-ʿAziz determined that his Kutama Berber forces were no longer sufficient and introduced a Turkish element to the Fatimid armies, consisting of both free Turks and slaves (*mamluks*). These new forces did not share the dynasty's Ismailism.

EMBELLISHING THE ESOTERIC CITY

Under al-Muʿizz and al-ʿAziz, the core monuments were constructed, primarily for the Ismaili community, within the walls of al-Qahira. Scholars have debated the extent to which the walled enclave of al-Qahira was restricted to the Fatimid court and their Ismaili retinue. Paula Sanders takes seriously Ibn Duqmaq's claim that Jawhar built the palace-city for al-Muʿizz "so that he and their friends and armies were separate from the general public," arguing that al-Qahira was meant as a distinct, reserved walled city, which served as a stage for the Fatimid's elaborate ceremonial practices.[51] Jonathan Bloom has asserted that, from the outset, the Fatimid city would have been accessible to the urban population as well as to the Fatimid court, particularly after the additional gates were added to the city's walls.[52] He asserts that al-Qahira was intended as a practical, temporary fort rather than an ideologically imbued ceremonial center.[53] However, it is clear that the form of al-Qahira was different from the previous Egyptian encampments of Fustat, al-ʿAskar, and al-Qataʾiʿ, in its inclusion of a wall, much like the earlier Fatimid palace-cities. The construction of the wall suggests that the Fatimids did, indeed, intend to keep the court distinct from the urban populations to the south, even if this separation was not always rigidly maintained.

Most importantly, the debate regarding the particularities of who was allowed to enter al-Qahira obscures the central issue of the role of the Fatimid palace-city. Even if non-Ismailis flooded its gates, to conduct business or visit its mosques, al-Qahira would have been experienced differently depending on the sectarian identity of its visitors.[54] Even if al-Qahira was intended as a temporary capital, on the road to conquering eastern Islamic lands, it would still hold a sacred status for the Ismailis, for whom the city's primary significance was as the dwelling place of the living Imam.[55] As such, it would have existed as a pilgrimage destination for the faithful throughout the world.

The sectarian distinction between the inhabitants of the walled city of al-Qahira and the southern Sunni majority was made explicit in Jawhar's first religious commission in Egypt—an open-air prayer space (*muṣallā*).[56] Built to the north of the walled city, near Bab al-Nasr, the *muṣallā* was built as far from the urban enclaves of Fustat-Misr as possible, while maintaining its accessibility to the residents of al-Qahira. Constructed in time for Fatimid troops to use during *ʿīd al-fitr* (the festival of breaking the fast), the *muṣallā* replicated the Prophetic tradition of praying in an open space for the festival (*ʿīd*) prayers. The practice was endorsed by the famed Ismaili judge al-Qadi al-Nuʿman, who dictated that the two festival prayers, *ʿīd al-fitr* and *ʿīd al-aḍḥā* (the festival of the sacrifice), should be held in an open place, rather than in a house or mosque.[57] In al-Qahira, *ʿīd* prayers in the *muṣallā* would have marked the Ismaili Fatimid celebration of the festival as meaningfully distinct from the practices of the Sunni-majority residents of Fustat-Misr.

The sectarian divide between the two cities and the two populations was expressed through spatial and temporal differentiations of practice. Not only did the

Ismaili residents of al-Qahira celebrate the *ʿīd* in this differentiated space, they did so based on their own calculations of the beginning of the holiday. Following Shiʿi custom, *ʿīd* began thirty days after the beginning of the lunar month, while Sunnis waited for a moon sighting to break their fast. So, in the first year of the Fatimid conquest, the Sunni population of Fustat-Misr celebrated *ʿīd* one day later than the Ismailis.[58]

Soon thereafter, the Fatimids would impose their distinct Shiʿi practices on the population, demanding that all Fatimid subjects break the fast according to Shiʿi calculations.[59] The religious orientation of the dynasty would also ring out from the minarets of the city when, beginning in March 970, Jawhar added the Shiʿi formula "Hurry to the best of works" (*ḥayya ʿalā khayr al-ʿamal*) to the call to prayer in Fustat-Misr, starting with the Mosque of Ibn Tulun.[60] Five a times a day, Muslims throughout the city would hear the new call, a frequent aural reminder of the sectarian change to the city echoing through its mosques.

As part of his effort to Ismailize his new city, Jawhar constructed a new congregational mosque for the walled al-Qahira, named for the brilliant light of the Imam. Known as al-Azhar ("the Radiant"), the first Fatimid mosque shared a name with the congregational mosque of al-Mansuriyya and established the tradition of architectural references to divine light in the new capital.[61] For the Ismaili Fatimids, light was a common metaphor both for the esoteric knowledge transferred from the Imam and as a symbol of the family of the Prophet. The significance of these concepts was made manifest in the architectural projects of the Fatimid period. Mosques within the walled palace-cities of the Ismailis acknowledged the importance of light in their epithets. Al-Azhar (root letters z-h-r) evokes radiance, brilliance, and a shimmering light. Later, the Mosque of al-Anwar (root letters n-ū-r) would be named after a physical manifestation of light—most closely translated as "illuminated." In the twelfth century, the Mosque of al-Aqmar (root letters q-m-r), "the Moonlit," would continue this tradition. Thus, within the walled city of al-Qahira, the relationship between light and architecture was made explicit in the naming conventions of the caliphal mosques. In contrast, beyond the boundaries of the city, mosques were called by more descriptive names, indicating the neighborhood in which they were constructed.

The form and function of al-Azhar at the time of its foundation is difficult to determine with precision.[62] Even the question of whether or not the original mosque featured a minaret is debated by scholars.[63] Later additions to the structure and its subsequent role as one of the primary centers of Islamic thought make a reconstruction difficult.[64] Even under early Fatimid rule, al-Azhar was repeatedly restored and changed. Much of the surviving Fatimid-era decoration is from the reign of al-Hafiz (r. 1130–49), postdating the foundation of the mosque. Al-Hafiz added keel arches, a dome in front of the mihrab, and lavish stucco carvings throughout (fig. 1.13).[65] According to K. A. C. Creswell's reconstruction of Jawhar's mosque, it was a hypostyle structure, measuring approximately 278 × 229 feet (85 × 70 meters), built as a series of three arcades

FIGURE 1.13
Cairo, Mosque of al-Azhar, begun 970; carved stucco decoration and dome added under the reign of al-Hafiz (r. 1130–49)

surrounding a central courtyard (figs. 1.14–1.15), a plan consistent with preexisting mosques in Egypt as well as many of those in the Maghreb and al-Andalus. The mosque consisted of five aisles parallel to the *qibla* wall, the wall facing Mecca, highlighted by a perpendicular transept that was both higher and wider than the rest of the sanctuary.[66] The roof was supported by pairs of columns, many of which were spolia from nearby Roman and Coptic Christian constructions, placed on bases to correct for differences in height to support the original, low roof (fig. 1.16).[67] Relative to the mosques of ʿAmr and Ibn Tulun in Fustat-Misr, al-Azhar was a small structure. Its size and its position within the walled Ismaili city, next to the palace, suggests that it was used primarily by the Ismaili members of the court and members of the *daʿwa*, though later, lessons offered there would draw non-Ismailis as well.

Under the long reign of the Imam-caliph al-ʿAziz, a larger Fatimid mosque was added to the cityscape. This time, it was in a new location, as far from the urban centers to the south as it could have been, next to the *muṣallā*, just outside the northern walls of

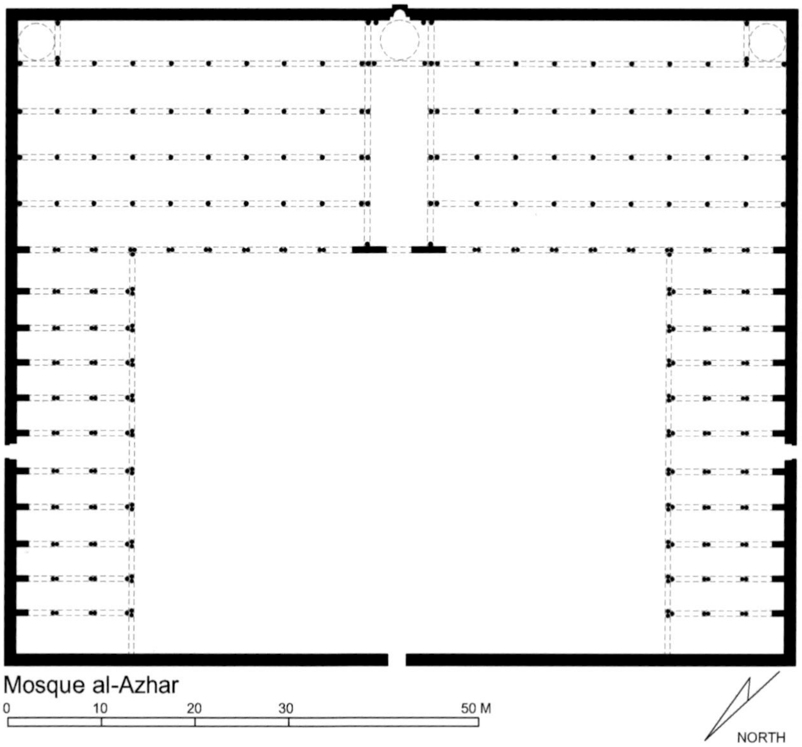

FIGURE 1.14
Cairo, Mosque of al-Azhar, plan, begun 970

FIGURE 1.15
Cairo, Mosque of al-Azhar, courtyard, begun 970

FIGURE 1.16
Cairo, Mosque of al-Azhar, interior, begun 970

al-Qahira.[68] The mosque was given the name al-Anwar ("the Illuminated")—an evocation of the significance of divine light in the figure of the Imam in Ismaili thought. Outside the walls of al-Qahira, on the route to the central lands of Islam, the mosque would have been the first building encountered by those Ismaili pilgrims who came to be within the presence of the Imam.

The Mosque of al-Anwar was built twenty years after the completion of al-Azhar and was more than twice the size of this first Fatimid mosque. Today, the mosque is known as the Mosque of al-Hakim, after the ruler who completed it.[69] For the sake of clarity, I will use this more familiar name to refer to this mosque in this and the following chapters. According to al-Maqrizi, al-ʿAziz began construction to the north of Bab al-Futuh, next to the open-air *muṣallā*, in Ramadan of 990. Its date of construction and location near the *muṣallā* suggest that it was linked initially with the *ʿīd* celebrations. Islamic jurists (*fuqahā*) moved from al-Azhar to the new mosque in the same year.[70]

As Paula Sanders has illustrated, through elaborate ceremonial processions, al-ʿAziz integrated this mosque into the Ismaili palace-city. Its location next to the *muṣalla*, a particularly significant space for the Ismailis and far from the urban centers of Fustat-Misr, emphasized this relationship, even if it was just beyond the northern walls.[71] In this same month, al-ʿAziz linked this space to the Fatimid palace through a procession for the *ʿīd* prayers. In the procession, the caliph rode wearing embellished brocade (*dībāj muthaqqal*), carrying golden swords, and wearing a golden belt. He was preceded by soldiers on elephants and was accompanied by horses with bejeweled saddles. Al-ʿAziz himself rode under a jeweled parasol (*miẓalla*), carrying a staff that belonged to the Prophet Muhammad.[72]

The ruler's movement from the palace to the northern prayer space was enlivened by the addition of benches (*masṭaba*s) that lined the way, providing seating for the muezzins and *fuqahā*, who recited "God is most Great" (*Allahu akbar*) as the ruler passed by them. The procession's allegorical significance for the Ismailis was made explicit as the seated Ismailis were arranged by rank. The addition of the benches, enlivened by the chanting of the faithful and the ranked Ismailis, created a dynamic, physical link between the palace and the new mosque.

Al-ʿAziz first used the mosque in Ramadan 991, when he pronounced the *khuṭba* and led the Friday prayers. On the following Friday, the ruler returned to al-Azhar to pray. The mosque is not mentioned again until 993, when al-ʿAziz is described leading a procession to the mosque from the palace to participate in the Friday prayers. In this description, al-ʿAziz rides on horseback, placing a *miẓalla* over his son's head, while the Imam-caliph rides without one.[73] The caliph walked with more than three thousand people, holding his cloak, a hooded robe (*taylasān*), and wearing riding boots (*hithaʿ*s). In the next year, he is once again described as praying in the new mosque.

It is clear from the accounts of the caliph praying in the mosque that the general form of the building was complete under al-ʿAziz. However, al-ʿAziz's son al-Hakim

FIGURE 1.17

Prosper Marilhat, *Ruins of the Mosque of al-Hakim*, Musée du Louvre, Paris, 1847

FIGURE 1.18

Cairo, Mosque of al-Hakim, begun 990, completed 1013. Photo by K. A. C. Creswell, Creswell Archive, Ashmolean Museum, Oxford University, EA.CA.2526

would later spend 40,000 dinars to finish the building. Therefore, it is difficult to determine exactly what existed in al-ʿAziz's time and what dates to al-Hakim's reign. Post-Fatimid developments make it particularly difficult to construct the building chronology of the mosque, as it was reconstructed several times in the medieval period, following a long period of disrepair and the eventual, controversial restorations by the Bohra Ismaili sect in 1979.[74] An idea of the ruined state of the building, with an indication of its inscriptional decoration, can be seen in a painting by the French Orientalist Prosper Marilhat, who visited Egypt in 1831–32 (fig. 1.17). Although we must be cautious of accepting such paintings as completely veracious, this depiction of the ruins of the Mosque of al-Hakim indicates the troubles of re-creating the interior construction while also demonstrating that the later minarets and bastions remained intact. Early twentieth-century photographs by Creswell show a similarly ruined mosque (fig. 1.18).

FIGURE 1.19
Cairo, Mosque of al-Hakim, plan, begun 990, completed 1013

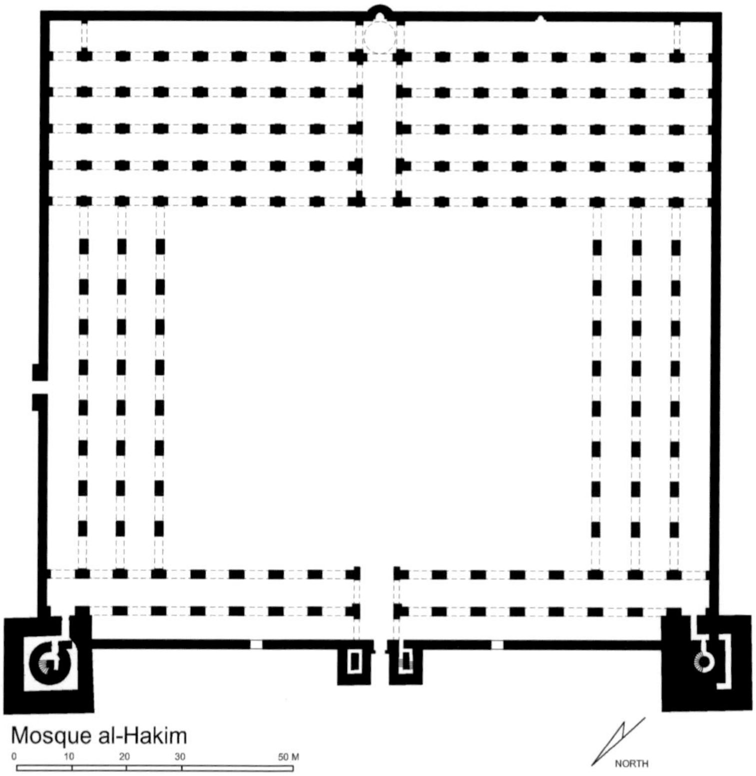

FIGURE 1.20
Cairo, Mosque of al-Hakim, begun 990, completed 1013; after the Bohra restoration of 1980, showing the restored courtyard and northern minaret, enclosed by the bastion of 1010

FIGURE 1.21
Cairo, Mosque of al-Hakim, begun 990, completed 1013; after the Bohra restoration of 1980

FIGURE 1.22
Cairo, Mosque of Ibn Tulun, 9th century

We can assume, however, that the basic form of the new mosque was completed under al-ʿAziz. The new mosque was more than twice the size of al-Azhar, at approximately 393 × 370 feet (120 × 113 meters). It consisted of a large, rectangular courtyard surrounded by pier-supported arcades with pointed arches and a five-aisle pier-supported prayer hall (figs. 1.19–1.21). Similar to its Maghrebi prototypes, the prayer hall of the mosque was punctuated by an axially articulated transept perpendicular to the mihrab, with three domes on the *qibla* aisle, facing toward the kaaba in Mecca, and a primary entryway immediately across from the mihrab. In addition to the primary entrance, the Mosque of al-Hakim contained twelve other entrances. Unlike the Mosque of al-Azhar, which was made up of a series of arcades, supported by columns, the Mosque of al-Hakim consists of large, square piers with engaged colonettes, similar to those found in the Mosque of Ibn Tulun (fig. 1.22).

Inscriptions inside the mosque introduce the hallmark style of floriated Kufic, departing both from the lively vegetal forms seen in al-Azhar and the austere Kufic script found in the earlier Mosque of Ibn Tulun (figs. 1.23–1.24).[75] In this elegant script,

FIGURE 1.23 (LEFT)
Cairo, Mosque of al-Hakim, begun 990, completed 1013; floriated Kufic detail before the Bohra restoration of 1980

FIGURE 1.24 (ABOVE)
Fragment from inscription at the Mosque of Ibn Tulun, Cairo, The David Collection, Copenhagen, 1/2002

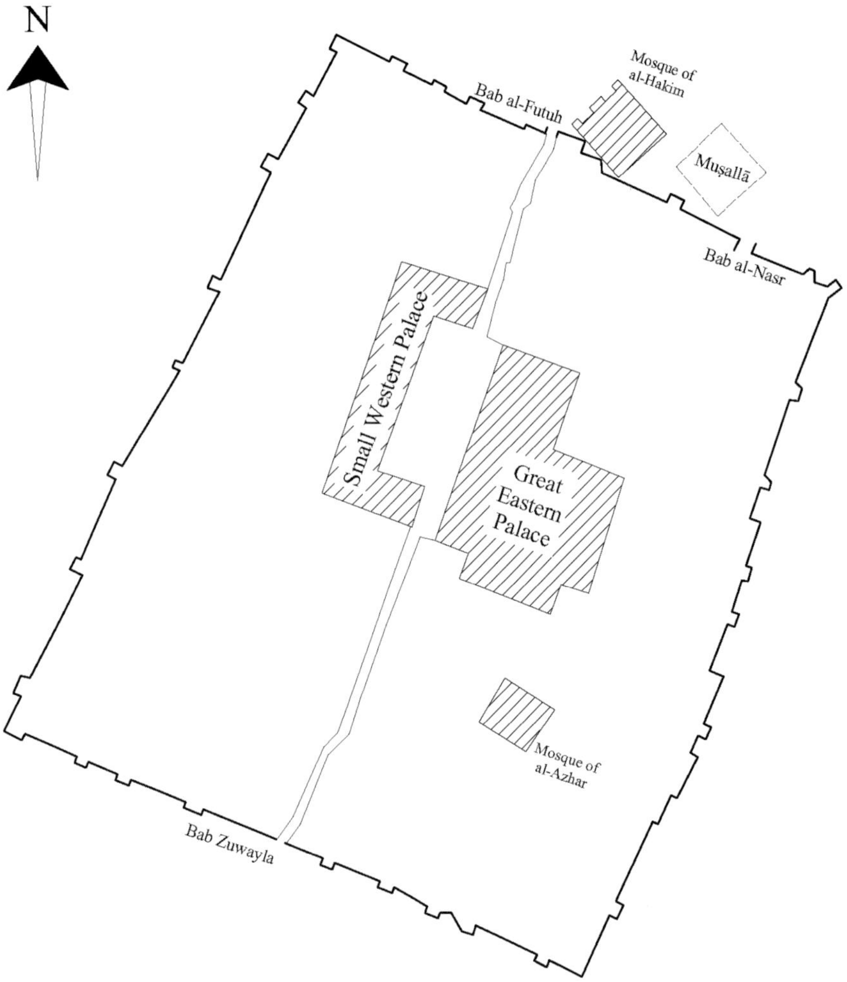

FIGURE 1.25
Map of al-Qahira, ca. 990

the forms of the letters are punctuated by interlaced vegetal scrolls that emanate from and envelop the Qur'anic text.

Even more important than these two mosques, al-Qahira contained the Fatimid palace. Certainly, there is nothing unique about an Islamic palace-city featuring a palace and mosque at its center. Indeed, these forms were shared by the Fatimids' rivals in al-Andalus and Iraq. However, unlike other caliphal domains, the palace-city of al-Qahira held a sacred status as the living Imam's domicile. Jawhar began construction of this most significant architectural project in advance of al-Muʿizz's arrival in the city. Located near the Mosque of al-Azhar in the walled city, the Fatimid palace initially consisted of a series of buildings known as "the Great Palace" (*al-qaṣr al-kabīr*), established under Jawhar and al-Muʿizz (fig. 1.25).[76] The *qaṣr al-kabīr* housed the ruler, most of the dynasty's official buildings, and the *turbat al-zaʿfarān*, where the bodies of the previous Imams were interred.

Later, al-ʿAziz sponsored a palatial renovation, adding the western, Lesser Palace (*al-qaṣr al-ṣaghīr al-gharbī*) and the Great Hall (*al-īwān al-kabīr*), which a tenth-century chronicler exclaimed was incomparable to anything else in the universe.[77] Less official than the eastern palace, the western palace served as residence to the caliph and his descendants. Although Jawhar began the palace, its final incarnation was an aggregation of many centuries of additions and changes. In particular, restorations during the reign of al-Mustansir (r. 1036–94) significantly added to the palace's grandeur, bringing it close to its final form. Between the two palaces was a rectangular parade ground (*bayn al-qaṣrayn*), which became the primary site of the Fatimids' elaborate ceremonies. Although nothing remains of the Fatimid palace, the contours of this ceremonial route endure today.[78]

Medieval sources laud the palace for its luxurious decor and rich ceremonial life, yet the forms and decoration are lost to time. Beyond the form of *bayn al-qaṣrayn*, we have few material remains from the Fatimid palace.[79] However, a few eyewitness accounts, dating to a slightly later Fatimid period, offer a firsthand glimpse into these lost structures, the most evocative of which comes from the eleventh-century Persian Ismaili traveler Nasir-i Khusraw (d. 1077). Nasir's description of the palace emphasizes its role as an Ismaili pilgrimage center. As an Ismaili convert, he held the Fatimid city in particularly high esteem.[80] And indeed, in his travelogue, only the universal Islamic pilgrimage centers of Mecca and Jerusalem receive attention similar to that which he lavished upon Cairo.[81] Within his description of the capital, Nasir reserves the most in-depth architectural description for the palace, attesting to its centrality for the Ismaili visitor. In addition, he describes the ruler's processions in great detail, demonstrating both the importance of ceremonies in the Fatimid context and his own devotional interest in the physical presence of the Imam.

As was the case at other caliphal palaces in al-Andalus and Iraq, the spectacle of people inside the structure, enlivening the spaces and emphasizing the power of the ruler, is what made the most vivid impression on this medieval traveler, rather than the structure itself.[82] According to Nasir, the palace was located in the center of al-Qahira, surrounded by open space. Central to the grandeur of the palace was the presence of one thousand watchmen, both mounted and on foot, who would enliven evening prayers by beating drums and blowing trumpets. Following the prayers, these same watchmen would patrol through the city. Nasir also records that twelve thousand servants worked in the palace, along with countless women and slave girls, with thirty thousand total individuals working there. The spectacle of human performance and organization was thus central to the experience of the Fatimid palace.

Nasir-i Khusraw also offers architectural descriptions that allow us to imagine the palace's structure. He writes: "Viewed from outside the city, the sultan's palace looks like a mountain because of all the different buildings and the great height. From inside the city, however, one can see nothing at all because the walls are so high."[83] The

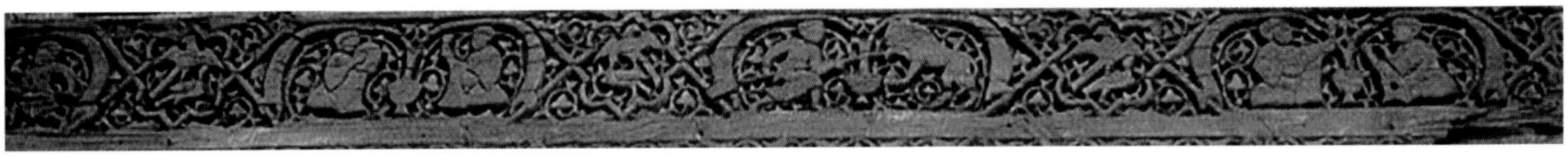

FIGURE 1.26
Carved wooden beam, believed to come from the Fatimid palace, 11th century. Cairo, Museum of Islamic Art

mountain-like height of the palace itself must have acted as a beacon, visible from a great distance by visitors and pilgrims who were approaching al-Qahira, even as it was difficult to see within the city. He then goes on to describe the palace itself, listing its ten gates and describing a subterranean passage through which the ruler could travel on horseback. He describes the palace walls as being made up of "rocks hewn to look like one piece of stone, and there are belvederes and tall porticos. Inside the vestibule are platforms."[84] He writes:

> As I entered the door to the hall, I saw constructions, galleries and porticos that would take too long to describe adequately. There were twelve square structures, built one next to the other, each more dazzling than the last. Each measured one hundred cubits [147 feet/45 meters] square and one was a thing sixty cubits [92 feet/28 meters] square with a dais placed the entire length of the building at a height of four ells [5 ½ feet/1.7 meters], on three sides all of gold, with hunting and sporting scenes depicted thereon and also an inscription in marvelous calligraphy. All the carpets and pillows were of Byzantine brocade and *būqalamūn* [a cloth with variegated colors], each woven exactly to the measurement of its place. There was an indescribable latticework balustrade of gold along the sides. Behind the dais and next to the wall were silver steps. The dais itself was such that . . . words do not suffice to describe it.[85]

Nasir must not have realized how much his repeated claims that the splendor of the palace could not be described would frustrate the modern art historian. However, the description does make it clear that the palace consisted of twelve regularly sized pavilions, decorated in hunting scenes. It was lavishly furnished with precious metals and rich textiles, presenting an impressive statement of Fatimid power and the court's taste for artistic splendor.

Although few traces of the Fatimid palace remain, a series of wooden beams, featuring scenes of courtly life, stand as our only material evidence of the structures described by Nasir-i Khusraw, likely dating to a slightly later Fatimid period.[86] Each beam measures between 7 and 12 inches (18 and 30 centimeters) wide and is several yards long (fig. 1.26). They are decorated with a floriated scroll background on which is a series of interlaced lobed polygons with scenes of musicians, cup bearers, falconers, animals, and the hunt (figs. 1.27–1.30)—evoking the hunting scenes described by Nasir and recalling the princely cycle scenes found at al-Mahdiyya and in al-Andalus and Iraq (figs. 1.4–1.6). The figures strike pinwheel poses, evoking a lively naturalism that is most

FIGURES 1.27–1.28
Carved wooden beam (details), believed to come from the Fatimid palace, 11th century. Cairo, Museum of Islamic Art

FIGURES 1.29–1.30
Carved wooden beam (details), believed to come from the Fatimid palace, 11th century. Cairo, Museum of Islamic Art

closely associated with the Fatimid style. Some even show suggestions of the paint that surely enlivened the forms in the tenth century (see fig. 1.27). As some of the few dateable examples of Fatimid art, the beams have been celebrated for their depiction of human forms. The dynamic figural poses against the floriated strap work have been used to identify a unique Fatimid style, in contrast to the conservative, abstracted forms of the Abbasid beveled style of Samarra (fig. 1.31).[87] In turn, these hallmarks of Fatimid style have been used to date other examples of woodwork and ivory.

A Crusader-era account of the Fatimid palace similarly focuses on the way that the palaces' residents and their devotion to the ruler animate the architectural form and contribute to the spectacle. Although it is written significantly later than the period under consideration here, the eyewitness account of Hugh of Caesaria, who visited Cairo during the Crusades, during the reign of Adid (r. 1160–70) offers another detailed account of the Fatimid structure. In his description, envoys are sent to renew a treaty with the caliph and he leaves a description of the "magnificence of the royal palace."[88] He describes Hugh of Caesaria and Geoffrey Fulcher visiting the palace, writing that they "were led through narrow passages entirely without light, preceded by a numerous and

FIGURE 1.31
Example of Samarra style C, the "beveled style," from the Ernst Herzfeld papers. Freer Gallery of Art and Arthur M. Sackler Gallery Archives. Smithsonian Institution, Washington, D.C., FSA A. 06 04.PF.23.096

noisy throng of attendants armed with swords. At each entrance they found noisy bands of armed Ethiopians who zealously showed their reverence to the sultan by repeated salutations."[89]

After winding through the dark, narrow passages, a revelation occurs as the passages open to

> a large and spacious court open to the sky which freely admitted the sun's rays. There, supported by columns of marble covered with designs in relief were promenades with fretted and gilded ceilings and pavements of various colored stones. Throughout the entire circuit royal magnificence prevailed. So elegant was both material and workmanship that involuntarily the eyes of all who saw it were ravished by the rare beauty and never wearied of the sight. There were marble fish pools filled with limpid waters; there were birds of many kinds, unknown to our part of the world. . . .[90]
>
> After passing through many winding passages and devious ways, whose wonders might well detail even the busiest men in contemplation, they reached the palace itself. Here still larger groups of armed men and throngs of attending satellites testified by their appearance and numbers to the incomparable glory of their lord. The very aspect of the palace gave indisputable proof of the opulence and extraordinary riches of the monarch. . . .[91]

> After being admitted to the inner part of the palace, their guide prostrated twice, showing a divinity due worship and a kind of abject adoration. Then for a third time bowing to the ground, he laid down the sword which he wore suspended from his neck. Thereupon the curtains embroidered with pearls and gold, which hung down and hid the thrown, were drawn aside with face unveiled. Seated on a throne of gold, surrounded by some of his privy counsellors and eunuchs, he presented an appearance more than regal. . . .
>
> With all reverence, the sultan approached him and, humbly imprinting a kiss upon the foot of the seated monarch, stated the reason for the envoys' visit.[92]

The Crusader's experience of the Fatimid palace is multisensory, based on the gradual revelation of the palace and its wonders. Although the author does not recognize it, the movement described here is evocative of the method of the gradual revelation of Ismaili knowledge itself, and the transition from the *ẓāhir* to the *bāṭin* in Ismaili thought. First, encountering the narrow, dark passageways of the city, enlivened by the Ethiopian soldiers, the visitor proceeds to the dramatic light of the courtyard, with its elegant workmanship, golden ceilings, and carved columns. Each passage contains new wonders, defined both by the elegance of the structure and the wonders of the animals within it. After winding through the preliminary buildings, the visitor finally encounters the palace itself, with even more performance of the spectacle of its attendance. Finally, the visitor moves from the outer structures of the palace to the guarded inner sanctum—a transition defined by the change from darkness to light—as the visitors and their guide reach the Imam himself, who is hidden from sight with a bejeweled veil. The veil is lifted from his face and his vizier bows down to kiss his feet.

For Ismailis, the experience of the palace would have been understood as a physical representation of the transition from the *ẓāhir* to the *bāṭin*—from the dark, narrow passageways of the street, to the increased light as one approaches the palace, until finally, God's earthly representative is unveiled in the center of this movement. The vizier's greeting of the ruler recalls the poems cited at the beginning of this chapter. In celebrating the importance of the Fatimid palace, the poets Ibn ʿIdhari and Ibn Haniʾ assert that the pilgrim kisses the corner of the palace, much as a pilgrim might kiss the corner of the kaaba. In William of Tyre's description, the vizier is able to kiss the body of the Imam directly—the most sacred of experiences for the Ismaili devotee.

The *bāṭin* significance of these forms would have been made explicit through one of the palace's primary functions as the locus of the Sessions of Wisdom (*majālis al-ḥikma*), through which the Ismaili doctrine and the *bāṭin* truths held by the Imam were spread gradually to its initiates. For Ismailis near and far, the Fatimid palace acted as a pilgrimage site not only by virtue of the Imam's presence but also as the site of these sessions. Within the protected walls of the Fatimid palace, the *majālis al-ḥikma* acted as the primary vehicle through which indoctrinated Ismaili missionaries educated less advanced Ismailis in the secrets of the faith within the presence of the living Imam.[93] Unlike other forms of learning in the Fatimid era, such as the debates (*munāẓarāt*) or the later establishment of the house of knowledge (*dār al-ʿilm*) during the reign of al-Hakim, the *majālis al-ḥikma* were reserved for members of the faith who had taken the Ismaili oath (*mīthāq* or *ʿahd*), which swore them to secrecy regarding their faith.[94] In one record of one of the gatherings, the Fatimid jurist al-Qadi al-Nuʿman gathered the Ismailis together within the palace to conduct the sessions. The gathering was so crowded, eleven people were killed in the crush.[95] After taking the oath, the Ismaili initiates could then learn the *bāṭin* aspects of the faith, for which the living Imam was the ultimate source and all-knowing authority. This process of this revelation of the hidden truths was a gradual one. For each stage of initiation into the *daʿwa*, more of the faith's *bāṭin* truths were revealed. These stages of revelation are echoed in the hierarchical arrangement of the palace itself.

The revelation of esoteric truths revealed to the Ismaili faithful was carried out through a system of allegorical interpretation (*taʾwīl*). In this system, Islamic law, the Qurʾan, hadith, and all other aspects of reality had a *bāṭin*, inner core, which could only be understood through allegorical interpretation. In describing this process, the tenth-century author al-Sijistani relied on a metaphor of wooden craftsmanship, for which the Fatimid dynasty is particularly well known (see figs. 1.26–1.30).[96] According to al-Sijistani, there are various types of wood in the world but unless a craftsman molds it into a specific shape, the wood is worthless. He argues that "the wood's worth and benefit become manifest only after it receives the craftsman's craftsmanship." Al-Sijistani applies this metaphor to explicate the relationship between Islamic revelation (*tanzīl*) and Ismaili allegorical interpretation (*taʾwīl*), arguing that as is the case with wood and other raw materials, a craftsman must work them for their worth to be revealed. Similarly, "the *tanzīl* consists of putting things together in words. Beneath these words lie the treasured meanings. It is the practitioner of the *taʾwīl* who extracts the intended meaning from each word and puts everything in its proper place. This is, then, the difference between the *tanzīl* and the *taʾwīl*."[97] In the same way that the craftsman shapes and manipulates wood in his workshop, the higher-level Ismailis developed the minds of and explicated the inner meaning of Ismaili *taʾwīl* to the next generation of Ismailis within the Fatimid palace via the *majālis al-ḥikma*.

Medieval descriptions suggest that the *majālis al-ḥikma* were organized in a hierarchical fashion that mirrored the structure of the Ismaili *daʿwa* as a whole and was reflected in the hierarchy of the palace structures. Al-Maqrizi writes:

> The *dāʿī* used to hold continuous sessions in the palace to read what was read to the saintly (*al-awliyāʾ*) and [collect] the duties connected with it. [The *dāʿī*] would hold a separate session for the *awliyāʾ*; another for the courtiers (*al-khāṣṣa*) and high officials as well as all those attached to the palaces as lackeys or in other capacities; a further

> session for the simple people and strangers in the city; a separate session for women in the mosque of [al-]Qahira called al-Azhar; and a session for the wives (*ḥurumū, scil.* [of the caliph]) and the noble women of the palaces.[98]

The separate sessions described here illustrate the staged revelation of *bāṭin* truths to the various levels of initiates—each of whom learned a bit at a time. The passage, along with the structure of the Ismaili mission itself, suggests that the experience of the palace and the city of Cairo itself would have been different for each segment of the population. Just as the *bāṭin* truths would be revealed gradually to Ismailis in the *majālis al-ḥikma*, so would the meaning of the palace change with the revelation of Ismaili truths. In al-Maqrizi's description of the *majālis al-ḥikma*, we also find a hierarchy of the architectural monuments within al-Qahira. In this model, the most important members of the Ismaili community received instruction in the palace itself. The less important members of Fatimid society—in this case, the women—met in the congregational mosque of al-Azhar rather than in the dwelling place of the Imam.

Further contributing to the sanctity of the palace was its containment not only of the living Imam and the *majālis al-ḥikma* but also the bodies of his ancestors in the *turbat al-zaʿfarān*, located in the southern part of the eastern palace. When al-Muʿizz traveled from al-Mansuriyya to Cairo with the bodies of the first three Imams, he carried the legitimacy of the empire and its physical links to the past. The bodies of the Imams acted as physical manifestations of the Fatimids' ʿAlid lineage and held special significance in their own right. The centrality and real power of the ancestors' physical presence was so crucial to Fatimid power, al-ʿAziz brought their bodies with him when he set out to reconquer Aleppo from the Byzantines.[99] The portability of the bodies attested to their role in supporting the Fatimids in warfare and also indicates al-ʿAziz's desire to expand the empire further east, moving the capital in the meantime.

The primary monuments under al-Muʿizz and al-ʿAziz, the Mosque of al-Azhar, Fatimid palace, and Mosque of al-Hakim, were built in the royal Ismaili city or, in the case of al-Hakim, in a space outside the walls but still linked to the palace-city, in what Irene Bierman has called a "sectarian space."[100] Aside from these projects, more minor or functional structures were also built outside the royal enclave, including small palaces in ʿAyn Shams, two aqueducts, and several pleasure pavilions.

Under these first two Cairene rulers, the dynasty's flagship construction projects were built *within* the walled city. However, patronage by lower-ranking members of the court did occur south of the Ismaili city. In particular, Fatimid women constructed their own mosque-tomb complexes to the south of al-Qahira in the Qarafa cemetery. In one early example, Durzan, the mother of al-ʿAziz, constructed a mosque complex built for the women of the dynasty, said to be built on the model of al-Azhar.[101] In this space, beyond the walled city, female patrons sponsored tombs for the less important members of the Fatimid lineage. Like the gendered hierarchy expressed in the description of the *majālis al-ḥikma*, building practices and locations varied depending on the status of the ruler, with the walled city of the highest status, close to the Imam, and lower status construction occurring within the existing urban fabric of the southern enclaves.[102]

At the same time that the primary function of the walled palace-city was to serve the needs of the Fatimid court and the Ismaili faithful, the administrative needs of the state continued to be executed beyond the walls of al-Qahira. The division in function between the palace-city and the areas outside the walled city can be characterized by the relationship of the *ẓāhir* to the *bāṭin*. The privileged *bāṭin* functions of the *daʿwa* and the Ismaili missions occurred in the new, royal city, where Ismaili missionaries would gather to attend the *majālis al-ḥikma*, receiving the esoteric Ismaili wisdom in proximity to the living Imam and the bodies of his ancestors.

Thus, from an art historical perspective, the Fatimid city existed as a site of material splendor that would be universally understood by the other caliphates and the Mediterranean courtly milieu. At its heart were forms universal to all Islamic powers—the congregational mosque and palace. However, much like the carved wood in al-Sijistani's metaphor, the deeper significance of Fatimid architectural forms would be revealed to the faithful through the Ismaili *ta'wīl*. We can read the procession of visitors through the palace, as described by William of Tyre and Nasir-i Khusraw, as a physical embodiment of the movement from the *ẓāhir* the *bāṭin*—a transition that would have been made explicit in the palace's *majālis al-ḥikma*.

Scholars have debated whether or not Cairo was meant to be a permanent capital for the Fatimids. Under al-Muʿizz and al-ʿAziz, it was likely a mere way station on the path toward conquering the east, much as al-Mahdiyya and al-Mansuriyya had been before the Egyptian conquest. However, the temporary nature of the capital did not inhibit the construction of elaborate monuments nor a rich symbolic elaboration of the city. Indeed, some of the most important Fatimid buildings were executed at this time—the walled city itself, the Mosque of al-Azhar, the world-renowned palace, and the Mosque of al-Hakim. For these early Fatimid rulers, the city and its buildings were constructed according to the esoteric aspects of the faith, with a focus on fulfilling the needs of the Ismaili faithful. This dynamic would change in the later projects of al-Hakim who, I will argue, would invest in Cairo as a permanent capital for the Fatimid caliphate and elaborated on the *ẓāhir* aspects of the faith.

2 A Contested Peace for the Churches

In art historical scholarship, the Fatimid era is often depicted as an apogee of interfaith tolerance, celebrated as a bygone golden age of religious cooperation, in which Christians, Jews, and Muslims were active and productive—if not equal—participants.[1] In this narrative, the persecuting reign of al-Hakim represents a psychotic break in an otherwise tolerant society. The Fatimid Imam-caliphs ruled over a diverse religious population in their new, Egyptian capital, numerically dominated by Sunni Muslims but with large populations of Christians and, to a lesser extent, Jews. A considerable number of the Fatimids' non-Muslim subjects occupied high-ranking posts in the administration and the Fatimid rulers generally allowed the Christian and Jewish religious minorities (*dhimmīs*) to practice their faiths openly.[2] However, even in the reigns of the first Egyptian Imam-caliphs, the status of *dhimmīs* was more complicated than this narrative suggests. Medieval Christian sources indicate a complex, persistent negotiation of power between the various urban religious communities and the Fatimid Imam-caliph, one in which the status of *dhimmī* monuments acted as a barometer for interfaith relations. This chapter complicates the narrative of early Fatimid tolerance by examining the status of Christian churches under the reigns of al-Muʿizz and al-ʿAziz. In contrast to the narrative that these two rulers ruled over an era of multifaith tolerance that al-Hakim later destroyed, an analysis of the architectural record demonstrates that their reigns were not free from religious conflict and that the status of churches played a potent role in the negotiation of religious identity and power.

Medieval Christian accounts suggest growing tensions between the populations of Fustat-Misr regarding the status of churches under al-Muʿizz and al-ʿAziz. A closer analysis of these sources reveals religious architecture to be a contentious battleground on which struggles over power, legitimacy, and caliphal favor were fought. In reading Christian medieval sources, it becomes clear that, contrary to the assumptions of Fatimid interfaith harmony, even in the reigns of al-Muʿizz and al-ʿAziz, religious power struggles were common, both between *dhimmīs* and Muslims as well as between the various sects of Muslims, Christians, and Jews.

The previous chapter argued that these rulers developed the Islamic monuments of Cairo according to Ismaili principles, with architectural patronage focused on filling

Detail of fig. 2.4

the religious needs of the Ismaili minority subjects. This chapter demonstrates that these principles were carried out in concert with a tolerance toward Christian monuments. However, this was a contested tolerance. Christian accounts of church restorations illuminate the complicated role of religious identity in the jockeying for status in the Fatimid court. In depicting the restoration of churches, the sources suggest that the Imam-caliphs' relative openness toward Christian monuments often drew the ire of the Sunni majority in Fustat-Misr. In these Christian tales of interfaith interactions, Coptic Monophysites struggle for caliphal favor against Jews, Muslims, and other Christian sects while the early Fatimid Imam-caliphs often unite with the Copts against oppressive urban masses.

THE STATUS OF *DHIMMĪS* AND THEIR BUILDINGS IN FATIMID EGYPT

Christians and Jews of the Fatimid dynasty, as in all medieval Muslim societies, were considered "People of the Book" (*ahl al-kitāb*) and, as such, held a special status as religious minorities. Throughout the medieval Muslim world, Christians and Jews generally were allowed to practice their religion in return for their proclamation of loyalty to the ruler and the payment of a special tax (*jizya*).[3] Within most medieval Islamic contexts, proscriptions against constructing and repairing non-Islamic religious buildings limited expressions of *dhimmī* faith—stipulations that were outlined in the so-called Pact of ʿUmar, which will be discussed in greater detail in chapter 4.[4]

After the Fatimid conquest of Egypt in 969, Christians and Jews in the Fatimid capital lived in relatively favorable conditions and even rose to high ranks in the Fatimid administration. Notably, following the conquest of Cairo, al-Muʿizz appointed as his vizier Yaʿqub ibn Killis, the famous Jewish convert to Islam, who continued to serve under al-ʿAziz.[5] After Yaʿqub died, al-ʿAziz later relied on the services of an unconverted Christian, ʿIsa ibn Nasturus. Under these early Fatimid rulers, the Christian communities flourished, as did their churches. The precise reasons for this relative openness in the Fatimid period is a matter of some conjecture. On the one hand, the Fatimids continued the patterns established by their Egyptian predecessors, who pragmatically incorporated *dhimmīs* into their administrative practices. On the other, perhaps the Fatimids' own minority status as Ismaili Shiʿa within a Sunni-dominated Egyptian context allowed for a greater integration of these factions.

Coptic Christians made up the largest *dhimmī* population in Fatimid Egypt. Coptic Christians embraced the Monophysite doctrine that Christ possessed a single divine nature. The Council of Chalcedon in 451 ratified the Orthodox Dyophysite position, which claimed a dual (human-divine) nature for Christ. Egyptian Christians loyal to the Byzantine Orthodox Church were in the minority and became known as Melkites (from the Syriac *malka* [king], referencing their allegiance to the Byzantine imperial church). The Copts, oppressed by their Dyophysite governors, welcomed the arrival of the Arab Muslim conquerors in 642.[6]

Following the Arab conquest, Egyptian Christian communities continued to be divided between the Coptic population, which was the largest community of Christians, and the Melkite population, which was much smaller, allied with the Byzantines, and typically appointed to higher posts in the Fatimid administration. Both were governed by distinct patriarchs. Christians tended to live in clusters within the urban fabric of Fustat-Misr but were increasingly integrated into the general population under the Fatimids, adopting Arabic as their primary language by the tenth century.

The Jewish community of Fustat was the other sizable *dhimmī* population at the time of the Arab conquest and under Fatimid rule.[7] The Jewish population is particularly well documented in the vibrant field of Geniza scholarship.[8] Indeed, some of the most intriguing and robust glimpses into life in the Fatimid period come from the Jewish community in the form of Geniza documents. These letters, court papers, contracts, and other documents were drafted by members of Jewish communities of the Islamic Mediterranean and were found in the Ben Ezra Synagogue in Fustat in the late nineteenth century. The corpus is an unofficial, unorganized treasure trove of information on medieval culture, commerce, family life, religion, and other topics. For the purposes of this study, the documents are significant in playing a crucial role in forming an understanding of Fatimid society as one in which Jews, Christians, and Sunni Muslims were integral and often powerful. They also illustrate the importance of international trade and immigration, presenting a picture of an urban bourgeois class that is often silent in other historic chronicles. However, because of the unsystematic nature of these documents, they often offer only glimpses into the specific historical context and, at the moment, give little information about the status of monuments. Therefore, they are not considered in depth here.

Unlike the Copts, who largely represented a native Egyptian community, Egyptian Jews had established themselves in the country through waves of immigration over many centuries. Since the time of the Arab conquest, there were large Jewish communities centered in Alexandria and in Fustat-Misr, near the old Roman Fortress of Babylon (Qasr al-Shamʿ). As trade flourished under the Fatimids and the reputation of the region's prosperity and relative tolerance grew, a new wave of Jews emigrated to the city. Like the Christian and Muslim communities, the Jewish community was further divided into distinct sects. Within Fustat-Misr, the Rabbanites represented the largest group, defined by their acceptance of rabbinical tradition. The Rabbanites were further divided into geographic divisions with separate congregations, the largest of which were the Palestinians, Babylonians, and the Maghrebis. The other major population of Jews were the Karaites, distinguished by their acceptance of the Bible as the sole source of religious knowledge. This group, though smaller in number, tended to be wealthier and part of the elite circle of merchants and Fatimid officials.[9] The Rabbanites and Karaites often came into conflict, jockeying for the support of Fatimid rulers, though they could also come together in times of crisis.[10]

Thus, the kaleidoscopic and contentious nature of Islamic sectarian identity in this period found its parallel in the complicated identities of Christian and Jewish sects. These diverse populations formed an integral part of Egyptian society, both influencing and participating in the local culture. However, there were often tensions between the various religious groups. Just as the Fatimids were defined by their Ismaili Shiʿism and struggled against their Sunni counterparts for caliphal authority, so, too, did the Coptic Monophysites claim superiority over the Melkites; meanwhile, and likewise, the struggle between the Rabbanites and Karaites partially defined the Jewish community.[11] Each group, in turn, vied for the powerful favor of the Fatimid ruler.

The Fatimid relationship to the *dhimmī* communities can be analyzed in both an imperial and an urban context. In the imperial context of the caliphate, the administration was open to Christian and Jewish elites and relied heavily on them. In addition, the Fatimid royal family included prominent Christians. Al-ʿAziz is known to have taken a Melkite Christian wife, who would become the mother of Sitt al-Mulk, the powerful half-sister of al-Hakim. This Christian wife's brothers occupied important posts; one brother, Orestes, sat as the Patriarch of Jerusalem while the other, Arsenius, became the Metropolitan of Misr and Cairo, showing the complicated intertwining of religious identities under the Fatimids.[12] In the urban context, the early Fatimid caliphs also showed great tolerance to the *dhimmī* communities by allowing them to practice their faith and maintain their religious structures.

The Ismaili belief system may have particularly encouraged this openness.[13] Certainly, the Fatimid privileging of the esoteric (*bāṭin*), explicated through allegorical analysis, allowed for greater interpretive flexibility. Their embrace of cyclical history, which accepted that all of the prophets were equally important, may have also cultivated a greater respect for the other strands of Abrahamic faith. Additionally, as Ismailis, the Fatimid Imams were the final sources of religious knowledge and therefore had to rely less heavily on Islamic jurists (*fuqahā*) and religious scholars (*ʿulamāʾ*), who may have advocated stricter measures against non-Muslims.[14]

Moreover, as Ismailis, the Fatimids were outsiders in their own lands. Only a minority of Egyptians were Ismaili or even Shiʿi. It is unclear how much of the Egyptian population converted to Shiʿism during the Fatimid reign but it was likely a small percentage of the population.[15] The religious difference between the Fatimids and the Sunni majority in Egypt can be seen in a letter of protection (*amān*), written by the general Jawhar and signed by local notables when he entered the city.

> I gave you the *amān* of God [. . .] and I take it upon me to fulfill what I have committed myself to give you—the *ʿahd* or pact of God and His inviolable *mīthāq* or covenant, together with his *dhimma*, or protection, and that of His Prophets and Messengers. [. . .] And you in turn shall act openly in accordance with his *dhimma*, coming out and submitting to me, and placing yourselves at my disposal until I cross the bridge into the city and alight in the blessed abode.[16]

Jawhar's use of the term *dhimma* to describe the protection he will offer the Sunni majority is evocative. *Dhimma* can refer to "obligation" or "duty of care" in Islamic law but was commonly used to refer to non-Muslims, even in the Fatimid period. For example, in *Da'ā'im al-Islām* (*The Pillars of Islam*), al-Qadi al-Nu'man uses the word *dhimma* in the context of describing jihad, where *dhimma* refers to the terms of submission.[17] Jawhar's use of the term to denote protection of the entire Sunni-majority population suggests that Sunnis hold a similar place in relation to the Ismaili Fatimids as did the Christian and Jewish communities.

THE SHARED ARTISTIC FORMS OF CHRISTIAN AND FATIMID EGYPT

Within the larger context of the medieval Mediterranean, scholars often characterize the long tenth century as an age of artistic exchange, production, and interfaith cooperation.[18] Intercourt gift giving, cooperation among local populations of Christians, Jews, and Muslims, and a pan-Mediterranean aesthetic taste characterize much of the discourse on Islamic artistic production in this period, with the Fatimid dynasty held up as a central actor in this cultural exchange. In the broader Mediterranean and Islamic context, the Fatimids were active participants in courtly, intellectual, and aesthetic culture, while locally they created a relatively tolerant context for their Christian and Jewish populations.

FIGURE 2.1
Early 10th-century stucco decoration from the Church of al-'Adhra' at Dayr Suryani in the Wadi al-Natrun monastic complex. (Photo: Herbert Ricke, 1929)

In the arts of medieval Islam, the artistic traditions of Muslims and Jews were often indistinguishable from one another. In the pre-Fatimid period, the mingling of shared forms between Islam and Christianity is demonstrated elegantly by the early tenth-century stucco decoration from the Church of al-'Adhra' at the Syrian Monastery in the Wadi al-Natrun monastic complex (fig. 2.1). With its undulating arabesques, executed in stucco, this example fits firmly within the tradition of the Abbasid ornamental mode that was based in Samarra but that spread as widely as the ninth-century Mosque of Ibn Tulun in Cairo and Samanid sites in Afghanistan and Nishapur.[19] Incorporating this ornamental mode, which was associated with an Abbasid imperial style, within a Christian monument suggests that Abbasid imperial design transcended religious boundaries. Indeed, the integration of crosses into the decorative program is the only indication that the stucco belongs within a Christian context.

FIGURE 2.2 (OPPOSITE)
Wooden screen in front of the haikal of the Church of Saint Barbara, Cairo, now in the Coptic Museum, Cairo

FIGURE 2.3 (RIGHT)
Detail, wooden screen in front of the haikal of the Church of Saint Barbara, Cairo, now in the Coptic Museum, Cairo

Shared visual forms between Christians and Muslims continued and flourished in the Fatimid period, during which the religions shared motifs and styles. For example, in woodwork, the screen in front of the haikal of the Church of Saint Barbara in Old Cairo recalls the wooden beams from the Fatimid palace (figs. 2.2–2.3; see figs. 1.26–1.30).[20] In both examples, delicate vegetal scrollwork occupies the background of each panel, while scenes of courtly life and princely pleasures animate the foreground. Like the Fatimid examples, the Saint Barbara screen depicts cross-legged, seated figures, musicians, and animals depicted in the mirror tradition, demonstrating shared artistic taste, and, likely, shared craftsmen between the Coptic Christian church and the Fatimid court.

Christian motifs are also found in the hallmark Islamic medium of luster ceramics, in which metallic oxides provide a shimmering, precious quality to ceramic objects. As in the case of woodwork, Fatimid luster objects are celebrated for their adoption of naturalistic, dynamic depictions of the human form.[21] Although luster production

FIGURE 2.4
Luster bowl depicting Coptic Priest, 11th century, Victoria and Albert Museum, C.49-1952

FIGURE 2.5
Luster fragment depicting Christ, 11th century, Cairo, Museum of Islamic Art, 5397/1

is generally limited to medieval Islamic realms, excavations in Fustat have unearthed Fatimid-era fragments depicting Christian subjects. One such example on a bowl shows a Coptic priest, painted in luster in his distinctive hooded robe and carrying a censor (fig. 2.4). A smaller fragment depicts Christ in luster (fig. 2.5), representing an example of the hybridity of medieval artistic practice. Although executed in luster, the figure of Christ recalls Byzantine prototypes for Christ Pantocrator, with his hand raised in blessing, cruciform nimbus, and a hint of a book displayed in his outstretched arm. Both examples demonstrate the blurred boundaries between "Christian" and "Islamic" arts. Although the scenes are resolutely Christian, the medium is quintessentially Islamic, pointing to the shared culture of the two religious traditions.

NEITHER SEEN NOR HEARD: CHRISTIAN MONUMENTS IN FATIMID EGYPT

When the Fatimids arrived in Egypt, they encountered a land with a long, rich history of Christian architectural production, with churches and monasteries located in both urban and remote areas of the country. As the birthplace of monasticism, Egypt was particularly rich in monasteries, many of which were famed as loci of miraculous events in the Christian tradition and were often situated in beautiful locations, featuring pleasant gardens, springs, and good views. In the early medieval period, Christian and non-Christian laity alike visited the monasteries as a form of recreation, taking advantage of their bucolic beauty and resort-like atmosphere. Christian sources even mention frequent visits by Islamic rulers to Christian monasteries, drawn in by their pleasant atmosphere and vistas.[22] Within the urban environment, most churches were located south of al-Qahira, in Fustat-Misr, particularly in the area next to Qasr al-Shamʿ (see fig. 1.12).[23]

Within certain contexts, the boundary between *dhimmīs* and the Muslim majority in Fatimid Cairo was permeable; in others, religious differences marked insurmountable divisions. Urban Christians, Muslims, and Jews often lived in the same neighborhoods, conducted business together, and even celebrated certain religious holidays together. At the same time, medieval Egyptian religiosity formed a central component of individual identity and group solidarity and difference. In medieval Egypt, festivals and other celebrations might unite religious communities. However, in central issues such as marriage, conversion, and death, an individual's religious identity could become a distinguishing trait of paramount importance. Indeed, in many ways, as we will see, the religious boundaries crossed in Fatimid courtly life were more strictly defined in the urban context.

Although there was a relative openness to the *dhimmī* communities in early Fatimid Cairo, relationships between the communities could be tense. In particular, sources record examples in which the Fatimid caliphs express discomfort of public expressions of *dhimmī* religions. For example, al-Maqrizi notes that al-ʿAziz halted public celebrations of Epiphany and the Feast of the Cross.[24] For the Coptic Christian community, the feast of Epiphany is celebrated six days in advance of the Feast of the Cross, in the Coptic month of Tūt (September). Medieval sources describe Christians processing from Fustat to the Church of Saint Peter, which was located on the Nile. As they walked, the participants held the visual signifiers of the Christian faith, carrying the Gospels, crosses, and burning incense, and chanting "Lord have mercy" (kyrie eleison).[25] The visual and aural audacity of the procession must have made a pronounced impression on the cityscape, in contrast to Islamic law, which often proscribed that Christian practice and construction could be neither seen nor heard. According to Islamic law, although churches could be repaired, new churches could not be constructed; visual and aural signs of Christianity—such as a cross or the ringing of bells—needed to be hidden from the population. These restrictions were carried over in the private sphere, as *dhimmī* houses were also required to be shorter than Muslim ones.

Christian communities and their spaces fared well under the Fatimid rulers, relative to other medieval contexts. However, delving into medieval sources on the role of churches in Fatimid Egypt reveals tensions surrounding the status of these spaces. Two sources of Coptic history offer invaluable insight into the tenor of Christian-Muslim relations in the Fatimid period. The most important of these sources, *Taʾrīkh baṭārikat al-kanīsa al-Miṣriyya* (*The History of the Patriarchs of the Egyptian Church*), was written by several authors over multiple centuries.[26] The section of most interest to the Fatimid historian is the volume containing information on the conquest of Egypt, in 539, through the year 1046. Although the book was originally attributed to the bishop Sawirus ibn al-Muqaffaʿ (d. ca. 1000), studies by Johannes den Heijer demonstrate that it was continued by Michael of Tinnis (d. 1056) and Mawhub ibn Mansur (d. ca. 1100).[27] The Fatimid period, under consideration here, is covered in the portion of the text composed by Michael of Tinnis. Originally recorded in the Coptic language and later translated into Arabic, the source integrates fact and fantasy with a dose of religious and ideological bias.[28] The particularities of chronology, so desired by historians, are often secondary to the fantastical and hagiographical tales in the text, which aim to promote the glory of God and the Coptic Christian community, in contrast to the more careful, seemingly straightforward chronologies, geographies, and encyclopedias written by Muslim historians of the time. However, although the dating and particularities of historical documentation can be unreliable in these accounts, the tales are invaluable in helping us tease out the values of the Christian community and the tenor of interfaith relations in the Fatimid period.

This study also draws on the eleventh-century accounts of the Melkite Christian, Yahya ibn Sa'id al-Antaki (d. 1065). Yahya's *Ta'rīkh* (History) is one of the few surviving contemporary accounts of the Fatimid dynasty.[29] His description of Egypt before 1014 constitutes one of the most important eyewitness accounts under the Fatimids. Though he left Egypt for Antioch as a result of al-Hakim's persecution of Christians, Yahya was well connected to some of the leading members of the Fatimid government and offers valuable insights into the administration. Another important, slightly later Christian source is *Ta'rīkh al-kanā'is wa al-adyira* (*The Churches and Monasteries of Egypt and Some Neighbouring Countries*), written in the late twelfth or early thirteenth century by the Armenian Christian Abu al-Makarim Sa'dallah Jirjis ibn Mas'ud.[30] The author relies on early Muslim geographies, including *Khiṭaṭ Miṣr* (Districts of Egypt) by al-Kindi (d. ca. 873) and *Al-Dīyārāt* (The monasteries) by al-Shabushti (d. ca. 1000), as well as Christian sources, such as *The History of the Patriarchs*, mentioned above. Medieval Muslim sources also deal with the Christian populations in great depth, although the most comprehensive of these, by al-Maqrizi, postdates this period by several hundred years.

Although the Fatimids are often considered as the most tolerant of Egypt's medieval dynasties, one of the most interesting references to an Islamic ruler's intimacy with Christian architecture predates the Fatimid arrival in Cairo. Abu al-Makarim describes the well-situated, beautiful Monastery of al-Qusayr, which was visited for worship and for pleasure by Christians and Muslims. He explains that a church within the complex contained an upper room, with four windows on four sides, built by Khamarawaih ibn Ahmad ibn Tulun (r. 884–96). Abu al-Makarim describes that in the church of the Apostles therein, there was:

> A picture of the Lady, carrying the Lord, with angels on the right and on the left, and pictures of all the twelve disciples, the whole being composed of tesserae of glass, and skillfully executed, as at Bethlehem, and some of these glass tesserae were gilded and some were colored. Khamārawaih, son of Aḥmad ibn Ṭūlūn, used to stand before these pictures and admire the beauty of their execution, and was much delighted

with them, especially with the picture of the Lady; so that he even built a *manẓarah* (belvedere) for himself at this monastery; that he might come there for recreation.[31]

This passage demonstrates the existence of Byzantine-style mosaics in an Egyptian context and the openness shown by the Tulunid ruler to the beauty of their form. Khamarawaih enjoys the monastery not only for its pleasant location, as did other rulers, but relishes the mosaic image, in spite of its overtly Christian subject matter. This instance is corroborated by al-Maqrizi, who notes the ruler's appreciation of the Christian image and his construction of a four-windowed *manẓara*, to enjoy the church fully.[32] This incident suggests that tolerance—and even appreciation—of Christian monuments existed even before the arrival of the Fatimids.

Medieval Christian authors universally approach the reigns of al-Muʿizz and al-ʿAziz with admiration. *The History of the Patriarchs* devotes far more attention to describing the church's association with Fatimid rulers than it had under the Abbasids, Tulunids, or Ikhshidids, suggesting an intimacy between the dynasty and the Coptic church that is acknowledged by virtue of the description's length. Both Abu al-Makarim and Michael of Tinnis refer to their reigns as a time of "great peace for the churches." Michael couches this peace in terms of the status of the physical churches (*biyaʾ*), equating the status of Coptic Christianity directly with the treatment of its monuments, demonstrating that the physical buildings existed as proxies for the Church as an entity.

In this time of peace, the source does record an instance of church destruction under al-Muʿizz. Immediately following the Fatimid conquest of Cairo, the Armenian general Jawhar demolished the Christian Khandaq Monastery. This structure was located within the walls of the newly built Fatimid enclave of al-Qahira, near what is now the Mosque of al-Aqmar. Most likely, Jawhar destroyed this monastery in his effort to build the new city. However, unlike later destructions under al-Hakim, Jawhar's church demolition was a matter of expediency rather than ideology, as he later allowed the church to be rebuilt to the north of the Fatimid city's walls. In addition, he transferred the bones buried within the monastery to the new location.[33]

Jawhar's removal and reconstruction of the Khandaq Monastery demonstrates his active role in constructing the Fatimid capital city. Soon after the bones of the Christians were moved outside the walls, they would be replaced by the bones of the Ismaili Imams in an attempt to reconsecrate the walled city as Ismaili. It also demonstrates an active interest in promoting religious identity through urban planning and construction within al-Qahira, which was quite distinct from the intermingling of Christian, Muslim, and Jewish spaces in Fustat-Misr.[34]

Jawhar removed the Khandaq Monastery in the service of creating an Ismaili space in the new walled city. However, Abu al-Makarim records early encounters between the first Fatimid caliph and the Christian community. He records that during his journey from al-Mansuriyya to Cairo, al-Muʿizz stayed in the Nahya Monastery in Giza for a period of seven months.[35] According to the account, not only did al-Muʿizz dwell in the monastery, he constructed waterworks to support a garden in its complex, complete with a well, water wheel, and a cistern for travelers.[36] Even if the account is apocryphal, it offers a fascinating glimpse into how the early caliph's relationship to Christianity was articulated in architectural terms. The implications of this account are, in fact, quite shocking. In Abu al-Makarim's tale, the Fatimid caliph not only lodges within a Christian retreat. Instead, in this account, the first direct act of Egyptian architectural patronage by Cairo's founding ruler was neither a mosque nor a palace, but rather additions to a Christian edifice.

A CONTESTED PEACE FOR THE CHURCHES: AN ANALYSIS OF THE MUQATTAM MIRACLE

Although Michael of Tinnis's documentation declares the reigns of al-Muʿizz and al-ʿAziz as a time of peace for Christian churches, he also records instances from their reigns that suggest this peace was contested. In particular, the famous tale of the Muqattam miracle can be analyzed to tease out the precarious state of this peace in early Fatimid Egypt.[37] The story of the miracle has different versions, but, as described in the Coptic tradition, a Fatimid caliph of Egypt became enraged by a Christian Biblical passage stating that mountains could be moved by faith alone (Matthew 17:20). In response, he demanded that a Coptic patriarch visibly demonstrate this claim of the Christian faith by making the Muqattam Mountain rise from the ground through prayer. After arrangements were made, an amazed Muslim ruler witnessed the mountain rise from the ground no less than three times before his own eyes. As a result of witnessing this miracle, the Fatimid ruler allowed the medieval Christian population of Cairo to restore two dilapidated churches in Fustat-Misr—the Church of Saint Mercurius in the Monastery of Abu Sayfayn and the Hanging Church (al-Muʿallaqa; figs. 2.6–2.7).

Michael of Tinnis situates the story within the context of an interreligious courtly encounter, which immediately and vividly evokes the multifaith character of the Fatimid administration. He begins by describing a struggle between Christians and Jews for caliphal favor at the Fatimid court that leads to a debate in a style typical of those that occurred in the court at this time.[38] According to the text, the Muslim ruler, al-Muʿizz, greatly admired the Coptic patriarch, Anba Abraham, and often sought his counsel in courtly affairs.[39] However, his vizier, Yaʿqub ibn Killis, a Jewish convert to Islam, was envious of the favor the caliph showed the Christian patriarch. He and his Jewish friend Musa requested a debate with Anba Abraham in front of the Muslim caliph. The Christian patriarch opted to ask the famous bishop Sawirus ibn al-Muqaffaʿ to debate on his—and, in effect, on Christianity's—behalf. According to Michael of Tinnis, the bishop Sawirus was gifted in Arabic and, on the insistence of the same ruler, al-Muʿizz, often debated with Muslim judges at the Fatimid court.

FIGURE 2.6
Exterior view of the complex of the Church of Saint Mercurius in the Monastery of Abu Sayfayn, Cairo, as seen today

FIGURE 2.7
Exterior view of the Hanging Church (al-Muʿallaqa), Cairo, as seen today

Within the description of the debate, *The History of the Patriarchs* includes an illuminating anecdote involving the famed Christian bishop. The anecdote begins with a Muslim judge, upon seeing a passing dog, asking the bishop the potentially inflammatory question of whether dogs are Muslim or Christian.[40] The Christian bishop reasons that on Fridays, Christians fast during the day and drink alcohol in the evening, but Muslims neither fast nor drink alcohol. Therefore, the bishop suggests that the question might be answered by placing meat and wine before the dog on Fridays to see which it consumes.[41] The foregone conclusion is that a dog will prefer the meat and is, therefore, Muslim. The Muslim noble audience is not offended by the objectionable conclusion that dogs are Muslim. Instead, "they marveled at the wisdom and at the strength of his answer and they departed from him."[42] Thus, the anecdote conveys an alliance between the Christian bishop and the enlightened Muslim members of the Fatimid court, who are not offended by the Christian's intellectual mastery.

In another tale that leads to an interfaith debate, the Jews Yaʿqub and Musa first seek to demonstrate their superiority over the Christians to gain the caliph's favor. Like the Christian bishop and patriarch, al-Muʿizz respected Musa, but Musa was envious of the attention and favor the caliph had bestowed on the Christian guests of the court. In order to discredit the Christians, Musa asks al-Muʿizz for permission to debate with the Christians, so al-Muʿizz arranges a meeting between the two. The Jewish Musa then prepares to debate the Christian bishop Sawirus, as the Muslim (Jewish-convert) vizier, Muslim caliph, and Christian patriarch look on. The story thus illustrates the intimacy among members of the Abrahamic faiths that evokes an aura of tolerance in the relationship between the Fatimid court and its religious minority subjects. However, as the story continues, this tolerance is tempered by conflicts between the faiths, with the aim of gaining the ruler's favor.

When it is finally time to debate, the Christian bishop refuses. He declares that it is unlawful to debate with a Jew in the presence of the caliph on account of the ignorance of Jews, citing Isaiah 1:3 to declare that God had attributed ignorance to the Jews, concluding that animals were more rational beings.[43] In this exchange, the Christian bishop constructs a hierarchy of faiths before the Fatimid caliph. Citing scripture, he concludes that beasts were more intelligent than Jews and that the Fatimid caliph should not bother with their ignorance. Once again, the account notes that the Muslim ruler stands in awe of the Christian bishop's astute, anti-Jewish logic.

The Jewish participants in this conversation do not take their humiliation lightly. They go on to seek their revenge on the Christian victors of this "debate," one that had finished before it had begun. It was within this context of interfaith struggles that the Muqattam miracle was conceived. As the defeated Jews recover from their embarrassment in front of the Fatimid caliph, they devise a plan to humiliate the Christians by discrediting a fundamental claim in their belief system. They inform an incredulous caliph that Christians believe their faith has such strong power that a person possessing it can tell a mountain to move and it will do so.[44]

Infuriated by the audacity of this notion that faith can move mountains, the Muslim caliph commands the Christian patriarch to demonstrate this miracle, lest all Christians under his rule be destroyed. The patriarch prays and fasts for three days, accompanied by other Christians in the Hanging Church. The account describes that on the third day of prayer, the Virgin Mary appeared to the patriarch and told him to find a one-eyed man carrying a jar of water on his shoulder, who will assist him in this miracle.

The patriarch finds this humble figure, named Samaan the Tanner, and together, they set about accomplishing this miracle.[45] Finally, the day arrives to demonstrate the miracle to the Fatimid caliph. A procession including al-Muʿizz, his army, his courtiers, Yaʿqub ibn Killis, and Musa approach the mountain and trumpets are sounded. Following the tanner's instructions, the crowd is divided. Christians take one side, including Samaan, who is hidden among the crowd. The caliph and his troops take the other. The patriarch and accompanying Christians recite "Lord have mercy" repeatedly, then prostrate themselves three times. Miraculously, each time the patriarch lifts his head and makes the sign of the cross, the Muqattam Mountain rises from the ground (fig. 2.8).

FIGURE 2.8
The Muqattam miracle remains a popular story for Copts in Egypt. Here, the event is illustrated in a carving on the Muqattam Hills, which is the site of several Coptic megachurches. The scene depicts the Copts, led by Samaan the Tanner, praying until the mountain itself rises from the ground. The Fatimid caliph, astride his horse, looks on in awe.

According to the text, the caliph, al-Muʿizz, as witness to this miracle, remained awestruck. Recognizing the validity of Christianity, he tells the patriarch that he has unrestricted freedom to request anything from him.[46] The patriarch refuses, but the offer is extended a total of three times. Refusing each time, the Christian patriarch's only response is to note that he wishes to protect the Fatimid state and give the caliph victory over his enemies. But when the caliph insists on granting a reward, the patriarch's request is simple and revealing—he asks first to rebuild the Church of Saint Mercurius, since it had previously been destroyed and now sat in ruins, used only for the storage of sugarcane. He also requests to restore the Hanging Church, since its walls had fallen and stood in a "state of decay."[47] The caliph agrees and offers the patriarch money to carry out the renovations, which the patriarch refuses, insisting that he only sought permission to do so.

In Abu al-Makarim's account, the story of the Muqattam miracle follows roughly the same trajectory, with a few differing elements. Most significantly, he ascribes the event to the reign of al-ʿAziz, under the sixty-second Syrian patriarch, Anba Ephraim. He also omits the story of the Christian-Jewish power struggle but includes an interfaith audience for the miracle itself. Abu al-Makarim also notes that both Muslims and Jews attempted to move the mountain before the Christians but were unsuccessful in their attempts. Like Michael of Tinnis's account, Abu al-Makarim's story ends with the request by the patriarch to rebuild the Church of Saint Mercurius, which, he notes, had been built by the Nile and turned into a sugarcane storehouse. As with the account in *The History of the Patriarchs*, Abu al-Makarim emphasizes the patriarch's rejection of the caliph's money to finance the restoration, but notes that he accepted his permission to restore both this church and other churches in Fustat.[48]

It is worth noting that the close alliance between the Coptic Christians and the early Fatimid caliphs can also be seen in the story that Alfred Butler encounters when he visits the complex of the Church of Saint Mercurius in the late nineteenth century.[49] Even at this later date, the story of the Muqattam miracle is associated closely with the rebuilding of the church, and Butler himself consults *The History of the Patriarchs* as a reference. In Butler's version of the tale, however, the Jews are conspicuously absent from the narrative. Butler compares the historical text to one told to him by a contemporary Coptic priest, who tells him that the caliph, al-Muʿizz, sent for the chief of the Christians and the chief of the Muslims and asked them to read from the Christian Gospels and the Qur'an. After hearing both holy texts, al-Muʿizz reached a shocking conclusion— "Muhammad does not exist" (*Muhammad mā fīsh*). He then

> ordered the mosque against the church of Anba Shanudah to be pulled down and the church of Abu Sifain [Saint Mercurius] to be rebuilt or enlarged in its place. The ruins of this mosque still remain between the two churches. The priest added that the khalif [al-Muʿizz] became Christian and was afterwards baptized in the baptistery beside the chapel of Saint John.[50]

In Butler's tale, the power of prayer, faith, and miracle, preserved in the account of *The History of the Patriarchs*, is replaced by the power of the word, readings from the Christian Gospels and the Qur'an. Butler's surprising tale of the dramatic conversion of al-Muʿizz is discussed more fully in the analysis below.

Returning to Michael of Tinnis's account of the tale, we see that in spite of the caliph's permission to rebuild the church, Christians encountered a violent resistance to this restoration from a segment of the Muslim population. He recounts that, when the caliph decreed that the church was to be restored, the "sellers who were there and the dregs of the people assembled said 'if we are all slain with one sword, we shall not allow anyone to place (one) stone upon (one) stone in this church.'"[51] When the patriarch informed al-Muʿizz of this resistance, the caliph went personally to the church and commanded the foundations to be dug. The resistance became even more brutal:

> An elder (*sheikh*), who used (to lead) in the prayers for those sellers in the mosque which was there . . . threw himself into the foundations and said "I desire to die today

> for the Name of God and not to let anyone build this church." When king al-Mu'izz was informed of this, he commanded that stones should be thrown upon him and that they should build over him. When lime and stones were thrown upon him, he wished to stand up, but the assistants did not allow him (to do so), since al-Mu'izz commanded that he should be buried in the foundation into which he had thrown himself. When the [Christian] patriarch saw this, he dismounted before his beast and threw himself before al-Mu'izz and besought him on behalf of him (the elder) until he (al-Mu'izz) commanded that the sheikh should be got up from the foundations.[52]

In this account, the Muslim population revolts against the religious tolerance of the caliph, who allies himself with the Christian community. Enraged at the Muslims' revolt against the reconstruction, the caliph commands the death of the sheikh. Ultimately, it is only the merciful benevolence of the Coptic patriarch that saves the emboldened Muslim. The source continues to note that following this dramatic event, the crowd halts their revolts and "all the churches in need of restoration" are rebuilt in Cairo and Alexandria.[53] This passage corroborates the nineteenth-century account, indicating the presence of a mosque near the church's location, as it mentions that the sheikh was from a nearby mosque. It is unclear whether this mosque was actually destroyed, or if the church was built next to the mosque, a more likely explanation.

Similar to Michael of Tinnis, Abu al-Makarim notes that when the patriarch began reconstruction, "the common people of the Muslims attacked him" and the patriarch had to send for the caliph, in this case al-'Aziz, for assistance.[54] The story goes on to recount that al-'Aziz

> commanded that a body of his troops and his [M]amelukes should go and stand by during the rebuilding of the fabric, and should repulse any who tried to hinder it and punish them as they deserved for opposing that which we have decreed to them. When the people saw this, they refrained from their attacks. Thus the work was begun.[55]

The various stories associated with the Muqattam miracle and the restoration of the complex of the Church of Saint Mercurius illustrate a number of points about caliphal-Christian relations and architectural patronage in the Fatimid period.[56] Each tale colorfully evokes the multireligious nature of the Fatimid court and society, illustrating the manner in which architecture served as a fulcrum of interfaith interaction, tolerance, religious ranking, and urban tension, as well as a literary device that could change to suit the times and agenda of the narrator. The interfaith tolerance for which the Fatimid period is known is demonstrated first in the very coming together of the participants in the debate. While clearly holding political authority, the caliph specifically invites Christian bishops to debate with Muslim judges and Jews in his court, and includes the various religions in the witnessing of the tests of faith.[57] Tolerance is more forcefully expressed in the way acts potentially incendiary to Muslims by Christian representatives lead instead to respect and recognition. Thus, in the story of the dog's preference, the Fatimid court could have been offended by the Christian bishop's association of the Muslim faith with the lowly creature, but instead ends with an appreciation of the Christian's intellectual mastery. The story suggests an alliance between the Christian bishop and the "enlightened" Muslim members of the court.

The corollary to a stronger Muslim-Christian alliance is that it occurred at the expense of Jewish participation in these stories. While well-regarded members of the Jewish faith are given the freedom to contest various assertions, consistently they, in the admittedly biased sources, fail to prevail. In the discussion of Sawirus ibn al-Muqaffaʿ, the Coptic bishop not only speaks Arabic well, suggesting the increasing Arabicization of the Christian population, but also writes many texts in Arabic, several of which are refutations against the Jews.[58] The caliph and his court are seen as reasonable and respectful of the Christian logic- and faith-based appeals for approval. The Christian minority in the early Fatimid era is not presented as a contemplative, insular community, but as one fully engaged with the politics of the court. In the struggle of religious minorities, the Jews are the ones who are cast off, and at times they appear vengeful, petty, and irrational.

Thus, the accounts illustrate the hierarchy of faiths in the struggle for power, with the Muslim caliph in charge, closely allied with Christians, who far outrank the Jews at court. Butler's tale takes this alliance to an extreme conclusion, as the priest suggests that al-Muʿizz finally converted to Christianity. Moreover, not only did the early caliph tolerate the reconstruction of a church, more scandalously, he allowed the destruction of a mosque. In the nineteenth-century priest's worldview, the Fatimid period stood as a "golden age" for their faith, and his story reflects a desire to claim the Fatimid ruler of Cairo as a member of his own group.[59] Conflict with the desires of another group—that of the urban masses—also emerges from the accounts. Michael of Tinnis's description of the aftermath of the miracle—the resistance of the crowds and the Muslim cleric who literally places himself in bodily opposition to the Christian restoration—suggests a tension between the Muslim populace and the Christian-Fatimid alliance. In direct contrast to the open dialogue between the Muslim judges and courtiers of the Fatimid palace depicted in the introduction to the tale of the Muqattam miracle, Christian reconstructions were often met with violent resistance by the urban populations. Unfortunately, in the medieval Christian sources about conflicts surrounding churches, the groups of protesters are often depicted as undifferentiated, Muslim mobs, without indication of sectarian or political affiliation.

Once again, it is difficult to unravel fact from fiction in the Coptic accounts. Certainly, al-Muʿizz never converted to Christianity. Likewise, for nonbelievers, the mountain never lifted as described. However, we can deduce from these tales that the rebuilding of churches was not easily accomplished in early Islamic Egypt, even under the "tolerant" reigns of the Fatimid caliphs. For the Christian recorders of the tale, it took moving a mountain to rebuild the dilapidated churches. Whether the reconstructions of the churches occurred under al-Muʿizz or al-ʿAziz, the tales reveal that the tolerance of the early Fatimid caliphs did enable a significant level of *dhimmī* architectural construction, though it was by no means without contestation.

COEXISTENCE AND CONFLICT: OTHER EXAMPLES OF CHURCH RESTORATION UNDER AL-MUʿIZZ AND AL-ʿAZIZ

This close analysis of the medieval sources of the tale has revealed that interfaith relations during the Fatimid period were not the stuff of fantasy but were quite complex. The relationship between the urban Muslim populace and the caliphate was often contentious, and religious architecture served as a battleground on which struggles over power, legitimacy, and caliphal favor were fought. In reading this tale of the Muqattam miracle, and other accounts of the treatment of churches under the early Fatimid caliphs, it becomes clear that interfaith power struggles were a common theme, both between Christians and Muslims, as well as between the various sects of Muslims, Christians, and Jews. Even in this age of relative interfaith tolerance, the barriers to church construction and renovation in Muslim-dominated society were pronounced. While the caliphs themselves may have indeed been open to the religious minorities in their realm, the negotiation over sacred spaces was not easily resolved.

Throughout *The History of the Patriarchs*, the reconstruction of churches is treated as one of the greatest challenges—and most admirable endeavors—for the Coptic patriarchs. The source records that the patriarch Abraham (r. 975–78) died penniless, despite having lived a life of wealth. The source celebrates that the patriarch had spent his entire fortune on alms and rebuilding churches, two acts that it commends as being particularly pleasing to God.[60]

Other medieval sources record examples of overt tensions between the urban Muslim populace and the Fatimid authorities, who were sometimes characterized as being allied with the *dhimmī*s. This finds expression in poem, recorded by al-Hasan ibn Bishr al-Dimashqi, as preserved by Ibn al-Athir:

> Be Christian. Today is the time of Christianity.
> Believe in nothing, but in the Holy Trinity.
> Yaʿqub is the father, ʿAziz is the son
> And for the Holy Ghost, Fadl is the one.[61]

In this sardonic critique of the Fatimid reign, the author proclaims that the Fatimid era was a "time of Christianity," implying that during this time Christians rose to prominence, at the expense of Muslims. Relying on the language of the Christian trinity, the author considers the Jewish-convert vizier Yaʿqub, Christian commander Fadl ibn

Salih, and the Fatimid caliph al-ʿAziz as operating in concert at the head of this heretical alliance.

At the same time that the Fatimids negotiated multireligious identities within their new capital, interfaith conflict characterized their efforts to expand further east. Christian Byzantium stood as the imperial barrier to the Fatimids' eastern ambitions under al-Muʿizz and al-ʿAziz, with particularly intense wars under the latter ruler.[62] The goal of the frequent frontier battles between these two imperial powers was the control of northern Syria, particularly Aleppo, with the Fatimids' eventual desire to conquer Baghdad for their cause. Yahya al-Antaki describes the battles and diplomatic missions carried out between the two dynasties, including a fleet of Egyptian warships that conducted an unsuccessful raid on the Byzantine coastline.[63]

At times, interreligious imperial conflict could lead to urban unrest, directed at imperial powers. Chronicles describe an event in 996, when a group of ships, docked in a port, preparing to be sent to fight the Byzantines at Tripoli, were destroyed by a fire. The local population blamed the Byzantine merchants for this event and rioted, killing 160 of them, while plundering a local Melkite and Nestorian church in retaliation. The Christian vizier ʿIsa ibn Nasturus, who was in charge of controlling the crowds, arrested many of the rioters, releasing one-third of them, killing another third, and beating the final third.[64] In this instance, as in the Muqattam miracle, the Fatimid officials acted as a buffer between the Christian population and the Muslim communities. Once again, urban unrest stood at odds with caliphal inclusiveness. The destruction of churches was the result.

Christian accounts are consistent in depicting the reigns of al-Muʿizz and al-ʿAziz as a good time for the Christian communities and their churches. However, accounts of church restorations make it clear that the Muslim population was often unhappy with the level of tolerance the Fatimid caliphs showed the *dhimmī* communities. These sources' depictions of the Fatimid caliphate do not portray oppression from the caliph. Rather, they portray a struggle for power among the Christians, Jews, and Muslims, as well as among multiple Christian sects. In this struggle, the sources depict the Christians and the Fatimid rulers as united against the other religious populations.

By integrating a consideration of al-Muʿizz's and al-ʿAziz's early patronage of new architectural and urban projects, as described in the previous chapter, with this consideration of the treatment of Christian monuments, a new picture emerges of this "golden age" of Fatimid patronage, and of the relationship between the caliphate and the urban populations. While the Fatimid caliphs' protection of *dhimmīs* and *dhimmī* monuments is often lauded for its inclusive, tolerant nature, in fact, such support was consistent with the early Ismaili development of the city. In addition, this tolerance did not always carry over to the urban populations. Christian sources demonstrate that the Fatimid alliance with religious minorities was often wildly unpopular with the Sunni population of Fustat-Misr, thereby complicating the dominant narrative of this era of tolerance.

3 Al-Hakim's Esoteric Urbanism

Al-Hakim bi-Amr Allah was the third Fatimid Imam-caliph in Cairo and the first to be born in the new capital city.[1] While his predecessors, al-Muʿizz (r. 953–75) and al-ʿAziz (r. 975–96), are celebrated for their roles in the development of Cairo and their inclusion and tolerance of their multireligious populations, al-Hakim is remembered most for his harsh persecution of his subjects and the wholesale destruction of churches, most notoriously that of the Church of the Holy Sepulcher in Jerusalem.[2] Architecturally, however, al-Hakim's reign was not merely destructive. He patronized several significant mosque projects during his reign, sponsored a *dār al-ʿilm* (house of knowledge), an observatory in the Muqattam Hills, and completed the mosque begun by his father, adding, and then concealing, the two famous minarets.[3] In addition, al-Hakim's birth connection to the city would bring about a deeper investment in the city's urban framework and architecture, transforming it from a way station on the road to conquering the east, to a significant, eventually permanent, capital in its own right.

Modern scholars read al-Hakim's cruelty, bizarre edicts, and large-scale destruction of churches and synagogues as evidence of his mental defects and despotism. Many medieval chronicles devote copious text to describing the reign of al-Hakim in great detail, attesting to its singularity. The eleventh-century Christian chronicler Yahya al-Antaki even regarded al-Hakim's unusual actions as possible evidence of a mental imbalance. Indeed, many of al-Hakim's actions do suggest eccentricity and mental instability. His penchant for wandering the streets of Fustat alone, his order to kill all dogs in Cairo, and his command to burn Fustat are among his most unusual acts. His cruelty and violence are well documented and rendered most puzzling by their capriciousness. In enacting his various edicts, al-Hakim often enforced, then retracted, then reinstated his commands, sometimes repeatedly.

While much of al-Hakim's reign was enigmatic, his demise was perhaps the most mysterious. After becoming increasingly ascetic in his practices, including reversing many of his prohibitions against Christians and Jews, al-Hakim was declared divine by a group now known as the Druze—who today make up a sizable religious minority population in both Lebanon and Syria. In 1021, al-Hakim disappeared on an evening walk in the Muqattam Hills of Cairo. His clothes were later found, marked with dagger

Detail of fig. 3.15

piercings. Today, many historians suspect that his sister Sitt al-Mulk ordered his assassination, but the Druze argue for his divinity, suggesting that he merely went into occultation and would appear again at the end of days.

The present study does not seek to reexamine al-Hakim's intent or mental state. It is impossible to psychoanalyze a man who lived one thousand years ago. However, the rich historical record surrounding al-Hakim's unusual reign allows for a deep exploration of the context of his architectural patronage, prompting us to ask: what does the *exception* to the Fatimid narrative of tolerance tell us about the larger context of Fatimid architecture?

The following two chapters are devoted to analyzing al-Hakim's architectural projects, integrating a discussion of his patronage with examples of his destruction. There are three distinct phases of al-Hakim's patronage. The first is considered in this chapter, which examines the early years of al-Hakim's reign, from the death of his father, al-ʿAziz, to his sponsoring of the completion of the mosque that now bears his name. In it, I argue that al-Hakim demonstrates a greater concern with the urban environment than had previously been seen in Fatimid Egypt, sponsoring caliphal mosque projects beyond the walls of al-Qahira, such as in the districts of al-Maqs and Rashida. However, these initial projects are executed in a fundamentally Ismaili Shiʿi idiom.

In this period, the early examples of the Imam-caliph's tyranny are directed at both Christians and Jews (*dhimmīs*) and the Sunni majority. This orientation is demonstrated in his architectural interventions, including the "golden curses" against the Companions of the Prophet Muhammad executed on the walls throughout al-Qahira and Fustat-Misr, and in the Ismaili symbolism on the remarkable stone towers of the Mosque of al-Hakim. While his early religious architectural patronage expanded beyond the courtly city, his early treatment of *dhimmī* monuments proceeded in a manner similar to that of his predecessors. By exploring the reactions and growing tensions surrounding architectural projects recorded in Christian sources, I demonstrate that the public pressure to destroy *dhimmī* monuments was building early in al-Hakim's reign.

THE HISTORICAL CIRCUMSTANCES OF AL-HAKIM'S EARLY REIGN

Al-ʿAziz died in 996, en route to one of the many battles on the Syrian frontier that would define his reign. Later that that day, his eleven-year-old son, al-Mansur, was declared caliph. The young ruler proceeded with his royal entourage, accompanied by the Fatimid army, to tend to al-ʿAziz's burial in the palace, among the Saffron Tombs (*turbat al-zaʿfarān*). At the front of the procession was the former ruler's body, carried on the back of a camel, trailed by the child ruler, accompanied by the might of the Fatimid army. The new caliph wore monochromatic clothing and a bejeweled turban, while carrying a lance and a sword.[4] The following day, the boy caliph entered the Great

Hall (*al-īwān al-kabīr*) of the Fatimid palace on horseback, wearing the same jeweled turban. He then proceeded to the golden throne of the Imamate, as his subjects kissed the ground before him. This eleven-year-old boy was now the Imam of the age to the Ismailis and the caliph of the mightiest Islamic empire and invested with the regnal title al-Hakim bi-Amr Allah ("the Ruler by God's Command").

During the first few years of his reign, the young al-Hakim ruled as a puppet of his powerful tutor, Barjawan.[5] Barjawan named a Christian, Fahd ibn Ibrahim, to a high-ranking post as his *ra'is*, demonstrating that in these early years of al-Hakim's reign, Christians continued to be incorporated into the Fatimid administration. Barjawan was largely occupied with continuing Fatimid campaigns against the Byzantines in Syria, until he was executed by the fifteen-year-old al-Hakim in 999.[6] What followed was one of the most compelling, enigmatic, and infamous reigns in early Islamic history.

Al-Hakim's reign was characterized by its cruelty and capriciousness. He murdered many members of his administration and persecuted his subjects. Michael of Tinnis described al-Hakim's demeanor, writing: "He grew up and became big and as a roaring lion seeking prey. He became more fond of shedding blood than a ferocious lion, so that a number [of people] counted them that were killed by his command and their number as eighteen thousand men."[7] Michael notes that the first person al-Hakim had killed was his tutor, Barjawan. According to his account, the young caliph tired of Barjawan, who had called the caliph "the lizard," following this insult with a call for his death, proclaiming that "the small lizard has become a great dragon."[8] Indeed, as al-Hakim came of age, his penchant for killing his subjects and those in his administration grew.[9]

Without question, al-Hakim reigned during a less stable period than his father or grandfather. Early in his reign, internal power struggles between the eastern and western elements of his military brought chaos to the empire. His reign also spanned a series of natural disasters and famines; indeed, many of his most harsh edicts are mentioned in association with these events. Politically, he faced the revolts of Abu Rakwa (1004–7) and the Jarrahids (1010), both of which challenged Fatimid legitimacy and the latter of which resulted in the declaration of a counter-caliph in Mecca. These revolts threatened the empire. However, despite these struggles, al-Hakim did not lose any of the Fatimid territories that had been won by al-Mu'izz and al-'Aziz.

The young caliph had a unique relationship to the Fatimid city, as he was the first of the Fatimid rulers to be born in Cairo.[10] While al-Mu'izz and al-'Aziz began their lives in the Maghreb, setting their sights on further expanding the empire toward the east, with Cairo likely being a mere way station on their road to conquering Baghdad, al-Hakim's empire was resolutely based in Cairo. As a result, his architectural projects focused on embellishing Cairo as a capital city. Likewise, his actions demonstrated a more direct interest in the city and its residents. Al-Maqrizi documented his early habits of processing through the streets of Cairo, often without the accompaniment of security forces, writing that, beginning in 1000, al-Hakim would ride through the city every night.[11] Consequently, al-Hakim ordered the illumination of the city streets and markets and sponsored the widening of the roads. Al-Maqrizi describes these urban improvements within the contexts of increased crowds and drunkenness, as the illumination of the streets meant that more people went out at night. Responding to this impropriety, al-Hakim ordered that women remain inside during the evenings and proclaimed that people should not loiter in front of shops.[12] These edicts can be considered as a sign of his puritanical leanings, but they also reveal al-Hakim's early engagement with the urban population beyond the Ismaili city's walls.[13]

ARCHITECTURAL PROJECTS BEYOND AL-QAHIRA

Just as al-Hakim's early reign was characterized by an increased engagement with the urban populace, so did his earliest architectural projects demonstrate a greater concern with the urban environment beyond the Ismaili enclave of al-Qahira. In 1003, al-Hakim ordered the completion of his father's Mosque of al-Anwar (now known as the Mosque of al-Hakim) and founded two new projects beyond the walls of al-Qahira. The first of these projects was the Mosque of al-Maqs, which was built on the banks of the Nile. Located to the west of the walled city and to the north of the primary urban centers, al-Maqs was a large area that had been settled prior to the Arab conquest (see fig. 1.12). The Mosque of al-Maqs was built next to a pavilion, from which the Imam-caliph had watched his naval fleet (*al-usṭūl*) sail on the Nile.[14] Little information is preserved regarding the mosque's foundation. However, the centrality of the mosque to al-Hakim's architectural vision is demonstrated in its inclusion in the endowment (*waqf*) of 1010, which is discussed in chapter 4.

In the same year, al-Hakim sponsored the construction of a new mosque in the Rashida district.[15] This mosque was built to the south of Fustat, in an area that had contained a Jacobite church surrounded by Christian and Jewish graves. Completed in 1005, the Mosque of Rashida was originally made of mud brick, then was later destroyed and rebuilt larger in stone.[16] Unlike the Mosque of al-Maqs, which seems to have been a relatively minor construction, the sources suggest that the Mosque of Rashida was a central monument during al-Hakim's reign. Al-Maqrizi refers to the Rashida mosque as "the Friday mosque of al-Hakim" (*al-jāmiʿ al-Ḥākimī*).[17] His description of Rashida's location depicts a sparsely populated, forgotten area prior to the mosque's construction. He describes it as an isolated place, cut off from religious observances and without religious connections.[18] The Rashida mosque was completed in Ramadan 1005, including the provision of candles and other furnishings. Al-Hakim rode to pray and offer the Friday sermon (*khuṭba*) there in the same year.

THE COMPLETION OF THE MOSQUE OF AL-HAKIM

In the same year, al-Hakim sponsored a third mosque project—the completion of the Mosque of al-Anwar, which had been begun by his father (and which later became known as the Mosque of al-Hakim). Al-Maqrizi describes the mosque as begun by al-ʿAziz's vizier, Yaʿqub ibn Killis, and situated outside Bab al-Futuh, and tells us that al-Hakim allotted 40,000 dinars for its completion.[19] The history of the mosque between al-ʿAziz's commission and al-Hakim's renovation is uncertain. While it must have been sufficient for the Fatimid armies, it is difficult to determine who patronized the mosque interior. For example, it is unclear whether the interior bands of inscription date to the reign of al-Hakim or to the reign al-ʿAziz. There are no associated foundational inscriptions for the verses inside the mosque, and the interior of the mosque itself lay in ruins for several centuries. Due to the uncertainty of their context, they will not be discussed here.[20] However, al-Maqrizi's report and the foundational inscriptions on the minarets confirm that the portal and two minarets were added at this time. Unlike the rest of the mosque, which was executed in stucco-covered brick and roughly hewn stone, the minarets and portal were crafted from finely carved stone. The addition of the richly carved stone elements, the large sum paid by the caliph for the renovation work, and al-Hakim's increasing incorporation of the mosque into his ceremonial practices suggest its growing significance in the Fatimid realm.[21]

The eleventh-century portal no longer exists in its original form.[22] At the time of Creswell's description of the mosque, a sixteenth-century mausoleum blocked the portal; later restorations re-created the portal according to his descriptions (figs. 3.1–3.2).[23] In addition to having a foundational inscription with the caliph's name and date of construction, the portal included carving that was, as Creswell described, "arabesque worked, so to speak, into the skeleton of a Classical entablature."[24] To the sides of the vaulted passageway were two niches with arabesque bands of decoration and carved lozenges. Certainly, the inclusion of the portal marked the mosque as distinct from the other congregational mosques in the city, which included neither monumental entrances nor prominent examples of writing on their facades.[25] It may also have connected the mosque to its Tunisian prototype, the Great Mosque of al-Mahdiyya, which also included a monumental entrance portal (see fig. 1.2).[26]

Descriptions of the Minarets at the Mosque of al-Hakim

The most interesting and famous additions to the mosque sponsored by al-Hakim were the two minarets on the northern and western corners of the facade, on either side of the portal. Many aspects of these minarets make them remarkable in the history of Islamic architecture. First, the existence of multiple minarets is, in itself, highly unusual. In the eleventh century, multiple minarets were found only at the mosques of Mecca, Medina, Damascus, and Jerusalem.[27] The varied shapes of the minarets were also unusual,

FIGURE 3.1
Cairo, Mosque of al-Hakim, showing the western minaret, encased by a bastion (1010), and a Mamluk-era tomb in front of the portal. The top of the minaret is also from the Mamluk era (14th century). Photo by K. A. C. Creswell, Creswell Archive, Ashmolean Museum, Oxford University, EA.CA.3092

FIGURE 3.2
Isometric drawing of the Mosque of al-Hakim, Cairo, ca. 1003, by K. A. C. Creswell

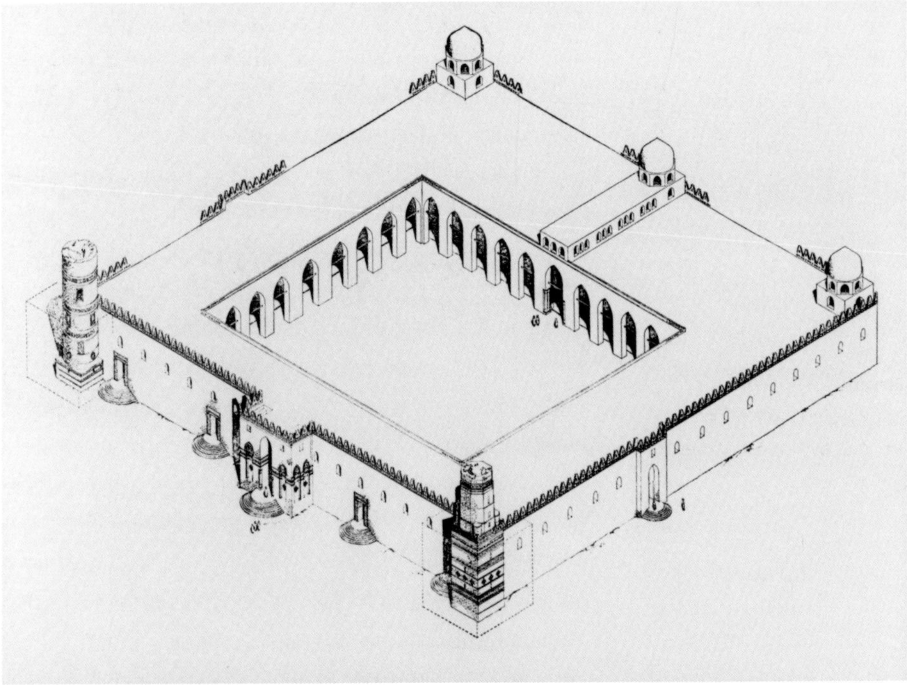

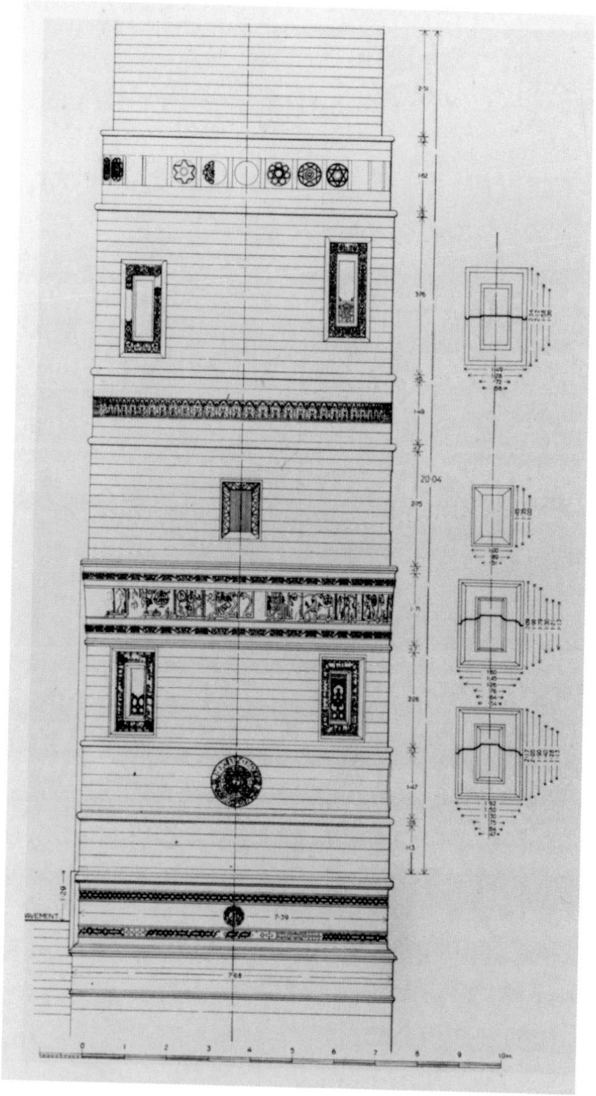

FIGURE 3.3
Elevation of northern minaret of the Mosque of al-Hakim, Cairo, ca. 1003, by K. A. C. Creswell

as were their different decorative and inscriptional programs, with distinct iconographic elements.

The northern minaret is a cylindrical tower, resting on a square base. Its diameter decreases slightly from bottom to top (fig. 3.3), and it is divided into eight bands, featuring a variety of circular medallions, pierced windows, blind windows, Qur'anic inscriptions, finely carved arabesques, and star- and rosette-shaped medallions (figs. 3.4–3.5; see figs. 3.17–3.18). The entrance to this minaret is on the southwestern side, facing the mosque courtyard. Surrounding the entrance is a lintel with a Qur'anic inscription, resting on top of two pilasters.[28] The inscriptions on both minarets, as throughout the mosque, are executed in the hallmark floriated Kufic style of the Fatimid court (fig. 3.6), in which letters are articulated with undulating vegetal tendrils that emanate from them and link them together.[29]

FIGURE 3.4 (LEFT)
Cairo, Mosque of al-Hakim, medallion featuring the word *Allah* on the northern minaret, 1003

FIGURE 3.5 (BELOW)
Cairo, Mosque of al-Hakim, five-pointed star on the northern minaret, 1003

FIGURE 3.6
Cairo, Mosque of al-Hakim, northern minaret, detail of floriated Kufic inscription, 1003

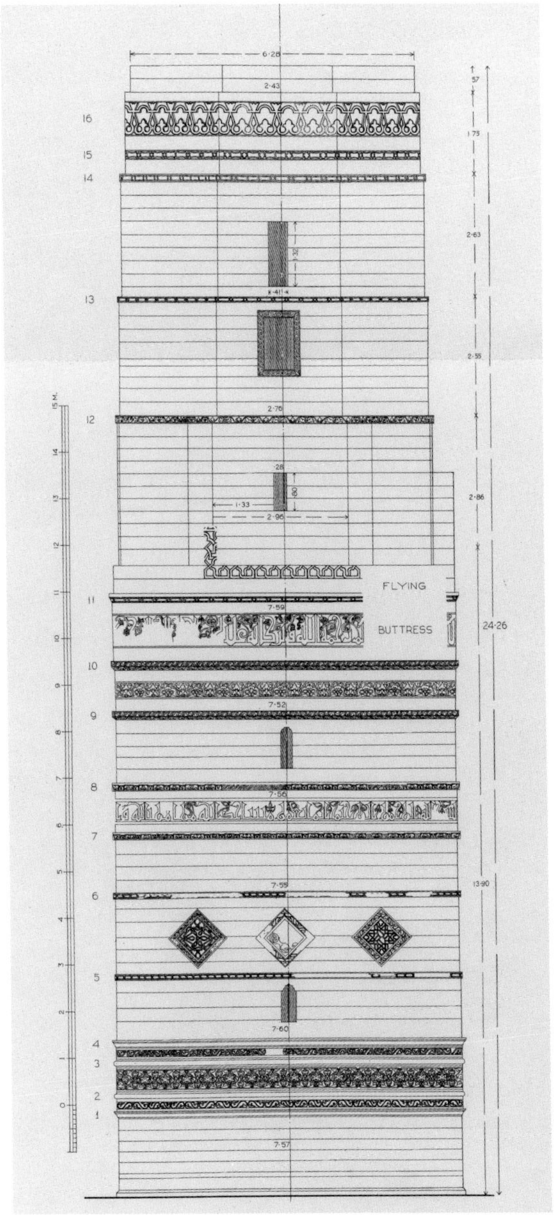

FIGURE 3.7
Elevation of the western minaret of the Mosque of al-Hakim, Cairo, 1003, by K. A. C. Creswell

The western minaret is markedly different in both form and inscriptional content (figs. 3.7–3.13), consisting of a cubical base, surmounted by five receding octagonal stories. These are decorated in arabesques, vegetal scrolls, embellished lozenges, narrow, unelaborated windows, and two bands of Qur'anic verse executed in the floriated Kufic style. The first octagonal story of the minaret features a semicircular buttress capped by a band of palmette scroll. Inside the inner staircase of the western minaret is a small room, often referred to as an oratory, which overlooks the mosque sanctuary (figs. 3.14–3.15).[30]

(CLOCKWISE FROM TOP LEFT)

FIGURES 3.8–3.10
Cairo, Mosque of al-Hakim, western minaret, 1003

(CLOCKWISE FROM TOP LEFT)

FIGURES 3.11–3.13
Cairo, Mosque of al-Hakim, western minaret, 1003

FIGURES 3.14–3.15
Cairo, Mosque of al-Hakim, room in western minaret, 1003

Open to the staircase on one side, the oratory also gives access to the roof of the mosque. Within this room are finely carved limestone walls and a flat, elaborately carved ceiling. The walls feature two niches, flanked by five-pointed stars and vegetal scrolls. The precise function of this room is an enigma. The presence of the five-pointed stars, with their evocation of light, makes it likely that this was a space that was used for esoteric (*bāṭin*) Ismaili purposes, though the precise nature of this is unclear. The Prophet had stated that "the Stars are a pledge to the world that it will not be drowned and my family are a pledge to the Community that it will not go astray," making it likely that the stars specifically evoked the family of the Prophet and thus were of particular significance to the Shiʿi faithful.[31] Prominent writing on the exterior of these minarets makes them particularly compelling monuments. These texts were meant to be read by anyone passing the monument. A close look at the inscriptional and ornamental content of the minarets of 1003 reveals content that would have been particularly meaningful for the Ismaili faithful who, as discussed in chapter 1, would gather as pilgrims in the Fatimid palace-city, just south of the mosque.

Scholarly Interpretation of the Minarets

Many scholars have written on the meanings of the minarets of 1003, though fewer have offered convincing explanations of the bastions of 1010, discussed in chapter 4. In his early consideration of the towers' significance, Jonathan Bloom focused on the unusual presence of two minarets, noting that other contemporary mosques had only one minaret positioned opposite the mihrab. Bloom noted that the exceptions were in the cities of Jerusalem, Damascus, Mecca, and Medina. Turning to a consideration of the development of the minaret in Islamic architecture, Bloom suggested the presence of two minarets marked the mosque as part of a pilgrimage network. In recent writings, however, Bloom has rejected this earlier interpretation and concluded that there is no discernible Ismaili meaning in the minarets' construction, nor did they serve to elevate Cairo to the status of the earlier cities. However, given the Ismaili-charged context of their construction, this seems unlikely. I accept Bloom's earlier claim that the two minarets marked the mosque as important for pilgrimage; however, I argue that it marked the mosque and the city of al-Qahira *itself* as a pilgrimage destination, rather than as part of a network of sites.

The analyses of Paula Sanders and Irene Bierman offer particularly useful insights into the Ismaili context in which the minarets were devised. Sanders considered the minarets in the context of the Fatimid "ritual city" and suggested that they must operate in both an esoteric and exoteric (*ẓāhir*) framework. She noted that the minarets' inscriptions link the mosque to the prayer of the rightly guided—the descendants of ʿAli and Fatima.[32] The Fatimid jurist al-Qadi al-Nuʿman wrote on these verses, interpreting them from both a *ẓāhir* and *bāṭin* perspective. In his book on Islamic law, *The Pillars of Islam*, representing the *ẓāhir* aspect of the faith, the jurist uses the Qur'anic verses found on the minarets of 1003 in his explication of the ranking of the mosques. He concludes that praying in the mosque of Mecca is worth one hundred thousand prayers; in Medina, ten thousand; in Jerusalem, one thousand; with a man praying in his own house counting for one.[33] However, in his companion book, *Taʾwīl al-daʿāʾim* (The allegorical interpretation of the pillars), which outlines the *bāṭin* meanings of Islamic practice, the jurist uses the exact same verses to demonstrate that mosque ranks are an allegory for the ranks of the Ismaili mission (*daʿwa*).[34] In this way, the verses on the minaret could be understood differently depending on the viewer's access to *bāṭin* Ismaili knowledge.

Like Bloom's earlier analysis, Sanders's writing recognized the unusual prominence given to the mosque. While Bloom noted the status of the mosque vis-à-vis the number of minarets, Sanders argued that the inscriptional content also elevated the mosque to the level of a pilgrimage site, only surpassed by those of Islam's most holy cities. However, in its pointed inclusion of verses central to Ismaili allegorical interpretation (*taʾwīl*), linking the mosque to the *daʿwa*, the concept of the mosque was a specifically Ismaili one. Irene Bierman has identified aspects of the 1003 minaret program that would have held particularly resonant meanings for the Ismaili faithful.[35] For example, the medallions, featuring concentric circles, operate as a "sign of Ismailism," mirroring the

FIGURE 3.16
Gold Fatimid dinar with concentric circle motif, from the reign of al-Muʿizz (r. 953–75)

memory devices of Ismaili philosophical writings of al-Sijistani and al-Qadi al-Nuʿman, in which concentric circle devices were used to illustrate the revelation of *bāṭin* truths through *taʾwīl*.[36] These forms are echoed in the Fatimid coin format, which would have spread this iconography far and wide (fig. 3.16). Moreover, the illegibility of the floriated Kufic itself may have visually supported the Fatimids' *bāṭin* beliefs.[37]

Additional aspects of the minarets' inscriptional content and form made them particularly relevant to Ismaili allegorical interpretation, emphasizing the *bāṭin* truths over the *ẓāhir* aspects of Islam emphasized by all. For example, the concentric circle device (fig. 3.17) containing the Qur'anic phrase "from the darkness into the light" surrounded by Qur'an 5:55: "Your only friend (*walīkum*) is God, and his Messenger, and the believers who perform the prayer and pay the alms and bend down [in prayer]." The pairing of these two verses is particularly illustrative of the key Ismaili belief in the relationship between the *bāṭin* and the *ẓāhir*. The inclusion of verse 5:55, which encircles the inner verse, emphasizes the *ẓāhir* aspects of Islam, focusing on acts universally embraced by Islam. Even within this verse, however, the inclusion of the word "ally" (*walī*) would be read with a specific meaning for the Ismaili readers. In this case, *walī* can be read as a reference to "Allies of God" (*awlīyāʾ Allāh*), a term most often used to refer to Ismailis. Moreover, as Bierman has argued, the inclusion of the concentric circle device itself operates as a "sign of Ismailism," based on the memory devices of their philosophical texts, making the *bāṭin* context of the verse particularly resonant.[38] For early Fatimid writers, concentric circle devices were used to illustrate the revelation of *bāṭin* truths through *taʾwīl*.[39]

Moving from the exterior of the circle to the interior—in Ismaili terms from the *ẓāhir* to the *bāṭin*—we find the phrase "from the darkness into the light" (*min al-ẓulumat*

FIGURE 3.17
Cairo, Mosque of al-Hakim, northern minaret detail, 1003, photo by K. A. C. Creswell, Creswell Archive, Ashmolean Museum, Oxford University, EA.CA.126

FIGURE 3.18
Cairo, Mosque of al-Hakim, grilled window on northern minaret, 1003, photo by K. A. C. Creswell, Creswell Archive, Ashmolean Museum, Oxford University, EA.CA.3172

ilā al-nūr).[40] This idea of illuminating the darkness was central to the Ismaili belief system, in which God turned darkness into light in much the same way the Ismaili Imam—in this case, al-Hakim—reveals the hidden truth to the faithful, illuminating the true meaning of Qur'anic verses such as those found on the minarets.[41] Given the proximity of the mosque to the Fatimid palace and the Ismaili Sessions of Wisdom (*majālis al-ḥikma*), the relationship between the *ẓāhir* and the *bāṭin* would have been instantly understood by the Ismaili visitors to the mosque.

It is likely that divine light imagery is also made manifest in the physical form of the minaret itself, which is embellished by inscriptions of Qur'an 24:35, the light verse (*āyat al-nūr*), (fig. 3.18). Although the verse is commonly found in Islamic art and architecture, it is a particularly important verse for the Ismailis, who understood the Imam and the hidden truths in metaphors of divine light.[42] Today, the grilled windows, surrounded by the *āyat al-nūr*, appear dark and lifeless, as they are obscured by the bastions of 1010. However, before their concealment, these windows would have embodied the Fatimid reliance on light imagery to convey *bāṭin* truths.

We can reconstruct how these windows would have appeared prior to the concealment by looking at the nearby Mosque of al-Aqmar ("the Moonlit"), which was built more than one hundred years later but used a similar technique of punctured stone (fig. 3.19). In the middle of al-Aqmar's famous facade are the familiar Fatimid concentric circles with the names of Muhammad and ʿAli, surrounded by a series of radiating flutes, evoking beams of light emanating from the sun. Similar to the grilled windows at the Mosque of al-Hakim, the medallion is punctured. As a result, light shines into the mosque.[43] More importantly, and most dramatically, light also shines *out* of the mosque to the street. The concentric circles glow for all who pass them and the mosque itself is the source of this light. Similarly, the grilled windows of the minarets of 1003 would have shone outward to the street. As glowing sources of light, surrounded by the light verse, the windows present the mosque and, by extension, the Fatimid palace in which the Imam resides, as the ultimate source of the light.[44] This surely would have been a particularly poignant expression of Ismaili belief to pilgrims entering the city from the northern gates and encountering the mosque as their point of entry to the city.

The inscriptions on the minarets of 1003 have a particular focus on celebrating the Prophet's family and underlining the supremacy of the Fatimid Imam. On the northern minaret, we find repeated references to "people of the house" (*ahl al-bayt*), a phrase that refers directly to the family of the Prophet and, by extension, the Fatimid rulers. Likewise, references to al-Hakim's "pure ancestors" reminded all passersby of his ʿAlid legitimacy. Moreover, on both the northern and western minarets, Qurʾanic verses are followed by the inscription: "This is what the slave of God al-Mansur Abu ʿAli, the Imam al-Hakim bi-Amr Allah, [C]ommander of the Faithful—may God's blessings be upon him and on his pure ancestors—orders Rajab of the year . . ."[45] The inscription cants out slightly, serving to display al-Hakim's name more prominently to visitors on the street. As with so much in the Ismaili city, this text can be understood on two levels. On one, the prominence of the ruler's name serves to glorify the Imam-caliph generally and fits within a long tradition of displaying the name of the ruler on his commissioned works. At the same time, the juxtaposition of the Imam's name with the preceding Qurʾanic verses also acted as a reminder to the Ismaili faithful to remember the *bāṭin* meaning of the verse, the source of which was the Imam himself.[46]

Signs of Ismailism and light imagery are less overt on the western minaret, which contains two large bands of Qurʾanic inscription (see figs. 3.9–3.11). The upper, larger inscriptional band contains verse 11:73 from Surat Hud: "The mercy of God and His Blessings be upon you. O people of the House (*ahl al-bayt*)! Surely He is all-laudable, all-glorious!"[47] Once again, *ahl al-bayt* refers specifically to the Fatimid dynasty as the people of the Prophet's house. As in the case of the northern minaret, the inscription is followed by a foundation text bearing al-Hakim's name, although in this case, the date is preserved as Rajab 393 (May 1003). The lower band contains a verse from Qurʾan 9:18: "Only he shall inhabit god's places of worship who believes in God and the Last Day,

FIGURE 3.19
Cairo, Mosque of al-Aqmar, 1125, demonstrating that Fatimid grilled windows would illuminate outward

and performs the prayer, and pays the alms, and fears none but God alone; it may be that those will be among the guided [*muhtadīn*]."[48]

This passage held particular significance to the Ismaili faithful, as the *muhtadīn*, like the *ahl al-bayt*, referred directly to the Prophet Muhammad's family.[49] Likewise, although acts such as performing the prayer and paying alms refer to the *ẓāhir* aspects of Islam and would be universally accepted by all Muslims, each of these acts had specific meanings in the Ismaili *ta'wīl*.[50] Although these pillars of the faith are required of all Muslims, they are commonly given a deeper explication in the Ismaili *ta'wīl* and are each related to the devotional practices of the Ismailis.[51] For example, the performance of charity (*zakāt*) is allegorically linked to the idea that more knowledgeable members of the *da'wa* should act as mentors for those less knowledgeable. Fasting (*ṣawm*) is understood to mean that the initiated should not reveal the Ismaili hidden truths. Most importantly for the present study, pilgrimage to Mecca is an allegory for pilgrimage to the Imam "because this is the house in which God resides."[52]

Although the allegorical interpretation of the Qur'an existed for Ismailis in every appearance of Qur'anic verse, the repeated presence of the Imam's name, references to the allies (*awlīyā'*), the *ahl al-bayt*, and the presence of Ismaili memory devices acted as reminders to the Ismaili faithful of the deeper explication of the Qur'anic passages. The centrality of the Imam in this interpretation can be seen in the Ismaili concept of the Imam as "the Speaking Qur'an" (*al-Qur'ān al-nāṭiq*), while the text itself, which is meaningful only through his interpretation, is known as "the Silent Qur'an" (*al-Qur'ān al-ṣāmit*).[53] The repetition of the Imam's name was, therefore, necessary to enliven these verses and make them resonate with the Ismaili faithful. Each verse, ordered into existence, as the mosque reminds us, by al-Hakim, would emphasize the ruler's role as the final interpreter and remind the *da'wa* initiates of the *bāṭin* meaning of the verses. This meaning, in turn, would be taught and approved in the nearby *majālis al-ḥikma* by the Imam al-Hakim himself.[54]

THE ESTABLISHMENT OF THE *DĀR AL-'ILM*

During this same period, in addition to patronizing the two new mosque projects—in al-Maqs and Rashida—and completing the mosque that now bears his name, al-Hakim also increased the prestige of Cairo through the establishment of a new house of knowledge (*dār al-'ilm*). Founded in 1005, within the walls of al-Qahira, the *dār al-'ilm* imported scholars from around the world to discuss various fields of science and knowledge.[55] It included Shafi'i and Maliki scholars, thereby allowing more non-Ismailis into the Fatimid palace-city. Unlike the *majālis al-ḥikma*, which was reserved for the promotion of esoteric Ismaili knowledge, the *dār al-'ilm* was devoted to all matters of knowledge and was open to Ismailis and non-Ismailis alike.[56]

Al-Maqrizi preserves al-Musabbihi's account of the *dār al-ʿilm*'s construction:

> The jurists took up residence there, and the books from the palace libraries were moved into it. People could visit it, and whoever wanted to copy something that interested him could do so; the same was true of anyone who wanted to read any of the material kept in it. After the building was furnished and decorated, and after all the doors and passages were provided with curtains, lectures were held there by Qur'an readers, astronomers, grammarians, and philologists, as well as physicians. Guardians, servants, domestics, and others were hired to serve there.
>
> Into this house they brought all the books that the commander of faithful al-Hakim bi-Amr Allah ordered to bring there, that is, the manuscripts in all the domains of science and culture, to an extent to which they had never been brought together for a prince. He allowed access to all this to people of all walks of life, whether they wanted to read books or dip into them. One of the already mentioned blessings, the likes of which had been unheard of, was also that he granted substantial salaries to all those who were appointed by him there to do service—jurists and others. People from all walks of life visited the House; some came to read books, others to copy them, yet others to study.[57]

With the creation of this universal center of learning, al-Hakim opened the city to a diversely sectarian population interested in both religious and secular learning. The text continues to note that the original location of the *dār al-ʿilm* was at the house of the Slav Mukhtar, which was most likely abutting the smaller, western palace, opposite the present location of the Mosque of al-Aqmar.[58] By creating this new center of learning, al-Hakim positioned Cairo as one of the great Islamic cities, rivaling the other caliphal capitals of Baghdad and Cordoba.[59]

As these examples make clear, the architectural and intellectual patronage of al-Hakim's early years was innovative and prolific. In this period, he sponsored the completion of one of the most important mosques in Islamic architectural history, including his addition of the symbolically charged minarets and striking portal. At the same time, he was the first caliph to extend his architectural patronage beyond the royal city, developing mosques in al-Maqs and Rashida and opening the Ismaili palace-city of al-Qahira to a larger public with the establishment of the *dār al-ʿilm*.[60]

AL-HAKIM AND THE *DHIMMĪS*

Al-Hakim's architectural projects in this early period were groundbreaking. However, in the first years of his reign, his treatment of *dhimmī* monuments proceeded similarly to that of his predecessors. Judging from the Christian chronicles, it appears that there was a period of peace early in his reign. Several accounts offer examples of al-Hakim visiting monasteries early in his caliphate, and several Christian and Jewish sources mention him positively. Michael of Tinnis notes that after the swearing in of the patriarch Zacharius, which occurred during al-Hakim's reign, the church remained "tranquil (and) in peace" for seven years.[61]

In another passage, Michael of Tinnis describes at length the conversion of the Muslim youth Ibn Raga to Christianity. When Ibn Raga's family learns of his shameful conversion, they try many techniques to get him to renounce his faith. Ibn Raga's family seeks counsel from the "good mediator" (*wāsiṭa khayr*) al-Hakim, his chief judge, and other members of the Fatimid court. Ultimately, al-Hakim sides with the Christian convert and commands him to be set free. Not only does this event suggest a Christian perspective of al-Hakim as a just ruler, it illuminates his early treatment of Christian architecture. After he was granted his freedom, Ibn Raga built a church dedicated to Saint Michael, which al-Hakim apparently permitted.[62]

The events that occur next follow the pattern seen in the reigns of al-Mu'izz and al-'Aziz. Michael of Tinnis describes that people of the Ramadiyat district in Fustat-Misr stole the precious wood of the church. Ibn Raga saw this and told them to return the wood or he would complain to the *wālī* (administrative official) of al-Qahira, demonstrating once again the role of the Fatimid court as mediator in urban sectarian disputes. When denied his request, Ibn Raga responded with a threat: "I shall go to al-Hakim bi-Amr Allah and he, if God will, will order the wood to be taken from where ye have put it and ye shall suffer harm from that."[63] The account of Ibn Raga suggests not only that there was a church constructed at some point in al-Hakim's reign, but that he followed in the footsteps of his predecessors by supporting the Christian builder over the Muslim masses who wished to plunder it. Based on the developments outlined by these sources, this event must have occurred early in al-Hakim's reign, in the time of peace for the churches. Al-Hakim's role as a "good mediator" and just ruler is echoed in other *dhimmī* sources. Yahya al-Antaki praises al-Hakim for providing "the kind of justice which his subjects had never known before. They slept in their homes secure in the possession of their properties."[64] The theme of al-Hakim's justice is likewise echoed in a Geniza fragment that praises al-Hakim as a "prince of justice."[65]

Al-Hakim's early reign does have a few aspects that suggest an emerging anti-*dhimmī* policy. Most notably, he killed the Christian administrator Fahd Ibn Ibrahim in 1003, arrested several Jewish and Christian secretary-scribes (*kuttābs*), and destroyed or converted a few churches.[66] However, the nature of these early church destructions was quite distinct from the demolition spree that would follow.

The earliest example of al-Hakim destroying a church was in the district of Rashida, on a site that had contained the graves of Christians and Jews.[67] The Mosque of Rashida, discussed earlier in this chapter, was then built in its place. Records indicate that for this destruction, al-Hakim allowed the Christians to rebuild elsewhere. Yahya al-Antaki and al-Maqrizi both suggest that the Christians had begun rebuilding a ruined church in the area when this was destroyed. Yahya writes that it was, indeed, a group of Muslims who attacked them and destroyed the building and other nearby churches, furthering the evidence that the urban populace was often in conflict with the Christians surrounding the issue of church restoration.[68]

Al-Maqrizi records that a dispute arose regarding whether the church had existed prior to the Muslim conquest, which suggests an application of the tenets of the Pact of ʿUmar (see chapter 4).[69] Yahya also notes that a group of Muslims attacked the Christians and destroyed the church and two others. At the same time, al-Hakim converted two other churches into mosques and forced Greek Melkites out of their own quarter to the Hamra and the whole area was made into one mosque.[70] Interestingly, however, in these early demolitions, the Christians were allowed to reconstruct their churches elsewhere, similar to the case of the Monastery of Khandaq during the foundation of al-Qahira. This suggests that it was part of a larger urban program of mosque construction rather than a targeted anti-*dhimmī* policy. Thus, the patronage of mosques outside the borders of al-Qahira, presumably intended to serve not only the Ismaili court but also the Sunni majority, was associated with the demolition of area churches.

CURSING SUNNISM ON THE WALLS OF CAIRO

Shortly after instituting his new architectural projects, al-Hakim changed the face of architectural structures throughout his capital city by ordering that curses denigrating the Companions of the Prophet Muhammad be inscribed throughout the city. Al-Maqrizi recorded that in the year 1005:

> In the month of November, there was written in the other mosques as well as the Old Mosque [Mosque of ʿAmr], inside and outside, on all walls, and on the doors of shops, cornerstones, tombstones and cenotaphs curses and insults directed against the Companions of the Prophet. They were inscribed and painted with a variety of colors and gold; that was done on the doorways of the bazaars and the doors of houses, having been forced to do so. People came from the outlying districts and estates to join the Ismaili mission (*daʿwa*). One day was set up for the men, another for the women. The crowds grew so large that in one session a number of persons died in the crush. When the pilgrimage caravan returned, those in it were assaulted and cursed by the masses, who asked them to insult and curse the Companions even while they refused.[71]

The cursing of the Companions of the Prophet was a Shiʿi practice, aimed at insulting the Sunni tradition. In this case, these insults were colorfully inscribed across the cityscape of al-Qahira and Fustat-Misr. The text does not tell us about the epigraphic style of these curses. However, its proclamation that these were executed in a "variety of colors and gold" demonstrates an attention to the aesthetic dimension of the curses, while the sheer scale of this project—on all the mosques "inside and outside," on shops, tombstones, and houses—points to a well-organized caliphal initiative. Once again, this act demonstrates a concern with the urban spaces in and beyond the royal city—a concern that was not seen under al-Mu'izz and al-'Aziz. However, this concern is manifested in a particularly Shi'i tradition, ultimately resulting in growing numbers of Egyptian converts to the Ismaili sect.

In this way, al-Hakim's early persecutions, as expressed in the built environment, were directed not only toward *dhimmīs* but perhaps also toward an effort at the Ismailization of the city and its inhabitants.[72] Indeed, in these early years of his reign, many of al-Hakim's persecutions and prohibitions are described in a particularly anti-Sunni context. Al-Maqrizi notes that in 1004–5, the Christians and Jews were ordered to wear a waistband (*zunnār*) and distinctive dress (*ghiyār*). He commanded that these markers should be black, as this was the color of the Abbasids.[73] Even seemingly bizarre edicts, such as the banning of *jirjir* (arugula) and *mulukhiyya* (a popular green Egyptian vegetable, also known as "Arab's mallow"), were associated with anti-Sunni sentiments because *mulukhiyya* had been favored by the Umayyad caliph Mu'awiya ibn Abi Sufyan and *jirjir* was associated with the Prophet's wife 'Aysha, who was also the daughter of Abu Bakr and had opposed the succession of 'Ali as caliph.[74]

THE ABU RAKWA REVOLT AS TURNING POINT IN AL-HAKIM'S REIGN

Al-Hakim's treatment of the Egyptian population and his architectural and urban projects in Cairo and Fustat shifted markedly following the revolt of the North African rebel known as Abu Rakwa. Born Walid ibn Hisham ibn 'Abd al-Malik ibn 'Abd al-Rahman, Abu Rakwa was named for the small leather water bottle (*rakwa*) he carried with him.[75] Abu Rakwa claimed to be a descendant of the Umayyads in Spain and an heir to 'Abd al-Rahman III. The power of the Cordoban Umayyads, who were once rivals to the Abbasid and Fatimid empires, had waned in the previous years, resulting in the rise of the regent al-Mansur and the demise of the Umayyad family in al-Andalus.[76] Sources suggest that the subsequent persecution of the Umayyad family partially motivated Abu Rakwa's flight from Spain to the Maghreb, where he sought to establish his own power, in contestation with the Fatimid dynasty.[77]

Abu Rakwa's mission was couched largely in sectarian terms, aimed at wresting power from the heretical Shi'i Fatimids and reclaiming it for the rightful Sunni heirs to the caliphate. He utilized al-Hakim's cursing of the Companions of the Prophet as a rallying point against the Fatimid rulers.[78] Relying on his anti-Fatimid message and his own Umayyad heritage as a source of legitimacy, Abu Rakwa traveled throughout North Africa, eventually settling in the old Sunni center of Qayrawan, from which he also traveled throughout the Islamic world, teaching the Qur'an and hadith and promoting Sunni doctrine. Eventually, Abu Rakwa gained the support of the Banu Qurra, a vehemently anti-Fatimid Bedouin tribe in Libya, and also brought the Berber Zanata to his anti-Fatimid, Sunni cause.[79]

This event not only points to the sectarian nature of the revolt but offers a window into the intended inter-caliphal audience for the Fatimid public text. The curses appeared on the walls of buildings in the Egyptian capital. However, the message spread to the rulers and populace of the Maghreb. The walls of Cairo had thus acted as a stage for articulating claims of sectarian legitimacy and caliphal competition.

Abu Rakwa's pro-Sunni, anti-Fatimid mission shook the dynasty to its core. His movement first caught the attention of the Fatimid caliph when he marched into Barqa, in Libya. After initial diplomatic efforts proved unsuccessful, al-Hakim sent troops to quash the rebellion. When the troops failed to contain the rebels, al-Hakim sent five thousand more men under the command of the Turkic general Yanal. In a shocking upset, the new Umayyad's forces defeated the mighty Fatimid armies in October 1004.[80] In celebration, Abu Rakwa declared himself a new caliph. He called himself al-Walid b. Hisham and the Umayyad Qa'im (a messiah-like figure). The Arab Banu Qurra and Berber Zanata recognized him as caliph in this same year. Abu Rakwa assumed the duties of caliphal authority, striking his new title, al-Nasir li-Din Allah, on coins in the realm and having the *khuṭba* read in his name. According to Yahya al-Antaki, upon Abu Rakwa's victory in Barqa, Sunnism was made victorious in all of his lands. Abu Rakwa's claim to Umayyad rule was mostly accepted by medieval chronicles and, apparently, also by the Fatimids. The Fatimids thus saw themselves as directly under threat from their Sunni Umayyad adversaries.

The scale of the threat of this revolt is demonstrated by the attention medieval chronicles pay to the episode. Almost all of the major chronicles discuss the revolt in some detail, indicating that the revolt was a true threat and that Abu Rakwa and his armies were not easily defeated.[81] The true urgency of the Abu Rakwa revolt became clear to al-Hakim when he advanced toward Cairo, besieging Alexandria and progressing as far as Giza. Abu Rakwa's swift conquest sent waves of panic throughout the Fatimid administration and, it would seem, the general population. Under the leadership of the general Fadl ibn Salih, Abu Rakwa was finally defeated. After fleeing to Nubia, where the Nubian king was paid to give him up, Abu Rakwa was captured and brought to Cairo, and executed in 1006–7. His revolt not only brought territorial losses for the Fatimids but also precipitated an economic crisis in Egypt; prices rose significantly and bread became scarce. Al-Hakim reacted by executing anyone found guilty of inflating prices or hoarding coins.[82]

Abu Rakwa did not look to the Sunni rulers of the Spanish Umayyads or the Abbasids for assistance in his quest for power but instead operated on a grassroots level in North Africa, appealing to the popular masses, who would support his own private, Sunni, Umayyad claim to the caliphate as an antidote to the heretical Shiʿi Fatimids. Although there is no evidence to suggest that Abu Rakwa garnered the general support of local Egyptian Sunnis, his reliance on tales of al-Hakim's anti-Sunni measures as a catalyst for revolt would mark a turning point in al-Hakim's treatment of the Sunni populations in Egypt and in the empire's strategy of gaining support throughout eastern Islamic lands. While much of the rebellion could be said to have been politically opportunistic, taking advantage of the region's economic hardship and al-Hakim's ill treatment of the North African tribes, the rhetoric of the revolt was based in sectarian divisions. Using al-Hakim's cursing of the Companions of the Prophet as an illustration of Shiʿi heresy, Abu Rakwa gathered enough Sunni sympathizers to pose a real threat to the powerful Fatimids. His surprising victories served as a wake-up call to the Fatimid ruler, altering the tenor of Sunni-Shiʿi relations in the years to come. Thus, Abu Rakwa's revolt marks a turning point in sectarian relations during the reign of al-Hakim—the aftermath of which will be discussed in the following chapter.

The early years of al-Hakim's reign brought about major changes in the conception of Cairo, the caliphate, and the Fatimid use of architecture. As the first caliph born in Cairo, al-Hakim demonstrated a deeper concern for urban affairs than either of his predecessors. Although his acts may have been erratic, during these early years the young caliph made the built environment of al-Qahira and Fustat-Misr a priority in his caliphate. He sponsored urban improvements, paraded through Fustat-Misr, and patronized religious monuments beyond al-Qahira in the mosques of Rashida and al-Maqs. At the same time, al-Hakim opened up the royal city and expressed a profound interest in universal learning through the establishment of the *dār al-ʿilm*, which welcomed non-Ismailis from the neighboring areas and, perhaps more importantly, made Cairo an important destination for scholars throughout the Islamic world.

Nevertheless, the caliph's attention to the urban centers was conducted in a previously established Ismaili idiom, with an apparent interest in Ismailizing the city. This trend was expressed in the built environment by the addition of the golden curses against the Companions of the Prophet Muhammad throughout the cityscape, including on the walls of the center of Sunni life, the Mosque of ʿAmr. At the same time, he constructed the explicitly Shiʿi towers at the Mosque of al-Hakim—whose unusual forms, illuminated qualities, and signs of Ismailism marked them as monuments to Ismaili Shiʿism.

Although this ruler is perhaps most infamous for his persecutions of *dhimmīs* and the large-scale destruction of their monuments, there is little evidence of this tendency early in his reign. Instead, although he initiates early edicts against them, these are instituted at the same time as anti-Sunni measures. Al-Hakim's treatment of Christian monuments in this period is consistent with that of his predecessors, as he allows the restoration and construction of churches. As was true under al-Muʿizz and al-ʿAziz, these allowances were often unpopular with the Sunni majority.

Most famously in this period, al-Hakim patronized the completion of the mosque now named for him, known at the time of the Mosque of al-Anwar, adding the monumental stone portal and innovative sculptural minarets to the facade. Although the mosque was technically outside the walls of al-Qahira, its location near the site of the prayer space (*muṣallā*) and the inclusion of specifically Ismaili symbols and inscriptions mark the space as resolutely Ismaili. The minarets' unusual prominence, two different shapes, and large-scale writing, along with the monumental portal, called attention to the mosque as a significant monument. Its incorporation of references to the Fatimids' ʿAlid lineage, signs of Ismailism, such as the concentric circle symbols, physical embodiment of divine light, and repeated use of the Imam's name, strongly resonate with the Ismaili *taʾwīl* of the selected verses and emphasize the prominence of the mosque and the Fatimid city. As it was located to the north of the city walls, on the road from the Islamic heartland, the mosque would have welcomed Ismailis visiting the city with a decorative program that would appeal to their faith and a nocturnally illuminated facade that would recall the divine light of the Imam, whose presence they had traveled to seek.

Certain aspects of the decorative program, such as the widespread use of stars and the unusual inclusion of a small room in the western minaret, remain enigmatic.[83] The former may be related to the divine light imagery and serve as symbols of ʿAli's family but may also have deeper symbolism. The form of the five-pointed star was later adopted by the Druze followers of al-Hakim as the primary symbol of their faith. These connections offer compelling questions for further exploration.

4 Construction, Destruction, and Concealment under the "Mad Caliph"

> There is ample evidence of his [al-Hakim's] commanding the good and prohibiting the bad, which none can deny, in the way he lives, devoting his nights and days to strengthening the word of truth, aiding the oppressed, building mosques, tearing down churches, preserving the communal prayer, applying the regulations of the law . . . reports of which have spread far and wide.
>
> —Hamid al-Din al-Kirmani on al-Hakim bi-Amr Allah

In the middle years of al-Hakim's reign, from 1007 to 1013, we encounter the two great enigmas of his architectural project—the construction of the austere bastions that concealed the minarets of the Mosque of al-Hakim and the wide-scale demolition of churches in his realm. Also in these years, al-Hakim engaged in the most cruel persecutions of the religious minorities in his realm. During this period, the predominantly Sunni urban center of Fustat-Misr was integrated into the Fatimid royal city through shifts in ceremonial practices; new architectural projects were consolidated and elaborated through renovations and endowments; the *dār al-ʿilm* grew as a locus of universal scholarship; and al-Hakim's new urban mosques were stripped of their overtly Shiʿi orientation. Why do these monumental acts of destruction, obscuration, and urban consolidation occur within the span of only a few years? It is my argument that the events that occurred between 1007 and 1013 were not simply the capricious acts of a mentally unbalanced, all-powerful ruler, but were part of a larger urban program, shaped by a constellation of forces, to reposition the role of Cairo and the Fatimid empire in the Islamic world. In this undertaking, architecture was instrumental in recasting the image of al-Hakim from the esoteric Imam of the Ismaili minority to an ideal Islamic ruler whose primary aim was "commanding the good and prohibiting the bad."[1] In Ismaili terms, this conceptual realignment is embodied in a shift from the esoteric (*bāṭin*) dimension of the faith emphasized in Ismaili practice to the exoteric (*ẓāhir*) acts of the faith, which were more universally accepted as Islamic.[2] These pivotal years of architectural and

Detail of fig. 4.2

urban patronage thus represent a conscious effort to situate Cairo as the universal capital of the Islamic world and al-Hakim as the Imam-caliph to all Muslims.

THE HISTORICAL CIRCUMSTANCES OF AL-HAKIM'S MIDDLE YEARS

As the previous chapter discussed, the revolt by Abu Rakwa, the claimant to the Umayyad throne, had threatened the legitimacy of al-Hakim's leadership and imperiled the Fatimids' hold on Egyptian lands. In many ways, the projects outlined in this chapter respond to the threat to the Fatimids posed by Abu Rakwa's revolt. Abu Rakwa utilized the Sunni legitimacy of his proposed Umayyad lineage to foment revolt in the Maghreb against the Ismaili ruler, coming within striking distance of Cairo. After the threat posed by Abu Rakwa subsided, al-Hakim instituted a policy of rapprochement with the Sunni majority of his realm. In 1007, he pardoned the Banu Qurra tribe, instrumental supporters of Abu Rakwa's revolt, and began to ease his own persecution of his Sunni subjects.

Al-Hakim's new conciliatory policies toward Sunnis in his realm altered the face of Cairo's and Fustat-Misr's buildings; specifically, as described in the previous chapter, al-Hakim ordered the removal of the curses denouncing the Companions of the Prophet that were inscribed in gold on mosque walls.[3] In a further apparent concession to the Sunni population, al-Hakim ordered that the Companions, especially Abu Bakr, be mentioned only in connection with their good deeds. In addition, the caliph permitted practices that resulted in a decrease in explicitly Shiʿi expressions throughout the fabric of the city. In 1009, he decreed his subjects could begin and end their fasting by sighting the moon, according to Sunni practices, rather than by Shiʿi calculations.[4] He also declared that muezzins would not be punished if they omitted the Shiʿi formula ("Hurry to the best of works"; *ḥayya ʿalā khayr al-ʿamal*) from the call to prayer, a requirement that had been in place since Jawhar's conquest of the city in 969. Concurrent with this Sunni rapprochement were the architectural projects under investigation in this chapter: the covering of the minarets of the Mosque of al-Hakim; the endowment (*waqf*) of the mosques of al-Azhar, Rashida, and al-Maqs, and the *dār al-ʿilm*; and the large-scale destruction of churches in his realm.

Two other revolts colored this middle period of Fatimid rule, threatening lands that carried crucial ideological symbolism for the Fatimids. On the frontier with the Byzantine empire, the Jarrahid revolt, led by Ibn al-Jarrah, would threaten Fatimid legitimacy in Palestine. As we have seen, the reigns of al-Hakim's forefathers had been defined by frequent wars with the Byzantines on the frontiers of Palestine and Syria. However, early in al-Hakim's reign, his mother's Christian brother, the patriarch of Jerusalem, helped broker a peace treaty that lasted until the destruction of the Church of the Holy Sepulcher circa 1010, though even during this ten-year truce, al-Hakim continued to increase Egypt's forces in the north. During this period, from 997 to 1010, it was the Jarrahids, leaders of the Bedouin Tayy clan, who held de facto power in Palestine, sometimes with the support of the Fatimid caliphs and sometimes allied with Byzantine forces. Ultimately, the Jarrahids attacked Fatimid-controlled Ramla, ushering in a rebellion against the Fatimids circa 1011.[5]

At around the same time as the Jarrahid revolt, an ʿAlid emir of Mecca, Abu al-Futuh, declared himself caliph with the support of Jarrahids in Palestine. The temporary caliph of Mecca minted coins (*sikka*) and declared himself the "Commander of the Faithful" (*amīr al-muʾminīn*) in the Friday sermon (*khuṭba*), both of which were important prerogatives of caliphal rule. With the Jarrahids in control of Palestine and the counter-caliph in Mecca, the annual hajj was limited. Eventually, al-Hakim sent gifts to the Jarrahids in sufficient quantities to lure them away from their support of the counter-caliph. In this struggle, Ibn al-Jarrah attempted to gain the support of the Byzantines, calling for the reconstruction of the Church of the Holy Sepulcher and installing a new patriarch in Jerusalem. The Jarrahids' opportunistic alliance with the Byzantines came to an end after the Byzantine emperor Basil II (r. 976–1025) failed to offer his support. In response, Ibn al-Jarrah allowed his armies to raid and pillage Christian homes in Palestine, confiscating their properties and forcing them to move to Byzantine territory.

Abu Rakwa had endangered Cairo itself, but the Jarrahid revolts threatened Fatimid power by encroaching upon their ideological claims to Islamic legitimacy—Jerusalem, the border with Christian Byzantium, and Mecca. As the Jarrahids first allied themselves with the Byzantines, the Fatimids were on the losing side of the jihad that would support their claim to the caliphate. As the Fatimids lost control of Mecca and Jerusalem, they lost their legitimacy as the rightful caliphs of Islam and their status as more powerful than the Abbasids, Spanish Umayyads, and other rival dynasties. Most importantly, at the heart of this struggle was the status of the Holy Sepulcher itself.

CONCEALING THE REVEALED: COVERING THE MINARETS AT THE MOSQUE OF AL-HAKIM

Al-Hakim's motivation for obscuring the innovative minarets of 1003 has been a matter of art historical debate.[6] The original double towers, with their Ismaili-oriented texts and unique symbols, were unusual from the outset. Even more bizarre was their covering only seven years later. Al-Maqrizi recorded that at the end of 1010 (AH 401) the singularly beautiful, intricately carved minarets were covered by bastions (*arkān*), which today stand as square towers encasing the original minarets (figs. 4.1–4.3).[7] The difference in aesthetics and message between the original and renovated towers is striking. Unlike the minarets of 1003, which relied on an extravagant use of ornamentation and Qurʾanic verses central to the Ismaili allegorical interpretation (*taʾwīl*) of the Qurʾan, the 1010 bastions were monuments of austerity. They featured a single band of Qurʾanic text that represented a marked change in message from the original towers.[8] Today,

(CLOCKWISE FROM TOP LEFT)

FIGURE 4.1
Cairo, Mosque of al-Hakim, western minaret enclosed by bastion, 1010. The top of the minaret is a later, Mamluk-era (14th-century) addition.

FIGURE 4.2
Cairo, Mosque of al-Hakim, northern minaret enclosed by bastion, 1010, later enclosed by Badr al-Jamali's 11th-century wall. The top of the minaret is a later, Mamluk-era (14th-century) addition.

FIGURE 4.3
Cairo, Mosque of al-Hakim, between the northern minaret of 1003 and the bastion of 1010

FIGURE 4.4
Minaret of the Great Mosque of Sfax, Tunisia, 9th century with 11th-century additions

FIGURE 4.5
Minaret of the Great Mosque of Qayrawan, Tunisia, 836

the inscription on the northern bastion can no longer be discerned, as the minaret was incorporated into the Fatimid walls of the city when they were expanded later in the eleventh century by Badr al-Jamali.[9] When the Armenian general rebuilt the walls of Cairo in stone, he expanded the perimeter of the city to the north, building the walls just to the north of the Mosque of al-Hakim. As the northern wall of the city came to abut the mosque, the northern minaret was encompassed within the new stone structure (see fig. 4.2). Therefore, the northern minaret was not covered once, but twice—first by al-Hakim, then by Badr al-Jamali. As Creswell has suggested, the slabs with Qur'anic inscriptions from al-Hakim's renovations were likely turned over and reused in this renovation, so it is impossible to read the northern minaret's inscription.[10] The tops of both minarets were destroyed in a fourteenth-century earthquake, so the finials we now see were replaced under the ruler Baybars II.

The western bastion from 1010, however, remains as a prominent feature of Islamic Cairo (see fig. 4.1). Disregarding the much later, distinctive Mamluk finial, in form the minaret resembles Islamic monuments in North Africa, such as the minarets of the Abbasid-style ninth-century Mosque of Sfax and Mosque of Qayrawan (figs. 4.4–4.5).[11] Its

FIGURES 4.6–4.7
Cairo, Mosque of al-Hakim, inscription on western bastion, 1010

elaborate, interlaced crenellation at roof height is reminiscent of the crenellations found at the Mosque of Ibn Tulun. The new tower is executed as two stacked cubes, the bottom wider than the top. Built of brick, the bastion is completely unadorned, with the exception of one narrow band of Qur'anic inscription executed in a restrained floriated Kufic style on a marble slab, approximately 17 feet (5.2 meters) above ground level (figs. 4.6–4.7).

Both bastions can be entered through a southeastern door that opens from the mosque's courtyard. Bracing arches support the towers and connect them to the original minarets of 1003 (see fig. 3.13), suggesting that the originals were purposefully preserved and accessible. At the time of Creswell's visit, one moved between the brick salients and original stone towers via an iron staircase that turned into a stone staircase as one ascended. However, when the historian Max van Berchem visited in 1888, he found a ramp leading between the two forms, which had possibly been replaced by the architectural historian Max Herz.[12]

Scholars have posited various reasons for the encasement of the exquisitely fashioned minarets of 1003—from a desire to add structural stability to the original towers, to a reluctance to destroy parts of a religious building, to a testament of al-Hakim's bizarre and capricious personality.[13] However, given the number of structures that were left unprotected and al-Hakim's penchant for changing the public message of his reign, these explanations seem unlikely. At the time of the renovation, major changes were underway in al-Hakim's architectural program, changes that illuminate the obscuring of the 1003 towers and al-Hakim's notorious legacy more generally. Most significantly, al-Hakim was engaged in the wide-scale destruction of churches and the *waqf* of major Islamic projects in his realm, including the Mosque of al-Azhar, the Mosque of al-Maqs, the Mosque of Rashida, and the *dār al-ʿilm*, suggesting a consolidation and Islamization of his architectural priorities.

Two interrelated elements of the new bastions are significant representations of al-Hakim's assertions of authority and a puritanical claim of Islamic universality. First, the new bastions are marked by an austere design. Second, the new inscriptions convey an increased emphasis on themes of justice and the universal acts of Islam, accepted by all Muslims, rather than the verses with allegorical significance to the Ismaili initiates. The new bastions omit the name of the Imam and instead feature harsh, recriminatory Qur'anic verses dealing primarily with hypocrites and unbelievers. Privileging the *ẓāhir* over the *bāṭin*, the 1010 towers focused on individual behavior and the Fatimid ruler's role as a purveyor of justice rather than as a holder of *bāṭin* truths.

The inscriptions contain verses not usually addressed in the Ismaili *taʾwīl* of the Qur'an. In particular, the inclusion of Qur'anic verses 24:26–28 relate directly to al-Hakim's increasingly puritanical edicts against women in his realm:

> Women impure are for men impure, and men impure are for women impure, and women of purity are for men of purity, and men of purity are for women of purity: these are not affected by what people say: for them there is forgiveness, and a provision honorable.

These verses recall the growing restriction on the movement of women during al-Hakim's reign. Increasingly, al-Hakim prohibited women from going outside, going so far as to ban the production of shoes for women. He also issued repeated injunctions against their visiting cemeteries.[14] Earlier Fatimid rulers could be characterized as laissez-faire in their dealings with the populace. In contrast, al-Hakim began to focus on a rigid, more extreme interpretation of Islamic law. This development of religious austerity was characteristic of his actions and architectural program in this time. Similar austerity can be seen in both the content and style of the new inscriptions.

The new inscription also included Qur'anic verse 62:9, urging the populace to observe the Friday prayers:

> O ye who believe! When the call is proclaimed to prayer on Friday [the Day of Assembly], hasten earnestly to the Remembrance of Allah, and leave off business [and traffic]. That is best for you if ye but knew.[15]

Although the Friday prayer mentioned in the new inscription band does have an Ismaili allegorical meaning, here its placement among verses without allegorical discussion and a lack of overt Ismaili symbolism emphasizes the importance of following Islamic law, rather than its *bāṭin* dimension.[16] One inscribed verse from the Qur'an (9:107) warns against those who "put up a mosque by way of mischief and infidelity—to disunite the Believers." As Irene Bierman and Paula Sanders have discussed, this verse may very well be an admonishment against the Jarrahid usurpers, who attempted to claim the holy cities of Mecca and Medina for themselves in 1010.[17]

Likewise departing from the distinctive 1003 design, the form of the newly enclosed minarets recalled older models of single-tower, square minarets encountered in Abbasid realms. Jonathan Bloom has shown that the single-tower minaret opposite the *qibla*, the direction Muslims face during prayer, is a style that was introduced in ninth-century Baghdad. It spread not only as a practical response for the need to call the faithful to prayer, but also as a visual symbol of Islamic power.[18] According to Bloom, in North Africa the presence of the minaret across from the mihrab specifically evoked allegiance to Abbasid Baghdad.[19] This precise form, consisting of a square, substantial tower tapering upward can be found throughout the North African Aghlabid context. The minarets in the mosques in Sfax, Sousse, and Tunis mimic this same basic form, indicating their fealty to the Abbasid ruler and operating as a visual sign of Sunnism more broadly (see fig. 4.4). For example, the Aghlabid minaret at the Great Mosque of Qayrawan is the earliest minaret in North Africa, dating to circa 836 (see fig. 4.5). Its placement in the mosque, situated in the center of the wall directly across from the mihrab, conforms to Bloom's identification of a Sunni mosque. Based on the lighthouse of Salakta, the minaret is made up of three levels, tapering as it rises from its massive base.[20] Like the bastions of the Mosque of al-Hakim, the minaret has an aesthetic that evokes austerity, solidity, and mass.[21]

Although Bloom identifies the use of this form in North Africa as a declaration of Abbasid fealty, it also acquired a more general identification of a Sunni mosque. For example, when, upon declaring the caliphate, ʿAbd al-Rahman III ordered the addition of a minaret to the Great Mosque of Cordoba, he opted for the square forms that characterized Sunni mosques of the time, even though he certainly was not allied with the Abbasids.[22] This form was not seen in the mosques of the Kharijites or of the ʿAlids in North Africa. Neither was it seen in the early mosques of the early Fatimids, who omitted the minaret altogether (see chapters 1 and 3), in favor of calling the faithful to prayer from the mosque's roof, in obedience to ʿAli's order.[23] It is significant, therefore, that the new bastions at the Mosque of al-Hakim so strongly evoke Sunni forms.

AL-HAKIM'S OTHER ARCHITECTURAL PROJECTS

At the same time that he obscured the original towers at the Mosque of al-Hakim, al-Hakim endowed the mosques of al-Azhar, Rashida, al-Maqs, and the *dār al-ʿilm*, guaranteeing their continuation and demonstrating that Cairo's architecture and urban development were central concerns of his rule. Al-Maqrizi recorded the *waqfiyya* (a document recording the details of the endowment) that was originally recorded by al-Musabbihi.[24] The text begins with an evocative glimpse of al-Hakim's realm. It notes that the endowment deed was verified by chief judge Malik ibn Saʿid al-Fariqi, along with the people of the Sessions of Wisdom (*majālis al-ḥikma*) and the judges of Fustat-Misr, suggesting that representatives of both the Ismaili and Sunni communities verified the document. It introduces al-Hakim as being in charge of "al-Qahira al-Muʿizziyya [al-Qahira of al-Muʿizz], Misr, Alexandria, Mecca, Medina, the military districts of Syria, Raqqa, Rahba, and the Maghreb, and all that he has conquered or will conquer east and west."[25] This list of territories emphasizes al-Hakim's recent victories over rebels in North Africa and in greater Syria over the short-lived Meccan counter-caliph.

The bulk of the record is devoted to the financing of the Mosque of al-Azhar, which Jawhar, under the patronage of al-Hakim's grandfather, al-Muʿizz, had established in the new Ismaili enclave of Cairo. It differentiates the institutions based on location, clarifying for the reader which mosques were inside the enclave and which were not. According to the document, al-Azhar and the *dār al-ʿilm* are part of the well-guarded Cairo (*al-Qāhira al-mahrūsa*); Rashida and al-Maqs, by contrast, are simply listed by name, emphasizing the distinction between the walled Ismaili enclave and the urban spaces outside its walls.[26] The document also suggests that al-Hakim's attention to these buildings had begun before the preservation of the document, as he had already endowed the *dār al-ʿilm* with books.

As is typical of medieval accounts, the endowment records preserve little of the projects' visual qualities and, beyond the covering of the minarets of 1003 with the bastions of 1010, it is impossible to determine what elements of the visual program of the Mosque of al-Hakim date to this period.[27] However, a pair of wooden doors, donated to the Mosque of al-Azhar during this period, is still extant, housed in the Museum of Islamic Art in Cairo (fig. 4.8). The doors are made up of a series of alternating vertical and horizontal carved panels. At the top is an inscription carved in a floriated Kufic form with typical Fatimid content: "Our master [*mawlānā*] commander of the faithful [*amīr al-muʾminīn*], the Imam al-Hakim bi-Amr Allah, Blessings of God on him and on his pure ancestors and descendants."[28] The panels below the inscription are carved in an archaizing Abbasid beveled style. The carved lines undulate into spirals at each end, leaving behind the vegetal ornamentation seen in the floriated Kufic that characterized earlier Fatimid carving. Instead, the forms moved into the pure abstraction that was typical of the older, more conservative style found in Abbasid realms and in Abbasid-style monuments, such as the Mosque of Ibn Tulun in Cairo. I would posit that this archaizing

FIGURE 4.8 (OPPOSITE)
Doors donated to the Mosque of al-Azhar by the Imam-caliph al-Hakim, 1010, Cairo, Museum of Islamic Art

Sunni style of carving is consistent with the shift to a more conservative, austere style in the bastions of the Mosque of al-Hakim. Indeed, the remaining material from these years of patronage suggest a concerted shift away from the more expressive, unique Fatimid aesthetics of the earlier periods to one that is more universally Islamic, with a particular nod to Sunni monuments.

Al-Maqrizi records several other instances of al-Hakim providing religious objects to Cairo's mosques. In 1013, he sent 814 Qu'ran manuscripts to the Mosque of Ibn Tulun along with 1,290 Qur'ans and a new silver chandelier to the Mosque of ʿAmr. In addition, he sponsored a survey of Cairo's mosques. When he discovered that almost 800 of them had no money, he provided 9,220 dirhams per month to support them.[29] The Mosque of al-Hakim was finally completed in 1013, when furniture was added and the prayers inaugurated. Al-Maqrizi preserves the report of al-Hakim donating a minbar, which was inscribed with an inscription, stating "He has ordered this minbar for the [M]osque of al-Hakim, built outside Bab al-Futuh in the year 403/1012–13." In the same year, al-Maqrizi reports that al-Hakim ordered 36,000 square cubits (54,000 square feet) of matting, curtains hung in the doors, four silver chandeliers, and many silver lamps. These renovations totaled 5,000 dinars.[30]

In this period, al-Hakim also sponsored another project in the Muqattam Hills—an observatory, which was ordered to be constructed in 1012. This project related both to the caliph's increasing practice of promenading to the Muqattam Hills at night and to his interest in science and intellectual pursuits, as seen in the earlier patronage of the *dār al-ʿilm*. Indeed, al-Hakim supported two of the most important scientists in the medieval Islamic world: Abu ʿAli al-Hasan ibn al-Haytham, the physicist, famous for his work on optics, and ʿAli ibn ʿAbd al-Rahman ibn Yunis, the astronomer. Al-Hakim was particularly interested in astronomy, and his court had its own royal astronomer, whose observations were made from this observatory at the top of the Muqattam Hills. From this base, Ibn Yunis and other astronomers compiled the information into an important scientific work, called *Zīj al-Ḥākimī al-kabīr* (The great astrological book of al-Hakim), named for the patron.[31]

Al-Hakim's substantial investment in the city's religious and intellectual spaces transformed Cairo from a way station on the path to Baghdad into a full-fledged Islamic center. These investments in Islamic building projects occurred at the same time as the demolishing of minority religious structures, suggesting that destruction and construction operated in tandem toward Islamizing the architectural framework of Cairo. The link between church destruction and Islamic renovation can be seen particularly clearly if we consider the Mosque of Rashida. As discussed in chapter 3, al-Maqrizi records that the mosque had been built in 1003 on a site where there had previously been a church. The Rashida area, located south of Fustat, had been full of churches, as well as graves of Christians and Jews. Al-Hakim's destruction of the churches in his realm would have certainly impacted the land surrounding the Mosque of Rashida, making this a particularly opportune time to endow the mosque. A similar dynamic is at work with the Mosque of al-Maqs. In one of the earlier cases of church destruction, al-Maqrizi records that the churches on the road to al-Maqs were destroyed. Just as al-Hakim claimed the lands for Islam through the destruction of minority monuments, he strengthened the Islamization through endowing the structure.

The Mosque of Rashida provides another glimpse into the dynamics of productive destruction. Only a few years after its completion and endowment, it was torn down. The brick structure built in 1003 was reconstructed in grander, more permanent stone in 1011.[32] Sources do not describe the aesthetics of the building beyond its brick construction, but it is significant that the destruction and reconstruction happened in the critical period of the reimagined minarets of the Mosque of al-Hakim. It also serves as evidence that the concealment of the minarets at the Mosque of al-Hakim was not simply carried out due to an apprehension about destroying the earlier towers.[33]

THE DESTRUCTION OF THE CHURCH OF THE HOLY SEPULCHER AND OTHER CHURCHES IN HIS REALM

As discussed in the previous chapter, in the first years of his reign, al-Hakim continued his predecessors' tolerance of the Christian population and their churches. However, al-Hakim's call to destroy the Church of the Holy Sepulcher in Jerusalem brought an end to this era of peace. In chapter 2, I argued that the popular fervor for church demolitions had already been on the rise during the reigns of al-Mu'izz and al-'Aziz. This fervor reached an unprecedented level in this second phase of al-Hakim's reign, starting with the destruction of the Church of the Holy Sepulcher.[34]

At the time of the church's demolition, Jerusalem was a Fatimid city, yet the church remained an important Christian pilgrimage site and was protected by a Fatimid treaty with the Byzantine empire, signed in 1000. Indeed, the church itself had a Byzantine origin, as it was the Byzantine empress Helena (d. ca. 330) who discovered the rock-hewn tomb of Christ in 326. A martyrium was then constructed around the discovered tomb between 326 and 336.[35] Al-Hakim's destruction of the church makes it impossible to reconstruct the original appearance of the monument, which is known primarily through textual and archaeological records. However, a corpus of images in various media indicate its form. A series of tenth-century ivories depict it as a cylindrical structure, typical of other Byzantine martyria.[36] One ivory from this group depicts the three Marys at the tomb of Christ (fig. 4.9). The cylindrical structure is similar to the reconstructed aedicula that marks the site of the tomb today (fig. 4.10). The church is also depicted in two mosaics in Jordan—one from Madaba (fig. 4.11) and the other from Umm al-Rasas. In these images, we can make out the rotunda, marking the site of the tomb, and the basilica, marking the site of the crucifixion. Likewise, a late seventh-century account of the Holy Land provided by the Frankish bishop Arculf describes a

FIGURE 4.9
Three women at the Church of the Holy Sepulcher, 10th-century ivory, northern Italy. The Metropolitan Museum of Art, New York, inv. no. 1993.19

FIGURE 4.10
Jerusalem, Church of the Holy Sepulcher, interior with a view of the aedicula and dome, as they appear today

rotunda with twelve columns, three aisles, and three recessed altars, with the sepulcher in the center, accompanied by a schematic plan of the church (fig. 4.12).[37] Arculf's plan and description corroborate textual evidence that a basilica was attached to the rotunda of the tomb, linking it with Golgotha, the site of Christ's crucifixion. Thus, the church housed the most central mysteries of the Christian faith, enclosing the site of Christ's crucifixion, burial, and resurrection in a single structure.

By the Fatimid period, the physical makeup and population of Jerusalem had changed significantly since its Islamic foundation by the Umayyads in the seventh century. This change was particularly notable during the time when the Abbasid caliph Harun al-Rashid (r. 786–809) controlled Jerusalem and the Carolingian emperor Charlemagne (r. 742–814), ruling from Aachen, invested heavily in the city. In this period, the increased presence of Latin Christianity changed the urban landscape of Jerusalem; as Abbasid investment in the city waned, the Carolingian investment in the city increased substantially. Charlemagne sponsored significant Christian structures within the city while re-creating his own city of Aachen as a new Jerusalem in the west. Within

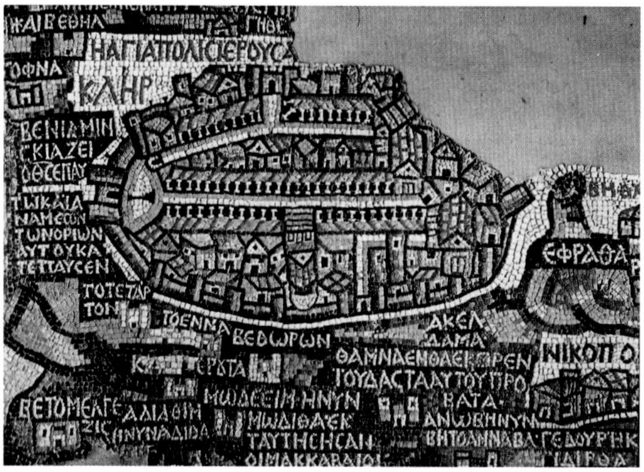

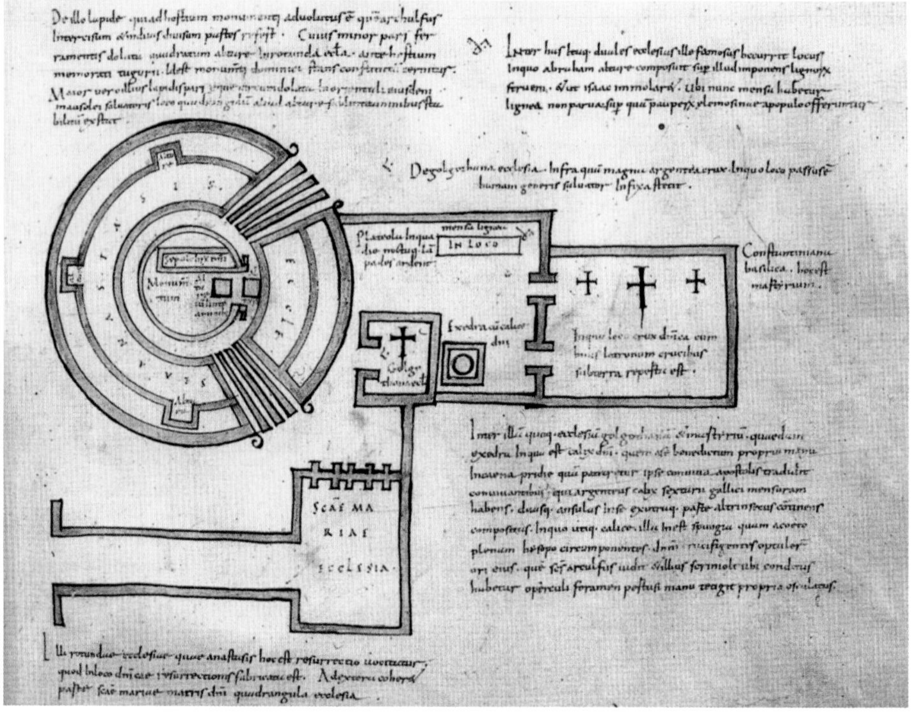

FIGURE 4.11
A 6th-century mosaic from the Church of Saint George in Madaba, Jordan, illustrating the major monuments of Jerusalem

FIGURE 4.12
Jerusalem, Church of the Holy Sepulcher, plan, by Arculf, ca. 670

Jerusalem itself, a complex for the Latin pilgrims was constructed near the Holy Sepulcher, adding to the mix of Christian confessional identities. Sources from the period suggest that many Christian monuments were in full operation with generous funding for their upkeep and with treasuries supplied by foreign Christian powers.[38]

Competition between Muslim and Christian populations in the city became particularly tense in the tenth century, when religious strife occurred on both imperial and local levels. Mob violence against Christians flared up on a scale large enough to be recorded by medieval historians. Al-Muqaddasi's description of the city during this time laments that everywhere, Christians and Jews "have the upper hand."[39] In particular, tales of wealth concentrated in church treasuries seemed to spawn urban upheavals. Much of the interfaith conflict centered on the status of religious spaces, particularly that of the Church of the Holy Sepulcher; for example, in 937, a mob attacked a group of Christians during a Palm Sunday procession and the Holy Sepulcher was set on fire, damaging its gates, the Anastasis rotunda, and Golgotha chapel.[40] In 966, mob violence again damaged the Holy Sepulcher and other Christian buildings in the city. Rioters set the doors and woodwork of the Holy Sepulcher on fire, destroying the roof of the basilica and the rotunda.[41] The rioting began in the architectural space but ended with the execution of the Christian patriarch.

Concomitant with the mob violence between the local populations of Jerusalem, strife intensified between the Byzantine empire and the Fatimids, with the Byzantines embarking on a series of raids against Muslim powers, which were couched increasingly in terms of a holy war between Christianity and Islam. In 964, the Byzantine emperor Nikephoros II Phokas (r. 963–69) proclaimed he would retake Jerusalem from the Muslims, and by 975, the Byzantine emperor John I Tzimiskes (r. 969–76) delivered a letter to the king of Armenia, noting his military endeavors to secure the city and situating the Holy Sepulcher at the heart of this struggle. Offering the details of his campaign, he wrote, "We were also intent on the delivery of the Holy Sepulcher of Christ our God from the bondage of the Muslims."[42] The emperor's focus on the monument and the need to liberate it from Muslim rule illustrates the historic centrality of the church in the spiritual, political, and ideological struggle for dominance between Islam and Christianity in a city that was of primary importance to both faiths. In the meantime, after the Fatimids conquered Damascus from the Byzantines, the emperor responded by converting a mosque to a church, then burning it to the ground.[43]

The tenth-century mob attacks on the Holy Sepulcher and the emperor's focus on the monument suggest that architectural space acted as a stage and proxy for religious rivalries, both locally and between empires.[44] Nevertheless, the reason for the destruction of the church at that precise moment is unknown. According to the Buyid chronicler Hilal al-Sabiʾ (d. 1056) as well as al-Maqrizi, al-Hakim was curious about the Christians who made a pilgrimage to the church every Easter. When the caliph inquired about this practice, one of his Ismaili missionaries (*dāʿīs*) informed him that the church was so significant to the Christians that the Byzantine emperor sometimes attended Easter celebrations in disguise and gave the church expensive gifts. The sources also lament that the Christians visited the church much as Muslims visited Mecca and that there was too much pomp surrounding this act. They suggest that al-Hakim was especially angered that Christian pilgrims regarded it as the locus of miracles, particularly the Holy Fire miracle.[45]

William of Tyre, a twelfth-century Latin resident of Jerusalem, offered one of the most provocative theories on the rationale for the Holy Sepulcher's destruction. William suggested that al-Hakim destroyed the church to counter rumors that he himself was a

Christian, on account of his Christian mother, noting that the patriarch of the time was a maternal uncle of the caliph. He concludes that "the caliph used this extreme measure to prove to the infidels that he was loyal to them."[46] Historically, it is contested whether al-ʿAziz's Christian wife was the mother of al-Hakim. However, even if the details are flawed, William's analysis illustrates the crucial concern with clarifying religious identity during al-Hakim's reign. It reminds us of the intimate connections between the early Fatimid caliphs and the Christian power structure. Even if al-Hakim's mother was not Christian, the fact remains that a member of the Fatimid royal family had been the patriarch of Jerusalem. Whether or not this figure was a blood relative, al-Hakim's destructions firmly distanced his rule from the often-unpopular interfaith alliances of his predecessors, alliances that were still resonant in the Crusader-occupied Jerusalem of William's time.

Ultimately, while the reasons for the destruction at this particular moment are lost to us, the results were clear: al-Hakim's destruction of the Holy Sepulcher asserted Muslim dominance over the contested city, putting a definitive end to the struggle over the sacred space that characterized earlier popular revolts and imperial warfare from the eighth to the tenth century.[47] Modern scholars might dismiss the destruction of the Holy Sepulcher as a symptom of al-Hakim's madness. However, medieval Muslim sources present a more complicated picture of the destruction. Ibn al-Qalanisi (d. 1160) noted that when the church was destroyed, Muslims "held long prayers of thanks giving." When word of the positive reaction to the destruction reached the caliph, he was overjoyed and was encouraged to demolish more churches in his realm.[48] The disdain for the church in contemporary Muslim thought is evidenced in medieval nomenclature, which refers to the church almost always as "the Garbage Heap" (*al-Qumāma*) rather than "the Resurrection" (*al-Qiyāma*).[49]

When al-Hakim razed the church, instead of collecting its precious objects for his own treasury he allowed the local population to plunder it as a way to garner support and make them complicit in the deed.[50] Yahya al-Antaki's report attests to the fervor of the plunder, noting that the church was "plucked up stone by stone," that everything was destroyed except the parts that would have been impossible to destroy or remove, and that its destruction was accompanied by the razing of other churches in Jerusalem, in addition to the desecration of a graveyard and a convent. This act of demolition, together with the acclaim it brought al-Hakim throughout the Muslim world, seems to have emboldened the caliph to embark on an intensified program of church destruction and persecution of Christians and Jews in the following years.

Among the major Egyptian Christian sources for the period, few discuss this momentous event in any detail. This is not entirely surprising, as Monophysite Coptic Christians, unlike the Orthodox Melkites, did not visit the church on pilgrimage.[51] In *The History of the Patriarchs*, Michael of Tinnis suggests that the destruction of the church was punishment for Christianity's misdeeds. His account notes that the Church was mostly concerned with a "love of silver and gold, and they sold the gift of God for money" and that God allowed the church's destruction for these misdeeds.[52] According to Michael, the order for the destruction of the Holy Sepulcher was composed by a Christian scribe, who then spent the rest of his days punishing his hand by lifting it up and striking the ground with it: "And he did not cease from this throughout the days of his illness until his fingers were cut to pieces and he died."[53]

Michael's account of the Holy Sepulcher's destruction points to the complicated nature of religious identity in the Fatimid era. On the one hand, Michael was a Christian, for whom a church marking the site of Christ's death and resurrection held obvious significance. On the other, he was a Coptic Christian, and his sect had splintered bitterly from the Byzantine Orthodox Church after the Council of Chalcedon in 451. Therefore, the destruction of the church was not blamed on the cruel Egyptian caliph but on the corruption of the Orthodox Melkites, who are implicitly contrasted with the righteous, Egyptian Copts.[54]

Relations between the Fatimids and Byzantines at the time of its destruction were relatively peaceful compared to the constant frontier wars that defined the reign of al-ʿAziz. However, reading between the lines of the historical sources suggests that the act *did* bring repercussions from the Byzantines, instituted partially through claims on sectarian space. In particular, it seems that, at some time after the church's destruction, the Byzantines closed the Mosque of Constantinople in retaliation. The closure is not mentioned explicitly in the sources, but we can infer it by the statement that the mosque was reopened during the truce with al-Hakim's successor, al-Zahir.[55] This episode suggests that religious spaces became pawns in imperial negotiations—the Mosque of Constantinople acted as a proxy for the Fatimid state, while the Holy Sepulcher was a stand-in for the Byzantine empire. Ultimately, the event was most highly publicized in the Western Christian world, where it acted as a rallying cry for wresting the Holy Land from Muslim hands.

Although the destruction of the Holy Sepulcher and the acclaim it garnered for al-Hakim seem to have bolstered the caliph in his intensified program of church destruction, it is difficult to piece together the demolitions that took place after the razing of the Holy Sepulcher. Many Muslim sources say simply that all the churches were destroyed. In analyzing this phenomenon, we are faced with the difficulty of discussing buildings that no longer remain and whose existence was not always recorded in medieval accounts. In examining some of the specific instances, I have relied particularly on the analysis of Abu Salih, an Armenian Christian who recorded the history of Egyptian churches in the late twelfth and early thirteenth centuries. As several of the churches and monasteries he documented were initially destroyed under al-Hakim and then rebuilt, his account allows for a consideration of key demolitions.

The Monastery of al-Qusayr offers a rare example of a dated Egyptian church destruction and, by all accounts, this event occurred after the destruction of the Holy

Sepulcher. The description of its demolition suggests a tide of public support for such acts. The monastery, a favorite location for the early rulers of Egypt, was particularly famous for its mosaic depictions of the Virgin Mary. However, according to al-Maqrizi, in 1010 al-Hakim ordered it razed; the subsequent plunder lasted several days. Abu Salih's record of this event corroborates the plunder: "A band of common people came here and seized the coffins of the dead, the timbers from the ruins."[56] The account's emphasis on grave robbery also recalls the account of the plundering of grave sites near the Church of the Holy Sepulcher. Abu Salih states that the grave robbers raided this church so extensively that al-Hakim finally had to put a stop to it—evidence of the role populist urban pressures played in the program of church destruction. The account suggests a popular fervor for destruction, with caliphal endorsement, in this middle period of al-Hakim's reign.

Abu Salih also mentions a church in al-Ashmunayn that had originally featured gilded mosaics and marble pillars but that was destroyed under al-Hakim. An account of the Nahya Monastery highlights the disparity between al-Hakim and his ancestors in the treatment of Christian structures. This monastery, described in chapter 2, housed al-Muʿizz on his way to Cairo and, according to Michael of Tinnis, was even embellished by the early caliph. However, this early site of interfaith contact was destroyed under al-Hakim.

Church destructions functioned as something more than an indicator of al-Hakim's personal anti-Christian zealotry. Instead, they appear as part of his political strategy of shoring up support for his rule and for the Fatimid caliphate through an architectural program aimed at further Islamization of the empire, oriented toward the Sunni majority. The case of the Church of Saint Mennas, located in al-Hamra, between al-Qahira and Fustat, provides the first of several examples of destruction as Islamization. Much of the information about the Church of Saint Mennas and its monastery comes to us through Abu Salih, who described it as having experienced various periods of decay and restoration prior to the Fatimid period. It also contained the bodies of many saints. He writes of one of its dependencies, the Church of Saint Theodore, that "this church was wrecked, and its columns were carried away and it was turned into a mosque, in the caliphate of al-Hakim; and a minaret was built for it."[57] According to Abu Salih, al-Hakim did not simply destroy the church. Rather, he changed its religious signifier by adding a minaret to the building. In Abu Salih's description, the Church experiences a pattern of disrepair and restoration, including purposeful demolition and repair. Abu Salih treats al-Hakim's rule as simply another chapter in the church's long and bumpy history rather than as a particularly ruthless period of destruction.

A similar pattern is seen in his description of the Monastery of Saint John the Baptist. Abu Salih recalls the beauty of the monastery and its ideal location, next to the Lake of al-Habash and the gardens sowed by al-ʿAziz's brother Tamim.[58] He notes that much of the populace enjoyed the monastery and the nearby royal gardens, suggesting the integration of these projects in a multiconfessional cityscape. Abu Salih recounts that "al-Hakim seized upon part of this monastery and church and rebuilt it as a mosque, with a minaret, and his name was inscribed on it." In these reconstructions, the addition of the minaret transformed the monuments from Christian to Muslim. Indeed, in most of Abu Salih's accounts, the churches destroyed by al-Hakim were turned into mosques, suggesting a larger movement to Islamize the city and country. The inclusion of al-Hakim's name in the new minarets resonates with the caliphal titles on the original Mosque of al-Hakim and al-Hakim's general use of the "public text."[59]

Christian sources often point to Muslims converting to Christianity as the main impetus for al-Hakim's persecution of Christians. William of Tyre's description of al-Hakim's links to Christianity highlights both the importance and complexity of religious identity in the medieval Islamic world. Moreover, the story of Ibn Raga in *The History of the Patriarchs* (discussed in chapter 3) reveals the high stakes of medieval conversion. Indeed, in the historical sources, we find many indications of Christians and Jews converting or pretending to convert to Islam. Yahya al-Antaki noted that al-Hakim relied heavily on Christians and Jews in his administration, but since they were so numerous, he tried to convert them. Ultimately, whether al-Hakim destroyed these buildings for popular appeal, financial gain, caliphal ambition, religious fervor, or a combination of all of these reasons, his actions seemed to have either garnered or been bolstered by popular support.

AL-KIRMANI AND THE FATIMID ZEITGEIST

Al-Hakim was a particularly active supporter of the Fatimid mission (*da'wa*), attempting to spread the Ismaili cause throughout the Islamic world.[60] One of the great paradoxes of the Fatimid empire is that the highly successful Ismailis' support for the efforts of the *da'wa* never resulted in the conversion of their Sunni subjects in great numbers. Due to the inherent secrecy of the *da'wa*'s efforts, it is difficult to discern the precise nature of their activity in Egypt, even as we know that their efforts were increasing in eastern Islamic areas. Non-Ismaili sources, such as al-Maqrizi and Yahya al-Antaki, were not privy to the workings of the Ismaili *da'wa* and therefore do not discuss the intricacies of the Fatimid *da'wa*. Ismaili sources, meanwhile, generally do not focus on historical details but on religious thought.[61]

However, recent publications have allowed us a glimpse into the workings and philosophies of the Fatimid-era *da'wa*.[62] The writings of al-Kirmani (d. 1021), the most important individual missionary (*dā'ī*) of al-Hakim's age and his chief apologist, have been translated by Paul Walker and offer tremendous insight into the Fatimid ideology during al-Hakim's reign. They provide further support for the idea that al-Hakim's architectural project was integral to and consistent with a wider program of political propaganda and a shift in Fatimid sectarian identity.

Originally from Iran, al-Kirmani was first active in eastern Islamic lands, eventually arriving in Cairo to serve at the Imam's court. A defender of al-Hakim, al-Kirmani attempted to spread the message of the ruler's rightful authority throughout the Islamic world. In particular, al-Kirmani defended the Fatimids against Sunni critics, who suggested that the Ismaili preference for the *bāṭin* over the *ẓāhir* was heretical. Sunni critics often disparaged the Fatimids as *bāṭiniyya* (favoring the *bāṭin*), suggesting that their allegorical interpretation of Islamic laws meant that they were not true Muslims, an accusation that gained particular currency during al-Hakim's reign.[63] According to these critics, the Fatimids privileged the esoteric dimension of Islam while ignoring the proscribed acts of the faith; once the inner truths had been revealed to the Ismaili initiates, they charged, Islamic practice was no longer necessary.[64] To counter this accusation, al-Kirmani wrote multiple tracts emphasizing the importance of uniting Ismaili *bāṭin* beliefs with lawful acts—what he referred to as double observance (*ʿibādatayn*).[65] An analysis of al-Kirmani's texts reveals a substantial shift in the dominant Ismaili philosophy during this time. It is impossible to determine whether al-Hakim responded to these changes or if al-Kirmani devised a philosophy to explain the shocking acts of the capricious caliph. However, it is clear that the religious and political ideology of the Ismaili Fatimids experienced a substantial transformation under al-Kirmani and that these changes are reflected in and supported by al-Hakim's architectural projects.

Certainly, al-Kirmani was not the first Ismaili *dāʿī* to outline the importance of Islamic acts and living in accordance with Islamic law. Prior to al-Kirmani, al-Qadi al-Nuʿman had outlined, in *Daʿāʾim al-Islām* (*The Pillars of Islam*), the proper way to balance the *bāṭin* dimensions of the faith with the required acts of Islam. However, al-Nuʿman and other early Fatimid thinkers stressed that ultimately the esoteric dimensions of the faith were most central. His accompanying work, *Taʾwīl al-daʿāʾim* (The allegorical interpretation of the pillars), therefore explicated the *true* nature of the pillars of Islam. Unlike al-Nuʿman, al-Kirmani argued against the primacy of the allegorical aspects of the faith, emphasizing the importance of the double observance of the *bāṭin* and the *ẓāhir* and arguing for the importance of Islamic acts even for those who might know their *taʾwīl*. He compares the performance of good acts, including for the Shiʿa, to the clothing of the soul. Referring to the Shiʿa, who have been indoctrinated into the *bāṭin* truths of the Ismailis, al-Kirmani asks his readers to imagine "how reprehensible of a person to be one of those in paradise alongside people who have struggled and worked righteous deeds (*ʿamal*), and while being amongst them, to rip off his clothes and expose his nakedness."[66] In this analogy, the shedding of the acts, which conceal the inner truths, is shameful and an insult to those in paradise.

Al-Kirmani characterizes the *bāṭin* and the *ẓāhir* as corresponding to knowledge and acts, respectively. He outlines the *ẓāhir* aspect of the faith, defining them as "acts requiring declarations by the tongue and works of the limbs and members, such as comprise the profession of faith, confession, purification, the call to prayer, the *iqāma* prayer, bowing, almsgiving, fasting, pilgrimage, jihad, acts of obedience and submission to the Friends of God."[67] These acts, recognized by all Muslims regardless of sect, are contrasted with *bāṭin* knowledge of God, the soul, and the heavens. Understanding the *bāṭin* truths requires guidance and careful initiation by the *dāʿīs*, who can slowly reveal the hidden knowledge to the initiates of the faith.

Perhaps the most revealing window onto the shift from *bāṭin* to *ẓāhir* under al-Hakim can be found in al-Kirmani's treatise *Al-Maṣābīḥ fī ithbāt al-imāma* (*Lights to Illuminate the Proof of the Imamate*). Paul Walker has noted that this was not the only treatise on the nature of the Imamate at this time. In fact, although they are rare in the Fatimid period in general, there are two works that prove the necessity of the Imamate dated to al-Hakim's reign.[68] This suggests a concerted effort on the part of the *daʿwa* to prove the nature of the Imamate. The precise date of al-Kirmani's treatise is not known, but it was most likely completed between 1011 and 1015 (AH 402–6) while he was in Iraq.[69] However, it is likely that al-Kirmani adapted it from writings prior to this. Therefore, the text can be considered as both a reflection of and a reaction to changes in Fatimid policies and thought, including al-Hakim's increasingly harsh edicts, his destruction of churches, and his growing popularity in some regions of the Islamic world. On the one hand, the text may be conceived of as an outline of al-Hakim's vision for the caliphate. On the other, it can be considered an apologist explanation of his acts. In either case, it offers valuable insight into the changing sectarian relations and claims of universal Islamic rulership during this period.

The treatise was written as a series of proofs, which first demonstrated the necessity of the Imamate and then proved that al-Hakim was the rightful Imam to all Muslims. In his proofs, al-Kirmani does not emphasize al-Hakim as the source of *bāṭin* knowledge but as a lawgiver and figure who commands his subjects in Islamic law. For the purposes of this study, the second half of the treatise is of particular interest. In it, al-Kirmani situates al-Hakim's Imamate in an intercultural context, noting that there were a series of "false Imams," which includes Shiʿi contenders as well as the Abbasid and Spanish Umayyad caliphs.

Unlike previous Ismaili treatises, this work was not aimed at the Ismaili initiates, but was addressed to the Buyid vizier in Baghdad, Fakhr al-Mulk, in an effort to win him over to the Fatimid cause. Though the Buyids themselves were Shiʿi, they did not recognize the Fatimid caliph as the living Imam and instead supported the Sunni Abbasid caliph. Rather than explicating the philosophical details of the Ismaili faith, the work acted as an overt piece of political propaganda, couched in terms of religious legitimacy and aimed at shifting the vizier's allegiance to the Fatimid cause. The many copies of the text suggest that it was meant to be distributed and read widely throughout the medieval Islamic world.

An analysis of this text supports the idea that the destruction of churches, endowment of mosques, and obfuscation of the minarets of the Mosque of al-Hakim were all integral to a wider program of political propaganda and a reconceptualization of Fatimid sectarian identity. In support of his argument that al-Hakim is the rightful Imam, al-Kirmani emphasizes that a key role for the Imam is to be a defender of morality and a commander of rightful Islamic acts. Al-Hakim, he argues, "commands the good and forbids the bad, applies the corporal punishments, preserves the borders, cares for the populace, revives the sunna, safeguards society."[70] These acts are consistent with *ẓāhir* laws accepted universally by all Muslim sects. The acts analyzed in al-Kirmani's text echo the inscriptional content of the new bastions at the Mosque of al-Hakim. He repeatedly notes that al-Hakim "safeguard(s) sexual relations and property." This is reminiscent of al-Hakim's harsh injunctions against women and the bastions' inclusion of Qur'an 24:26–28, which prescribes "women impure . . . for men impure" and warns the reader not to enter other people's houses without permission. Al-Kirmani expands upon this theme:

> Because of being distracted by having to defend one's womenfolk and property, that would lead to ruin, destruction and the obstruction of the entry to houses for the worship of God. Accordingly, the path of reason requires that, in fulfillment of the wisdom of God among what He made and created in order to populate the next world, humans should have regulations and judgments that function in accord with its stipulations, in order to keep the gates of sedition shut. Hence, the regulations, which are the law, and the works are necessary.[71]

Al-Kirmani pointedly claims that al-Hakim commands the good and forbids the bad *more* effectively than his Umayyad and Abbasid rivals. He writes:

> There is ample evidence of [al-Hakim's] commanding the good and prohibiting the bad, which none can deny, in the way he lives, devoting his nights and days to strengthening the word of truth, aiding the oppressed, *building mosques, tearing down churches, preserving the communal prayer, applying the regulations of the law and confirming them and the corporal punishments*, extending justice to the masses, and acting with respect to them with clemency and charity to the extent that the countries whom the protection of his orders include are in the cradle of security at home, neither evil nor sadness touches them. There is evidence for his prohibiting the bad, *reports of which have spread far and wide*, from his closing down the sources of depravity and dissolution, which are permitted quite openly in their cities by those who claim the Imamate among the family of Umayya and the family of ʿAbbas. *There is much evidence of his jihād* [Holy War] *in the service of God and the preservation of the borders*, and his familiarity with commoners and his discouraging the word of the false and what pertains to short-changing the law that his ancestor Muhammad brought.[72]

In his seminal study on commanding the good and prohibiting the bad, Michael Cook identifies al-Hakim as the single Fatimid caliph to concern himself with this injunction, while other rulers who embraced the *bāṭin* dimensions of the faith did not.[73] The realignment of the Fatimid city, including the construction, renovation, and endowment of Islamic monuments, the increasing importance of the center for secular and Sunni learning in the *dār al-ʿilm*, and the massive, often popular, destruction of churches can thus be seen in the new importance Ismaili thought accorded to the *ẓāhir*.

Instead of emphasizing the Fatimid Imam-caliph as the center of *bāṭin* knowledge for his Ismaili initiates, al-Kirmani expands the impact of al-Hakim's reign beyond the Fatimid court by promoting his support of good, universally Islamic acts, his commitment to "command[ing] the good and forbid[ding] the bad," and even his "familiarity with commoners" and his "building mosques, tearing down churches." The text suggests a shift in the image of the Imam from a storehouse of *bāṭin* knowledge to a purveyor of Islamic justice, one who, by commanding good and forbidding bad, fulfills a central prerogative of any Islamic ruler.

Architectural patronage and destruction are key components of this claim of legitimacy. In particular, "building mosques" and "tearing down churches" are considered as part of al-Hakim's program of Islamic justice. Here, they are considered as a core prerogative of an Islamic ruler. References to jihad and preserving borders point to his wars with the Byzantine empire on the Muslim frontiers, while frequent references to his demolition of churches suggest that this program of destruction was an overt declaration of his right to claim the title of the "Commander of the Faithful" (*amīr al-muʾminīn*)—the one true caliph to rule all Muslims. In addition to references to building mosques, the text later commends al-Hakim for the "spending of his funds for religiously commendable purposes," a claim that was supported by his endowment of mosques in this period.

Al-Kirmani specifically suggests that tearing down churches was a central aspect of al-Hakim's Islamic legitimacy, considered in the vein of "commanding the good and prohibiting the bad," and regarded it, alongside mosque construction, as a core caliphal prerogative. He notes that this is in direct contrast to the permissive nature of the families of the Umayyads and Abbasids. Al-Kirmani's text suggests that al-Kirmani, by addressing the Buyid ruler, was striving for a broader-based Islamic support for al-Hakim's rule, in this case, appealing to a Twelver Shiʿi figure.

The relation of al-Hakim's acts to a puritanical interpretation of Islamic law is demonstrated by comparing his deeds with the tenets set forth in the so-called Pact of ʿUmar, a treaty between Sophronius (d. 638), the patriarch of Jerusalem, and the second caliph, ʿUmar ibn Khattab (r. 633–44), outlining the rights and responsibilities of Christians under Muslim rule. Although modern scholars have debated the precise dating of this pact, it is based on the treaties made by ʿUmar as he conquered lands dominated by Christians and Jews.[74] The pact is not a neutral document; it was certainly doctored over time to suit the changing values of Islamic societies. None of the preserved versions of the text date to the period under consideration here. However, an analysis of versions of the pact demonstrate that many of al-Hakim's edits were not anathema; rather, they were consistent with a puritanical interpretation of Islam that existed in various periods in the middle ages. In all versions of the text, the treatment of churches is of central importance, as can be seen in the decree that Christians may not repair dilapidated houses of worship or build new ones.

One version of this pact is in the form of a letter from the Christians:

> When you came to us we asked of you safety for our lives, our families, our property, and the people of our religion on these conditions; to pay tribute out of hand and be humiliated; not to hinder any Muslim from stopping in our churches by night or day, to entertain him there three days and give him food there and open to him their doors; to beat the *nāqūs* [a board beaten to announce the prayer] only gently in them and not to raise our voices in them in chanting; not to shelter there, nor in any of our homes, a spy of your enemies; *not to build a church, convent, hermitage or cell, nor repair those that were dilapidated, nor assemble in any that is in a Muslim quarter*, nor in their presence; not to display idolatry nor to invite it, nor show a cross on our churches, nor in any of the roads of markets of the Muslims . . . to tie the *zunnār* [waistband] round our waists; to keep to the religion; not to resemble Muslims in dress, appearance . . .[75]

The prescriptions of the Pact of ʿUmar, including the requirement that Christians wear distinctive clothing and the banning of the beating of the *nāqūs* and other public displays of Christianity, correspond with many of al-Hakim's anti-*dhimmī* (religious minorities, see chapter 2) edicts. Another version of the pact restates these prohibitions regarding overt displays of religion and further declares that Christians are not to engage in Easter or Palm Sunday processions. These restrictions relate directly to the pomp and unseemly ceremony that al-Hakim learned had been taking place at the Church of the Holy Sepulcher, engendering his wrath. Whether or not the final form of the pact was codified at the time of Fatimid rule, it is significant that many of the acts most strongly condemned by the caliph were also condemned in this Sunni text and that previous Fatimid rulers' relative tolerance of *dhimmī* religious expression and architectural construction, in fact, ran counter to ʿUmar's example. Although the pact does not call for the destruction of any of the existing churches, it does challenge the precedent of permitting church repair established by al-Hakim's Fatimid predecessors, under whom many churches were restored and new structures built. It is clear from the accounts of church destructions under al-Hakim that many of them resulted from violations of the basic tenets of the pact.

Another example of the codification of behavior toward *dhimmī*s and the emphasis on proper acts during the medieval period can be seen in accountability (*ḥisba*) manuals, which were used by Islamic market inspectors (*muḥtasibs*) to supervise the practicalities of Islamic markets and their moral behavior.[76] The caliph ʿUmar himself was considered the first to perform the role of *muḥtasib*, ensuring that the markets ran properly and looking after public morals according to Islamic law.[77] Fatimid sources demonstrate the increasing prominence of the *muḥtasib* in their administrative system, with al-Maqrizi describing robes of honor and a turban being given to a *muḥtasib*, whose name was read out in the Mosque of Ibn Tulun and the Mosque of ʿAmr.[78] Al-Hakim himself is said to have taken on the position of the *muḥtasib* during his reign, a claim that is not entirely surprising given his demonstrated interest in morality and the urban environment.

Although the earliest preserved *ḥisba* manual from the eastern Islamic realm, written by al-Shayzari (d. 1193) in the twelfth century, postdates al-Hakim's reign, it sheds new light on al-Hakim's destruction of churches and on the tension between Ismaili esoteric faith and Islamic law. Many of the harsh prescriptions and demolitions of al-Hakim's reign are, in fact, consistent with a puritanical strain of medieval Sunni thought. Al-Hakim's edicts during this time were consistent with the treatment of the *dhimmī*s prescribed in al-Shayzari's text. He outlines the sumptuary laws that should be applied to *dhimmī*s, describing their distinctive dress. He asserts that Christians should tie a *zunnār* and wear a cross around their neck while Jews should wear red or yellow cords. *Dhimmī* women should wear one white shoe and one black. All *dhimmī*s should wear a metal neck-band in the public baths, to be distinguished from the Muslim population. The distinction between *dhimmī*s and Muslims in public spaces was of paramount concern to the *muḥtasib*, resulting in harsh sumptuary laws that were consistent with al-Hakim's persecuting laws.

In architecture, the *muḥtasib* should ensure that "their [*dhimmi*] buildings should not be higher than those of the Muslims." Their lodgings and places of worship must also be offered to any Muslims who require them. In their acts, they

> should not jostle Muslims on the main road, but should rather use the side streets. They should not be the first to give a greeting nor be welcomed in meetings . . . they must not be allowed to display any alcoholic drinks or pigs, to recite the Torah or Bible openly, to ring the church bells, to celebrate their festivals or to hold funeral services in public.[79]

In other words, expressions of religious faith—including conspicuous architectural presence—must be hidden in favor of the Muslim majority. Ostentatious display of these acts—such as the pilgrimages to the Church of the Holy Sepulcher in this period of increasing Latin presence—would have been particularly problematic.

At times, al-Shayzari specifically conceptualizes the role of the *muḥtasib* as embracing the outward laws of Islam, as opposed to the esoteric dimensions of the Ismaili faith. For example, he explains that the *muḥtasib*'s duty to oversee mosques and ensure that people pray diligently is "in order to show the characteristic outward forms of the religion and the sign of Islam" and that doing so "is especially important in this time of many innovations, differing sects, various forms of the *bāṭiniyya* and those who have declared the destruction of Islamic law and the abolition of the norms of Islam."[80] Another treatise on the *ḥisba* by the Sunni scholar al-Ghazali (d. 1111), written in the

Seljuq context, echoes these sentiments, noting, "the strange thing is that the Shiʿites have gone to extremes in this, and have stated that it is not permitted to order good until the infallible appears, their Imam of truth."[81]

AN ANALYSIS OF AL-HAKIM'S ARCHITECTURAL PROGRAM DURING THE MIDDLE PERIOD

Al-Kirmani's treatise and later *ḥisba* literature illuminate a consistency in al-Hakim's architectural program: while the early years of his reign were characterized by an Ismaili orientation, in which Christians, Jews, and Sunnis alike faced persecution, these middle years promoted the concept of al-Hakim as the ruler of the universal Islamic community (*umma*) and the one true caliph. The destruction of the Holy Sepulcher and the other churches in his realm acted as a sign of this legitimacy.

It would seem that many of these changes were done in response to Abu Rakwa's swift incursions into the Maghreb and advancement into Egypt, which sent waves of panic throughout the Fatimid administration until his capture and execution in 1007 (AH 397). Although there is no evidence that local Egyptian Sunnis supported Abu Rakwa's revolt, his claim to legitimacy as an Umayyad ruler and his apparent pro-Sunni rhetoric prompted a shift in al-Hakim's treatment of the Sunni populations in Egypt and the imperial strategy to build support throughout the eastern Islamic lands. Abu Rakwa's bid for the resurrection of a Sunni Umayyad caliphate was not directed at the preexisting rulers of the Umayyads or the Abbasids but at the grassroots. He appealed to the populations in the Maghreb who would support his own caliphate as an antidote to the heretical Fatimids. Indeed, it does not seem that Abu Rakwa received much of a reaction at all from the Umayyads in al-Andalus or the Abbasids. In this sense, his revolt was primarily a local one against the Fatimids that wielded the rhetoric of sectarian difference.

As part of a rapprochement with the Sunni majority of his empire and beyond, al-Hakim began to shift the urban expression of religion away from the esoteric dimensions of the Ismailis toward a more universally accepted form of Islam: his subjects could begin and end their Ramadan fast according to Sunni practices rather than by Shiʿi calculations and the city's muezzins were no longer required to use the Shiʿi formula in the call to prayer.[82] The architectural projects in this middle period of al-Hakim's reign were part of this reorientation. The removal of the "golden curses" denouncing the Companions of the Prophet from the walls of Cairo's mosques made the urban space more inclusive of all Muslims, as did the encasement of the esoterically oriented Shiʿi messages of the minarets of the Mosque of al-Hakim within austere towers inscribed with Qur'anic verses concerned with exoteric acts. The central role of architecture in conveying al-Hakim's universal legitimacy and the empire's inclusiveness of the whole *umma* is further evident in his endowment of the mosques of al-Azhar, al-Maqs, and Rashida as well as the growing importance of the *dār al-ʿilm*.

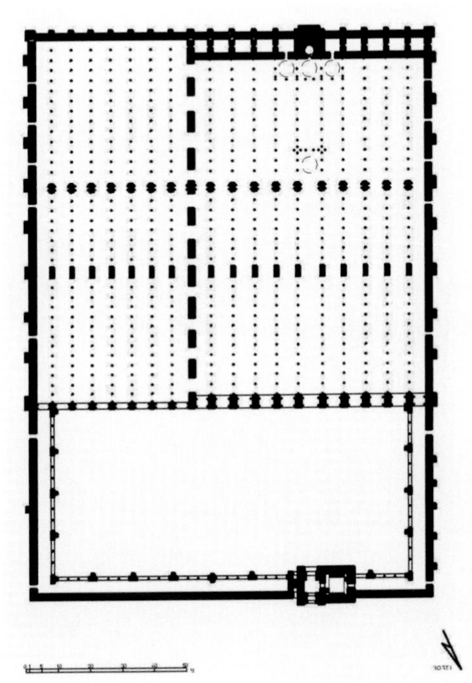

FIGURE 4.13
Great Mosque of Cordoba, plan after al-Mansur's additions, 987/8

The obscuring of esoteric Ismaili practice in favor of those accepted by all Muslims finds a corollary in the imperial ceremonies of this period. As Paula Sanders has argued, al-Hakim increasingly integrated the urban centers of Fustat-Misr into his ritual processions. The reorientation of the city and the ceremonial merging of al-Qahira and Fustat-Misr can be seen in 1012, when al-Hakim led the Friday prayers during Ramadan not at al-Azhar—the primary Fatimid mosque of the walled Ismaili enclave—but at the Mosque of al-Hakim, his newly endowed Mosque of Rashida, and the Sunni Mosque of al-ʿAmr in Fustat. As he processed from mosque to mosque, al-Hakim engaged directly with the urban masses. On one of these Fridays, al-Hakim stopped so frequently on his procession from al-Azhar, spending time to talk and laugh with his subjects, that he did not return to the palace until sunset.[83]

Today, al-Hakim is most notorious for his destruction of the Holy Sepulcher—an act most closely associated with his madness. However, he was certainly not unique in his reliance on church destruction to assert Islamic legitimacy. Twenty years prior to the destruction of the Holy Sepulcher, al-Mansur, the Umayyad chamberlain (*ḥājib*) to the caliph Hisham II (r. 996–1009 and 1010–13) and the de facto ruler of al-Andalus from 978 until 1002, engaged in a similar demolition. In 997, al-Mansur infamously razed the Christian shrine of Santiago de Compostela. At the same time, al-Mansur sponsored a major renovation to the Great Mosque of Cordoba, adding eight eastern aisles in the typical double horseshoe style of the mosque (figs. 4.13–4.14). Ibn ʿIdhari noted that

FIGURE 4.14
Great Mosque of Cordoba, al-Mansur's additions, 987/8

al-Mansur favored solidity over ornamentation—an austerity that is similar to that of the 1010 additions to al-Hakim's mosque.[84]

Like the Holy Sepulcher, Santiago de Compostela had been a crucial site of Christian pilgrimage in Spain. After destroying the shrine, al-Mansur brought its bells to the Great Mosque of Cordoba, where they were used as mosque lamps, overtly connecting architectural destruction and construction in the renovations to the mosque.[85] Al-Maqqari, preserving the account of Ibn Hayyan, linked the two acts together, celebrating that the mosque's addition was "rendered still more meritorious by the circumstance of Christian slaves from Castile and other infidel countries working in chains at the building instead of the Moslems, thus exalting the true religion and trampling down polytheism."[86]

Indeed, this chapter of Spanish Umayyad rule was defined primarily by conflict rather than coexistence (*convivencia*). Under al-Mansur's leadership, the Spanish Umayyads launched a series of fifty-six campaigns against Christian polities on the frontier of the empire, bringing the empire to the height of its power.[87] Al-Mansur's reign relied on the rhetoric of jihad, allowing him to gain the support of Berber recruits from North Africa.[88] During al-Mansur's reign, the Fatimids were under a peace treaty with the Byzantine empire and the Abbasids were experiencing stagnation. Al-Mansur used this to proclaim himself as the legitimate defender of the faith. Perhaps al-Mansur's jihadi rhetoric and the legitimacy al-Mansur gained through his campaigns acted as a competitive impetus for al-Hakim's destruction of the churches in his own realm.[89]

Al-Hakim's destruction of churches thus may be seen, as al-Kirmani's text suggests, as part of a larger claim for legitimacy beyond the confines of the Fatimid empire, establishing al-Hakim's caliphate as a rival to those in Cordoba and Baghdad. Our meager historical records of Abu Rakwa's revolt do not mention al-Mansur's destruction of Santiago de Compostela. However, I would suggest that, as the Umayyads were on al-Hakim's doorstep, tales of their successful destruction of the holy shrine may have inspired his own demolition of the Holy Sepulcher.

During this crucial chapter of al-Hakim's reign, his rapprochement with his Sunni subjects and his attempts at making ideological inroads with Muslims throughout the Islamic world bore fruit in terms of increasing his influence and popularity in Abbasid territory. In 1010, shortly after al-Hakim had several churches destroyed, the Iraqi governor Qirwash ibn Muqallad pledged his allegiance to al-Hakim rather than to the Abbasid caliph, reading the *khuṭba* in the name of al-Hakim and striking coins in the name of the Fatimid empire. The centrality of al-Hakim's role in destroying churches is noted in the text of this *khuṭba*: "Thanks to God Who by His light dispels the flood of anger and by His majesty demolishes the pillars of graven images and by His power causes the sun of righteousness to rise in the west."[90] By evoking pillars of graven images that al-Hakim destroyed, Qirwash uses the ruler's program of church destruction as a rallying cry to the Muslim faithful. Although Qirwash was forced to retract his earlier message of support just one month after offering it, the pronouncement demonstrated the increasing popularity of the Fatimid caliph beyond Egyptian lands as a result of his demolition of Christian monuments.[91]

While his predecessors, al-Muʿizz and al-ʿAziz, explicitly sought control of the eastern lands of Islam through military incursions, al-Hakim focused on ideological gains in Abbasid territories through increasing the activities of the *daʿwa* and other propagandistic efforts. Yahya al-Antaki noted his nonmilitary propaganda in the Abbasid realm, writing: "[Al-Hakim] drew most of the people of distant places to support him and follow him. He was recognized in the prayer in al-Kufa and his propaganda reached the gate of Baghdad and into the city of al-Rayy. He sent many splendid articles to the governors and rebels in the districts of Iraq to win them to his side."[92] Yahya also mentions al-Hakim's eastern ambitions, noting that when a visiting merchant had his goods confiscated, he praised the caliph by claiming that the ruler would soon hold Baghdad and expand his territory. This pleased al-Hakim so much that he gave the merchant thousands of dinars.[93]

The impact of al-Hakim's ideological program outside Egypt is reflected in the chants that Shiʿi protesters shouted in Baghdad in 1008, "Ya Hakim! Ya Mansur!" referring to the Ismaili caliph as the preferred ruler.[94] Two years later, around the same time that Qirwash pledged his loyalty to al-Hakim, ʿAli al-Asadi, the chief of the Banu Asa, also proclaimed his allegiance to the Fatimid caliph in Hilla. The increasing popularity of al-Hakim in the Abbasid realm was a critical threat to the Abbasids and the Shiʿi

Buyids who controlled them. In the year after Qirwash issued (and then was forced to retract) his allegiance to al-Hakim, the Abbasid caliph al-Qadir (r. 991–1031), under the Buyid vizierate of Fakhr al-Mulk, gathered important members of his empire, including various Twelver Shiʿi leaders and members of the *ashrāf* (those who claim descent from the Prophet Muhammad), and compiled a manifesto accusing the Fatimid dynasty of destroying Islam. In 1011, this decree was read at all of the mosques in Abbasid territory. The so-called Baghdad Manifesto marked a turning point in Fatimid history, confirming that the dynasty posed a substantial threat to the Iraqi-based leadership. It underscored the importance of the claim to ʿAlid descent for Fatimid power and the importance of uniting Sunnis and Shiʿis against them. At the same time as the manifesto was drafted, al-Qadir and Fakhr al-Mulk encouraged the Muʿtazili philosopher al-Istakhri to write a treatise against Ismaili doctrine.[95]

The intellectual and doctrinal realignment of the Fatimids under al-Hakim, as outlined by al-Kirmani, offers a new interpretation of the addition of the brick bastions to the Mosque of al-Hakim in 1010, only seven years after the construction of the original towers. To recall, the original towers of 1003 (described in chapter 3) contained verses and symbols that were resonant with esoteric Ismaili beliefs and central to the Ismaili *taʾwīl* of the Qurʾan. Their grilled windows shone outward to the Cairene street, making the towers, and its symbols and verses, a source of light. The minarets were visually different from any others of the time, making them distinctively Fatimid and, therefore, distinctly Ismaili. The light, the Imam's oratory, and the esoteric dimensions of the towers were masked by the bastions of 1010, which were sparse in decoration, constructed of brick rather than stone, and bore only a band of Qurʾanic verse. These verses, which did not appear in the Ismaili *taʾwīl*, were harsh recriminations directed at impure individuals and nonbelievers, with a focus on performing the acts of Islam without indication of the deeper, *bāṭin* significance of these acts. Resembling Sunni minarets, such as those found in the Sunni centers of Qayrawan and Sfax, the bastions built in 1010 contained nothing that would signal to the viewer that there was anything distinct about the religious convictions of the Fatimids. This shift to emphasizing the *ẓāhir* corresponds to al-Hakim's claim to be an ideal Islamic ruler to the entire Islamic *umma*, Shiʿi and Sunni, in Cairo and beyond.

If, however, the initial Ismaili message was no longer consistent with al-Hakim's imperial goals and claims for the universal caliphate, then why did he not simply tear down the first towers? We know from the case of the Mosque of Rashida that al-Hakim certainly did not hesitate to pull down mosques when they needed to be constructed; if he did not want the original minarets' messages to be preserved, he could have simply removed them. Their preservation, therefore, suggests a potent ideological purpose. Here I posit that the obscuring of the original minarets was meant to stand as a visual manifestation of the revised Fatimid official ideology: just as each action prescribed by Islamic law contained a deeper, inner, and true meaning that could be reached through

Ismaili allegorical interpretation, with the Imam at the center of this allegorical system, so do the menacing warnings of the austere bastions mask an inner Ismaili core. In this way, like the circular memory devices of Ismaili philosophers, the minarets themselves became material manifestations of this fundamentally Ismaili belief system, writ large on the Cairene cityscape.[96]

The emphasis on architecture, growing concern with projects beyond the royal city, openness to Sunnis, and emphasis on the universal Islamic *umma* suggests a major transformation in architectural patronage under al-Hakim. His persecution of Christians and the destruction of Christian monuments in this period were not antithetical to his generous patronage, endowment, and restoration of Islamic monuments. On the contrary, they were part of the same impulse toward a broadly conceived Islamic system of urban development, which was defined by al-Kirmani as the proof of al-Hakim's rightful place as a universal Islamic ruler. Cairo was no longer simply a center for the Ismaili faithful or a way station for the expanding empire. Instead, by promoting the image of al-Hakim as the commander of Muslims in Egypt and beyond, it was reinterpreted and restructured as an Islamic capital to rival Cordoba and Baghdad.

5 Rebuilding the Fatimid City

> Your resurrection (*qiyāma*) has taken place, your era of concealment [of the inner meaning] has run its course.
>
> —Al-Akhram on the divinity of al-Hakim

The final years of al-Hakim's reign were the most enigmatic and disruptive. During these years (from 1017 to 1021) the ruler reversed many of his edicts against the Christian and Jewish religious minority (*dhimmī*) populations—a decision that, medieval sources show, was often unpopular. Most notably, a new religious movement, which became known as the Druze, began to preach that al-Hakim was God incarnate. The rise of the Druze, the reversal of anti-*dhimmī* edicts, and a dramatic succession of conflicts meant that al-Hakim's reign would end in turmoil. Few building projects can be dated to al-Hakim's late years, but the events of this period would have a dramatic impact on the architectural projects of al-Hakim's successor, his son al-Zahir (r. 1021–36).

Following al-Hakim's mysterious disappearance in 1021, al-Zahir succeeded him as Imam-caliph. While his father's, grandfather's, and great-grandfather's most important architectural projects had been in Cairo, al-Zahir's most significant architectural undertaking was the restoration of the monuments of the Haram al-Sharif in Jerusalem (fig. 5.1). This chapter considers al-Zahir's architectural projects in Jerusalem as a response to his father's destruction of the Church of the Holy Sepulcher and the chaos of his late reign. Al-Hakim's architectural interest in Jerusalem had been predominantly destructive. Nevertheless, his attention to the city would have productive results for eleventh-century Jerusalem, as his successor lavished unprecedented architectural attention on the city. Al-Zahir's renovations of the monuments on the Haram al-Sharif announced an intimate relationship between the Fatimid dynasty and the sacred site—one that had not existed since the Umayyad era. Visitors to the platform saw elaborately refurbished monuments and encountered the ruler's name inscribed throughout. Inside the Aqsa Mosque, visitors marveled at the new Fatimid arches and domes, embellished with glittering mosaics. These new forms sanctified the Aqsa Mosque as the site of the Prophet's arrival on his night journey (*isrā'*) and reminded viewers of the Haram

Detail of fig. 5.8

FIGURE 5.1
Jerusalem, the Dome of the Rock and Aqsa Mosque on the Haram al-Sharif, view from the Mount of Olives

al-Sharif's central role in the Prophet's ascension (*miʿrāj*). The distinct architectural form and inscriptional content of the renovations emphasized an orthodox Islamic view of man's encounter with the divine and insisted on the mortality of the late ruler, in direct contrast to Druze doctrine regarding al-Hakim's divinity and occultation.

THE CHAOS OF AL-HAKIM'S LATER YEARS: THE REVERSAL OF ANTI-*DHIMMĪ* EDICTS AND THE RISE OF THE DRUZE

The final years of al-Hakim's life brought about a tumultuous upheaval for the Fatimids. During this period, the ruler became increasingly ascetic, with sources describing him as unbathed and clad in simple clothes.[1] He rode exclusively on a donkey and took increasingly frequent nocturnal walks through the city and into the Muqattam Hills. However, from a historical, biographical, and architectural standpoint, these years are the most difficult to chronicle and explain.

As discussed in the previous chapter, al-Hakim had used architectural patronage to appeal to the broader Muslim community at a time when there was growing tension within the Ismaili ranks. Al-Kirmani provided a frank description of the chaos he encountered in Cairo, describing the atmosphere as "dark with pervasive clouds," the Sessions of Wisdom (*majālis al-ḥikma*) canceled, and the mission (*da'wa*) as lost, confused, and powerless. According to his text, the *da'wa* was plagued by infighting and chaos ruled the day.[2]

Of particular concern for the dynasty, in 1014 al-Hakim named his cousin Ibn Ilyas, rather than his son al-Zahir, as his successor. Given that Fatimid legitimacy was based on patrimonial lineage, this proclamation was radically destabilizing. Even al-Hakim's apologist missionary (*dāʿī*), al-Kirmani, stressed that the Imam must have male offspring as proof of his rightful claim to the Imamate. Despite the oddity of al-Hakim naming his cousin as his successor, for the next seven years Ibn Ilyas would appear with al-Hakim in ceremonial events, and his name was even written on coins and stitched into the dynasty's official state textiles (*ṭirāz*).[3]

Further compounding the instability, the *daʿwa* was torn apart when, in 1017, a new doctrine began to circulate through the Fatimid capital, declaring that al-Hakim himself was divine.[4] Led by al-Darazi and Hamza ibn ʿAli, this burgeoning Druze movement believed that al-Hakim had superseded the Prophet Muhammad as God's representative on earth.[5] According to the Druze teachings, the messiah had arrived in the form of al-Hakim, and so Islamic law, based on the teachings of the Qur'an and hadith, should be abandoned in recognition of a new age.[6] The Druze's extreme interpretation of the ruler's divinity was based on the esoteric (*bāṭin*) aspects of the Ismaili faith. To the individuals proclaiming al-Hakim's divinity, the exoteric (*ẓāhir*) practices of Islam were no longer necessary, as only the Imam and the *bāṭin* truths held by him mattered. Al-Akhram, in the passage that began this chapter, celebrated that that the ruler's *qiyāma* had occurred and that the era of concealment of the *bāṭin* had ended. As a result, al-Hakim's new age "completely abrogated the sharia of Muhammad."[7] In addition to the growing problems in the *daʿwa* associated with the rising Druze movement, these last years of al-Hakim's reign were marked by a series of crises, including the flooding of the Nile and conflicts between the black, Turkish, and Berber regiments of the Fatimid military. The conflicts culminated in the catastrophic burning of Fustat in 1020.[8] Whether the caliph ordered this act or was simply complicit in it, it is clear that the relationship between the two cities of al-Qahira and Fustat-Misr took a dramatic and devastating turn in this period.

During this tumultuous chapter, in 1015/6, al-Hakim commissioned the construction of a small mosque, known as al-Lu'lu'a ("the Pearl"), in the northeastern sector of the Qarafa cemetery, near the Muqattam Hills (figs. 5.2–5.3), where the caliph was spending increasing amounts of time. Like the Mosque of al-Hakim, this small mosque stood in ruins for centuries, until it was reconstructed by the Bohra Ismailis, who gave it its present form. The Mosque of al-Lu'lu'a was an unusual structure, whose overall impression was one of height. It consisted of a tall tower, with three vaulted rooms, each of which measured approximately 9.8 × 16.4 feet (3 × 5 meters), and featured a mihrab. The Mosque of al-Lu'lu'a consisted of a rubble core, which was dressed by roughly hewn blocks (*talālāt*) from the nearby Muqattam Hills, making the monument appear to rise organically from al-Hakim's favorite mountain—an effect that was heightened by the fact that its ground floor emerged directly from the rock outcropping.[9] The facade of al-Lu'lu'a

FIGURE 5.2
Cairo, Mosque of al-Lu'lu'a, at the base of the Muqattam Hills, 1015/6. Photo by K. A. C. Creswell, Creswell Archive, Ashmolean Museum, Oxford University, EA.CA.2557

FIGURE 5.3
Cairo, Mosque of al-Lu'lu'a, 1015/6. Photo by K. A. C. Creswell, Creswell Archive, Ashmolean Museum, Oxford University, EA.CA.3196

featured three arches, with the middle higher than the other two, a form that prefigured that of the Mosque of al-Aqmar, built one hundred years later. Creswell noted that while the stones were "well laid and fairly well dressed on the outer face" they were "very badly laid and roughly dressed on the inner," indicating hasty construction, little internal use, or even intentional austerity, related to al-Hakim's late asceticism.

The construction of this unusual structure in the Qarafa cemetery recalled the earlier construction of the Qarafa Mosque by Durzan and Sitt al-Mulk (al-ʿAziz's wife and daughter respectively).[10] However, unlike the Qarafa Mosque, which mirrored the caliphal forms inside al-Qahira, the Mosque of al-Lu'lu'a was commissioned by the caliph himself and departed radically from a traditional hypostyle form. Once again, the function of this mosque remains uncertain. Al-Maqrizi described it in *Al-Khiṭaṭ*, recording:

> This mosque is situated at the foot of the mountain and still remains. It stood in ruins [*kharāban*], and was rebuilt by al-Hakim bi-Amr Allah who named it al-Lu'lu'a. It is said that the building took place in the year 406 [1015/6]. It is well built.[11]

Thus, al-Maqrizi's account gives us little historical context, other than a date, and an indication that a ruined mosque had existed on this site. Considering that it was sponsored by the caliph in one of his favorite locations, one wonders if perhaps it was used privately by the wandering ruler. The emphasis on height and its square tower form recall the bastions of the Mosque of al-Hakim. However, little decoration or inscriptional evidence remains to offer a clue to its purpose.

The intense persecution of *dhimmīs* and large-scale destruction of *dhimmī* monuments under al-Hakim in the period discussed in the previous chapter (1007–13), resulted in mass conversions to Islam and Christian emigration to Byzantine territory.[12] Moreover, these efforts were supported by some members of the Muslim community. However, al-Hakim enigmatically reversed course circa 1021. *The History of the Patriarchs* preserves the details of this change, outlining that, for years, Christians had been unable to visit churches. The situation was so desperate, they would often offer bribes to go at night to ruined churches to hide the vestments within.[13] The text recorded that after three years of being kept from their ruined churches, Christians began to restore them, reconsecrate them, and pray in them. When al-Hakim was informed of this, he turned the other way, allowing the Christians to restore their monuments without interference.[14]

Later, the source discusses al-Hakim's more direct reversal of his previous policies toward Christians, whereby he allowed them to restore their churches and even to convert back to Christianity. According to the source, this change was inspired by al-Hakim's personal relationship with a monk known as Bimin. After befriending the Christian, al-Hakim sent a decree to the Christian community

> authorizing the opening of all the churches which were in his kingdom and their restoration, and that there should be returned to them the timber, pillars, and bricks which had been taken from them and the lands and the gardens, which belonged to them all in the land of Misr.[15]

The text even links al-Hakim's increasing asceticism to the influence of Christian clergy, as the caliph, impressed by this, remarks that the community reveres the patriarch even though he is dressed humbly. The source records that al-Hakim allowed the Christians to stop wearing the distinctive dress (*ghiyār*) and large crosses, granting them permission to once again strike the board beaten to announce the prayer (*nāqūs*) in their churches.[16]

Yahya al-Antaki notes three specific instances of al-Hakim granting permission for church reconstruction, all dating to the year 1020. The first decree allowed for the Monastery of al-Qusayr to be rebuilt, permitted the reestablishment of its endowment (*waqf*), and granted permission for Christians to congregate there again. Yahya also specifies that al-Hakim allowed the reconstruction of churches in and around Jerusalem and Lydda, and the reestablishment of their *waqfs*. Later that year, al-Hakim permitted all converted Christians to return to their faith. Significantly, while modern scholars deride al-Hakim's destruction of Christian monuments and persecution of religious minorities, medieval Muslim sources often praise him for the obliteration of *dhimmī* structures and his harsh edicts that led to mass conversions, criticizing instead his reversal of these persecutions.[17]

THE REIGN OF AL-ZAHIR

In 1021, al-Hakim mysteriously disappeared after going for one of his customary walks in the Muqattam Hills.[18] Although his knife-slashed clothes were discovered, his body never was. For the Druze, the absence of his body was a divine sign indicating that al-Hakim had not died but had gone into occultation, to return at the end of days. Some sources suggest that al-Hakim's powerful sister Sitt al-Mulk (r. 1021–23) had him killed to put an end to the chaos of his late reign. After his disappearance, Sitt al-Mulk took control of the Fatimid state, and under her guidance as regent, al-Hakim's son al-Zahir rather than Ibn Ilyas, al-Hakim's named successor, came to the throne.[19] Together with his aunt, al-Zahir condemned those who proclaimed al-Hakim's divinity or who deviated from Islam, imprisoning and killing many members of the Druze movement, though many of them escaped to the Levant.[20]

As al-Maqrizi describes it, al-Zahir's reign contrasted dramatically to al-Hakim's. It was characterized by celebrations, the imbibing of alcohol, and general revelry.[21] In his policy regarding *dhimmī* monuments, al-Zahir stressed the importance of Qur'anic verse 2:256, "There is no compulsion in religion"; non-Muslims were allowed to restore their churches and synagogues, and those who had converted to Islam by force were allowed to return to their original faiths. *The History of the Patriarchs* tells us that under al-Zahir churches were rebuilt and made even better than they were before al-Hakim's reign.[22] However, the source mentions little else about al-Zahir, and certainly nothing comparable to the pages devoted to al-Mu'izz, al-'Aziz, or al-Hakim. This relative absence of

FIGURE 5.4
Jerusalem, Dome of the Rock and Dome of the Chain, established 691/2

information about al-Zahir's reign is shared among medieval Islamic accounts as well. Yahya al-Antaki's account ends before al-Zahir comes to power, and al-Maqrizi devotes far fewer pages to al-Zahir than to his predecessors.[23] As a result, the historical details of al-Zahir's reign are particularly sparse, though he was generally known as a politically incompetent and hedonistic ruler.[24]

Architecturally, al-Zahir's most important project was the reconstruction of Jerusalem, an act that ushered in a new chapter of Islamic patronage in the holy city. Prior to al-Hakim's destruction of the Holy Sepulcher, we have little record of patronage by the early Fatimid caliphs in Jerusalem. Al-Muʿizz and al-ʿAziz do not appear to have sponsored major projects in the city, which is somewhat surprising, given their interest in expanding their rule farther east. Instead, most of these early caliphs' architectural projects were focused on the new capital in Cairo. Unlike his predecessors, al-Zahir patronized few major architectural projects in Cairo, with perhaps the most remarkable Egyptian commission being his addition of the *ziyāda*, the extra space between a mosque and the outer wall, to the Mosque of al-Hakim.[25] Al-Zahir's architectural priorities were instead expressed on an international stage, with a particular focus on rebuilding Jerusalem in the wake of his father's destruction of the Holy Sepulcher.[26]

Today, the monuments of the Haram al-Sharif in Jerusalem stand as some of the most iconic structures in the history of Islamic art, with the Dome of the Rock and Aqsa Mosque at its center (see figs. 5.1 and 5.4–5.5). Scholarly analysis of Islamic Jerusalem often focuses on the monuments of the Haram al-Sharif at the time of its foundation,

FIGURE 5.5
Jerusalem, Aqsa Mosque, established 705. Much of the current form of the mosque dates to the reign of al-Zahir, 1035. The exterior of the mosque includes additions by the Crusaders and Ayyubids (in the 11th or 12th century).

under the Umayyad caliphate (661–750), even though after the construction of the Dome of the Rock in 691/2, the Umayyads controlled the city only for a little more than fifty years.[27] Instead, it was under al-Zahir that many of the pre-Crusader monuments of the Haram al-Sharif were renovated and rebuilt.

Al-Zahir's efforts to embellish Jerusalem's Islamic monuments stand in direct contrast to the detachment shown by rulers in the previous centuries. Following the Abbasids' defeat of the Umayyads in 750 and the subsequent move of the caliphal capital from Damascus to Baghdad, Jerusalem's imperial sponsorship had declined dramatically, even as the city grew as a site of local Muslim devotion. While the accounts of earlier Abbasid rulers' patronage suggest a reluctance to invest heavily in Jerusalem, al-Zahir did so lavishly.[28] His efforts indicate that al-Zahir made a conscious decision to prioritize Jerusalem as a patronage site rather than simply continue regular maintenance, particularly because the early eleventh century was a time of great turmoil for the Fatimids.

BEFORE THE FATIMIDS: ISLAMIC JERUSALEM IN THE EIGHTH THROUGH TENTH CENTURIES

In order to appreciate just how radical al-Zahir's investment in Jerusalem was, we must understand its dormancy as a patronage center for the three hundred years before his reign. In the history of Islamic art, the Umayyads are celebrated for developing Jerusalem as an Islamic city, establishing and embellishing Islam's most famous early monuments, including the Dome of the Rock and the Aqsa Mosque.[29] However, after the Abbasids seized control of the caliphate in 751, and until the Fatimids gained control in 973, Jerusalem played a far more peripheral role, since the new caliphs relocated their capital away from Damascus to the eastern cities of Baghdad and Samarra. Sources that mention Jerusalem in the Abbasid period offer a hazy account of imperial interest in the city, but suggest a waning imperial concern with patronizing Jerusalem's architecture. They record that the Abbasid caliphs al-Mansur (r. 754–75) and al-Mahdi (r. 775–85) visited the city but do not mention any visits by subsequent Abbasid rulers.[30]

The decreased imperial interest in the city was exacerbated by a number of serious earthquakes, which led to major structural damage of the monuments on the Haram al-Sharif. Records suggest that Jerusalem's Muslim residents often rallied to demand the restoration of monuments in the face of caliphal indifference. This dynamic is in contrast to the top-down mode of imperial patronage that is often assumed for medieval architecture. For example, records of al-Mansur's first visit to the city in 758 indicate that he found the monuments on the Haram al-Sharif and the former Umayyad palace in ruins, following earthquake damage in 746. The Aqsa Mosque was also in ruins, with its eastern and western parts destroyed. When the local Muslim inhabitants of the city approached the caliph, requesting that he finance the restoration of the mosque, the caliph replied that he had no money, instead ordering the removal of the gold and silver

FIGURE 5.6
Jerusalem, Aqsa Mosque, Umayyad-era mihrab, under restoration, showing the original decoration that survived the earthquakes and subsequent restorations by the Abbasids

that embellished the doors. These repurposed precious metals were then turned into the dinars and dirhams that financed the restoration of the monument.[31] This incident suggests that within a span of fifty years, the city's Islamic buildings had lost the premier status they held at the time of their foundation. Instead, it was the Muslim population in Jerusalem, rather than the caliph, that acted as the protector of these structures. The central mosque had become such a low priority to the Abbasid ruler that he was willing to pluck off the rich decor of the iconic structure. Indeed, this dismantling was the only way he would agree to its restoration.

A similar dynamic of caliphal disinterest in Jerusalem's monuments is seen under al-Mansur's successor, al-Mahdi. In 771, there was another earthquake in Jerusalem. The tenth-century geographer al-Muqaddasi reports that the entire Aqsa Mosque was destroyed except a small portion near the mihrab (fig. 5.6).[32] Like his father, al-Mahdi insisted that the Abbasid treasury had no money to rebuild it. Instead, he commanded that his governors and commanders should each build a colonnade in the structure,[33] suggesting that once again, the reigning caliph refused to finance the renovation of Islamic monuments in Jerusalem. Instead, he marshaled his courtiers to repair the building, with each aisle of the new mosque sponsored by one of his officials.[34] Al-Mahdi determined that al-Mansur's mosque had been too narrow and not much used, so the builders should "curtail the length and increase the breadth."[35] This was the mosque that al-Muqaddasi encountered in his visit in 985. In his 1930s excavations at the Aqsa Mosque, Robert Hamilton found the archaeological record to be consistent with al-Muqaddasi's description of the mosque as made up of a wide central nave and a dome, with parts of the older mosque incorporated into the structure.[36] The form of al-Mahdi's renovations to the Aqsa Mosque would last into the tenth century.

The next major event in the Abbasid patronage of Jerusalem's structures was during the reign of al-Ma'mun (r. 813–33), who sponsored eastern and northern gates on the Haram al-Sharif and the refurbishment of the Dome of the Rock.[37] Like his predecessor, al-Ma'mun refused to invest his own funds in the project, but the rebuilding

FIGURE 5.7 (OPPOSITE)
Fatimid-era restorations to the Dome of the Rock, Jerusalem, ca. 1027

nevertheless asserted his presence in the city. Al-Maʾmun's renovations maintained the aesthetic style and architectural framework of the Umayyad originals. In fact, this aesthetic sense was so consistent that in the Dome of the Rock's inscriptional band, al-Maʾmun simply replaced ʿAbd al-Malik's name with his own. The edited inscription mimics the gold Kufic lettering of the Umayyad original. The lettering appears more compressed, due to the altered letter lengths, but otherwise the name of the Abbasid caliph looks as if it could have been a part of the Umayyad original. Indeed, although the Umayyad caliph's name was replaced, the foundational date was unaltered.[38] Changing the name within the Umayyad inscription not only proclaimed the Abbasid ruler as the renovator of the site but erased the Umayyad history of the site, associating the very foundation of the Dome of the Rock with Abbasid patronage. Al-Maʾmun's investment in Jerusalem was also visible in the Aqsa Mosque. Nasir-i Khusraw described a bronze portal said to have been sent from Baghdad and bearing al-Maʿmun's name within the confines of the mosque.[39]

In the tenth century, Abbasid control of Jerusalem waned as the Egypt-based Tulunid and Ikhshidid dynasties took control of the city.[40] The historical details of this period are particularly murky, but it seems that the city gained greater significance in Islamic thought. Sufis (Muslim mystics) increasingly traveled to the city, focusing their practices around the Haram al-Sharif. By the time the Tulunids and Ikhshidids came to power, the Haram al-Sharif had seen a proliferation of commemorative structures, added at some point in the eighth and ninth centuries, most likely initiated by local Muslims, pilgrims, and Sufi travelers. While it is unclear what role the rulers played in patronizing these monuments, the fact that the bodies of deceased Ikhshidid rulers were transported to Jerusalem to be interred within the confines of the holy city signals the city's rising status.[41] Given the lack of written documentation of imperial patronage in this period, it is likely that the new structures represented a grassroots effort by the local population to embellish the sacred city, suggesting an intimate connection between the populace and the city's sites.

AL-ZAHIR'S RECONSTRUCTION OF ISLAMIC JERUSALEM

Following al-Zahir's assumption of the Fatimid throne in 1021, Jerusalem's architectural framework changed dramatically. Unlike the Abbasids, the Fatimids in this period made their presence felt throughout the city. The Dome of the Rock was repaired (fig. 5.7) and inscriptions naming the Fatimid ruler were added to the Haram al-Sharif. The Aqsa Mosque was reconstructed, with its dome and arches receiving an elaborate mosaic program addition (figs. 5.8–5.10). The city's reconstruction extended beyond the Haram al-Sharif as the city's walls were rebuilt and shortened. Al-Zahir also allowed the Byzantine emperor Romanos III Argyros (r. 1028–34) to rebuild the Church of the Holy Sepulcher, and the church's new form and identity brought a different orientation to the city and

FIGURE 5.8
Jerusalem, Aqsa Mosque, view of the sanctuary looking toward the Fatimid archways and dome (*maqṣūra*), renovated ca. 1035

FIGURE 5.9
Jerusalem, Aqsa Mosque, detail of the Fatimid-era archway, with inscription at the top, ca. 1035

FIGURE 5.10
Jerusalem, Aqsa Mosque, view of archways and the *maqṣūra*, renovated ca. 1035

the distinct stamp of Byzantine patronage. By the end of al-Zahir's reign, the two sacred spaces of Jerusalem would have intimate imperial associations, with the Fatimids claiming the Haram al-Sharif and the Byzantines claiming the Holy Sepulcher.

The changes made to the Haram al-Sharif platform in the eleventh century emphasized the site's connection with the miraculous event of the Prophet Muhammad's *isrā'* and *mi'rāj*. An analysis of the projects sponsored by al-Zahir suggests a change in the meaning of Jerusalem for the Fatimid empire. Earlier scholars have noted that, whereas during the Umayyad era the significance of the Haram al-Sharif primarily derived from its association with the first and second Jewish temple and as its association with the prophets, in the Fatimid era its significance was due to its close association with the Islamic ascension story.[42] I argue that this change in meaning was a reaction to the internal threats of the heretical Druze movement that emerged at the end of al-Hakim's life. To counter the Druze's declaration of al-Hakim's divinity and occultation, the monuments of Jerusalem emphasized the particular holiness of the Prophet Muhammad by celebrating his ascension to heaven.

Although al-Zahir sought to stabilize the empire, his reign was tumultuous. The Fatimid control of Palestine had never been entirely secure and was often struck by plague, famine, and frequent Bedouin insurrections as well as Byzantine incursions.[43] Particularly troubling for the Fatimids was that not all of the Muslim population in Jerusalem accepted the Fatimid rulers as the legitimate caliphs.[44] Riots against the empire broke out throughout the realm as the young caliph sought to solidify his rule.[45] However, even within the context of unrest, wars, and plague, the Fatimid ruler prioritized the reconstruction of Jerusalem, suggesting an ideological reason for his architectural patronage. At the beginning of al-Zahir's reign, Jerusalem's architecture was in great peril. The Holy Sepulcher lay in ruins following his father's cataclysmic act. An earthquake in 1033 had severely damaged the Islamic monuments on the Haram al-Sharif. In response, al-Zahir supported a full-scale rehabilitation of the Islamic monuments on the Haram al-Sharif. Not since the Umayyad period had Jerusalem's monuments received such enthusiastic support. That these restorations were done in a period of strife for the Fatimids only serves to emphasize al-Zahir's commitment to Jerusalem's monuments.

Although visitors to the Aqsa Mosque today will encounter many Crusader-era additions, at its core, the mosque preserves many of al-Zahir's renovations (see figs. 5.8 and 5.11).[46] Based on restoration work undertaken in the 1920s and the description of the mosque by Nasir-i Khusraw (discussed below), scholars have determined that the Fatimid structure was made up of seven aisles of arcades running perpendicular to the *qibla* wall, the wall facing Mecca. Each of these aisles consisted of eleven arches, with the exception of two on either side of the central aisle. The central aisle of the Fatimid-era mosque was distinguished from the other aisles, as it was twice the width and featured a clerestory, gabled roof, and dome.[47] Thus, it appears that the mosque of al-Zahir was significantly more narrow than the Abbasid-era mosque of al-Mahdi, even as it possessed many of the same basic features.[48]

Restoration work on the Aqsa Mosque in the 1920s uncovered a splendid Fatimid-era mosaic and painted decoration in the dome and its supporting arches. The lavish mosaic program, dating to the reign of al-Zahir, is executed in the pendentives leading to the dome, the drum of the dome, and in the archway leading to this space, an assemblage that I will refer to as the mosque's *maqṣūra* (see figs. 5.8–5.10 and 5.12–5.14).[49] The mosaic program here clearly harks back to that of the Umayyads, such as in ʿAbd al-Malik's Dome of the Rock. Indeed, at the time of the restoration, mosaics were used infrequently

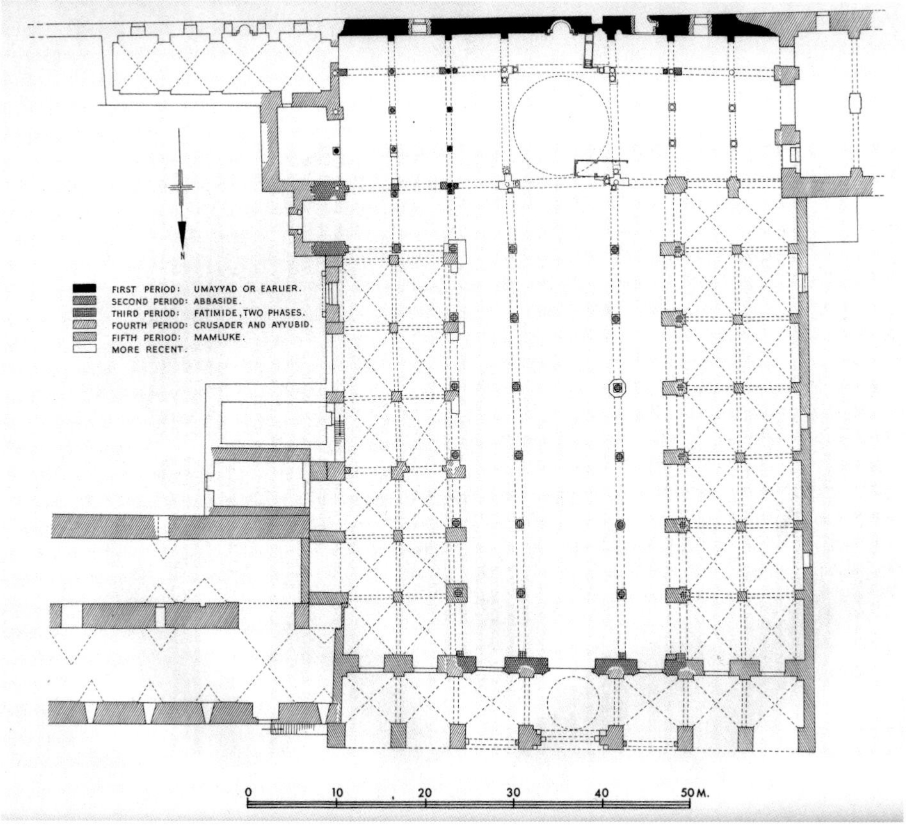

FIGURE 5.11
Plan of the Aqsa Mosque, K. A. C. Creswell

in Islamic architecture.[50] Their inclusion in the mosque renovation, with clear references to the Dome of the Rock, linked the Fatimid-era program to the Umayyad prototype.[51] However, the precise forms depicted here do not have a precedent. In the monumental archway, large-scale vegetal motifs sprout from small vases. The vegetal tendrils mimic those found in the Dome of the Rock, but on a much larger scale and with unusual floral motifs capping them off.

At the top of the archway, above the Umayyad-inspired mosaic program are two bands of golden inscriptions (see fig. 5.9). The inscription includes the first appearance of Qur'anic verse 17:1 on the platform, associating the mosque directly with the "masjid al-Aqsa" described in the Qur'anic account of the Prophet's night journey. The inscription reads:

> In the name of God, the Compassionate, the Merciful, Glory to the One who took his servant for a journey by night from the masjid al-haram [the mosque in Mecca] to the masjid al-Aqsa [the farthest mosque] whose precincts we have blessed . . . has renovated its construction our lord Ali Abu al-Hasan the Imam al-Zahir li'Aziz din Allah, Commander of the Faithful, son of al-Hakim bi-Amr Allah, Commander of

FIGURE 5.12
Jerusalem, Aqsa Mosque, recessed roundels in the *maqṣūra*, renovated ca. 1035

> the Faithful, may the blessing of God be on him, and his pure ancestors, and on his noble descendants. By the hand of ʿAli ibn ʿAbd al-Rahman, may God reward him. The [job] was supervised by Abu al-Qasim Husaini may God help him.[52]

While the style of the floral decoration on the arch recalls the Umayyad past, the inscription links the work directly with the mosque's Fatimid patrons. It identifies ʿAli ibn ʿAbd al-Rahman as the mosaicist, declaring that the work was done by a Muslim Arab, rather than by the Byzantine craftsmen (to whom art historians often ascribe mosaic work). It also indicates the involvement of the Fatimid vizier Abu al-Qasim Husaini as the overseer.

The inscription links the mosque with the "masjid al-aqsa" described in the Qur'an as the destination of the Prophet's *isrāʾ*, thereby asserting the mosque's direct connection with the *isrāʾ* and the Prophet's subsequent *miʿrāj*. In doing so, it commemorates the mosque's significance as the site of one of the most important miracles in the history of the faith and the site from which a direct connection was made between humanity and God. After making this connection explicit, the inscription goes on to name not only the

FIGURE 5.13
Jerusalem, Aqsa Mosque, recessed roundel in the *maqṣūra*, renovated ca. 1035

FIGURE 5.14
Jerusalem, Aqsa Mosque, recessed roundels in the *maqṣūra*, renovated ca. 1035

current ruler of the Fatimid empire (al-Zahir) but ties him directly to his controversial father (al-Hakim). Moreover, it includes the specifically Shiʿi practice of calling for the blessings of God, the "pure ancestors" and "noble descendants"—formulae that would have been absent from the Sunni projects of the Umayyads and Abbasids. In this way, while the decorative form of the mosaics carries on the traditions of the past, the inscriptional content adds a purely Fatimid stamp on this holy space.

In addition to the inscriptional program on the archway, the Fatimid restoration embellished four highly unusual recessed roundels, elaborated with mosaic decorations, on the pendentives of the Aqsa Mosque (figs. 5.12–5.14). Each of these is composed of four concentric circles, executed on alternating planes of silver and gold. Moving from the outside of the circle inward, we find alternating palm fronds and eight-pointed stars on a silver background, a series of depictions of the peacock eye motif on a gold background, and alternating rectangular and ovoid lozenges on a silver background, with a multi-lobed golden form in the center. By articulating circles in a recessed format, the domes have a trompe l'oeil effect, suggesting an even deeper recession; these devices are unprecedented in the history of Islamic art.[53]

NASIR-I KHUSRAW'S DESCRIPTION OF THE FATIMID-ERA HARAM AL-SHARIF

A thorough description of the Haram al-Sharif platform in the Fatimid period is offered by the Persian Ismaili poet and philosopher Nasir-i Khusraw, whose vivid descriptions of the Fatimid palace were discussed in chapter 1.[54] Nasir's account begins in 1046, as he set out for the hajj, and includes lengthy descriptions of many Islamic cities, Jerusalem among them.[55] Traveling during the reign of the Fatimid ruler al-Mustansir (r. 1029–1094), Nasir provides a firsthand account of al-Zahir's restored monuments and explicates the sacred associations of eleventh-century Jerusalem. In his introduction to the city, Nasir refers to the city as "*quds*" (holy) and identifies the Haram al-Sharif as the site of the Prophet's *isrā'* and *mi'rāj*. He emphasizes Jerusalem's distinction as a pilgrimage destination, noting that Muslims could perform the rituals of hajj in Jerusalem if they could not make it to Mecca.[56] Pilgrims would have been particularly plentiful in the time of his visit, as the Fatimid ruler had advised Egyptians to forgo the hajj to Mecca on account of famine in that city. Nasir also presented the city as a pilgrimage center for Christians and Jews, whom he describes visiting the city's churches and synagogues.

Nasir focuses his detailed description on the Haram al-Sharif, the entirety of which he refers to as a "*masjid*" (mosque).[57] He takes the reader on a walking tour of the platform, describing what he sees as he moves through the space, beginning with a description of how, as he approached the Haram al-Sharif, he beheld a gateway "adorned with designs and patterned with colored glass cubes set in plaster. The whole produces an effect dazzling to the eye. There is an inscription on the gateway, also in glass mosaic, with the titles of the sultan of Egypt. When the sun strikes this, the rays play so that the mind of the beholder is absolutely stunned."[58] This vivid description tells us that mosaic decoration was present on the gates of the Fatimid-era platform. It demonstrates that the name of the Fatimid ruler and his titles were displayed prominently as one entered the Haram al-Sharif, overtly connecting the Fatimid ruler to patronage of the sacred space. The account does not provide the ruler's name, however, so it is unclear whether the inscription named al-Zahir, the restorer, or al-Mustansir, the ruler at the time of Nasir's visit.[59]

This is not the only instance of the ruler's name being prominently displayed on the Haram al-Sharif. In his description of the Dome of the Rock, Nasir inventories the furnishings of the space and notes: "There are many silver lamps here, and on each one is written its weight. They were donated by the sultan of Egypt. . . . They said that every year the sultan of Egypt sends many candles, one of which was this one, for it had the sultan's name written in gold letters around the bottom."[60] Once again, Nasir does not name the ruler, but he describes the patronage as occurring annually, indicating that the candles must have featured the name of al-Mustansir, the Fatimid ruler at the time of his visit.

Nasir's account suggests that, unlike the tepid, occasional support of Jerusalem offered in the previous centuries, the Fatimids were committed to the regular upkeep of the holy sites. The presence of the ruler's name on the gates and soft furnishings of the

Dome of the Rock made the imperial support of Islamic architecture visible to visitors to the site, suggesting that imperial legitimacy was gained through architectural patronage. The practice of prominently featuring the ruler's name on the Haram al-Sharif is consistent with the Fatimid promotion of the public text in Cairo. While the reliance on mosaic decoration continued the Umayyad traditions of design, the prominence of names and titles in public spaces carried on a well-established Fatimid prerogative.[61]

In describing the reconstructed Aqsa Mosque, Nasir offers lengthy descriptions of its measurements, providing quantitative data about the columns and other architectural details. He also pays particular attention to cataloging the soft furnishings within the structure, noting the presence of Maghrebi carpets, lamps, and lanterns. He writes:

> In that place is a skillfully constructed edifice with magnificent carpets and an independent staff who are always attendant. On the outside again, along the southern wall and beyond the corner, there is an uncovered courtyard about 200 ells long [1 ell is approximately the length of a man's arm from the middle finger to the elbow]. The length of the mosque along the west wall is 420 ells, with the *maqṣūra* to the right along the south wall; it [the mosque] is 150 ells wide. It has 280 marble columns supporting a stone arcade, the tops and bottoms of which are decorated and the joints filled with lead so that the construction is extremely tight. Between every two columns is a distance of six ells, and the ground is flagged in colored marble tile, the joints again caulked in lead. The *maqṣūra*, in the middle of the south wall, is large enough for sixteen columns and an enormous dome inlaid in tile, as has been described. It is filled with Maghrebi carpets, lamps, and lanterns each hung by a separate chain.[62]

Although modern studies note that these numbers are inaccurate, if not absurd, they allow his readers to imaginatively enter the space.[63] This sense of immediacy is strengthened by his assertion that the descriptions are based on measurements he took himself and drawings he made while on the site.[64] His focus on detailed data related to the Aqsa Mosque may also indicate its special role as a pilgrimage mosque, as he similarly details the dimensions and numbers of columns of the mosques in Mecca and Medina but does not do the same for the mosques of Cairo and other cities. Nasir's account provides data, descriptions of the furnishings, insight into the religious associations of the site, and occasional information regarding the inscriptions on the site. What it lacks, however, is art historical detail regarding the new elaborate Fatimid mosaic program in the mosque. While frustrating for the art historian, such a lack of detail is typical of medieval accounts.[65] Although our medieval geographer fails to mention this elaborate mosaic program, his descriptions can help us contextualize the visual program of the new *maqṣūra*, particularly the inscriptional content and the curious inclusion of the recessed roundels in the pendentives, which will be discussed below.

THE FATIMID *MAQṢŪRA*: ENSHRINING THE PROPHET'S *ISRĀʾ*

Today, the monuments of the Haram al-Sharif are venerated in Islam due to their association with the Prophet Muhammad's *isrāʾ* and *miʿrāj*. Based on Qurʾanic passages and hadith, it is believed that Muhammad was miraculously transported by night from Mecca to Jerusalem on a heavenly steed named al-Buraq.[66] From Jerusalem, he ascended to heaven to meet with God. This is not only one of the most important episodes in the Islamic tradition, celebrating the moment that the Prophet was in direct contact with the divine, but it is also the moment that most distinctly marks Jerusalem and the Haram al-Sharif in particular as sites of Muslim veneration. Much ink has been spilled in attempting to determine exactly when the Dome of the Rock became known as the precise spot from which Muhammad ascended to heaven.[67] Although today and for much of premodern period, the *isrāʾ* and *miʿrāj* are the events most closely associated with Islam's veneration of the site, this link was not always emphasized in Islamic tradition. Nasir's description does not designate the Dome of the Rock specifically as the site of the Prophet's ascension, but it does make it clear that by the Fatimid era, the Haram al-Sharif was associated intimately with both the *isrāʾ* and *miʿrāj*. In documenting the religious significance of the Haram al-Sharif, Nasir introduces the Aqsa Mosque as "the spot to which God transported Muhammad from Mecca on the night of his heavenly ascent."[68]

Nasir's description of the Haram al-Sharif also illustrates the proliferation of domes, gates, and small commemorative structures on the sacred platform (fig. 5.15).

FIGURE 5.15
Aerial view of the Haram al-Sharif today, with a view of the domes and gates that proliferate that platform

FIGURE 5.16
Jerusalem Dome of the Prophet on the Haram al-Sharif. The present form dates to the 16th or 17th century. However, Nasir-i Khusraw's 11th-century account describes a similar dome present on the Fatimid-era platform.

As Oleg Grabar has demonstrated, the addition of numerous commemorative structures marking the sacred spaces of Islam means that the appearance of the platform had changed substantially between the Umayyad era and the Fatimid era.[69] Nasir describes the platform as having four domes near one another, the largest of which was the Dome of the Rock.[70] Three of these domes he associates directly with the story of the *miʿrāj.* He writes:

> They say that on the night of the ascent into heaven the Prophet first prayed in the Dome of the Rock and placed his hand on the Rock. As he was coming out, the Rock rose up because of his majesty. He put his hand on the Rock again, and it froze in its place, half of it still suspended in the air. From there the Prophet went to the dome that is attributed to him and mounted the Buraq, for which reason that dome is so venerated.[71]

Thus, although the Dome of the Rock is not mentioned as the precise spot from which the Prophet ascended into heaven, it is characterized as marking an important moment in the *miʿrāj* story. A similar meaning is ascribed to the Dome of the Prophet (fig. 5.16), which commemorates the spot on which Muhammad mounted his sacred steed, al-Buraq. In addition to these two domes, Nasir asserts that the Dome of Gabriel is the spot where "Buraq was brought . . . for the Prophet to mount." In this way, the domes on the platform of the Haram al-Sharif are understood as commemorating key moments in the *miʿrāj* story.

Given the historical context and religious associations of the eleventh-century Haram al-Sharif, how might we make sense of the inscriptional program and recessed roundels in the renovated Aqsa Mosque's *maqṣūra*? As mentioned, the roundels are unique in the history of Islamic art.[72] Their recession into the pendentives is made more pronounced by the concentric circles, which have a trompe l'oeil effect, making the forms appear even more three dimensional, resembling miniature domes surrounding a larger, central dome. Indeed, the domes throughout the Haram al-Sharif utilized similar circular forms to accentuate their verticality, leading the viewer's gaze and contemplation toward the heavens (see figs. 5.14 and 5.17). I would posit that their presence in the new *maqṣūra* may have operated on a number of levels for the visitors to the mosque.

Visitors walking into the Aqsa Mosque would have instantly recognized the domed *maqṣūra* as a special space in the mosque, through its architectural distinction and glittering mosaics. In effect, this assemblage functioned as a shrine within the congregational mosque and sacralized this particular space as the hallowed spot to which the Prophet was transported on his *isrāʾ*—the first part of the Prophet's miraculous journey. Progressing through the Fatimid-era arch into the domed *maqṣūra,* visitors first encounter Qurʾanic verse 17:1, which explicitly addresses the *isrāʾ* (see fig. 5.10). The verse's presence within this structure reminds the visitor that he is standing on the very spot to which

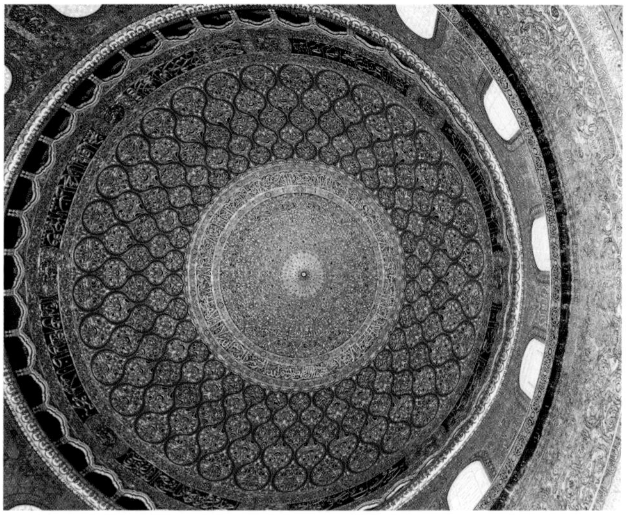

FIGURE 5.17
Jerusalem, Dome of the Rock, 691/2, view looking up at dome, demonstrating the use of circular motifs to lead the eye upward

the Prophet was transported during the miraculous event. Progressing through the arch, the visitor turns up to face the mosaics in the recessed roundels, which move the eye toward heaven and function as trompe l'oeil miniature domes. With a single large dome surrounded by recessed roundels, the *maqṣūra* may have reminded the viewer of the various commemorative structures, as described by Nasir, that mark the most sacred spaces on the platform, relating to the second part of the Prophet's journey—the *miʿrāj* (see figs. 5.15–5.16). Seen as a whole, then, the new Fatimid *maqṣūra* may have functioned as a microcosmic representation of the most sacred significance of Jerusalem in Islam.

The new orientation of the mosque furthered this sacralization of space within the building. Unlike al-Mahdi's plan for al-Aqsa, which emphasized its width, the mosque under al-Zahir was longitudinal, evoking the basilica plan of Christian churches in Jerusalem. Like the earlier version of the Holy Sepulcher, which had been destroyed by al-Hakim, the Aqsa Mosque utilized a basilica plan, whose nave culminated in a domed space, marking the most sacred spot in the structure. It also relied on Christian architectural vocabulary, in including potent symbols, executed in mosaic, on the pendentives of the dome. In a Christian context, these spaces would have been occupied by iconographically significant human figures. In the Aqsa Mosque, these forms preserve semiotic potency but in an aniconic language, as is appropriate to mosque architecture.

Of course, these forms might have had particular resonances for Shiʿi visitors to the space. First, the concentric circle motif recalls the concentric circles found throughout Fatimid art, as discussed in chapter 3. In particular, in its glittering evocation of precious materials, the domes' mosaic decoration recalls al-Maqrizi's description of the sunburst decoration (*shamsa*), made by al-Muʿizz for the kaaba in Mecca.[73] Al-Maqrizi records the display of the *shamsa* in the Fatimid palace, with an open-work golden ball, inside of which were pearls the size of dove's eggs in red, yellow, and blue precious stones, surrounded by the hajj verse from the Qur'an (*sūrat al-ḥajj*) in emeralds. The adornment of sacred spaces in precious materials, executed in a series of concentric circles, was thus an established Fatimid practice.[74] For an Ismaili worshipper, the presence of these circles may have also evoked the relationship of the *bāṭin* to the *ẓāhir* and the many levels of creation, as outlined in the Ismaili memory devices discussed in chapter 3.

The *miʿrāj* itself was interpreted allegorically by Ismailis, for whom the story of the *isrāʾ* and *miʿrāj* had a number of esoteric meanings.[75] The *isrāʾ* was understood as an allegory for the ranks of the *daʿwa*, while the *miʿrāj* was understood in terms of an individual's gradual initiation into the *bāṭin* truths of the faith, as outlined in al-Qadi al-Nuʿman's *Asās al-Taʾwīl* (The foundation of allegorical interpretation).[76] As Elizabeth Alexandrin has highlighted, for Ismailis, the *isrāʾ* and *miʿrāj* were interpreted in a Neoplatonic framework, as an allegory for the Universal Soul's ascension toward the Universal Intellect, resulting in the gradual perfection of the individual on a microcosmic level.[77] This ascent is, in turn, modeled by the Prophet Muhammad's ascension.[78] Thus, for Ismailis, the *miʿrāj* narrative functioned as an allegory for the gradual perfection of the human individual and was regarded as a spiritual rather than physical ascent. Perhaps these unusual forms functioned as meditative aids for Ismailis to contemplate the relationship of the macrocosm and microcosm, in the relationship between the Prophet's *miʾrāj* and the individual's spiritual ascent toward the perfected universal form. Scholarship on Fatimid understandings of these events are quite nascent but may yield more concrete interpretations in the future.[79]

Much of al-Zahir's reign was devoted to undoing the damage of al-Hakim's late days and restoring order in the wake of the chaos caused by the rising Druze movement. Given the turmoil of this chapter in Fatimid history, al-Zahir would have had a particularly strong motivation for promoting this orthodox Islamic episode that describes the Prophet's direct encounter with God. Attempting to wipe away the heresy of the Druze proclamation of al-Hakim's divinity and occultation, al-Zahir invested lavishly in this commemoration of the Qur'anic argument for the Prophet's primacy within the faith. In Islam, the ruler does not ascend to heaven; only the Prophet is capable of this feat.

If al-Zahir was concerned with distancing the Fatimids from the heresy of the Druze movement and reversing the excesses of al-Hakim's late reign, why did he include his father's name in the inscription? The *maqṣūra*'s inscription asserts that the renovation was carried out by "the Imam al-Zahir li'Aziz Din Allah, Commander of the Faithful, son of al-Hakim bi-Amr Allah, Commander of the Faithful." It is unusual for a Fatimid inscription to include both the name of the reigning caliph and the name of his father.[80] However, including both names in this inscription also serves to discredit the Druze heresy. It proclaims al-Zahir, rather than his cousin Ibn Ilyas, as the rightful successor. Naming the order of rightful succession in the inscription asserts that, contrary to Druze proclamations, al-Hakim was indeed dead. In effect, the inscription asserts that there was nothing unusual in the transference of power from al-Hakim to al-Zahir—a statement that could not be further from the truth.

AL-ZAHIR AND THE RESTORATION OF CHRISTIAN JERUSALEM

Al-Zahir's attempt at mitigating the damage of al-Hakim's reign can be seen not only in his renovations of the Haram al-Sharif but also in his accommodation of Christian monuments in the city. In general, al-Zahir's reign ushered in a new period of peace with the Byzantine empire—a peace that was predicated in part on the control of sacred space.[81] Yahya al-Antaki records that, in 1023, the patriarch of Jerusalem, Nikephoros I, wrote to the Byzantine emperor, to inform him that the Church of the Holy Sepulcher was being repaired. This renovation was conducted not on behalf of the Byzantine ruler but on behalf of al-Zahir's regent and aunt, Sitt al-Mulk, as a way to reverse a trade embargo.[82] A few years later, the emperor Constantine VIII (r. 1025–28) proposed a new agreement. The mosque in Constantinople would be reopened, with the sermon said in the name of the Fatimid ruler. In return, the Fatimids would allow the Byzantines to rebuild the Church of the Holy Sepulcher.[83] At the same time, the Byzantine empire lifted its trading embargo against the Fatimids. The 1030 treaty between al-Zahir and Romanos III Argyros allowed the Byzantine emperor to rebuild the Church of the Holy Sepulcher, but at his own expense, while the mosque in Constantinople was reopened with the Friday sermon delivered in al-Zahir's name.[84] The treaty also allowed the Byzantines to reconstruct other destroyed churches in Jerusalem and to reestablish the Christian patriarch.[85] This episode of imperial negotiation demonstrates the centrality of religious architectural space in medieval diplomacy. By the eleventh century, the Byzantine and Fatimid empires claimed religious monuments as their own, whether or not they had built them.

While treaties with the Byzantines allowed for the reconstruction of the Holy Sepulcher and other destroyed churches, sources suggest that some church destruction continued under al-Zahir. In particular, several churches were destroyed in the process of reconstructing the city's walls.[86] Unlike his father, who was ideologically motivated, however, al-Zahir seems to have ordered the destruction of churches according to the pragmatic needs of urban restoration.

In 1033, three years after the treaty between the Fatimids and the Byzantines was signed, a catastrophic earthquake complicated the reconstruction of the Holy Sepulcher. The earthquake left many of the remaining monuments in Jerusalem in ruins, including Islamic structures on the Haram al-Sharif. Al-Zahir financed the restoration of the Haram al-Sharif in 1034 and 1035, but the Holy Sepulcher would have to wait until the 1040s, when Byzantine emperor Constantine IX Monomachos (r. 1042–55) undertook its completion.[87] Most likely, the reconstruction of the monument was carried out by Byzantine craftsmen from Constantinople working in partnership with a local Jerusalem-based group. Based on a plan devised by a Byzantine architect in Constantinople, the new church was considerably smaller than the one destroyed by al-Hakim, consisting only of the rotunda and courtyard.[88] Thus, the eleventh-century Holy Sepulcher had a significantly curtailed visual and spatial impact on the cityscape of Jerusalem. In addition to its smaller footprint, the new Holy Sepulcher was given an altered orientation, which placed it in clear distinction from and subservient to the monuments of the Haram al-Sharif. Under the Umayyads, the primary entrance of the Christian complex faced the Haram al-Sharif, thereby placing the Islamic space and the Christian structure in conversation with one another. In contrast, the eleventh-century entrance to the Holy Sepulcher was constructed on the north side of the building. This new orientation made it less visible from the monuments of the Haram al-Sharif and vice versa. Furthermore, looking at the new Holy Sepulcher from the Haram al-Sharif, only the domes could be seen, and processional access to the building became highly restricted.[89] In this way, the spatial conversation between the two buildings was broken as the Islamic and Christian monuments began to operate in their own, distinctive orbits.

The role of Jerusalem changed dramatically in the post-Umayyad, pre-Crusader period. Throughout the centuries of Abbasid rule, the monuments of the Haram al-Sharif were of little interest to the rulers in Baghdad. However, the local population of Jerusalem was invested in the status of the Islamic structures and called on the distant rulers to restore them, though their calls were met with a lukewarm reception. In the Fatimid era, during the destructive and turbulent reign of al-Hakim, Jerusalem once again rose in status. It further grew in stature under al-Zahir, who oversaw the renewal of the Haram al-Sharif in concert with the Byzantine renewal of the Holy Sepulcher. These renovations both symbolized a new era of peace between the polities and served to distinguish between Islamic and Christian spaces. In this period, each empire used buildings as proxies in the struggle for political and religious legitimacy.

To our modern sensibilities, the destruction of the Holy Sepulcher appears to be a most violent act—a transgressive suppression of artistic expression and religious devotion. However, destruction can also act as a potent catalyst—in this case, al-Hakim's destructive reign prompted his successor's constructive investment in and reconceptualization of Jerusalem itself, an act that called increasing attention to Jerusalem as a global stage and battleground for architectural patronage—one that would have dramatic repercussions in the decades and centuries to come.

Conclusion

Architecture played a pivotal role in negotiating power within the kaleidoscope of religious identities in the early Fatimid period (909–1036). The reign of al-Hakim bi-Amr Allah, who is often dismissed as a psychotic anomaly in Fatimid history, was, in fact, a particularly transformative period in terms of setting the architectural priorities of the dynasty and solidifing the status of Cairo and Jerusalem in the Islamic world. Although scholars often see the establishment of Cairo as a major turning point for the Fatimids, in fact, the architectural projects there initially were carried out according to Fatimid precedent in Tunisia, in which the requisite mosque and palace were constructed at the center of a walled palace-city. In form, this was the same urban composition established by rival Islamic caliphates in Spain and Iraq. However, in meaning, it was utterly different. In the Fatimid model, the city was a sacred space, sanctified by the presence of the living Imam, who dwelled in its palace. Thus, the palace itself was the most sacred space in the new walled city. The early Fatimid rulers al-Muʿizz and al-ʿAziz built their greatest monuments for this Ismaili population, according to the esoteric dimensions of the Ismaili faith. The audience was not only the Ismaili court but also the pilgrims who would travel from throughout the world to be in the presence of the Imam and to study the esoteric (*bāṭin*) teachings of the faith at the Sessions of Wisdom (*majālis al-ḥikma*), held within the palace. It was this distinctly Ismaili function of the city with which the first Egyptian Imam-caliphs were concerned; as a result, their most important architectural projects were focused on the walled city of al-Qahira.

At the same time that al-Muʿizz and al-ʿAziz built monuments focused on the Ismaili functions of the city, they showed a pragmatic tolerance of their religious minorities (*dhimmīs*), particularly their Christian communities. A close reading of Christian sources from this period demonstrates that they exhibited a tolerance toward the construction and renovation of Christian monuments in their realm and an openness to the *dhimmīs* who staffed their administration. However, although modern scholars celebrate the rulers' tolerance, the sources illustrate growing tensions between Muslim and Christian communities regarding the caliphs' support of Christian architectural projects.

The reigns of al-Muʿizz and al-ʿAziz are often contrasted to that of al-Hakim, who is frequently considered the single exception to the Fatimid model of tolerance. Architecturally, al-Hakim is infamous for his demolition of the Church of the Holy Sepulcher in Jerusalem and his enigmatic veiling (by the stone bastions visible today) of the remarkable minarets at the Mosque of al-Hakim. However, an evaluation of al-Hakim's notorious projects in light of his complete architectural program, within the context of changing local and imperial sectarian relations, reveals that architecture was an integral component in a new articulation of caliphal identity—one in which the role of the Fatimid ruler as caliph to all Muslims was emphasized over his role as the Imam to the Ismaili minority.

Unquestionably, the reign of al-Hakim was unusual. Modern scholars read his cruelty, bizarre edits, and large-scale destruction of churches and synagogues as evidence of his mental defects and despotism. Many medieval chroniclers devote copious text to describing the reign of al-Hakim in great detail, attesting to its singularity and, in the case of Yahya al-Antaki, even questioning his sanity. Of course, it is impossible to examine the intent or mental state of a medieval figure. However, the singularity of al-Hakim's reign allows for a deeper exploration of the context of his architectural patronage, allowing us to ask: what does the *exception* to the Fatimid narrative of tolerance tell us about the larger context of Fatimid architecture?

Al-Hakim's patronage program can be divided into three distinct phases. In the first, the new caliph ordered the completion of the Mosque of al-Hakim, including the construction of the famous minarets. These unique towers emphasize the esoteric dimension of Ismaili Shiʿism, displaying evocative signs of the faith, divine light imagery, and Qur'anic verses whose *bāṭin* meanings were to be interpreted through Ismaili *ta'wīl*. Unlike his predecessors, al-Hakim demonstrated a greater concern for the urban sphere, engaging more directly with its population, and sponsoring two major mosques beyond the walls of al-Qahira. The first, the Mosque of al-Maqs, was built to the northwest of the royal palace-city while the Mosque of Rashida was constructed to the south of Fustat-Misr, at the site of former Christian cemeteries. These mosques and others in al-Qahira and Fustat-Misr acted as billboards for an anti-Sunni message from the ruler, as sites of the "golden curses" condemning the Companions of the Prophet Muhammad. Within this early period, al-Hakim also established the house of knowledge (*dār al-ʿilm*) in the royal city, thereby promoting the Fatimid city as an international center of learning for Ismailis and non-Ismailis alike, increasing its status as a caliphal capital and rivaling a similar institution founded ten years earlier in a Buyid suburb of Baghdad. His architectural projects in the capital ultimately reflect the growing importance of the palace-city itself to the first caliph born inside its walls. Although the caliph's treatment of the capital began to change in these early years, the changes occurred within an Ismaili framework. Meanwhile, he continued his predecessors' tolerance of churches, despite a growing outcry from Muslims against them.

These dynamics shifted in the wake of the Abu Rakwa revolt. Alarmed by the extent of this Sunni threat, which promoted the heresy of al-Hakim's "golden curses" to gain support, the caliph instituted a rapprochement with the Sunni majority of the city. He ordered the erasing of the curses and banned anyone from speaking badly about these Sunni figures from the formative era of Islam. The middle years of al-Hakim's reign brought a radical shift in the Fatimid message. Architecturally, the shift is demonstrated in al-Hakim's response to growing religious tensions, culminating in the mass destructions of *dhimmī* monuments, including the Church of the Holy Sepulcher in Jerusalem. While al-Hakim obliterated churches throughout his realm, he sought to guarantee the perpetuity of his own architectural monuments by establishing endowments (*waqfs*) for the mosques of al-Azhar, al-Maqs, and Rashida, and the *dār al-ʿilm*.

The change in tone between the early and middle periods is most clearly articulated in the addition of stone bastions to conceal the minarets of the Mosque of al-Hakim in 1010. In this act, the Ismaili messages and symbolism of the original towers were obscured by an austere encasement, featuring a line of Qur'anic verse expressing harsh recriminations to non-believers. Ultimately, the change in message is consistent with a recasting of the ruler from the esoteric Imam of the Ismailis to the universal caliph of Islam, whose legitimacy was demonstrated in his efforts to "command the good and forbid the bad." These efforts were not only aimed at the Muslims in his Egyptian realm but at claiming the caliphate for the Fatimid cause, seen most vividly in al-Kirmani's letters to the Buyid emir in Baghdad. Although al-Hakim's persecution of *dhimmīs* and destruction of churches was extreme, a comparison of his acts with the codification of church treatment in the Pact of ʿUmar and the *ḥisba* manuals of the Islamic market inspectors (*muḥtasibs*) demonstrates that the religious basis for the destructions, and the messages of the new bastions, were consistent with a puritanical strain of Sunni Islam that may have been intended to be of broad appeal to the entire Islamic community (*umma*).

A consideration of this complete historical and architectural context allows for a reinterpretation of the addition of the bastions to the original minarets. Clearly, the Fatimid message and aesthetic had changed dramatically between the construction of the original towers and the construction of the bastions. Just as the imperial message and caliphal priorities shifted from the esoteric aspect of Ismailism to the action-oriented, universally understood Islamic law (*sharīʿa*), the minarets' Ismaili symbolism was concealed by the unadorned, action-oriented verses of the new bastions. These new towers blended with the many square Sunni towers that existed throughout the Islamic world, rather than expressing the innovative Ismaili decorative program of the 1003 towers. In this way, the minarets became visual representations of the fundamental Ismaili paradigm of the hidden (*bāṭin*) and the visible (*ẓāhir*), with the harsh warnings of the austere bastions hiding the *bāṭin* core of Ismaili belief. Perhaps these two layers of the minarets would have been accessible to members of the mission (*daʿwa*), who could visit the interior of the towers as a physical, didactic display of the relation between the *bāṭin* and *ẓāhir*. This middle period of al-Hakim's reign represents a consistent ideological shift in Fatimid intellectual history and an effort to appeal to the Islamic *umma* in Egypt and abroad. In many ways, these years represent the apex of Fatimid power, in which the patronage and decimation of architectural projects were instrumental tools in claiming caliphal authority and establishing Cairo as an Islamic center to rival Abbasid Baghdad.

The final years of al-Hakim's reign are another turning point in the role of architecture and caliphal ambitions, characterized by enigmatic architectural patronage and a crisis in the *daʿwa*. The priorities of both the early and middle periods were once again changed, as the Imam-caliph became increasingly ascetic, and less focused on universal Islamic rule. Meanwhile, the rise of the Druze movement threatened and splintered the Ismaili *daʿwa*. At this time, al-Hakim reversed many of his anti-*dhimmī* laws, allowing for the reconstruction of churches, engaged in increasingly frequent nighttime walks through the Muqattam Hills, and, perhaps most enigmatically, named his cousin Ibn Ilyas as his successor in 1013. In these later years, al-Hakim's interest in asceticism and wanderings in the Muqattam Hills led to the patronage of the small, enigmatic Mosque of al-Lu'lu'a at the base of the Muqattam Hills, in the Qarafa cemetery. Unlike the congregational mosques of his earlier reign, this small mosque (*masjid*) was apparently intended for more private use, perhaps serving a similar function to the small oratory in the western minaret of the Mosque of al-Hakim. Although the precise context of this late commission remains a mystery, with little historical or inscriptional record, al-Hakim's sponsorship of a small project in the Qarafa can be considered an early example of the development of the Qarafa cemetery as a site of Fatimid patronage of smaller shrine and mausolea projects.

Although al-Hakim is noted as the exception to the Fatimid age of religious unity and tolerance, the reality was far more complicated. In the shifting dynamics of sectarian relations, architecture often acted as a battleground on which religious wars were waged. Ultimately, the struggle for religious legitimacy and power was not limited to the Egyptian context but defined this period of Islamic history in general. Indeed, the Abbasid caliphate encountered similar dynamics in the tenth and eleventh centuries. Controlled by the Shiʿi Buyids and inhabited by a multisectarian population, the Abbasid world was frequently destabilized by sectarian strife. Although no buildings remain for the Abbasids from this period, textual sources document that the mosques of Baghdad played an equally important role in defining religious identity, acting, at times, as billboards upon which was displayed the cursing of the first three caliphs and the Companions of the Prophet, as in the Fatimid context.[1]

The impact of al-Hakim's reign is seen most directly in the rebuilding of Jerusalem under his successor, al-Zahir. As a response to al-Hakim's cataclysmic destruction of the Holy Sepulcher, unprecedented attention was lavished on the city, with an architectural argument for a shared, orthodox vision of the city's role in Islam. This chapter of Jerusalem's history is often forgotten, due to the tumult of the Crusades in the following centuries, but al-Zahir's renovations suggest a reimagining of the role of the city and its architecture prior to this moment—one that was precipitated by destruction.

Fatimid Egypt is often treated as a unique case in both Islamic and art historical studies. It stands alone as the only medieval Shi'i caliphate and is, therefore, often approached as a fascinating, but ultimately isolated, chapter in Islamic architectural history.[2] Alternatively, scholars approach the dynasty teleologically, investigating the Fatimids primarily in terms of their contribution to the development of a distinctively Islamic Egyptian architecture. Indeed, the relative richness of architectural remains and historical sources for the Fatimids, combined with the uninterrupted development of Cairo as an architectural center, has contributed to the isolation of Egypt as a topic of study. This current study has demonstrated that the Fatimid architectural program was not only an Egyptian phenomenon but was conducted on an international stage, concerned largely with claiming legitimacy over the Islamic world. As the unified caliphate of the early Umayyad and Abbasid periods splintered into the rival caliphates of the tenth and eleventh centuries, architecture played a crucial role in defining imperial identities and ambitions.

The period under consideration here represents the Fatimid empire at its apogee. Indeed, al-Hakim was the last Imam-caliph to rule supreme over a vast empire. In contrast, al-Zahir faced many hardships—plague, Bedouin revolts, and financial crises. These crises would ultimately weaken the role of the Fatimid Imam-caliph, culminating in the long reign of al-Mustansir. Under al-Mustansir, the administrative power of the empire would be transferred away from the Imam-caliph to powerful viziers, while the Imam-caliph acted as the religious figurehead for the dynasties.[3] The nature of architectural patronage changed radically in this second half of the Fatimid dynasty. Once focused on hallmark projects such as congregational mosques and palaces, caliphal patronage moved instead to smaller mosques and, especially, a proliferation of small, often elaborately decorated, shrines, in the cemeteries to the south of al-Qahira.[4]

The reconstruction of Islamic Jerusalem by al-Zahir was a profoundly influential, yet momentary, chapter in the city's history. Al-Hakim's destruction of the Holy Sepulcher had had a resounding impact not only on the Fatimid history of the city but in the history of the world. His attack would act as a rallying cry to the Latin Crusaders to wrest the city from Muslim hands. For the next centuries, Jerusalem was the disputed territory of the Crusades, and would bloodily change hands between Muslim and Christian polities.

Narratives of tenth-century tolerance—both in the context of the Fatimids and the Cordoban Umayyad courts—are often couched in terms of a temporal relativism. The Fatimids and Umayyads did, indeed, create interfaith utopias when we compare them to what we know of the postcaliphal period. Religious communities lived together peacefully, relative to the brutality of the Crusades; coexistence was the standard in the tenth-century Islamic world if we compare it to the vicious persecution of Jews in medieval Latin Europe or their forced expulsion in the Spanish Reconquest of 1492.[5] Even in the Islamic context, the Cordoban Umayyads and the Fatimids oversaw a period of enlightened coexistence if we compare their reigns to the puritanical spirit of the later Almoravids and Almohads, or to the persecution of religious minorities under the Mamluk sultanate.[6] Ultimately, our notions of medieval utopias or dystopias reflect our own modern identities, tempting us to read the caliphal period as an era of enlightenment, one that mirrors our own contemporary hope for a global, cooperative coexistence in a multicultural, interfaith society.[7]

Of course, the reality of medieval coexistence was complicated, defined by both coexistence and conflict. This study contributes to a body of recent scholarship that examines architecture's role in negotiating interfaith relationships in medieval Islam.[8] As Stephennie Mulder has demonstrated for later medieval Syria, the approach toward architectural patronage could be "pragmatically ecumenical," even in times of sectarian strife.[9] Finbarr Flood has pointed to dangers of "flattening the topography of highly contoured landscapes" throughout the medieval period in India.[10] The balance between tolerance and intolerance, coexistence and conflict was often precarious and needs to be explored with historical precision.

The Fatimid period was neither a utopia nor a dystopia. However, an understanding of a tenth-century golden age has tended to obscure the complications of this narrative and the central role architecture played in articulating religious identity and competition. As a result, a persecuting ruler like al-Hakim can be dismissed easily as a madman. This line of thinking has caused us to overlook what was perhaps the most influential architectural act in the medieval world—the destruction of the Church of the Holy Sepulcher in Jerusalem. Instead of dismissing this act, this study demonstrates that destruction played a generative role in medieval architectural patronage. In destroying the Holy Sepulcher, al-Hakim, the "image breaker," became an "image maker."[11] This destruction rang out throughout the medieval world, serving as a catalyst for the Fatimid reimagining of Jerusalem and, eventually, an inspiration for the Crusades. It was also entirely consistent with the rest of al-Hakim's architectural program.[12]

Moreover, although some scholars have suggested that the nature of medieval Islamic texts reveals little information about art or architecture, a close consideration of diverse medieval sources demonstrates that these universal Islamic forms were not arranged without meaning.[13] This study highlights conscious architectural choices based on specific historical circumstances, challenging the idea that medieval Islamic architecture was simply a haphazard combination of unified Islamic forms. This type of analysis is often reserved for later Islamic empires, but it is equally relevant for the period of competing caliphates. The meanings and audiences of medieval Islamic architecture were extraordinarily complex. Scholarly debate on the Fatimids often centers around whether ordinary Egyptians could understand the esoteric meanings of Ismaili messages.[14] However, this debate does not exist for western medieval architecture, in which it is assumed that peasants, kings, monks, and nuns could all experience and interpret art differently. The present study suggests that this rich complexity existed in the context of medieval Islamic architectural history, even if we are yet in the beginning stages of decoding these meanings.

NOTES

Introduction

1. This act is described in al-Muqaffaʿ, *Taʾrīkh baṭārikat al-kanīsa al-Miṣriyya (The History of the Patriarchs of the Egyptian Church)*, 2:128/194.

2. In modern Arabic, *al-Qahira* is simply the term used for what is known in English as *Cairo*. Throughout this text, however, I use the terms *Cairo* and *al-Qahira* differently. I use *Cairo* to indicate the capital city and its environs in general. I use *al-Qahira* to specifically discuss the walled palace-city to the north of Fustat-Misr that was reserved primarily for the Ismaili faithful.

3. Scholars have increasingly critiqued this model in historical scholarship on Spain and Egypt, though it remains pervasive in art historical scholarship. See Feliciano, "Review of Arts of Intimacy," 395; Shenoda, "Re-Envisioning Persecution," 411–30.

4. The modern concept of a "clash of civilizations" was first hypothesized by Samuel Huntington, who argued that in a post–Cold War context, conflict would be based largely on religious identity. This concept was applied by Bernard Lewis to conflicts between the Middle East and the West. See Huntington, *Clash of Civilizations?* and Lewis, "Roots of Muslim Rage."

5. The boundaries of medieval sectarian belief were not static. Sectarian difference was sometimes more clearly articulated than others. For a study on the blurring of sectarian boundaries in the architecture of medieval Syria, see Mulder, *Shrines of the ʿAlids in Medieval Syria.*

6. For an articulation of the role of art and architecture in caliphal competition, see Necipoğlu and al-Asad, *Topkapı Scroll*, 93–95.

7. For a discussion of the art and architecture of the three caliphates, see Anderson and Pruitt, "Three Caliphates, a Comparative Approach," 223–49. For a consideration of Islamic aesthetics in the service of sectarian competition in a later period, see Tabbaa, *Transformation of Islamic Art during the Sunni Revival.* For an alternate view of the same period, see Mulder, *Shrines of the ʿAlids in Medieval Syria.*

8. This distinguishes them from other branches of Shiʿism, for example, the more numerous Twelver Shiʿa. However, it is beyond the scope of this book to consider these differences. For the development of Imami Shiʿism, see especially Crone, *God's Rule*, chapter 10.

9. The potential for conflict between the *ʿulamāʾ* and the ruler could directly impact architectural projects. Cordoban Umayyad accounts suggest that ʿAbd al-Rahman III was criticized publicly by a judge (*qāḍī*) for skipping Friday prayer to oversee the construction of his new palace-city, Madinat al-Zahraʾ. Al-Maqqarī, *Analectes sur l'histoire et la littérature des arabes d'Espagne*, 1:375; al-Maqqarī, *Azhār al-riyāḍ fī akhbār ʿiyāḍ*, 2:270, as cited in Ruggles, *Gardens, Landscape, and Vision in the Palaces of Islamic Spain*, 60. Similarly, the caliph removed the gold and silver ceilings of an elaborate pavilion in the complex when it was deemed too elaborate. Al-Maqqarī, *Analectes*, 1:377–78; al-Maqqarī, *Azhār*, 2:28–82; al-Nubāhī, *Histoire des juges d'Andalousie intitulée kitab al-Markaba al-ʿUlya*, 71, as cited in Ruggles, 67.

10. For an application of this relationship to Fatimid art, see Bierman, *Writing Signs*, chapter 3.

11. For a discussion of the relationship between the *bāṭin* and *ẓāhir* in the early Fatimid empire, see especially Daftary, *Ismāʿīlīs: Their History and Doctrines*, 137–39; Halm, *Fatimids and Their Traditions of Learning*, 41–55.

12. For a consideration of the Ismaili community under the Fatimids, see Walker, "Ismāʿīlī Daʿwa and the Fāṭimid Caliphate."

13. Crone, *God's Rule*, 83.

14. Crone, 197–218.

15. Fierro, *ʿAbd al-Rahman III*, 71, 76.

16. Fierro, 121. The Abbasids, although Sunni, traced their lineage to the Prophet's family. Due to this genealogy, they had gained support from the party of ʿAli, whose support had allowed them to conquer the Umayyads in 750. In turn, the Cordoban Umayyads embraced Malikism, rejecting the Hanafism of the Abbasids, which they suspected as having Shiʿi leanings. ʿAbd al-Rahman III and al-Hakam II were active in patronizing biographical dictionaries that stressed that al-Andalus was a Sunni society, in which the *ʿulamāʾ* played a central role, in contrast to the Fatimids.

17. The Fatimids were Seveners (*sabaʿēa*), meaning that they believed it was the seventh Imam who had gone into occultation; however, they also believed that each age had a living Imam who could rightfully rule.

18. See Cahen, "Buwayhids or Būyids," 1:1350–57; Mottahedeh, *Loyalty and Leadership in an Early Islamic Society.*

19. For the purposes of this study, the term *dhimmī*s will refer broadly to minority populations of Christians and Jews living under caliphal rule.

20. For a discussion of sources, see Walker, *Exploring an Islamic Empire*, 152–69.

21. See Walker, 164–69;

Rabbat, "Architects and Artists in Mamluk Society," 30–37; Rabbat, "Medieval Link," 29–57.

22. Walker, "Al-Maqrīzī and the Fatimids," 88.

23. Al-Maqrīzī, *Al-Mawā'iẓ wa-l-i'tibār bi dhikr al-khiṭaṭ wa-l-āthār* (2002–3 edition); Al-Maqrīzī, *Itti'āẓ al-ḥunafā' bi-akhbār al-a'imma al-Fāṭimiyyīn al-khulafā'*. For translations of *Itti'āẓ* for much of al-Hakim's reign, see Walker, *Caliph of Cairo*.

24. In addition, the Abbasids had encouraged the circulation of tracts that looked Ismaili but portrayed the sect in a negative light.

25. Some caution must be reserved for these sources, however, as they have been copied and circulated several times since their medieval origins. Moreover, as the Institute has stated that its mission is to elevate the role of Ismailis in history, this purpose could influence the type of works they publish.

26. Some of the most intriguing glimpses into life in the Fatimid period come from the Jewish community in the form of Geniza documents. These letters, court papers, contracts, and other documents were drafted by the Jewish communities of the Islamic Mediterranean and were found in the Ben Ezra Synagogue in Fustat in the late nineteenth century. The corpus is an unofficial, unorganized treasure trove of information on medieval culture, commerce, family life, religion, and other topics. For the purposes of this study, the documents are significant in supporting an understanding of Fatimid society as one in which Jews, Christians, and Sunni Muslims were integral and often powerful. They also illustrate the importance of international trade and immigration, presenting a picture of an urban bourgeois class that is often silent in other historic chronicles. However, because of the unsystematic nature of these documents, they can often offer only glimpses into the specific historical context and, at the moment, give little information on the status of monuments. Goitein, *Mediterranean Society*; Rustow, *Heresy and the Politics of Community*.

27. From the tenth to eleventh centuries, there was a movement for translating texts from Coptic to Arabic. Rubsenson, "Translating the Tradition," 4–14. For a discussion of this document in the context of a common intellectual life, see Griffith, "Kitāb Miṣbāḥ al-'Aql of Severus Ibn al-Muqaffa'," 15–42. For a history of the patriarchs, see den Heijer, *Mawhub ibn Mansur ibn Mufarrig et l'historiographie copto-arabe*; Swanson, *Coptic Papacy in Islamic Egypt*.

Chapter 1. The City Illuminated

1. He is describing Hugh of Caesaria's visit to Cairo in the eleventh century. Tyre, *History of Deeds Done beyond the Sea*, 320.

2. For a discussion of the Fatimid treasury, see especially Ibn al-Zubayr, *Book of Gifts and Rarities*, 103–5, 163, 218.

3. For the esoteric dimensions of the Ismaili city, see especially Sanders, *Ritual, Politics, and the City in Fatimid Cairo*, chapter 3, and Bierman, *Writing Signs*, chapter 3.

4. This phrase was recorded by al-Qadi al-Nu'man in his *Iftihah*, translated in Haji, *Founding the Fatimid State*, 68.

5. For a discussion of the Fatimids prior to their conquest of North Africa, see Halm, *Empire of the Mahdi*; Brett, *Rise of the Fatimids*.

6. This caused an early schism for the Ismailis. Those who challenged al-Mahdi's claim became the Qarmatians, who established their own state in Baharin and acted as antagonists to the Fatimids through much of their reign. The details of this schism are unclear but discussed in Walker, *Exploring an Islamic Empire*, 20.

7. Walker, *Orations of the Fatimid Caliphs*, 17.

8. For a discussion of art and architecture under the Aghlabids, see Anderson, Fenwick, and Rosser-Owen, *The Aghlabids and Their Neighbors*, and Lézine, *Architecture de l'Ifriqiya*.

9. Bloom, *Arts of the City Victorious*, 19.

10. Brett, *Fatimid Empire*, 50–54. See also García-Arenal, *Messianism and Puritanical Reform*, introduction, chapters 1, 3, 6.

11. Al-Mahdiyya was founded in 912 and completed in 920. For a discussion of al-Mahdiyya, see Bloom, *Arts of the City Victorious*, 22–32; Lézine, *Mahdiya*. See also Bloom, "Origins of Fatimid Art"; Bloom, "Meaning in Early Fatimid Architecture."

12. Al-Muqaddasī, *Aḥsan al-taqāsīm fī ma'rifat al-aqālīm* [*The Best Divisions for Knowledge of the Regions*], 17.

13. Bloom, "Origins of Fatimid Art," 22.

14. The palace consisted of an eastern and western section, surrounding a central square—a form that would be repeated in the palace-city at al-Qahira.

15. Lézine, *Mahdiya*. See also Talbi, "Al-Mahdiyya."

16. This link is made by al-Qadi al-Nu'man (d. 974), who proclaims in his *Da'ā'im al-Islām* that 'Ali "saw a tall *mi'dhana* (minaret) and ordered it torn down because the call to prayer should not be given from a place higher than the roof of the mosque, because it would enable the muezzin to see within the privacy of the homes around the mosque, so it is not permited." Al-Qāḍī al-Nu'mān, *Da'ā'im al-Islām*, 147. Discussed in Bloom, *Minaret*, 138. Bloom discusses the proliferation of Umayyad minarets in the ideologically charged landscape of North Africa in Bloom, *Minaret*, chapter seven, "The Triumph of the Cordoban Minaret in the Maghreb"; Nasser Rabbat suggests that the presence or absence of a minaret at al-Azhar is more murky in Rabbat, "Al-Azhar Mosque," 50.

17. For a discussion of the portal, see Bloom, "Origins of Fatimid Art," 23.

18. Ibn 'Idhārī, *Al-Bayān al-mughrib fī akhbār al-Andalus wa-al-Maghreb*, 188. Trans. in Sanders, *Ritual, Politics, and the City in Fatimid Cairo*, 40–41. Irene Bierman has theorized the relationship between Ismaili and non-Ismaili spaces in Bierman, *Writing Signs*, chapter 1.

19. For a discussion of the princely cycle, see Grabar, *Formation of Islamic Art*, 154–56.

20. For a discussion of *ṭirāz*, see Sokoly, "Textiles and Identity"; Rabbat, "Ṭirāz"; Sanders, "Robes and Honor in Fatimid Egypt."

21. A similar evocation of Abbasid palatial forms is seen in Madinat al-Zahra', which recalled Abbasid Samarra. Ruggles, *Gardens, Landscape, and Vision in the Palaces of Islamic Spain*, 86–109. Little remains of al-Mansuriyya today, which is known primarily through archaeological excavations. For a discussion of al-Mansuriyya's construction in the context of the Fatimid victory over the Kharijite rebel Abu Yazid, see Brett, *Fatimid Empire*, 45.

22. Al-Muqaddasī, *Aḥsan al-taqāsīm fī ma'rifat al-aqālīm*, 17. Jonathan Bloom notes that al-Muqaddasi's link between the two cities must be taken with a grain of salt. At the time of al-Mansuriyya's foundation, little remained of the round city of Baghdad. Moreover, he claims that the Fatimids would not have been interested in hearkening back to a form established by their archrivals. Bloom, *Arts of the City Victorious*, 37. However, although the city lay in ruins, tales of the round city remained. Moreover, the Cordoban Umayyads also evoked Abbasid forms—in this case, Samarra, in their contemporary city, Madinat al-Zahra'. Most likely, the adaptation of Abbasid form by both dynasties was an architectural expression of their caliphal ambitions. For the Fatimids, it was also likely a reminder of their ambition to conquer the east, including Baghdad. For a discussion of medieval memories of Baghdad, see Cooperson, "Baghdad in Rhetoric and Narrative."

23. From Ibn Hānī, *Tabyīn al-ma'ānī fī sharḥ dīwān Ibn Hānī al-Andalusī al-Maghribī*, nos. 9, 12, 13, and 15, as translated in Sanders, *Ritual, Politics, and the City in Fatimid Cairo*, 41.

24. On Madinat al-Zahra', see Ruggles, *Gardens, Landscape, and Vision in the Palaces of Islamic Spain*, chapter 4; Fierro, "Madinat al-Zahara', el paraíso y los Fatimíes"; Triano, "Madīnat al-Zahrā': Triumph of the Islamic State"; Triano, "Madīnat al-Zahrā': Transformation of a Caliphal City"; Almagro, "Dwellings of Madīnat al-Zahrā'."

25. Ruggles, *Gardens, Landscape, and Vision in the Palaces of Islamic Spain*, 86–109.

26. A similar dynamic in competitive titulature might also be seen in the Cordoban Umayyad coins from the time, which use the title "Imam" to describe the ruler.

27. Walker, "Identity of One of the Ismaili Da'is Sent by the Fatimids to Ibn Hafsun," 387–88. The minbar no longer exists but al-Idrisi says it was worked on for seven years and that the Kutubiyya Mosque in Marrakech is thought to preserve its form.

28. Fierro, "Plants, Mary the Copt, Abraham, Donkeys and Knowledge," 126–27.

29. Bloom, *Minaret*, 148–49.

30. See Dodds, "Great Mosque of Córdoba," 18–23; Khoury, "Meaning of the Great Mosque of Cordoba in the Tenth Century," 81–83.

31. Khoury, "Meaning of the Great Mosque of Cordoba in the Tenth Century," 85–86. 'Uthman's Qur'an and its relationship to the Great Mosque of Cordoba is discussed in al-Idrīsī, *Description de l'Afrique et de l'Espagne*, 210–11; Dessus-Lamare, "Le mushaf de la Mosquée de Cordoue et son mobilier mécanique," 552–75; Grabar, "Notes sur le mihrab de la Grande Mosquée de Cordoue," 115–22.

32. For a discussion on the shared culture of the courts, see Grabar, "Shared Culture of Objects"; Hoffman, "Pathways of Portability."

33. See Lev, "Fāṭimid Imposition of Ismā'īlism on Egypt"; Bloom, "Mosque of the Qarafa in Cairo."

34. Bianquis, "Autonomous Egypt from Ibn Ṭūlūn to Kāfūr," 117.

35. Prior to the Arab conquest of Egypt, the central city of the region was Alexandria, with its strategic location on the Mediterranean Sea and Nile Delta. However, the Arab conquest of 641 moved the center of the country to the south, to the inland Byzantine fortress of Babylon, located on the shores of the Nile. For a discussion of pre-Fatimid Babylon and Fustat, see Kubiak, *Al-Fusṭāṭ*; Sheehan, *Babylon of Egypt*. See also the numerous excavation reports of George Scanlon listed in the bibliography.

36. For a discussion of pre-Fatimid Cairo, see Sheehan, *Babylon of Egypt*; Kennedy, "Egypt as a Province in the Islamic Caliphate"; Butler, *Arab Conquest of Egypt, and the Last Thirty Years of the Roman Dominion*; Creswell, *Muslim Architecture of Egypt*, volume 1; Sayyid, *La capitale de l'Égypte jusquà l'époque fatimide*, 19–35.

37. See, for example, al-Maqrīzī, *Itti'āẓ al-ḥunafā' bi-akhbār al-a'imma al-Fāṭimiyyīn al-khulafā'*, 1:103–7. Other sources and the content of the letter are discussed in Lev, *State and Society in Fatimid Egypt*, 15–16.

38. Ravaisse, "Essai sur l'histoire et sur la topographie du Caire d'après Makrizi," 415–19; Creswell, *Muslim Architecture of Egypt*, 1:20; Sayyid, "Grande palais fatimide au Caire."

39. The walls of Jawhar's city were constructed of mud brick and supposedly wide enough for two horsemen to ride next to one another. Creswell preserves this account from Ibn Duqmaq (d. 1406) in Creswell, 1:21. The walls seem to have been built rather hastily, measuring approximately 3608 feet (1100 meters) on the east-west axis and 3772 feet (1150 meters) on the north-south side. Some sources suggest that these walls must have been built overnight, but as Jonathan Bloom has pointed out, walls of this size must have taken some time to construct. Bloom, *Arts of the City Victorious*, 55.

40. Creswell, *Muslim Architecture of Egypt*, 1:22.

41. Al-Maqrīzī, *Al-Mawā'iẓ wa-l-i'tibār bi dhikr al-khiṭaṭ wa-l-āthār* (2002–3 edition), 3:454–61; Creswell, *Muslim Architecture of Egypt*, 1:22.

42. For a list of gates, see Creswell, *Muslim Architecture of Egypt*, 1:23–34.

43. On the *khalīj*, see Sheehan, *Babylon of Egypt*, 79–86.

44. Al-Muqaddasī, *Aḥsan al-taqāsīm fī ma'rifat al-aqālīm*, 193–215.

45. The status of Mecca at this time is described in Wensinck and Bosworth, "Makka."

46. However, the caliph choked off food to this region and the Meccans were forced to proclaim their fealty. Ibn al-Athīr, *Al-Kāmil fī'l ta'rīkh*, viii, 491, cited in Wensinck and Bosworth, "Makka."

47. Al-Maqrīzī, *Itti'āẓ al-ḥunafā' bi-akhbār al-a'imma al-Fāṭimiyyīn al-khulafā'*, 1:134.

48. The sanctity of the Imam's city resulted in the elaboration of what Paula Sanders has called the "ritual city." Sanders, *Ritual, Politics, and the City in Fatimid Cairo*, 39–82.

49. Medieval sources are not in agreement regarding the meaning of "al-Qahira." It is usually thought to refer to "the victorious" but may also be named for the planet Mars (al-Qahir), which was in ascendance when the new city was begun. Creswell, *Muslim Architecture of Egypt*, 1:21–23. The first coin minted with this name dates from 394/1003–4, when the city was called al-Qāhira al-Maḥrūsa (al-Qāhira "the Well-Protected"). See Bloom, *Arts of the City Victorious*, 53.

50. This period of Fatimid rule was a relatively prosperous and stable time, tied closely to the bounty of the Nile's floods. As Egypt's prosperity was bound so tightly to the level of the Nile, its measurement was an event for celebration and commemoration by the Fatimid state. The strong Fatimid economy was further supported by vibrant international trade, based on Egypt's access to both the Mediterranean and Indian Ocean trade routes. For a discussion, see Sanders, *Ritual, Politics, and the City in Fatimid Cairo*, 99–104.

51. Sanders, 42.

52. Bloom, *Arts of the City Victorious*, 58.

53. Bloom, "Ceremonial and Sacred Space in Early Fatimid Cairo," 96.

54. Here, I accept Irene Bierman's argument that Fatimid space, which she distinguishes as being either "public" or "sectarian," could mean different things to different audiences. Bierman, *Writing Signs*, 1–10.

55. Indeed, even for the eleventh-century Ismaili author Nasir-i Khusraw, who lauds Cairo and all of its accomplishments, Cairo was understood as being constructed as an "army camp" whose grandeur developed gradually. Nasir-i Khusraw, *Book of Travels*, 57.

56. Al-Maqrīzī, *Al-Mawāʿiẓ wa-l-iʿtibār bi dhikr al-khiṭaṭ wa-l-āthār* (2002–3 edition), 1:451; al-Maqrīzī, *Ittiʿāẓ al-ḥunafāʾ bi-akhbār al-aʾimma al-Fāṭimiyyīn al-khulafāʾ*, 1:113.

57. Al-Qāḍī al-Nuʿmān, *Taʾwīl al-daʿāʾim* (1967 edition), 1:322, cited in Sanders, *Ritual, Politics, and the City in Fatimid Cairo*, 50. The Cordoban Umayyads similarly gathered for *ʿīd* prayers at *muṣallā*s in Cordoba and Madinat al-Zahraʾ, suggesting that it was a caliphal prerogative to declare a continuation with Prophetic practice and use *muṣallā*s. This differs from Nasser Rabbat's assertion that in the tenth century the *muṣallā* was not a common feature for Sunni cities. Rabbat, "Al-Azhar Mosque," 52. While certainly true for most Sunni cities, it would seem that the *muṣallā* was an important form for the caliphates. For the Cordoban Umayyads, the *ʿīd* prayers were not led by the caliph, but by preachers (*khuṭabāʾ*s), while the caliph looked on from his *majlis* (a courtly gathering). For Umayyad *muṣallā*s, see Safran, *Second Umayyad Caliphate*, 95.

58. Al-Maqrīzī, *Ittiʿāẓ al-ḥunafāʾ bi-akhbār al-aʾimma al-Fāṭimiyyīn al-khulafāʾ*, 1:116. For a consideration of the significance of this difference, see Sanders, *Ritual, Politics, and the City in Fatimid Cairo*, 45.

59. Al-Maqrīzī, *Ittiʿāẓ al-ḥunafāʾ bi-akhbār al-aʾimma al-Fāṭimiyyīn al-khulafāʾ*, 1:116. For a discussion, see Sanders, *Ritual, Politics, and the City in Fatimid Cairo*, 45.

60. Al-Maqrīzī, *Ittiʿāẓ al-ḥunafāʾ bi-akhbār al-aʾimma al-Fāṭimiyyīn al-khulafāʾ*, 1:120–21; Lev, *State and Society in Fatimid Egypt*, 17; Sanders, *Ritual, Politics, and the City in Fatimid Cairo*, 45.

61. Ground was broken on al-Azhar in 970. The first Friday prayer was conducted in al-Azhar in 971 and the first *khuṭba* given in 972. Al-Maqrīzī, *Al-Mawāʿiẓ wa-l-iʿtibār bi dhikr al-khiṭaṭ wa-l-āthār* (2002–3 edition), 4:91–92.

62. For discussions of al-Azhar, see al-Maqrīzī, *Al-Mawāʿiẓ wa-l-iʿtibār bi dhikr al-khiṭaṭ wa-l-āthār* (2002–3 edition), 4:90–107; Flury, *Ornamente der Ḥākim und der Azhar Moschee*; Creswell, *Muslim Architecture of Egypt*, 1:36–64; Bloom, *Arts of the City Victorious*, 59–65; Rabbat, "Al-Azhar Mosque"; Walker, "Fatimid Institutions of Learning."

63. Bloom, *Minaret*, 138; Rabbat suggests that the presence or absence of a minaret at al-Azhar is more murky in Rabbat, "Al-Azhar Mosque," 50.

64. For the phases of construction, see al-Maqrīzī, *Al-Mawāʿiẓ wa-l-iʿtibār bi dhikr al-khiṭaṭ wa-l-āthār* (2002–3 edition), 4:90–107, and Rabbat, "Al-Azhar Mosque."

65. See Creswell, *Muslim Architecture of Egypt*, 1:53–58.

66. Jonathan Bloom suggests that this ceiling may, in fact, have been raised during the reign of al-ʿAziz. Bloom, *Arts of the City Victorious*, 63.

67. Creswell notes that the original roof was only 22.7 feet (6.9 meters) high. Creswell, *Muslim Architecture of Egypt*, 1:45.

68. There seems to be some dispute as to the exact date of construction. Qalqashandi wrote that the mosque was begun by the vizier Ibn Killis in 379/989 and completed by al-Hakim in 396/1006 and Ibn Aybak writes that al-Hakim began construction in 392/1001. See Sayyid, *Capitale de l'Égypte jusquà l'époque Fatimide*, 334. However, it is likely that al-Maqrizi's account from the Fatimid contemporary al-Musabbihi are the most reliable. Al-Maqrīzī, *Al-Mawāʿiẓ wa-l-iʿtibār bi dhikr al-khiṭaṭ wa-l-āthār* (2002–3 edition), 4:107–26.

69. In medieval sources, it is also sometimes called al-Khuṭba. See for example al-Maqrīzī, *Al-Mawāʿiẓ wa-l-iʿtibār bi dhikr al-khiṭaṭ wa-l-āthār* (2002–3 edition), 4:107.

70. Al-Maqrīzī, *Al-Mawāʿiẓ wa-l-iʿtibār bi dhikr al-khiṭaṭ wa-l-āthār* (2002–3 edition), 4:108.

71. Paula Sanders convincingly argues for the role of ceremonial processions in linking these spaces in Sanders, *Ritual, Politics, and the City in Fatimid Cairo*, 48–52.

72. Al-Maqrīzī, *Al-Mawāʿiẓ wa-l-iʿtibār bi dhikr al-khiṭaṭ wa-l-āthār* (2002–3 edition), 1:267. A translation of this text is found in Sanders, *Ritual, Politics, and the City in Fatimid Cairo*, 49.

73. Al-Maqrīzī, *Ittiʿāẓ al-ḥunafāʾ bi-akhbār al-aʾimma al-Fāṭimiyyīn al-khulafāʾ*, 1:272.

74. For a post-Fatimid summary of the mosque's history, see Al-Maqrīzī, *Al-Mawāʿiẓ wa-l-iʿtibār bi dhikr al-khiṭaṭ wa-l-āthār* (2002–3 edition), 4:114–20. For a discussion of Bohra renovations, see Sanders, "Bohra Architecture and the Restoration of Fatimid Culture"; and Sanders, *Creating Medieval Cairo*, chapter 4. In the Ayyubid period, the mosque was used as the primary congregational mosque of the city, as the Shafiʿi *madhhab* allowed for only one Friday mosque. They converted the structure into a madrasa, which continued to be used in the Mamluk period. Medieval restorations discussed by al-Maqrizi include the earthquake and restoration of the minarets in 703/1303. The earthquake caused the top parts of the minarets/roofs and walls of the mosque to fall down. Al-Maqrizi reports that Emir al-Ruknu al-Deen Baybars al-Jashankir restored it, adding a new roof and whitewash, making several endowments (*waqfs*) with proceeds from Giza and al-Saʿeed and Alexandria, instituting studies of the four Islamic schools within the mosque.

75. For a discussion of the use of floriated Kufic, see Tabbaa, *Transformation of Islamic Art during the Sunni Revival*, 55–57; Tabbaa, "Transformation of Arabic Writing: Part 2, the Public Text," 121–26; Blair, "Floriated Kufic and the Fatimids"; O'Kane, "Monumental Calligraphy in Fatimid Egypt"; Shehab, "Fatimid Kūfī Epigraphy on the Gates of Cairo."

76. Ground was broken on palace construction in January 973. Al-Maqrīzī, *Al-Mawāʿiẓ wa-l-iʿtibār bi dhikr al-khiṭaṭ wa-l-āthār* (2002–3 edition), 4:91; al-Maqrīzī, *Ittiʿāẓ al-ḥunafāʾ bi-akhbār al-aʾimma al-Fāṭimiyyīn al-khulafāʾ*, 1:112. In the nineteenth century, Paul Ravaisse proposed the locations of the various palace parts, based on al-Maqrizi's description of the city. These plans are an invaluable tool in envisioning how the palaces may have looked in the Fatimid period. Although Ravaisse's reconstructions suggest a planned regularity to the construction, it is likely that in al-Muʿizz's time, the eastern palace was a jumble of functional constructions rather than a centrally planned entity. However, al-ʿAziz's smaller western palace may have been more regularly planned. Ravaisse, "Essai sur l'histoire et sur la topographie du Caire d'après Makrizi."

77. Al-Maqrīzī, *Al-Mawāʿiẓ wa-l-iʿtibār bi dhikr al-khiṭaṭ wa-l-āthār* (2002–3 edition), 2:298.

78. For a discussion of the 1125 Mosque of al-Aqmar in the context of this space, see Behrens-Abouseif, "Facade of the Aqmar Mosque in the Context of Fatimid Ceremonial"; Williams, "Cult of ʿAlid Saints in the Fatimid Monuments of Cairo. Part I: Mosque of Al-Aqmar," 37–52.

79. The Fatimid palace no longer remains. The library and treasury were dismantled and sold by the Ayyubids and the palace was divided and given as land grants to Fatimid commanders. Eventually, the palace fell into a state of disrepair. See Walker, *Exploring an Islamic Empire*, 89–90.

80. Though it is not clear when Nasir-i Khusraw converted to Ismailism, his treatment of Ismaili sites in the text makes it most likely that he had already converted at the time of his journey. See page xii of W. M. Thackston's introduction in Nasir-i Khusraw, *Book of Travels*.

81. Cairo is described in Nasir-i Khusraw, *Book of Travels*, 56–74. As a comparison, in his description of Mecca and Jerusalem, the sacred sites of the kaaba and the Haram al-Sharif are given the most detailed description.

82. As a comparison, see the description of the Byzantine envoy's visit to the Abbasid court in Baghdad in 917. Ibn al-Zubayr, *Book of Gifts and Rarities*, 150–54.

83. Nasir-i Khusraw, *Book of Travels*, 58.

84. Nasir's description also records that outside the city, there was "another palace connected to the harem palace by a passageway with a reinforced ceiling." This connected palace most certainly did not exist under the time period under consideration here.

85. Nasir-i Khusraw, *Book of Travels*, 73.

86. The beams were found reused in the Maristan of Qalawun (ca. 1280), a Mamluk structure located on Bayn al-Qasrayn, and they now reside in the Museum of Islamic Art in Cairo. See Hampikian and Cyran, "Recent Discoveries Concerning the Fatimid Palaces Uncovered during the Conservation Works on Parts of Al-Ṣāliḥiyya Complex."

87. For a discussion of the Fatimid style, see Ettinghausen, "Painting in the Fatimid Period"; Ettinghausen, "Early Realism in Islamic Art"; Grabar, "Imperial and Urban Art in Islam."

88. Tyre, *History of Deeds Done beyond the Sea*, 2:315.

89. Tyre, 2:319. The passage describes Shawar as the sultan but in the Fatimid context, his position is usually referred to as vizier (*wazīr*).

90. Tyre, 2:319.

91. Tyre, 2:320.

92. Tyre, 2:320–21.

93. Paul Walker has explicated the nature of the al-Muʿizz and al-ʿAziz–era *majālis al-ḥikma*, distinguishing them from the institution of universal learning, the *dār al-ʿilm*, founded by al-Hakim in 1005 (see chapter 3 of this book). Walker has shown that although later medieval historians and modern historians use the terms *dār al-ʿilm* (house of knowledge) and *dār al-ḥikma* (house of wisdom) interchangeably, they conflate two distinct institutions. Walker, "Fatimid Institutions of Learning."

94. Halm, "Ismaili Oath of Allegiance (*ʿahd*) and the 'Sessions of Wisdom' (*majālis al-ḥikma*) in Fatimid Times."

95. This event occurred in 995. See al-Maqrīzī, *Al-Mawāʿiẓ wa-l-iʿtibār bi dhikr al-khiṭaṭ wa-l-āthār* (2002–3 edition), 1:391. See also Halm, "Ismaili Oath of Allegiance (ʿahd) and the 'Sessions of Wisdom' (Majālis al-Ḥikma) in Fatimid Times," 102.

96. For a discussion of Fatimid woodwork, see Pauty, *Catalogue général du Musée arabe du Caire*; Contadini, *Fatimid Art at the Victoria and Albert Museum*, 111–12; O'Kane, *Treasures of the Islamic Art in the Museums of Cairo*, 59.

97. Poonawala, "Ismāʿīlī Taʾwīl of the Qurʾān," 206.

98. Al-Maqrīzī, *Al-Mawāʿiẓ wa-l-iʿtibār bi dhikr al-khiṭaṭ wa-l-āthār* (2002–3 edition), 1:391. Translated in Halm, "Ismaili Oath of Allegiance (ʿahd) and the 'Sessions of Wisdom' (Majālis al-Ḥikma) in Fatimid Times," 102–3.

99. Bianquis, "Autonymous Egypt from Ibn Ṭūlūn to Kāfūr," 117. This event occurred in 996.

100. Bierman, *Writing Signs*, 4.

101. Bloom, "Mosque of the Qarafa in Cairo." For a response, see Rāghib, "Mosquée d'al-Qarāfa et Jonathan M. Bloom."

102. See Cortese and Calderini, *Women and the Fatimids in the World of Islam*, 166–69; Bloom, "Mosque of the Qarafa in Cairo," 7–20. Although the Qarafa cemetery was a location for women's patronage under the early Egyptian caliphs, it became a site of caliphal patronage under later Fatimid rulers. On the development of the Qarafa, see especially Williams, "Cult of ʿAlid Saints in the Fatimid Monuments of Cairo. Part II: Mausolea."

Chapter 2. A Contested Peace for the Churches

1. The catalog of a recent exhibition on the arts of Fustat typifies the art historical view of the relationships between religious communities, noting that the three faiths in Fustat created a culture of cosmopolitanism that "foreshadowed the rich diversity of modern global urbanism." Vorderstrasse and Treptow, *Cosmopolitan City*. Likewise, a recent exhibition of Fatimid art at the Aga Khan Museum in Toronto suggests that the "world of the Fatimids was diverse and inclusive," and states as its mission to bring "to light a selection of artifacts that bear witness to the religious tolerance and cultural achievements of the Fatimid dynasty." Aga Khan Museum, museum label for *The World of the Fatimids*, Toronto, March 10–July 2, 2018. Historical studies often adopt this stance as well. Samuel Samir has called the Fatimid period a "golden age for the *Dhimmīs*" and that the Fatimid period was "probably the best in their [Egyptian Christians'] history under Arab rule"; Samir, "Role of Christians in the Fāṭimid Government Services of Egypt to the Reign of Al-Ḥāfiẓ," 177–78. In his seminal work on interreligious relations in the medieval Mediterranean, S. D. Goitein suggests that the Fatimid empire was characterized by a "spirit of tolerance and liberalism." Goitein, *Mediterranean Society*, 1:29. In contrast, he characterizes al-Hakim's large-scale destruction of Christian and Jewish monuments as a "fit of religious insanity" and describes the ruler as "the interesting psychopathic caliph, who ordered the destruction of churches and synagogues." Goitein, 21 and 34. The notion of Fatimid tolerance has become more nuanced in historical studies but has not been integrated into art historical investigations. The special volume of *Medieval Encounters* 21 (2015) is dedicated to reexamining non-Muslim communities in Fatimid Egypt. In it, Maryann Shenoda astutely observes that modern notions of tolerance cannot be applied to medieval societies. Shenoda, "Re-Envisioning Persecution," 413. Modern understanding of the Fatimid tolerance of religious minorities is paralleled in studies of Islamic Spain, mirroring the debate surrounding the merits and limits of the Convivencia narrative. See Dodds, Menocal, and Balbale, *Arts of Intimacy*; Robinson, "Talking Religion, Comparatively Speaking," "Arts of Intimacy," and "Qurtuba"; Soifer, "Beyond Convivencia," 19–35.

2. The reliance by members of the Fatimid administration on Christians and Jews in many ways continued a pattern established by the Tulunids and Ikhshidids. In contrast, the Abbasid caliph al-Mutawakkil had previously replaced all Christian administrators in Egypt with Muslims. Dridi, "Christians of Fustat in the First Three Centuries of Islam," 37.

3. For a consideration of *dhimmīs* in medieval Islam, see Friedmann, "Dhimma"; Griffith, *Church in the Shadow of the Mosque*. For *dhimmīs* in Fatimid Egypt, see Samir, "Role of Christians in the Fāṭimid Government Services of Egypt to the Reign of Al-Ḥāfiẓ"; Wilfong, "Non-Muslim Communities"; den Heijer, Lev, and Swanson, "Fatimid Empire and Its Population"; Saleh, "Government Relations with the Coptic Community in Egypt during the Fatimid Period"; Mikhail, *From Byzantine to Islamic Egypt*; Cohen, *Under Crescent and Cross*.

4. For a discussion, see Ward, "Taqī al-Dīn al-Subqī: On Construction, Continuance, and Repairs of Churches and Synagogues in Islamic Law."

5. For a discussion of al-ʿAziz, see Walker, "Al-ʿAzīz bi-Llāh"; Halm, *Kalifen von Kairo*, 119–66.

6. For a considerations of the Coptic community in Egypt, see Atiya, "Ḳibṭ"; Swanson, *Coptic Papacy in Islamic Egypt*; Wilfong, "Non-Muslim Communities"; den Heijer, Lev, and Swanson, "Fatimid Empire and Its Population"; Brett, "Al-Karāza al-Marqusīya"; Mikhail, *From Byzantine to Islamic Egypt*.

7. See Goitein, *Mediterranean Society*; Cohen, *The Voice of the Poor in the Middle Ages*; Rustow, *Heresy and the Politics of Community*, 2008; Bareket, *Fustat on the Nile*.

8. See especially Goitein, *Mediterranean Society*; Rustow, *Heresy and the Politics of Community*.

9. For a discussion of the Jewish communities, see Bareket, *Fustat on the Nile*, 9–16; Stillman, "Non-Muslim Communities," 200.

10. Rachel Milstein has commented on the art historical expression of this relationship, noting "the bitter polemics between Rabbinic Jewry and the Karaites over the reading and interpretation of the Bible remind us of the contemporary debate over the Qur'an between Sunnites and Shiʿites, which brought about the evolution of the *naskhi* [a type of cursive] script by Ibn Muqla and Ibn al-Bawwab." Milstein, "Hebrew Book Illumination in the Fatimid Era," 230.

11. Although the Jewish communities were distinguished by these sectarian divisions, recent studies in Geniza documents suggest that the communities were more intertwined than previously thought. See Rustow, *Heresy and the Politics of Community*, 2014, 243–48.

12. For a discussion of Sitt al-Mulk, see Halm, "Destin de la princess Sitt al-Mulk"; Lev, "Fatimid Princess Sitt al-Mulk"; Cortese and Calderini, *Women and the Fatimids in the World of Islam*, 51–58.

13. The relative freedom of the religious minority communities of the Fatimid realm is particularly contrasted to the harsher treatment of minorities in later Egyptian history. In particular, during the reign of Sultan al-Nasir Muhammad, riots against the Christian communities of Egypt led to widescale destruction of churches and resulted in mass conversion. This is described in al-Maqrīzī, *Al-Mawāʿiẓ waʾl-iʿtibār biʾdhikr al-khiṭaṭ waʾl-āthār*, as cited in Behrens-Abouseif, "Locations of Non-Muslim Quarters in Medieval Cairo," 119 and 124. Al-Maqrizi suggests that as a result of these fourteenth-century destructions, the churches of Qasr al-Shamʿ, which were more remote, and therefore less effected, were some of the only preserved churches, resulting in a more pronounced Christian identity in that area of the city. Behrens-Abouseif, 125.

14. For other considerations of why *dhimmīs* fared particularly well under the Fatimids, see Swanson, *Coptic Papacy in Islamic Egypt*, 48; Saleh, "Government Relations with the Coptic Community in Egypt during the Fatimid Period," 214–21; Samir, "Role of Christians in the Fāṭimid Government Services of Egypt to the Reign of al-Ḥāfiẓ," 189–91; den Heijer, Lev, and Swanson, "Fatimid Empire and Its Population," 338–40.

15. See Lev, "Fāṭimid Imposition of Ismāʿīlism on Egypt," 313–25, and Bloom, "Mosque of the Qarafa in Cairo," 12–15.

16. Brett, "Al-Karāza al-Marqusīya," 38.

17. Brett, 40.

18. For a consideration of courtly interchange in artistic production in this time, see Hoffman, "Pathways of Portability," and Grabar, "Shared Culture of Objects."

19. Abbot Moses, under whom the stucco works were carved, had been to Baghdad circa 927. Thomas, "Christians in the Islamic East," 367–68; see also Hunt, "Stuccowork at the Monastery of the Syrians in the Wādī Naṭrūn."

20. Hunt, "Churches of Old Cairo and Mosques of al-Qāhira," 325–26, and Jenkins, "Eleventh-Century Woodcarving from a Cairo Nunnery." Many parallels can be drawn from the woodwork published by Edmond Pauty, *Bois sculptés d'églises coptes (époque fatimide)*; Pauty, *Catalogue général du Musée arabe du Caire*. See also O'Kane, *Treasures of Islamic Art in the Museums of Cairo*, 59.

21. The vibrant naturalism of Fatimid luster led Richard Ettinghausen to deem these examples of early Islamic realism, particularly when considered in comparison to the abstraction seen in Abbasid luster. Ettinghausen, "Painting in the Fatimid Period"; Ettinghausen, "Early Realism in Islamic Art." See also Grabar, "Imperial and Urban Art in Islam."

22. It is beyond the scope of this book to discuss the rich tradition of Coptic monastic architecture outside Cairo. For a discussion, see Bolman, *Red Monastery Church*; Bolman and Godeau, *Monastic Visions*; Gabra and Vivian, *Coptic Monasteries*; Evelyn-White, *Monasteries of the Wadi 'n Natrun*; Saleh, "Church Building, Repair, and Destruction in Fatimid Egypt"; al-Shābushtī, *Al-Dīyārāt*.

23. For an archaeological analysis of this area, see Sheehan, *Babylon of Egypt*. For the churches in general, see Gabra and Eaton-Krauss, *Treasures of Coptic Art in the Coptic Museum and Churches of Old Cairo*; Hunt, "Churches of Old Cairo and Mosques of al-Qāhira"; AlSayyad, *Cairo*, 19–38. From the time of the Arab conquest, Egyptian Christian communities were brought into Fustat-Misr to serve the administrative needs of the Arab conquerors. Kubiak, *Al-Fusṭāṭ*, 125.

24. Al-Maqrīzī, *Itti'āẓ al-ḥunafā' bi-akhbār al-a'imma al-Fāṭimiyyīn al-khulafā'*, 1:72, 1:242. Al-Maqrizi does note, however, that he allowed these to be celebrated again. Al-Maqrīzī, 1:276.

25. Al-Maqrīzī, *Al-Mawā'iẓ wa-l-i'tibār bi dhikr al-khiṭaṭ wa-l-āthār*, 1:715–29. This event is discussed in Mikhail, *From Byzantine to Islamic Egypt*, 244.

26. Al-Muqaffa', *Ta'rīkh baṭārikat al-kanīsa al-Miṣriyya (The History of the Patriarchs of the Egyptian Church)*.

27. From the tenth to the eleventh century, there was a movement for translating texts from Coptic to Arabic. See den Heijer, *Mawhub ibn Mansur ibn Mufarrig et l'historiographie copto-arabe*; den Heijer, "Coptic Historiography in the Fāṭimid, Ayyūbid and Early Mamlūk Periods," 86.

28. The source is used frequently by those interested specifically in Coptic history, although usually the historical facts are separated from the miraculous tales. This use can be seen in the series of books on the Coptic papacy published by the American University in Cairo Press. Davis, *Early Coptic Papacy*; Swanson, *Coptic Papacy in Islamic Egypt*; Jirjis, *Emergence of the Modern Coptic Papacy*.

29. Yaḥyā ibn Sa'īd al-Anṭākī, *Ta'rīkh (Histoire de Yahya-ibn-Sa'īd d'Antioche)* Vols. 18, 23, and 47. Yahya's account is discussed at length in Forsyth, "Byzantine-Arab Chronicle of Yahya b. Sa'id al-Antaki."

30. Abū Ṣāliḥ, *Churches and Monasteries of Egypt and Some Neighbouring Countries*. For a discussion of the authorship of this source, see Atiya, "Abū al-Makārim."

31. Abū Ṣāliḥ, *Churches and Monasteries of Egypt and Some Neighbouring Countries*, 148–50. For a consideration of *manẓaras* in al-Andalus, see Ruggles, "Eye of Sovereignty."

32. Al-Maqrīzī, *Al-Mawā'iẓ wa-l-i'tibār bi dhikr al-khiṭaṭ wa-l-āthār* (2002–3 edition), 4:2. Al-Maqrizi does not mention the mosaics, however, but only that Ibn Tulun would gaze upon the pictures of Mary.

33. After the monastery was moved, this area became known as al-Khandaq and became an important Christian quarter, particularly following the destruction of churches under al-Hakim. Al-Maqrīzī, 2:290, 2:507.

34. Although the walled Fatimid city existed for the Ismaili court and its retinue, it would have also contained Christian quarters for their armies. Al-Maqrizi described two quarters (*ḥārat al-Rūm*), housed not by urban Christians of Fustat-Misr but by the Greek, Christian mercenary armies employed by the Fatimids. One of these was northeast of Bab Zuwayla and the other was to the south of Bab al-Nasr. Al-Maqrīzī, 2:5, 2:8, 2:14, 2:464, 2:471, 2:511. See also Behrens-Abouseif, "Locations of Non-Muslim Quarters in Medieval Cairo," 122.

35. According to Abu Salih, al-Mu'izz stayed in the monastery for seven months, which seems like an absurdly long amount of time for a ruler who was surely eager to move to his new capital. Abū Ṣāliḥ, *Churches and Monasteries of Egypt and Some Neighbouring Countries*, 181.

36. Abū Ṣāliḥ, *Churches and Monasteries of Egypt and Some Neighbouring Countries*, 181. The author notes that the "well is now filled up, and the cistern is disused" and the garden became a "waste."

37. The Muqattam miracle remains a central story for Coptic Christians. Michael Swanson has noted that it is "known to every Coptic child," commemorated through three additional days of fasting near Christmas, and recited in Coptic churches every December 2. Swanson, *Coptic Papacy in Islamic Egypt*, 48. Architecturally, it is also celebrated in a series of churches, which have become pilgrimage sites for the Coptic community. See Pruitt, "Miracle of Muqattam," 277–78. Maryann Shenoda has analyzed the text to explicate the relations between the Coptic community and its Fatimid rulers in Shenoda, "Displacing Dhimmī, Maintaining Hope." See also Swanson, *Coptic Papacy in Islamic Egypt*, 50–52; Saleh, "Church Building, Repair, and Destruction in Fatimid Egypt," 179–80.

38. The interfaith debate described was typical of the Fatimid period. For a discussion, see al-Muqaffa', *Ta'rīkh baṭārikat al-kanīsa al-Miṣriyya (The History of the Patriarchs of the Egyptian Church)*, 2:93–94/137–39.

39. Maryann Shenoda suggests that this patriarch actually reigned prior to al-Mu'izz's caliphate, adding another layer of dating problems to the text. Shenoda, "Displacing Dhimmī, Maintaining Hope," 593.

40. Al-Muqaffa', *Ta'rīkh baṭārikat al-kanīsa al-Miṣriyya (The History of the Patriarchs of the Egyptian Church)*, 2:92–93/138.

41. In this case, the bishop refers to the lightly fermented alcohol *nabīdh*, al-Muqaffa', 2:93/138.

42. Al-Muqaffa', 2:93/138.

43. The text of Isaiah 1:3 is: "The ox hath known its owner, and the ass hath known the manger of its master, but Israel hath not known Me." Al-Muqaffa', 2:93/139. The anti-Jewish rhetoric is also found in a modern account of the story, which records: "In spite of the fact that he [Ya'qub ibn Killis] espoused Islam, he still sided with Judaism, because he did not adopt Islam out of belief in it but for the sake of the governmental office. Now this Jew hated Christians very much, especially because he has a Christian rival who was dear to the caliph. This Jew feared that the caliph would appoint the Christian as minister instead of him. This man's name was Quzman ibn Mina, and had the title Abul Yumn ("Fortunate One")." See 117th Pope and Patriarch of Alexandria and the See of St. Mark, *Biography of Saint Samaan the Shoemaker "the Tanner" Mattaos*, 45. This account is recorded in a brochure available at the site of the modern megachurch in the Muqattam Hills, dedicated to the miracle outlined here. For a discussion, see Pruitt, "Miracle of Muqattam," 277–78, 289.

44. This is a reference to Matthew 17:20, which reads: "He replied, 'Because you have so little faith. Truly I tell you, if you have faith as small as a mustard seed, you can say to this mountain, "Move from here to there," and it will move. Nothing will be impossible for you.'"

45. Samaan tells the patriarch that he had plucked his own eye out, after experiencing lust. He lived a life of destitution, carrying water to poor people he encountered during the day. Pruitt, "Miracle of Muqattam," 285.

46. The pattern of demonstrating miracles to a ruler who then grants favors to the Christians is also seen in an earlier passage in which Ibn Tulun's son Khamarawaih is shown a miracle by the Christians and they are treated kindly by him. Al-Muqaffa', *Ta'rīkh baṭārikat al-kanīsa al-Miṣriyya (The History of the Patriarchs of the Egyptian Church)*, 2:77/113–14.

47. Al-Muqaffa', 2:96/144.

48. Abū Ṣālih, *Churches and Monasteries of Egypt and Some Neighbouring Countries*, 116–18.

49. Butler also recounts various legends associated with the church in Butler, *Ancient Coptic Churches of Egypt*, 124–28.

50. Butler, 128.

51. Al-Muqaffa', *Ta'rīkh baṭārikat al-kanīsa al-Miṣriyya*, 2:96/145.

52. Al-Muqaffa', 2:96/145.

53. Al-Muqaffa', 2:96/145.

54. Abū Ṣālih, *Churches and Monasteries of Egypt and Some Neighbouring Countries*, 117.

55. Abū Ṣālih, 117. This theme is continued in the author's description of the eventual burning of the church in 1168. He records: "The cause of the burning of this church was that the Christians had brought many gifts to it and had made for it many splendid vessels; so the Muslims desired to pillage it thoroughly, but were unable to do this. Then a large multitude of them assembled and gave way to their fury, and set fire to the church, so that nothing remained except the walls and a small chapel within it, which was not burnt."

56. Maryann Shenoda has argued that the account is a subversive attempt to critique the status of *dhimmīs* in the Fatimid order. She notes that the story, "with its emphasis on the 'unthinkable,' works to displace *dhimmī* social status as relegated upon Copts by Islamic governance. Overturning the social order, Coptic *dhimmīs* instill fear in the hearts of their Muslim rulers." Shenoda, "Displacing Dhimmī, Maintaining Hope," 600. While I agree that the account presents the Christian faith as superior to the Islam of the caliphs, it also suggests a closeness of the Copts to the Fatimid caliph and a desire for an association with Cairo's founders.

57. Disputes between Islamic rulers and the populace in the rebuilding of churches is also encountered in pre-Fatimid Egypt. In 938, the ruler of Egypt, Muhammad ibn Tugh, was offered money to allow the restoration of the Church of Anba Shenouta. When he consulted various jurists, they differed in their opinion of the subject. Ultimately, the jurist who had supported the restoration was assaulted by a mob. Ibn Ḥajar, *Raf' al-Iṣr*, 554–55. See also Tritton, *Caliphs and Their Non-Muslim Subjects*, 53–54, and Lev, *State and Society in Fatimid Egypt*, 184–85. This instance is interesting, in that it occurs in the pre-Fatimid period, which suggests that even the pre-Fatimid rulers of Egypt were quite open to the *dhimmī* population. It also highlights that the involvement of jurists in the decisions of the state resulted in differing, often anti-*dhimmī*, opinions, which supports the idea that the Fatimids were able to be more tolerant, as they did not have to bow to the authority of the *'ulamā'* and other religious officials.

58. The fact that not only Jews but also Nestorian Christians come under attack speaks to a finer-grained political contentiousness within Christian sects.

59. This modern view of a Fatimid-Coptic alliance can also be seen in the overt references to the Fatimid Mosque of al-Aqmar in the nineteenth-century construction of the Coptic Museum. For a discussion of the Coptic Museum, see Bierman, *Writing Signs*, 144–45.

60. Al-Muqaffa', *Ta'rīkh baṭārikat al-kanīsa al-Miṣriyya (The History of the Patriarchs of the Egyptian Church)*, 2:99/150.

61. Al-Hasan ibn Bishr al-Dimashqi, as quoted in Ibn al-Athīr, *Al-Kāmil fi'l ta'rīkh*, IX, 48–49, translated in Assaad, *Reign of al-Hakim bi-Amr Allah*, 41–42.

62. For a discussion of early mosques constructed in a Christian context, see Guidetti, *In the Shadow of the Church*.

63. Forsyth, "Byzantine-Arab Chronicle of Yahya b. Sa'id al-Antaki," 2:434.

64. This incident is described in al-Maqrīzī, *Itti'āẓ al-ḥunafā' bi-akhbār al-a'imma al-Fāṭimiyyīn al-khulafā'*, 1:290.

Chapter 3. Al-Hakim's Esoteric Urbanism

1. The most complete biography and analysis of al-Hakim is Walker, *Caliph of Cairo*. See also Assaad, *Reign of al-Hakim bi-Amr Allah*; Sacy, *Exposé de la religion des Druzes*; Ess, *Chiliastische*

Erwartungen und die Versuchung der Göttlichkeit; Halm, "Nachtrichten zu Bauten der Aglabiden und Fatimiden in Libyen und Tunesien," 129–57; Bianquis, "Al-Ḥākim bi Amr Allāh ou la folie de l'unité chez un souverain fatimide," 107–33; Bianquis, "Al-Hakim bi-Amr Allah"; de Smet, "Interdictions alimentaires du calife fatimide al-Ḥākim," 53–70.

2. On the destruction of churches, see Saleh, "Government Relations with the Coptic Community in Egypt during the Fatimid Period," 77–98; Saleh, "Church Building, Repair, and Destruction in Fatimid Egypt," 177–96; Pruitt, "Method in Madness"; Canard, "Destruction de l'église de la résurrection par le calife Hakim et l'histoire de la descente du Feu Sacré," 16–43.

3. For a discussion of the *dār al-ʿilm* and observatory, see Walker, "Fatimid Institutions of Learning," 179–200. For the sake of clarity and simplicity, I am using the term *minaret* for these towers. Jonathan Bloom has shown that this term might not mean precisely what we mean in the modern era (as a tower from which the call to prayer was called). For the evolution of the term, see Bloom, "Mosque of al-Ḥākim in Cairo," 20, and *Minaret.*

4. Al-Maqrīzī, *Ittiʿāẓ al-ḥunafāʾ bi-akhbār al-aʾimma al-Fāṭimiyyīn al-khulafāʾ*, 2:3–5.

5. Barjawan became even more powerful after the defeat of his foe, the powerful army general, Ibn ʿAmmar, after which he was assigned to a new high-ranking administrative post—*wāsiṭa* (intermediary). For a discussion of this post, see Lev, "Wāsiṭa."

6. Described in al-Maqrīzī, *Al-Mawāʿiẓ wa-l-iʿtibār bi dhikr al-khiṭaṭ wa-l-āthār* (2002–3 edition), 2:25–29.

7. Al-Muqaffaʿ, *Taʾrīkh baṭārikat al-kanīsa al-Miṣriyya (The History of the Patriarchs of the Egyptian Church)*, 2:121/183.

8. Al-Muqaffaʿ, 2:121/183.

9. The source also describes a link between royal prestige and murder, noting that if al-Hakim wanted to kill someone, he would first grant him money and robes of honor, before having him beheaded. Al-Muqaffaʿ, 2:121/183.

10. Al-Hakim was born in the Fatimid palace in 985.

11. Al-Maqrīzī, *Ittiʿāẓ al-ḥunafāʾ bi-akhbār al-aʾimma al-Fāṭimiyyīn al-khulafāʾ*, 2:14–15.

12. Al-Maqrīzī, 2:38–40.

13. For a synopsis of al-Hakim's edicts at this time, see Walker, *Caliph of Cairo*, 197–219; Assaad, *Reign of al-Hakim bi-Amr Allah*, 84–85, 93–107. See also Bianquis, "Al-Hakim bi-Amr Allah."

14. Al-Maqrīzī, *Al-Mawāʿiẓ wa-l-iʿtibār bi dhikr al-khiṭaṭ wa-l-āthār* (2002–3 edition), 4:130–46. The mosque is no longer extant, though it was in al-Maqrizi's time. He documents some of its later restorations. See also Creswell, *Muslim Architecture of Egypt*, 1:106; Sayyid, *Capitale de l'Égypte jusquà l'époque fatimide*, 19.

15. Al-Maqrizi preserves al-Musabbihi's account of its construction, noting that it was built by al-Hakim on 17 Rabīʿ I 393 (January 27, 1003).

16. Al-Maqrīzī, *Ittiʿāẓ al-ḥunafāʾ bi-akhbār al-aʾimma al-Fāṭimiyyīn al-khulafāʾ*, 2:45.

17. This is preserving the account of al-Musabbihi.

18. This is also described in Yaḥyā ibn Saʿīd al-Antaki, *Taʾrīkh (Histoire)*, 23:404.

19. This is based on the account by al-Musabbihi. Al-Maqrīzī, *Al-Mawāʿiẓ wa-l-iʿtibār bi dhikr al-khiṭaṭ wa-l-āthār* (2002–3 edition), 4:108. The mention of the famous vizier illustrates that it was not only the Fatimid caliph who made the decisions on the construction of monuments. Rather, the vizier and other members of the court would have also played active roles. For a discussion on the nature of medieval Islamic patronage, see the conclusion of this book.

20. For a discussion and interpretation of the interior inscriptional program, see Bloom, "Mosque of al-Ḥākim in Cairo," 18–20; Sanders, *Ritual, Politics, and the City in Fatimid Cairo*, 58–59.

21. For a discussion of ceremonial practices, see Sanders; Canard, "Cérémonial Fatimite et le cérémonial Byzantin," 355–420.

22. Creswell notes that the tomb was called the Mausoleum of Badr al-Jamali, named for the twelfth-century Fatimid vizier. In fact, the tomb was most likely built in the sixteenth century. Creswell, *Muslim Architecture of Egypt*, 1:68.

23. Creswell described the original portal as 50.8 feet (15.5 meters) wide, projecting 20.2 feet (6.16 meters) from the mosque and pierced by a tunnel-vaulted passage. Creswell, 1:68.

24. Creswell, 1:69.

25. About the mosque's foundational inscription, Creswell writes that "Sir Gardner Wilkinson, about 1831, saw a Kufic inscription of al-Hakim over the doorway at the back of this entrance passage . . . its contents agree with al-Maqrizi's account with the addition of the actual month Ragab to the year 393 [May/June 1003], but not word for word. . . . Miss Rogers in 1880 records its fate as follows: 'A few years ago most of the stones bearing this interesting historical record fell to the ground, with a quantity of masonry and rubble, and stopped up the entrance.' On hearing of the accident, Mr. E. T. Rogers, having obtained permission from H. E. Nubar Pasha to collect the fragments, caused them to be conveyed to the Ministry of Foreign Affairs. But the Ministry of Waqfs would not consent either to replace the fallen stones or to remove the remaining ones, on which the rest of the legend is inscribed." Creswell, 1:71.

26. For a discussion of the links to North Africa, see Bloom, "Origins of Fatimid Art," 30–38; Bloom, "Mosque of al-Ḥākim in Cairo," 15–17.

27. For a discussion of the minarets within a comparative context, see Bloom, "Mosque of al-Ḥākim in Cairo," 20–26.

28. For a full catalog of the minarets' inscription, see the appendix in Bloom, "Mosque of al-Ḥākim in Cairo."

29. For a debate on the originality of floriated Kufic script, see Bierman, *Writing Signs*, 127; Blair, "Floriated Kufic and the Fatimids"; Tabbaa, *Transformation of Islamic Art during the Sunni Revival*, 55–57; Tabbaa, "Transformation of Arabic Writing: Part 2, the Public Text," 122–25.

30. Creswell records the measurements of this oratory as 4.1 feet (1.3 meters) deep × 3.6 feet (1.1 meters) wide × 8.3 feet (2.5 meters) high. Creswell, *Muslim Architecture of Egypt*, 1:100. See also Behrens-Abouseif, *Minarets of Cairo*, 121.

31. For a discussion, see Goldhizer, Arendock, and Tritton, "Ahl al-Bayt."

32. Sanders, *Ritual, Politics, and the City in Fatimid Cairo*, 55.

33. Al-Qāḍī al-Nuʿmān, *Daʿāʾim al-Islām*, 1:149. For the comparative merit of mosques, see also Kister, "'You Shall Only Set Out for Three Mosques,'" 173–96.

34. Al-Qāḍī al-Nuʿmān, *Taʾwīl al-daʿāʾim* (1967 edition), 1:225–26, 3:60.

35. Bierman, *Writing Signs*, 62–70. For another interpretation of the Ismaili significance of this symbol, see Williams, "Cult of ʿAlid Saints in the Fatimid Monuments of Cairo. Part I: Mosque of Al-Aqmar," 36–37.

36. Bierman, *Writing Signs*, 62. Their most important primary sources are al-Sijistānī, *Kashf al-maḥjūb*; al-Qāḍī al-Nuʿmān, *Iftitāḥ al-daʿwa wa ibtidāʾ al-dawla*; al-Qāḍī al-Nuʿmān, *Daʿāʾim al-Islām* (1951–60 edition); al-Qāḍī al-Nuʿmān, *Taʾwīl al-daʿāʾim* (1967 edition). For discussion of the philosophers, see Walker, *Early Philosophical Shiism*; Walker, *Wellsprings of Wisdom*; Poonawala, "Al-Qāḍī al-Nuʿmān and Ismaʿili Jurisprudence," 117–43.

37. Yasser Tabbaa has argued that this illegibility was the basis of the transformation of writing in the Sunni Revival. See Tabbaa, "Transformation of Arabic Writing: Part 2, the Public Text," 119–47; Tabbaa, *Transformation of Islamic Art during the Sunni Revival*, 57–72.

38. Irene Bierman sees the earliest examples of this device replicated in the city of al-Mansuriyya and in the coin reform of al-Muʿizz. Bierman, *Writing Signs*, 62–63.

39. Bierman refers specifically to diagrams in al-Sijistani's *Kitāb al-yanābīʿ* (which was translated by Paul Walker as *The Wellsprings of Wisdom*) and diagrams in Corbin, *Trilogie Ismaélienne*.

40. For a discussion of the use of light in Fatimid architecture, see Williams, "Cult of ʿAlid Saints in the Fatimid Monuments of Cairo. Part I: Mosque of al-Aqmar," 45–47. Blair and Bloom, *God Is the Light of the Heavens and the Earth*. For a comparative context, see Robinson, "Power, Light, Intra-Confessional Discontent, and the Almoravids," 22–45. For light imagery under the Seljuqs, see Yalman, "ʿAla al-Din Kayqubad Illuminated."

41. Bierman notes that this is also related to God's utterance at the time of the world's creation—"be" (*kun*)—thereby turning darkness into light. Bierman, *Writing Signs*, 83.

42. For a discussion of its appearance in Islamic architecture, see Dodd and Khairallah, *Image of the Word*, 84–86, and Graham, "Light in the Qur'an and Early Islamic Exegesis," 43–60.

43. Doris Behrens-Abouseif has interpreted the pierced windows of the minarets of 1003 as allowing light to shine in, for example. Behrens-Abouseif, *Minarets of Cairo*, 121.

44. This is in contrast to the *lux nova* of the Gothic age in Europe, in which light is similarly used as a metaphor for the divine presence. However, the *lux nova* of a Gothic cathedral shines in rather than out.

45. This inscription is truncated. The complete date is preserved on the western minaret.

46. A similar use of the Imam's name can be seen in descriptions of the *majālis al-ḥikma*, when participants would bow to have the Imam's name, which had been inscribed on documents, touch their heads. In this instance, it was the presence of the Imam's name that allowed for the true revelation of the hidden knowledge. Walker, "Fatimid Institutions of Learning," 13.

47. Translation from Arberry, *Koran Interpreted*, 248.

48. Translation from Arberry, 209.

49. This is linked to the idea of the family of the Imam being rightly guided (*al-mahdiyyīn*). See Bloom, "Mosque of al-Ḥakim in Cairo," 19.

50. Sanders notes that in particular, praying and paying alms are associated with the *daʿwa* and the Imam. Sanders, *Ritual, Politics, and the City in Fatimid Cairo*, 65.

51. For Ismaili *taʾwīl*, see Poonawala, "Ismāʿīlī Taʾwīl of the Qurʾān," 199–22; al-Qāḍī al-Nuʿmān, *Taʾwīl al-daʿāʾim* (1967 edition).

52. Al-Qāḍī al-Nuʿmān, *Taʾwīl al-daʿāʾim* (1967 edition), 1:25–27; Fyzee, *Book of Faith*, 29–32. See also Daftary, *Ismāʿīlīs: Their History and Doctrines*, 222.

53. Poonawala, "Ismāʿīlī Taʾwīl of the Qurʾān," 210. See also Daftary, *Ismāʿīlīs: Their History and Doctrines*, 222. For an overview of the use of allegory in Shiʿism generally, see Bar-Asher, "Shīʿism and the Qurʾān."

54. Although early studies by Jonathan Bloom embraced the Ismaili dimension of these minarets, in his more recent text, he dismissed the Ismailism of the inscriptions by noting that "although Ismaili adepts were trained at seeing the hidden meanings behind outward appearance, such meanings would have been lost to virtually all other eyes since so few adopted the Ismalii beliefs of the rulers." Bloom, *Arts of the City Victorious*, 7. However, given the location of this monument, so close to the palace and the *majālis al-ḥikma*, Ismaili pilgrims would have been a large population of the visitors to this space.

55. This is in contrast to the later proliferation of madrasas, which were schools devoted to the study of Sunni Islamic law.

56. Walker, "Fatimid Institutions of Learning," 189.

57. Al-Maqrīzī, *Ittiʿāẓ al-ḥunafāʾ bi-akhbār al-aʾimma al-Fāṭimiyyīn al-khulafāʾ*, 2:56. Translated in Halm, *Fatimids and Their Traditions of Learning*, 74.

58. Halm, 74.

59. The Abbasid caliph al-Maʾmun (r. 813–33) had a similar institution, which had been the center of the Greek-Arabic translation phenomenon and included an observatory. However, Heinz Halm has suggested that the actual model for this was the *dār al-ʿilm* established in a Shiʿi suburb of Baghad in 991 or 993. Halm, 73.

60. The opening of the city and integration of architectural projects beyond the walled city is consistent with Paula Sanders's contention that al-Hakim had explicitly urban concerns and was the first ruler to integrate Cairo and Fustat in his ceremonial practices. Sanders, *Ritual, Politics, and the City in Fatimid Cairo*, 52–67.

61. Al-Muqaffaʿ, *Taʾrīkh baṭārikat al-kanīsa al-Miṣriyya* (*The History of the Patriarchs of the Egyptian Church*), 2:139/210.

62. Al-Muqaffaʿ, 2:109/163.

63. Al-Muqaffaʿ, 2:109/163.

64. Yaḥyā ibn Saʿīd al-Anṭākī, *Taʾrīkh* (*Histoire*), 23:186. Translated in Assaad, *Reign of al-Hakim bi-Amr Allah*, 84.

65. Goitein, *Mediterranean Society*, 1:36.

66. Al-Maqrīzī, *Ittiʿāẓ al-ḥunafāʾ bi-akhbār al-aʾimma al-Fāṭimiyyīn al-khulafāʾ*, 2:44; see also Assaad, *Reign of al-Hakim bi-Amr Allah*, 94.

67. Al-Maqrīzī, *Al-Mawāʿiẓ wa-l-iʿtibār bi dhikr al-khiṭaṭ wa-l-āthār* (2002–3 edition), 4:126.

68. Yaḥyā ibn Saʿīd al-Anṭākī, *Taʾrīkh (Histoire)*, 23:465.

69. Al-Maqrīzī, *Al-Mawāʿiẓ wa-l-iʿtibār bi dhikr al-khiṭaṭ wa-l-āthār* (2002–3 edition), 4:129.

70. Yaḥyā ibn Saʿīd al-Anṭākī, *Taʾrīkh (Histoire)*, 23:465–66. Al-Maqrizi also preserves a story from Ibn Abi Tayy in his "History of Aleppo" that in 393/1003, Jacobite Christians were building a church, angering the Muslims. In response, the Christians argued that the church predated Islam. In the end, three churches were destroyed to build three mosques in this area. Al-Maqrīzī, *Al-Mawāʿiẓ wa-l-iʿtibār bi dhikr al-khiṭaṭ wa-l-āthār* (2002–3 edition), 4:127–28.

71. Al-Maqrīzī, *Ittiʿāẓ al-ḥunafāʾ bi-akhbār al-aʾimma al-Fāṭimiyyīn al-khulafā*, 2:59, translated in Walker, *Caliph of Cairo*, 66. For a discussion of the semantic content of this event, see Bierman, *Writing Signs*, 76–77. Yahya al-Antaki also discusses this event, noting that al-Hakim publicly condemned the first three Rashidun caliphs, the Companions of the Prophet, and all Abbasid caliphs in 395/1004–5 but reversed these decisions after the Abu Rakwa revolt. Yaḥyā ibn Saʿīd al-Anṭākī, *Taʾrīkh (Histoire)*, 23:468, 23:480.

72. The tradition of cursing the first three caliphs and the Companions of the Prophet was not only limited to sectarian conflict in the Fatimid context but also occurred in the Shiʿi-Sunni conflicts in Abbasid Baghdad. See Makdisi, *Ibn ʿAqīl et la résurgence d'Islam traditionaliste au XIe siècle*, 312.

73. Al-Maqrīzī, *Ittiʿāẓ al-ḥunafāʾ bi-akhbār al-aʾimma al-Fāṭimiyyīn al-khulafāʾ*, 2:53. The *ghiyār* was a distinctive clothing worn by *dhimmīs*. Its exact definition was variable and al-Maqrizi was not specific about what it looked like. In some medieval sources, the *ghiyār* was described as a piece of cloth in a designated color, draped over the shoulder. In others, it is used as a more general term to describe distinctive clothing worn by *dhimmīs*. It is thought to be a possible inspiration for the distinctive badge worn by Jews in Christian Europe. See Perlman, "Ghiyār."

74. Al-Maqrīzī, *Ittiʿāẓ al-ḥunafāʾ bi-akhbār al-aʾimma al-Fāṭimiyyīn al-khulafāʾ*, 2:53. Al-Maqrizi also notes that *al-mutawakkiliyya* was banned. Clearly, this was named for the Abbasid caliph, al-Mutawakkil, and, therefore, was an anti-Abbasid act. However, exactly what *al-mutawakkiliyya* is has been lost to history.

75. His use of the water bottle might also indicate his Sufi inclination. Van Nieuwenhuyse, "Uprising of Abū Rakwa and the Bedouins against the Fāṭimids," 246, 248.

76. Abu Rakwa's flight from Spain to North Africa, where he sought to establish his own power, mirrors the earlier flight of the Spanish Umayyad ʿAbd al-Rahman I from Syria to Spain in the wake of the Abbasid revolution.

77. Many medieval historical accounts discuss this event. See especially al-Maqrīzī, *Ittiʿāẓ al-ḥunafāʾ bi-akhbār al-aʾimma al-Fāṭimiyyīn al-khulafāʾ*, 2:60–66; Ibn al-Athīr, *Al-Kāmil fīʾl taʾrīkh*, 8:42–46; Yaḥyā ibn Saʿīd al-Anṭākī, *Taʾrīkh (Histoire)*. For a discussion of events, see Walker, *Caliph of Cairo*, 169–73; Sanders, *Ritual, Politics, and the City in Fatimid Cairo*, 57–60; Bloom, "Mosque of al-Ḥākim in Cairo"; Lev, *State and Society in Fatimid Egypt*, 27–30; van Nieuwenhuyse, "Uprising of Abū Rakwa and the Bedouins against the Fāṭimids." For a discussion of Abu Rakwa's teaching of the Qur'an, see Assaad, *Reign of al-Hakim bi-Amr Allah*, 135.

78. Yahya al-Antaki records that this was actually the entire reason for Abu Rakwa's revolt. Given that the cursing occurred at approximately the same time, it is unlikely that this was the single reason, but certainly, it must have been used in Abu Rakwa's propaganda. Yaḥyā ibn Saʿīd al-Anṭākī, *Taʾrīkh (Histoire)*, 23:290–92.

79. Both groups had been hostile to the Fatimids prior to Abu Rakwa's rebellion. The Banu Qurra had previously been oppressed by al-Hakim while the Berber Zanata had never accepted the Fatimids as the rightful caliphate.

80. The recorded Islamic date is Dhu'l-Hijja 395.

81. For a discussion of the medieval sources, see Walker, *Caliph of Cairo*, 168, and Assaad, *Reign of al-Ḥākim bi-Amr Allah*, 135–45.

82. Al-Maqrīzī, *Ittiʿāẓ al-ḥunafāʾ bi-akhbār al-aʾimma al-Fāṭimiyyīn al-khulafāʾ*, 2:144–46.

83. Although it is impossible to know what this room contained, it is tempting to think it may have been used by the Imam or housed an Ismaili relic, or an item belonging to the Imam, similar to the overtly Sunni relic of ʿUthman's Qur'an page at the Great Mosque of Cordoba. However, I have not yet found evidence for this. For a discussion of ʿUthman's Qur'an, see Khoury, "The Meaning of the Great Mosque of Cordoba in the Tenth Century," 80–98. As it opened up to the roof, it could also be a space from which the Imam appeared. The meaning and purpose, for now, remain elusive.

Chapter 4. Construction, Destruction, and Concealment under the "Mad Caliph"

1. For a discussion of this concept in Islamic history, see Cook, *Commanding Right and Forbidding Wrong in Islamic Thought* (2010 edition).

2. Early efforts at creating new systems of Fatimid law can be seen in the writings of al-Qadi al-Nuʿman. Al-Qāḍī al-Nuʿmān, *Daʿāʾim al-Islām*, 2 vols., and al-Qāḍī al-Nuʿmān, *Taʾwīl al-daʿāʾim*, 3 vols. (1995 edition).

3. This edict would be repeated by al-Hakim several times during his reign, suggesting that there were Shiʿi contingencies within Cairo who continued this practice.

4. Al-Maqrizi records this event in AH 399. Al-Maqrīzī, *Ittiʿāẓ al-ḥunafāʾ bi-akhbār al-aʾimma al-Fāṭimiyyīn al-khulafāʾ*, 2:78.

5. For a discussion of these revolts, see Gil, *History of Palestine*, 370–73; Walker, *Caliph of Cairo*, 176–77; Canard, "Djarrāḥids"; Assaad, *Reign of al-Hakim bi-Amr Allah*, 150–51.

6. "Concealing the Revealed" is a play on the title of one of the most important works by the Ismaili philosopher al-Sijistani, which can be translated as "Revealing the Concealed." Al-Sijistānī, *Kashf al-maḥjūb*.

7. Al-Maqrīzī, *Al-Mawāʿiẓ wa-l-iʿtibār bi dhikr al-khiṭaṭ wa-l-āthār* (2002–3 edition), 4:110.

Creswell also suggests that the four mausolea that he found in ruins in the Qarafa cemetery might also date from the year 1010. However, there is very little information about these monuments. Creswell, *Muslim Architecture of Egypt*, 1:107.

8. The inscriptions on the interior of the Mosque of al-Hakim are more difficult to discuss in any detail, as we do not have foundational inscriptions suggesting when they were added. Samuel Flury had identified two stages—the first from the original construction under al-ʿAziz and the second from a later date. Jonathan Bloom suggests that the interior verses may have been executed at some time between the addition of the salient and the completion of the mosque in 1013. Flury, *Ornamente der Ḥākim und der Azhar Moschee*, 13–15; Bloom, "Mosque of al-Ḥākim in Cairo," 20.

9. Discussions about Badr al-Jamali's reign and the post-Fatimid history of the mosque are provided in al-Maqrīzī, *Al-Mawāʿiẓ wa-l-iʿtibār bi dhikr al-khiṭaṭ wa-l-āthār* (2002–3 edition), 4:112–26.

10. Creswell, *Muslim Architecture of Egypt*, 1:87.

11. For an in-depth consideration of minaret construction, see Bloom, *Minaret*. See especially chapter 7 for the development of the North African minaret.

12. Creswell, "Great Salients of the Mosque of al-Hakim at Cairo," 574; van Berchem, "Notes d'archéologie arabe: Monuments et inscriptions fatimites," 439–41.

13. Irene Bierman, Paula Sanders, and Jonathan Bloom have all tackled the question of the changing semantic content of the minarets and their covering. Irene Bierman notes that the new bastions take on a military appearance and, along with Paula Sanders, argues that the new bastions served as a warning to Rashid li-Din Allah, the *sharīf* of Mecca and counter-caliph who led the Jarrahid movement. Bierman, *Writing Signs*, 93–95; Sanders, *Ritual, Politics, and the City in Fatimid Cairo*, 59–60. Jonathan Bloom recognizes the stark difference in tone between the two minarets but does not consider the 1010 bastions in great detail, unlike his meticulous analysis of the 1003 towers. Bloom, "Mosque of al-Ḥākim in Cairo," 19–20; Bloom, *Arts of the City Victorious*, 78–81.

14. Al-Maqrīzī, *Ittiʿāẓ al-ḥunafāʾ bi-akhbār al-aʾimma al-Fāṭimiyyīn al-khulafāʾ*, 2:38.

15. For a complete compilation of the inscriptions at the Mosque of al-Hakim, see Bloom, "Mosque of al-Ḥākim in Cairo," 34–36.

16. The inclusion of Qur'an 24:27 also recalls al-Hakim's particular concern with justice in his empire: "Enter not houses other than your own, until ye have asked permission and saluted those in them: that is best for you in order that ye may heed [what is seemly]. If ye find no one in the house, enter not until permission is given to you: if ye are asked to go back, go back: that makes for greater purity for yourselves: and Allah knows well all that ye do."

17. The full verse is: "And there are those who put up a mosque by way of mischief and infidelity—to disunite the Believers—and in preparation for one who warred against Allah and His Messenger aforetime. They will indeed swear that their intention is nothing but good; But Allah doth declare that they are certainly liars." For the connection to the Jarrahid revolt, see Sanders, *Ritual, Politics, and the City in Fatimid Cairo*, 59–60; Bierman, *Writing Signs*, 94–95.

18. Bloom, *Minaret*, xvii.

19. Bloom, 115.

20. Bloom, 119.

21. For a discussion of Aghlabid monuments, see Lézine, *Architecture de l'Ifriqiya*; Anderson, Fenwick, and Rosser-Owen, *Aghlabids and Their Neighbours*.

22. For documentation of other square towers throughout Spain, see Bloom, *Minaret*, 145.

23. Bloom, 125.

24. Al-Maqrīzī, *Al-Mawāʿiẓ wa-l-iʿtibār bi dhikr al-khiṭaṭ wa-l-āthār* (2002–3 edition), 4:96–99. A French translation is also found in Sayyid, *Capitale de l'Égypte jusquà l'époque fatimide*. Although al-Maqs is included in the *waqf*, it is important to note that it was financed separately and the details of its form are not preserved. There is an unusual detail that suggests that the original lamps of the Mosque of Rashida were replaced by more expensive silver lamps, decorated with animals. The Fatimid style is certainly known for its animal decoration (see palace beams, for example), but it would be quite unusual to have animals decorating the interior of a mosque.

25. Al-Maqrīzī, *Al-Mawāʿiẓ wa-l-iʿtibār bi dhikr al-khiṭaṭ wa-l-āthār* (2002–3 edition), 4:127.

26. Al-Maqrīzī, 4:96. For these, he gives the proceeds of *Dār al-ḍarb, qaysariyyat al-suf*, and *dār al-kharq al-jadīda*, all of which were located in Fustat-Misr.

27. For a discussion of artistic analysis in medieval Egyptian sources, see Rabbat, "ʿAjīb and Gharīb"; Rabbat, "Architects and Artists in Mamluk Society."

28. See van Berchem, "Notes d'archéologie arabe."

29. Al-Maqrīzī, *Ittiʿāẓ al-ḥunafāʾ bi-akhbār al-aʾimma al-Fāṭimiyyīn al-khulafāʾ*, 2:96.

30. Al-Maqrīzī, *Al-Mawāʿiẓ wa-l-iʿtibār bi dhikr al-khiṭaṭ wa-l-āthār āthār* (2002–3 edition), 4:110.

31. Halm, *Fatimids and Their Traditions of Learning*, 76; Walker, "Fatimid Institutions of Learning," 197.

32. Al-Maqrīzī, *Al-Mawāʿiẓ wa-l-iʿtibār bi dhikr al-khiṭaṭ wa-l-āthār* (2002–3 edition), 4:127. Later biographers suggested that the mihrab was incorrect and that this was the reason for its destruction. See Walker, *Caliph of Cairo*, 150–51. Canard, "Destruction de l'Église de la Résurrection par le calife Hakim et l'histoire de la descente du feu sacré," 21.

33. Bloom has suggested that this apprehension might be the reason for preserving the 1003 towers, but clearly this is not the case. Bloom, *Arts of the City Victorious*, 79.

34. Sources disagree on the precise date of the razing of the church. Yahya al-Antaki provides the year 1009 (AH 399). *The History of the Patriarchs* offers the year 1010 (AH 400). Muslim sources generally place the destruction in 1007 (AH 398) and Christian sources suggest a slightly later date of 1009 or 1010. For Muslim historians, the most complete accounts are given by Sibt al-Jawzi and Ibn al-Qalanisi. Both accounts rely on the lost contemporary account of Hilal al-Sabiʾ. See Saleh, "Church Building, Repair, and Destruction in Fatimid Egypt," 180–81. Anti-*dhimmī* measures had been instituted earlier than the massive church destructions, as al-Hakim forced the Christians to wear the *ghiyār* (a distinctive dress designated for *dhimmīs*), outlawed wine and all the vessels used to make wine, killed pigs, and enacted other harsh sumptuary laws beginning, it seems, in 1004 (AH 395).

35. For a recent study on the church, see Morris, *Sepulchre of Christ and the Medieval West from the Beginning to 1600*. For a reconstruction of the fourth-century monument, see Abel and Vincent, *Jerusalem nouvelle*.

36. This centrally planned construction, executed around a rock cropping, was echoed in the construction of the Dome of the Rock by ʿAbd al-Malik in 691/2. See Grabar, *Dome of the Rock*, 59–102; Avner, "Dome of the Rock in Light of the Development of Concentric Martyria in Jerusalem." For a discussion of the Byzantine source material, see Shalev-Hurvitz, *Holy Sites Encircled*.

37. Macpherson, *Pilgrimage of Arculfus in the Holy Land*, 5–6. For an illustration of the changing plans of the Holy Sepulcher, see Ousterhout, "Rebuilding the Temple," 67–69.

38. Much has been written in western literature on the relationship between the Abbasids and the Carolingians during the reigns of Harun al-Rashid and Charlemagne. However, Arabic sources do not discuss this relationship. See Gil, *History of Palestine*, 285. While the facts surrounding the relationship between Harun al-Rashid and Charlemagne are unclear, a Latin account points to the role of architecture in establishing a ruler's presence. A Benedictine monk recorded the story of Charlemagne visiting the Holy Sepulcher with Harun al-Rashid. The Carolingian ruler covered the monument in gold and inscribed his name on it, indicating its association with the empire. From Benedictus Monachus's *Chronicon*, cited in Gil, *History of Palestine*, 285–87. For a discussion of Charlemagne in Jerusalem, see Gabriele, *Empire of Memory*, 73–96.

39. Al-Muqaddasī, *Description of Syria, Including Palestine*, 37.

40. While mob violence occurred within the city, which was under Berber control, the Ikhshidid ruler, Kafur, sent support for the Christians. See Goitein and Grabar, "Al-Ḳuds."

41. Al-Muqaddasī, *Description of Syria, Including Palestine*, 37.

42. For the full text, see Walker, "'Crusade' of John Tzimisces in the Light of New Arabic Evidence," 319–20, and Peters, *Jerusalem*, 243. For a synopsis of Byzantine raids at this time, see Gil, *History of Palestine*, 344–48.

43. Elisséeff, "Ḥimṣ."

44. The jockeying for confessional control of architecture may have been made visually manifest when a mosque was constructed on top of a section of the Holy Sepulcher, directly claiming the space for Islam. The details of this act are lacking. It is discussed in Grabar, *Shape of the Holy*, 142. Van Berchem connected an inscriptional fragment with this mosque. Van Berchem, *Matériaux pour un corpus inscriptionum arabicarum*, 52–67. However, I was unable to find direct evidence for this addition. See also Goitein and Grabar, "Al-Ḳuds."

45. Canard, "Destruction de l'Église de la Résurrection par le calife Hakim et l'histoire de la descente du feu sacré," 21; al-Maqrīzī, *Ittiʿāẓ al-ḥunafāʾ bi-akhbār al-aʾimma al-Fāṭimiyyīn al-khulafāʾ*, 2:75. Marlis Saleh has recently suggested that the year 400 of the Islamic calendar, in which this was carried out, was particularly significant in Ismaili thought. Saleh, "Church Building, Repair, and Destruction in Fatimid Egypt," 188. Rage at false miracles echoes the sentiments seen in *The History of the Patriarchs* in the description of al-Muʿizz's rage at the belief that Christians could move mountains through faith alone (see chapter 2).

46. Tyre, *History of Deeds Done beyond the Sea*, 1:66.

47. Although sources suggest that the Holy Sepulcher was completely destroyed, material evidence suggests that some parts of the church survived. See Shepard, "Holy Land, Lost Lands, Realpolitik," 527; Avni and Seligman, "New Excavations at the Church of the Holy Sepulchre Compound," 158–60; Biddle, *Tomb of Christ*, 73.

48. Ibn al-Qalānisī, *Dhayl taʾrīkh Dimashq*, 67–68, as cited in Saleh, "Church Building, Repair, and Destruction in Fatimid Egypt," 118, and Assaad, *The Reign of al-Hakim bi-Amr Allah*, 107.

49. The origin of this story is a bit unclear, as all records of it are from later sources. Al-Harawi, who visited Jerusalem in 1173, says it was called this because the garbage from the area was stored there. Hillenbrand, *The Crusades*, 317. Of course, this nomenclature was likely not so innocent. By referring to the location of Christ's burial and resurrection as "the Garbage Heap" (*al-Qumāma*), the Muslim chroniclers implicitly reject the resurrection itself, thereby attacking one of the core differences between the Christian and Muslim understanding of Jesus.

50. The richness of the church was well known and increased significantly under Charlemagne who, in the year 1000, was said to have embellished it with gold, jewels, and added a large gold cross. Benedictus Monachus's *Chronicon*, cited in Gil, *History of Palestine*, 285–87.

51. As discussed in chapter 2, Coptic Christians held Monophysite beliefs (that Christ is at once divine and human), differing significantly from their Orthodox Byzantine counterparts. This caused the two communities to splinter following the Council of Chalcedon in 451. The division was so strong that the Copts, oppressed by the Byzantine governors, welcomed the arrival of the Arab conquerors, despite their Muslim beliefs. See Wilfong, "Non-Muslim Communities," 178.

52. Al-Muqaffaʿ, *Taʾrīkh baṭārikat al-kanīsa al-Miṣriyya* (*The History of the Patriarchs of the Egyptian Church*), 2:100/177. He also describes other scams by the Church, including adding sediment to the wine. The theme of punishment is echoed by William of Tyre, who notes that "as the kingdom of Egypt gradually became more powerful, it seized the provinces and countries as far as Antioch; the Holy City, among others, fell under its sway, subject to the same laws. Under this headship the troubles of the Christians were slightly relieved, just as the prisoners are oft times allowed to enjoy some measure of relaxation. Finally, however, as a just punishment for the wickedness of man, al-Hakim became caliph of that realm." Tyre, *History of Deeds Done beyond the Sea*, 66.

53. According to the account, the author of letter was a Nestorian Christian named Ibn Shirin. Al-Muqaffaʿ, *Taʾrīkh baṭārikat al-kanīsa al-Miṣriyya* (*The History of the Patriarchs of the Egyptian Church*), 2:128/194. Yahya al-Antaki records that al-Hakim gave the order to Yarukh (Ya'qub ibn Killis's son-in-law) in Ramla. See Gil, *History of Palestine*, 373. Although most of the church was razed, the pillars supporting the dome remained standing. See Morris, *Sepulchre of Christ and the Medieval West from the Beginning to 1600*, 134.

54. Al-Muqaffa', *Ta'rīkh baṭārikat al-kanīsa al-Miṣriyya (The History of the Patriarchs of the Egyptian Church)*, 2:127/193. Michael of Tinnis's association of the event with church corruption continues, as he notes that the destruction occurred contemporaneously with al-Hakim's imprisonment of a corrupt patriarch. He reports that al-Hakim attempted to feed the patriarch to hungry lions, but they miraculously resisted him. Out of rage, al-Hakim sent a decree to Jerusalem, ordering the destruction of the church.

55. It is difficult to know exactly when the closure of the mosque occurred, but it is reasonable to conclude that it took place after al-Hakim's reign. The closure is not mentioned directly in the sources, but one can infer its closure from al-Maqrizi's suggestion that it was reopened under al-Zahir. Al-Maqrīzī, *Itti'āẓ al-ḥunafā' bi-akhbār al-a'imma al-Fāṭimiyyīn al-khulafā'*, 2:176. For a discussion of the Mosque of Constantinople, see Anderson, "Islamic Spaces and Diplomacy in Constantinople." See also Runciman, "Byzantine 'Protectorate' in the Holy Land"; Reinert, "Muslim Presence in Constantinople"; Durak, "Through an Eastern Window."

56. Al-Maqrizi in Abū Ṣālih, *Churches and Monasteries of Egypt and Some Neighbouring Countries*, 308. Abū Ṣālih, 147.

57. Abū Ṣālih, 102–8. The source notes that it was restored initially in 725, following a complaint that women and children were harassed while traveling from the churches in Egypt (Misr), resulting in many deaths. In this initial restoration, a water wheel, garden, and a large tank were added. However, this was very controversial even in these early years. Abu Salih notes that "much opposition was made by evil-minded Muslims during the finishing of this church and so the Christians explained that it rightfully belonged to this Church and was not a new building." He also records various periods of destruction of the church in the post-Fatimid period, particularly under the Ayyubids.

58. Abu Salih describes the pavilion: "the roof of which is supported by pillars. The pavilion is beautifully designed, skillfully constructed and adorned, and decorated with paintings; near it is a well called Bir Naja'i, beside which grows a tall sycamore affording much shade; and here the people assemble to enjoy the shade, and saunter around the spot when the Nile is high and the lake is full, and also when the crops are green and the flowers are blooming. Near the aforesaid sycamore is the bridge which leads to many roads, and at which men set lines for fishing during the day of high Nile; and this is a pretty sight." Al-Maqrizi echoes the sentiment that this monastery was a very popular place that people would visit for amusement. He notes, as translated by Evetts: "The Monastery of St. John lies on the bank of the Lake of al-Habash, near to the Nile, and beside it are gardens, some of which were laid out by the Emir Tamim ibn al-Mu'izz and a pavilion built on pillars, of fine architecture, with paintings, also constructed by the Emir Tamim. Near the monastery is a fountain called the Fountain of Mammati; near this stands a great sycamore, under which people assemble and drink, and this place is a place of constant amusement, dancing, and pleasure, and is equally pleasant in the days of the rise of the Nile when the lake is filled, and during the time when the fields are full of crops and all green and flourishing; it is much resorted to by the people, who amuse themselves here. Poets have sung of the beauty and charm of this district and this monastery is now called Monastery of al-Tin." This monastery was later restored toward the end of al-Hakim's reign. Abu Salih suggests that the monastery was under the watch of the restorer's nephew, who then became a Muslim and desecrated it by adding many mihrabs to it (in the text, these are referred to as *qiblas*, which only indicates the direction of Mecca). Abū Ṣālih, 127–28 and 309.

59. Bierman, *Writing Signs*, 75–95.

60. For a discussion of the *da'wa* under al-Hakim's reign, see Walker, "Ismaili Da'wa in the Reign of the Fatimid Caliph Al-Ḥākim."

61. Walker, 162. Walker notes that the shift in Ismaili policy at this time can also be seen in a change in al-Hakim's reliance on the family of al-Qadi al-Nu'man. Early in his reign, he employed members of the famous judge's family as the chief judges of the empire. In 1008, however, he named someone outside the Nu'man family, Malik ibn Sa'id al-Fariqi, as the chief judge, suggesting a shift in the nature of Ismaili thought at this time. As the nature of Fatimid religious identity changes during this time, the population of Fustat-Misr seems to have become more involved in the *da'wa*; sources suggest growing attendance at the Sessions of Wisdom (*majālis al-ḥikma*).

62. The Institute of Ismaili Studies is consistently publishing on this topic. Among the most useful studies are Daftary, *Mediaeval Isma'ili History and Thought*; Daftary, *Ismā'īlīs: Their History and Doctrines*; Haji, *Founding the Fatimid State*; Ibn al-Haytham and Ja'far ibn Ahmad, *Advent of the Fatimids*; Hamdani, *Between Revolution and State*; Haji, *Founding the Fatimid State*; Halm, *Fatimids and Their Traditions of Learning*; Walker, *Exploring an Islamic Empire*.

63. Walker, *Ḥamīd al-Dīn al-Kirmānī*, 65.

64. Walker, 121.

65. Walker, 4.

66. Walker, 71.

67. Walker, 74.

68. Al-Kirmānī, *Al-Maṣābīḥ fī ithbāt al-imāma* [*Master of the Age*], 4.

69. Al-Kirmānī, 17.

70. Al-Kirmānī, 114.

71. Al-Kirmānī, 60.

72. Al-Kirmānī, 114. Emphasis added.

73. Cook, *Commanding Right and Forbidding Wrong in Islamic Thought*, 302.

74. On the Pact of 'Umar, see Tritton, *Caliphs and Their Non-Muslim Subjects*; Friedmann, *Tolerance and Coercion in Islam*; and Levy-Rubin, *Non-Muslims in the Early Islamic Empire*. The precise dates of the codification of this pact are debated. However, Griffith notes that it seems to have "reached its classical form" by the ninth century. Griffith, *Church in the Shadow of the Mosque*, 15.

75. Tritton, *Caliphs and Their Non-Muslim Subjects*, 5–6. Emphasis added.

76. See Cahen, Talbi, Mantran, Lambton, and Bazmee Ansari, "Ḥisba."

77. Al-Shayzarī, *Book of the Islamic Market Inspector* (*Nihāyat al-rutba fī talab al-ḥisba*), 16.

78. Al-Maqrīzī, *Itti'āẓ al-ḥunafā' bi-akhbār al-a'imma al-Fāṭimiyyīn al-khulafā'*, 2:135.

79. Al-Shayzarī, *Book of the Islamic Market Inspector* (*Nihāyat al-rutba fī talab al-ḥisba*), 121–22 and 127. The manual also includes other acts that were adopted by al-Hakim, such as prohibiting women from lamenting or wailing at funeral ceremonies and, in fact, discouraging them from attending burials altogether. Compare with al-Hakim's acts of 1013, as described in al-Maqrīzī, *Itti'āẓ al-ḥunafā' bi-akhbār al-a'imma al-Fāṭimiyyīn al-khulafā'*, 2:93–94.

80. Al-Shayzarī, *Book of the Islamic Market Inspector* (*Nihāyat al-rutba fī talab al-ḥisba*), 128.

81. Al-Shayzarī, 149.

82. Al-Maqrīzī, *Itti'āẓ al-ḥunafā' bi-akhbār al-a'imma al-Fāṭimiyyīn al-khulafā'*, 2:78; Yaḥyā ibn Sa'īd al-Anṭākī, 23:490, 23:499. This is discussed in Sanders, *Ritual, Politics, and the City in Fatimid Cairo*, 57–58. Many of these edicts were later repealed, suggesting either a capriciousness of the caliph or an internal conflict within the Fatimid administration. Yahya al-Antaki suggests that al-Hakim did this to identify who had Sunni beliefs, so he could get rid of them. Given the general trend in his administration and the openness of the *dār al-'ilm* to Sunni scholars, this seems an unlikely cause. Moreover, the fact that he once again permitted the prayers in 400/1009–10 suggests that this was not the case. Yaḥyā ibn Sa'īd al-Anṭākī, 23:499.

83. Sanders, *Ritual, Politics, and the City in Fatimid Cairo*, 60.

84. For a consideration of al-Mansur's additions to the Great Mosque of Cordoba, see Dodds, "Great Mosque of Córdoba," 23–24; Safran, *Second Umayyad Caliphate*, 104–5; Hillenbrand, "Medieval Córdoba as a Cultural Centre," 132–33. Al-Mansur's reign is discussed in Ibn 'Idhārī, *Al-Bayān al-mughrib fī akhbār al-Andalus wa-al-Maghrib*, 287–88.

85. Similar bells can today be seen in the Mosque of Qarawiyyin in Fez.

86. Dodds, "Great Mosque of Córdoba," 24, from al-Maqqarī, *History of the Mohammedan Dynasties of Spain* (*Nafḥ al ṭīb min ghuṣn al-Andalus al-raṭīb*), 196.

87. For a discussion of al-Mansur's reign, see Chalmeta, "Al-Manṣūr"; de la Puente, "Carcterización de Almanzor."

88. This campaign began following critiques by the religious scholar (*'ulamā'*) that he wasn't orthodox enough. In response, al-Mansur destroyed much of the library of al-Hakam II, including works of philosophy and astronomy. Chalmeta, "Al-Manṣūr."

89. Similar measures were carried out by the Abbasid caliph al-Mutawakkil (r. 847–61), who instituted similar sumptuary laws and ordered the destruction of Christian monuments while also patronizing architectural projects.

90. Cited in Walker, "Ismaili Da'wa in the Reign of the Fatimid Caliph Al-Ḥākim," 173.

91. See Assaad, *Reign of al-Hakim bi-Amr Allah*, 111; Walker, *Caliph of Cairo*, 219–26; Walker, *Ḥamīd al-Dīn al-Kirmānī*, 16–24. Walker asserts that although al-Hakim's popularity spread outside Cairo, those closest to al-Hakim recognized the difficulty of defending the caliphate. For example, al-Kirmani's arrival in Cairo was met by a crisis in the Ismaili *da'wa*, culminating in the shutting down of the *majālis al-ḥikma*.

92. Forsyth, "Byzantine-Arab Chronicle of Yahya b. Sa'id al-Antaki," 227.

93. Forsyth, 228.

94. Al-Maqrīzī, *Itti'āẓ al-ḥunafā' bi-akhbār al-a'imma al-Fāṭimiyyīn al-khulafā'*, 2:65.

95. Walker, *Ḥamīd al-Dīn al-Kirmānī*, 14–15. Ultimately, the anti-Fatimid treatises composed by the Abbasids at this time became inextricably part of later Sunni histories on the Fatimids, making it particularly difficult to ascertain accurate information on the dynasty.

96. In fact, the idea of concealing *bāṭin* truths is central to the Shi'i defense of *taqīyya* (literally, prudence or fear, but refers to the concealment of religious belief under the threat of persecution). It is possible that the masking of the *bāṭin* cores to resemble Sunni minarets could also be related to this concept.

Chapter 5. Rebuilding the Fatimid City

1. Al-Maqrīzī, *Itti'āẓ al-ḥunafā' bi-akhbār al-a'imma al-Fāṭimiyyīn al-khulafā'*, 2:117. For an analysis of this period, see Walker, *Caliph of Cairo*, 239–62; and Assaad, *Reign of Al-Hakim bi-Amr Allah*, 182–92.

2. Walker, "Ismaili Da'wa in the Reign of the Fatimid Caliph al-Ḥākim," 178, based on descriptions in Husayn, *Ṭa'ifat al-durūz*, 52, and Ghalib, *Majmua'at rasā'il al-Kirmānī*, 113–14.

3. Al-Maqrīzī, *Al-Mawā'iẓ wa-l-i'tibār bi dhikr al-khiṭaṭ wa-l-āthār* (2002–3 edition), 4:182–83.

4. For an exploration of the Druze, see Abu-Izzeddin, *Druzes*; Obeid, *Druze and Their Faith in Tawhid*; Hodgson, Tekindağ, and Gökbilgin, "Durūz"; Sacy, *Exposé de la religion des Druzes*; and Walker, *Caliph of Cairo*, 250–61.

5. The Druze now comprises a sizeable religious minority in both Syria and Lebanon.

6. These early Druze not only abandoned the sharia but also the Ismaili *bāṭin* interpretations of the Qur'an. Hodgson, "Durūz."

7. This was uttered by Hamza al-Labbad, see Bryer, "Origins of the Druze Religion," 250; and Crone, *God's Rule*, 210–11.

8. Al-Maqrīzī, *Al-Mawā'iẓ wa-l-i'tibār bi dhikr al-khiṭaṭ wa-l-āthār* (2002–3 edition), 3:337.

9. For a discussion and images of the structure before Bohra renovations, see Creswell, *Muslim Architecture of Egypt*, 1:113–15. The practice of integrating religious structures into the fabric of the Muqattam Hills was one that was also practiced by Christians. Abu al-Makarim describes a Church of Saint John beneath the Monastery of al-Qusayr, built into the Muqattam Hills and "hewn out in the rock with the pickaxe." Abū Ṣālih, *Churches and Monasteries of Egypt and Some Neighbouring Countries*, 146.

10. Al-Maqrīzī, *Al-Mawā'iẓ wa-l-i'tibār bi dhikr al-khiṭaṭ wa-l-āthār* (2002–3 edition), 2:288–94; Bloom, "Mosque of the Qarafa in Cairo"; Cortese and Calderini, *Women and the Fatimids in the World of Islam*, 166–68.

11. Al-Maqrīzī, *Al-Mawā'iẓ wa-l-i'tibār bi dhikr al-khiṭaṭ wa-l-āthār* (2002–3 edition), 4:887. See

Creswell, *Muslim Architecture of Egypt*, 1:115.

12. Among those who emigrated during this time was the Fatimid chronicler Yahya al-Antaki, whose history of the Fatimid dynasty remains one of our best sources on the period. See Yaḥyā ibn Saʿīd al-Anṭākī, *Taʾrīkh* (*Histoire*) and Forsyth, "Byzantine-Arab Chronicle of Yahya b. Saʿid al-Antaki."

13. Al-Muqaffaʿ, *Taʾrīkh baṭārikat al-kanīsa al-Miṣriyya* (*The History of the Patriarchs of the Egyptian Church*), 2:135/204.

14. Al-Muqaffaʿ, 2:137/207.

15. Al-Muqaffaʿ, 2:137/207–8. Interestingly, the more reliable account of Yahya al-Antaki also attributes al-Hakim's reversals to a personal relationship with a monk. In the case of Yahya's account, the friendly monk was known as Salmun, from the Monastery of Saint Catherine. Yahya also sees a Christian precedent in al-Hakim's adoption of ascetic clothing, noting that he wore wool as though an apprentice to the monk Salmun.

16. Al-Muqaffaʿ, *Taʾrīkh baṭārikat al-kanīsa al-Miṣriyya* (*The History of the Patriarchs of the Egyptian Church*), 2:137/208.

17. Marlis Saleh has documented the various medieval writings on al-Hakim's actions. She notes that the inconsistency of the caliph's acts was most condemned. Ibn Khallikan complained, "he was constantly doing and undoing." Ibn Taghribirdi conurs that al-Hakim's worst quality was that he would "do something, then undo it, then do its opposite." Al-Suyuti noted that "al-Hakim was the worst caliph; no one worse ruled Egypt after the Pharaoh. Among his faults is that he was fickle in words and deeds; he destroyed the churches of Egypt then restored them, and destroyed the [Church of the Holy Sepulcher] then restored it." In contrast, many of the medieval scholars praise the prohibitions themselves. Saleh, "Government Relations with the Coptic Community in Egypt during the Fatimid Period," 250–51. See also Saleh, "Church Building, Repair, and Destruction in Fatimid Egypt," 189.

18. Medieval sources are in great disagreement over the details of al-Hakim's death. For a discussion, see Walker, *Caliph of Cairo*, 260, and Assaad, *Reign of al-Hakim bi-Amr Allah*, 182–92.

19. For a consideration of Sitt al-Mulk's fascinating story, see Cortese and Calderini, *Women and the Fatimids in the World of Islam*, 117–27; Halm, "Destin de la princess Sitt al-Mulk"; Lev, "Fatimid Princess Sitt al-Mulk."

20. Al-Maqrīzī, *Ittiʿāẓ al-ḥunafāʾ bi-akhbār al-aʾimma al-Fāṭimiyyīn al-khulafā*, 2:181. See Walker, *Caliph of Cairo*, 268. Lev, *State and Society in Fatimid Egypt*, 36–37.

21. Lev, *State and Society in Fatimid Egypt*, 38–42.

22. Al-Muqaffaʿ, *Taʾrīkh baṭārikat al-kanīsa al-Miṣriyya* (*The History of the Patriarchs of the Egyptian Church*), 2:137/209.

23. Al-Maqrīzī, *Ittiʿāẓ al-ḥunafāʾ bi-akhbār al-aʾimma al-Fāṭimiyyīn al-khulafā*, 2:124–35.

24. Ibn Muyassar, *Akhbār Miṣr*, 2–5; Bianquis, "Al-Ẓāhir li-Iʿzāz Dīn Allāh."

25. For a discussion of the *ziyāda*, see O'Kane, "Ziyada of the Mosque of al-Hakim and the Development of the Ziyada in Islamic Architecture"; Creswell, *Muslim Architecture of Egypt*, 1:115–17.

26. Oleg Grabar devoted a chapter to the "Fatimid City" in Grabar, *Shape of the Holy*, 135–69. Jonathan Bloom also discusses it in Bloom, *Arts of the City Victorious*, 81–83.

27. While most scholarship on the architecture of the Haram al-Sharif focuses on the time of their foundation, Oleg Grabar and Gülru Necipoğlu have both tackled the subject of Islamic Jerusalem's changing meaning. See Grabar, *Shape of the Holy*; Grabar, *Dome of the Rock*; and Necipoğlu, "Dome of the Rock as Palimpsest." For recent scholarship on Umayayd-era Haram al-Sharif see Milwright, *Dome of the Rock and Its Umayyad Mosaic Inscriptions*.

28. For a consideration of Abbasid Jerusalem, see Grabar, *Shape of the Holy*, 161–63.

29. The bibliography on Umayyad Jerusalem is vast. See especially Kaplony, *Ḥaram of Jerusalem*; Creswell, *Early Muslim Architecture*, 1:65–380; Rosen-Ayalon, *Early Islamic Monuments of al-Ḥaram al-Sharīf*; Milwright, *Dome of the Rock and Its Umayyad Mosaic Inscriptions*; Rabbat, "Dome of the Rock Revisited"; Gil, *History of Palestine*; Blair, "What Is the Date of the Dome of the Rock?"; Johns, "Archaeology and the History of Early Islam"; van Berchem, *Matériaux pour un corpus inscriptionum arabicarum*, vol. 2. For post-Fatimid Jerusalem, see Burgoyne, *Mamluk Jerusalem*. For a more comprehensive overview of sources, see Grabar, *Dome of the Rock*, and Grabar, *Shape of the Holy*; Necipoğlu, "Dome of the Rock as Palimpsest"; and Rabbat, "Meaning of the Umayyad Dome of the Rock."

30. In fact, al-Mansur visited Jerusalem twice. Once after his hajj in 758 and a second time in 771, to put down a revolt. For a summary of caliphal visits, see Goitein and Grabar, "Al-Ḳuds." Oleg Grabar has suggested that these early visits may have been due to the temporary change to the hajj route. During al-Mansur's and al-Mahdi's reigns, the route passed through Jerusalem. However, by the reign of al-Ma'mun, the route bypassed the city. Grabar, *Dome of the Rock*, 127.

31. Mujir al-Din, *Histoire de Jérusalem et d'Hebron*, 59–60.

32. Al-Muqaddasī, *Description of Syria, Including Palestine*, 41–42.

33. Al-Muqaddasī, 41.

34. Al-Muqaddasi couches the restoration in the context of religious competition in Jerusalem. Prior to discussing the restorations under al-Mahdi, he argues that the mosque's proximity to the Holy Sepulcher made it even more beautiful than the mosque in Damascus. Al-Muqaddasī, 41. His account of the mosque's comparison to the beauty of the Holy Sepulcher echoes his famous statement that the Dome of the Rock was constructed so that the Holy Sepulcher would not "dazzle the minds" of resident Muslims.

35. This account is recorded by Muthir al-Gharam, as cited in Le Strange, *Palestine under the Moslems*, 92–93.

36. Hamilton, *Structural History of the Aqsa Mosque*, 72. For reconstructions of the Aqsa Mosque, in addition to Hamilton's work see Grabar, *Shape of the Holy*, 117–22; and Creswell, *Early Muslim Architecture*, 1:373–80. Al-Mahdi's visit took place during a time of intense wars with the Byzantine empire. This visit is briefly mentioned in al-Ṭabarī, *History of al-Ṭabarī* (*Taʾrīkh*), 215.

37. Under the reign of

al-Ma'mun, Jerusalem had suffered a widescale famine, resulting in a drastic decrease in its Muslim population. The Christian patriarch used this as an opportunity to repair the Church of the Holy Sepulcher, suggesting that even before the destruction of al-Hakim, repair of the building did not come easily. This is recorded by Sa'id al-Bitriq, as discussed in Gil, *History of Palestine*, 295, and by Eutychius, as cited by Goitein and Grabar, "Al-Ḳuds."

38. This inscription is published in Grabar, *Shape of the Holy*, 60–68, and Grabar, *Dome of the Rock*, 96.

39. Nasir-i Khusraw, *Book of Travels*, 35.

40. The Tulunid and Ikhshidid rulers did not seem to have made visits to Jerusalem. Grabar, *Shape of the Holy*, 136. For a discussion of these groups, see Bianquis, "Autonomous Egypt from Ibn Ṭūlūn to Kāfūr."

41. Grabar also notes that there is a series of inscriptions from 913 and 914 on the beams from the ceiling, most likely recording repairs or restorations most likely patronized by the mother of the caliph al-Muqtadir, under the oversight of Labid. See Grabar, *Dome of the Rock*, 127. This is also mentioned in al-Muqaddasī, *Description of Syria, Including Palestine*, 45.

42. Grabar, *Shape of the Holy*, 57.

43. For a summary of events, see Gil, *History of Palestine*, 336. In addition to the Byzantines, various tribes rose up against the Fatimids during this period, including the group of Palestinian Bedouins, called the Banu Tayy, led by the Banu'l Jarrah, the Qarmatians and other Arab tribes in Syria. Many sources discuss the Fatimids' conquest of Palestine. For a summary, see Gil, 337.

44. Gil, 352–53.

45. Details for the beginning of al-Zahir's reign are difficult to make out. We have very thorough accounts preserved by al-Musabbihi but these stop in 1025, at the peak of unrest. See Lev, *State and Society in Fatimid Egypt*, 38.

46. Much of the determination of the dating was carried out by R. W. Hamilton and during the renovations by Mimar Kemalettin. See Hamilton, *Structural History of the Aqsa Mosque*; Creswell, *Early Muslim Architecture*, 1:121–22; and Yavuz, "Restoration Project of the Masjid al-Aqsa by Mimar Kemalettin."

47. Creswell, *Early Muslim Architecture*, 1:121–22.

48. For a reconstruction, see Grabar, *Shape of the Holy*, 150; Creswell, *Early Muslim Architecture*, 1:119–26; Hamilton, *Structural History of the Aqsa Mosque*, 70–74.

49. Grabar has referred to this assemblage as a "triumphal arch." Grabar, *Shape of the Holy*, 149. The mosaic program as a whole was studied by Henri Stern in "Recherches sur la mosquée Aqsa et ses mosaiques." I use the term *maqṣūra* here to distinguish the space formally from the rest of the mosque. It is the term used by Nasir-i Khusraw in his description of the mosque. However, it should not be understood as a space that was reserved for royalty, as is usually the case for *maqṣūras*. For a discussion of *maqṣūras*, see Mostafa, "Early Mosque Revisited."

50. The practice is rare enough that one wonders if, in fact, the same mosaicists may have been used for the reconstruction of the Haram al-Sharif and the Holy Sepulcher, which would have also had a new mosaic program. See Ousterhout, "Rebuilding the Temple," 70–71.

51. The most famous post-Umayyad use of mosaics in Islamic architecture is found at the Spanish Umayyad Great Mosque of Cordoba. In this case, the use of mosaics most likely hearkened back to Umayyad production. On the Great Mosque of Cordoba, see Jerilynn Dodds, "Great Mosque of Córdoba"; Khoury, "Meaning of the Great Mosque of Cordoba in the Tenth Century"; Ruggles, "Stratigraphy of Forgetting." On Umayyad revivals, see Flood, "Umayyad Survivals and Mamluk Revivals."

52. Translation in Grabar, *Shape of the Holy*, 151. See also Hamilton, *Structural History of the Aqsa Mosque*, 9; van Berchem, *Matériaux pour un corpus inscriptionum arabicarum*, 2:381–92.

53. Nasir-i Khusraw offers commentary on the effect of light at different times of day, noting that "when all the doors are opened, the inside of the mosque is as light as an open courtyard. However, when the wind is blowing or it is raining, the doors are closed, and then light comes from skylights." Nasir-i Khusraw, *Book of Travels*, 35. The different effects of the light would have also been emphasized by the opening and closing of the oculi on the front of the arch.

54. Although he would later become a major figure in Ismaili thought, it is not clear whether his conversion to Ismailism occurred before or after his voyage. See Nasir-i Khusraw, *Book of Travels*, xii, and Nanji, "Nāṣir-i Khusraw."

55. The travelogue is also particularly valuable for its description of Cairo and Mecca. Nasir-i Khusraw entered Jerusalem on the fifth of Ramadan 438 (March 5, 1047). Nasir-i Khusraw, *Book of Travels*, 27.

56. Nasir-i Khusraw, 27. The account does not suggest that Jerusalem was meant to overtake Mecca as a pilgrimage center, as in the Umayyad-era Ibn Zubayr controversy. Nasir-i Khusraw describes the rock outcropping in the Dome of the Rock as the first *qibla*, but not as the site of the Prophet's ascension. Nasir-i Khusraw, 20–30. However, he refers to the Aqsa Mosque as "the spot to which God transported Muhammad from Mecca on the night of his heavenly ascent [*mir'āj*] and thence to heaven." Nasir-i Khusraw, 34.

57. At first he refers to the Aqsa Mosque itself as "*maqṣūra*," to distinguish it from the Haram al-Sharif, then later he calls it "*masjid al-Aqsa*" (Aqsa Mosque).

58. Nasir-i Khusraw, *Book of Travels*, 28. Nasir-i Khusraw calls it "David's Gate" but Oleg Grabar identifies it as the "Gate of the Chain" in *Shape of the Holy*, 146.

59. Nasir-i Khusraw simply names him as the "*sulṭān*" of Egypt. Nasir-i Khusraw, *Book of Travels*, 28.

60. Nasir-i Khusraw, 32. He also describes the stairway in the Ghorid Station, in which the arcade "is inscribed in gold and fine calligraphy, 'By the order of Prince Layth al-Dawla Nushtakin the Ghorid.' They say that this Layth al-Dawla was a slave of the sultan of Egypt and that he had these stairs and gangways built." Nasir-i Khusraw, 34. Nasir records a similar system of patronage in his description of the shrine of Abraham at Hebron, in which there is a "prayer carpet said to have been sent by a prince of the army who was a slave of the sultan of Egypt." Nasir-i Khusraw, 36.

61. For an analysis of the Fatimid public text, see Bierman, *Writing Signs.*

62. Nasir-i Khusraw, *Book of Travels*, 34.

63. For example, Creswell notes that his measurements are "manifestly absurd." Creswell, *Early Muslim Architecture*, 1:121.

64. His description of the mosque is found in Nasir-i Khusraw, *Book of Travels*, 34. Amusingly, after noting that he measured and drew the site himself, he concludes his description of Jerusalem by noting that "among the strange things I saw in the Jerusalem sanctuary was a walnut tree." Nasir-i Khusraw, 43. For modern studies of the site, see Creswell, *Early Muslim Architecture*, 1:373–80; Hamilton, *Structural History of the Aqsa Mosque*; and Kaplony, *Ḥaram of Jerusalem.*

65. For a discussion on medieval Arabic sources' consideration of artistic practice, see Rabbat, "ʿAjīb and Gharīb."

66. The episode is described in Qur'an 17:1, which says: "Praise Him who made His servant journey in the night (*isrā*) from the sacred sanctuary (*al-masjid al-ḥarām*) to the remotest sanctuary (*al-masjid al-aqṣā*)."

67. For discussions, see Mourad, "Symbolism of Jerusalem in Early Islam"; Amikan Elad, *Medieval Jerusalem and Islamic Worship*, 48–50; Grabar, *Shape of the Holy*, chapter 2; Rabbat, "Meaning of the Umayyad Dome of the Rock"; and Grabar, *Dome of the Rock.*

68. Nasir-i Khusraw, *Book of Travels*, 34.

69. For a reconstruction of the Fatimid-era platform, see Grabar, *Shape of the Holy*, chapter 4.

70. It is not clear whether the Dome of the Rock itself was associated with the spot of the Prophet's ascension at this time. Nasir-i Khusraw does not associate it with the *miʿrāj* but only as the site of the first *qibla*. See Grabar, *Dome of the Rock*, 143–57.

71. Nasir-i Khusraw, *Book of Travels*, 39.

72. The closest parallel I have found is in the roundels often found in the pendentives of Ottoman-era mosques, most notably that of the Suleymaniye Mosque. However, these roundels, in addition to being five hundred years later, are not recessed.

73. The *shamsa* is described in al-Maqrīzī, *Ittiʿāẓ al-ḥunafā' bi-akhbār al-a'imma al-Fāṭimiyyīn al-khulafā'*, 1:140–42.

74. The *shamsa*'s evocation of the Ismaili memory device is argued in Bierman, *Writing Signs*, 74. See also Bloom, "Mosque of al-Ḥākim in Cairo," 27, and Sanders, *Ritual, Politics, and the City in Fatimid Cairo*, 47.

75. There is vast potential for Ismaili symbolism in these roundels that could perhaps be elucidated in the future. For example, the four roundels circling a central dome could evoke the family of the Prophet *or* people of the house (*ahl al-bayt*) circling around the central figure of Muhammad or even the Mahdi. For a discussion of the *ahl al-bayt* as illuminated figures in the ascension narrative, see Colby, "Early Imami Shiʿi Narratives and Contestation over Intimate Colloquey Scenes in Muḥammad's Miʿrāj," 145.

76. Al-Qāḍī al-Nuʿmān, *Asās al-Ta'wīl*. For an analysis of the *miʿrāj* in this text, I rely on Alexandrin, "Prophetic Ascent and Initiatory Ascent in Qāḍī al-Nuʿmān's *Asās al-Ta'wīl*." Thank you to Christiane Gruber for pointing me toward this text.

77. Alexandrin, 159.

78. Alexandrin sees this as operating in parallel with Abraham's ascent narratives. Alexandrin, 159.

79. Amir-Moezzi has also written on the Twelver Shiʿi context, noting that in preexistence, the *ahl al-bayt* are described as "silhouettes of light revolving around the Throne of the All-Merciful." With five domes, shimmering in their unique mosaic form, the Aqsa forms could have also evoked the family of the Prophet. Amir-Moezzi, *Spirituality of Shiʿi Islam*, 140. This tradition is, at times, even described as being articulated in silver and gold. Amir-Moezzi, 166.

80. It is, in fact, *so* unusual that Caroline Williams named the inscription on the Mosque of al-Aqmar in Cairo (1125) as the *only* example of this formula. She interprets this much later inscription in the context of a twelfth-century succession crisis. See Williams, "Cult of the ʿAlid Saints in the Fatimid Monuments of Cairo. Part I: Mosque of al-Aqmar," 43.

81. Shepard has shown that the Byzantine interest in restoring the Holy Sepulcher was based on the increase in Christian pilgrims (mostly from the Latin west) to the Holy Land that inspired imperial investment in the church. Shepard, "Holy Land, Lost Lands, Realpolitik."

82. Yaḥyā ibn Saʿīd al-Anṭākī, *Ta'rīkh* (*Histoire*), 47:468–69, as cited in Shepard, 530. Shepard argues that her concern was most likely increasing Fatimid intervention in Aleppo.

83. See Shepard, 531; Reinert, "Muslim Presence in Constantinople," 139; Jacoby, "Bishop Gunther of Bamberg, Byzantium and Christian Pilgrimage to the Holy Land in the Eleventh Century," 120.

84. Al-Maqrīzī, *Ittiʿāẓ al-ḥunafā' bi-akhbār al-a'imma al-Fāṭimiyyīn al-khulafā'*, 2:176. See Lev, *State and Society in Fatimid Egypt*, 40; Runciman, "Byzantine 'Protectorate' in the Holy Land." For a discussion of the mosque in Constantinople, see Anderson, "Islamic Spaces and Diplomacy in Constantinople." For a consideration of Muslim presence in Constantinople, see Durak, "Through an Eastern Window"; Reinert, "Muslim Presence in Constantinople."

85. In addition to the negotiation over architectural spaces, the Byzantines called for the Fatimids to stay out of the affairs of Aleppo and to stop giving aid to the rulers of Sicily. See Lev, *State and Society in Fatimid Egypt*, 40–41. He mentions Yahya al-Antaki as his major source on the topic of restoring monarchy; Lev, 165. Reconstruction was also mentioned in al-Maqrīzī, *Ittiʿāẓ al-ḥunafā' bi-akhbār al-a'imma al-Fāṭimiyyīn al-khulafā'*, 2:183.

86. Grabar, *Shape of the Holy*, 139; Hamilton, *Structural History of the Aqsa Mosque*, 73.

87. See Ousterhout, "Rebuilding the Temple."

88. On his visit in 1047, Nasir-i Khusraw describes "much gold" in the decoration of the church, depicting various prophets. These were most likely added during the renovations of the 1040s. Nasir-i Khusraw, *Book of Travels*, 38; Ousterhout, "Rebuilding the Temple," 78.

89. Grabar, *Shape of the Holy*, 142.

Conclusion

1. Makdisi, *Ibn ʿAqīl et la résurgence de l'Islam traditionaliste au XIe siècle*, 312; Bierman, *Writing Signs*, 175–76. This also found its parallel in the cursing of the Imams from the minbars of the Cordoban Umayyad-controlled Maghreb.

2. See, for example, Bierman, *Writing Signs*, and Bloom, *Arts of the City Victorious.*

3. For a discussion of this period, see Brett, *Fatimid Empire*, chapters 8 and 9.

4. See especially Williams, "Cult of ʿAlid Saints in the Fatimid Monuments of Cairo. Part II: Mausolea," 39–60; Bloom, *Arts of the City Victorious*, chapter 5.

5. For a comparative study, see Cohen, *Under Crescent and Cross.* For a discussion of the persecution of religious minorities in medieval Latin Europe, see Nirenberg, *Communities of Violence.*

6. In his seminal work on the Geniza, Shelomo Dov Goitein situates the "classical Geniza" period of the tenth to thirteenth century as the apogee of interfaith relations in the Mediterranean; he contrasts this early "spirit of tolerance and liberalism" with the growing "intolerance and fantaticism" of the thirteenth century. Goitein, *Mediterranean Society*, 1:29.

7. The casting of premodern Islam as "tolerant" in opposition to modern Islam has been considered and problematized by Flood, "From the Prophet to Postmodernism?," 43, and Watenpaugh "Resonance and Circulation," 1238–39.

8. This narrative is particularly well explored in the art and architecture of Islamic Spain. See Dodds, Menocal, and Balbale, *Arts of Intimacy*; Robinson, "Talking Religion, Comparatively Speaking," "Arts of Intimacy," and "Qurtuba"; and Soifer, "Beyond Convivencia," 19–35.

9. Mulder, *Shrines of the ʿAlids in Medieval Syria*, 267.

10. Flood, *Objects of Translation*, 266.

11. Joseph Koerner wrote on the context of iconoclasm during the Protestant Reformation: "Especially when they seek to publish their endeavors, image breakers become image makers." Koerner, "Icon as Iconoclash," 164. For a consideration of the way image destruction brings greater prominence to the work of art in an Islamic context, see especially Flood, "Between Cult and Culture," Flood, "Idol Breaking as Image Making in the Islamic State," and Harmanşah, "ISIS, Heritage, and the Spectacles of Destruction in the Global Media."

12. Of course, in many ways, destruction has often been at the crux of Jerusalem's architectural identity. From the destruction of the Jewish Temple, longing for what was gone was a central defining feature of the city. A modern example of this dynamic is in the 1967 fire at the Aqsa Mosque. After the Six Day War, an Australian Christian extremist set the mosque on fire, destroying the exquisite Salah al-Din minbar, in the hopes that this destruction would expedite the second coming of Christ. For a discussion of the rebuilding of the minbar, see Singer, *Minbar of Saladin*.

13. See, for example, Hillenbrand, *Islamic Architecture*, 26–30; Blair and Bloom, "Mirage of Islamic Art," 171.

14. Bloom, *Arts of the City Victorious*, 7; Behrens-Abouseif, *Minarets of Cairo*, 116.

BIBLIOGRAPHY

MEDIEVAL SOURCES

Abū Ṣāliḥ. *The Churches and Monasteries of Egypt and Some Neighbouring Countries, Attributed to Abū Ṣāliḥ the Armenian* [*Ta'rīkh al-kanā'is wa al-adyira*], translated by B. T. A. Evetts. Oxford: Clarendon Press, 1895.

Adamnan, Abbé de Seghine. *The Pilgrimage of Arculfus in the Holy Land*, translated and annotated by James Macpherson. London: Palestine Pilgrims' Text Society, 1895.

Ibn al-Athīr, ʿAlī ʿIzz al-Dīn. *Al-Kāmil fī'l ta'rīkh*. Beirut: Dār al-kitāb al-ʿarabī, 1967.

Ibn al-Haytham, Jaʿfar ibn Ahmad. *The Advent of the Fatimids: A Contemporary Shiʿi Witness: An Edition and English Translation of Ibn al-Haytham's Kitāb al-munāẓarāt*, translated by Wilferd Madelung and Paul Ernest Walker. Ismaili Texts and Translations Series, vol. 1. London: Tauris, 2000.

Ibn al-Qalānisī. *Dhayl ta'rīkh Dimashq*, edited by H. F. Amedroz. Beirut: Maṭbaʿat al-ābā' al-yasūʿiyyīn, 1908.

Ibn al-Zubayr, Aḥmad ibn al-Rashīd. *Book of Gifts and Rarities: Kitāb al-hadāyā wa al-tuḥaf*, translated by Ghādah Ḥijjāwī al Qaddūmī. Harvard Middle Eastern Monographs 29. Cambridge, MA: Harvard University Press, 1996.

Ibn Aybak al-Dawādārī. *Kanz al-durar wa-jāmiʿ al-ghurar. Vol. 6: Al-Durra al-muḍiyya fī akhbār al-dawla al-fāṭimiyya*, edited by Ṣalāḥ al-Dīn al-Munajjid. Cairo: Qism al-dirāsāt al-Islāmīyah, al-ma ʿhad al-almānī lil-āthār bi-al-Qāhirah, 1961.

Ibn Duqmāq, Ibrāhīm ibn Muḥammad. *Kitāb al-intiṣār li-wāsiṭat ʿaqd al-amṣār*. Cairo: al-Maṭbaʿah al-kubrā al-amīrīyah, 1893.

Ibn Ḥajar. *Rafʿ al-Iṣr*, edited by R. Guest, in his edition of Kindī, *Governors and Judges of Egypt*. Leiden: Brill, 1912.

Ibn Hānī. *Tabyīn al-maʿānī fī sharḥ dīwān Ibn Hānī al-Andalusī al-Maghribī*, edited by Zāhid ʿAli. Cairo: Maṭbaʿat al-maʿārif wa-maktabatihā, 1933.

Ibn Ḥawqal, Abū'l-Qāsim ibn ʿAlī. *Kitāb ṣūrat al-arḍ*, edited by J. H. Kramers, second edition. Leiden: Brill, 1967. First published in 1938 by Bibliotheca Geographorum Arabicorum.

Ibn ʿIdhārī. *Al-bayān al-mughrib fī akhbār al-Andalus wa-al-Maghrib*, edited by R. P. A. Dozy. Leiden: Brill, 1848.

Ibn Khallikān, Aḥmad ibn Muḥammad. *Ibn Khallikān's Biographical Dictionary*, translated by M. de Slane, 4 vols. New York: Cosimo Classics, 2010.

———. *Wafayāt al-aʿyān*, edited by Iḥsān ʿAbbās. Beirut: Dār ṣādir, 1968.

Ibn Miskawayh, and Aḥmad ibn Muḥammad. *The Concluding Portion of the Experiences of the Nations: The Eclipse of the ʿAbbasid Caliphate*, 5 vols. Oxford: Basil Blackwell, 1920.

al-Idrīsī, Muḥammad ibn Muḥammad. *Description de l'Afrique et de l'Espagne* [*Al-Maghreb wa al-Sūdān wa Miṣr wa al-Andalus*], edited and translated by R. Dozy and M. J. de Goeje. Leiden: Brill, 1968.

Idrīs ʿImād al-Dīn. *ʿUyūn al-akhbār*, edited and translated by Shainool Jiwa as *The Founder of Cairo: The Fatimid Imam-Caliph al-Muʿizz and His Era*. London: Tauris in association with the Institute of Ismaili Studies, 2013.

al-Jawdharī, Abū ʿAlī Manṣūr al-ʿAzīzī. *Sīrat al-ustādh Jawdhar*, translated by M. Canard as *Vie de l'ustadh Jaudhar*. Algiers: Alger Carbonel, 1958.

———. *Sīrat al-ustādh Jawdhar*, edited and translated by Hamid Haji as *Inside the Immaculate Portal: A History from Early Fatimid Archives*. London: Tauris in association with the Institute of Ismaili Studies, 2012.

al-Kirmānī, Ḥamīd al-Dīn Aḥmad ibn ʿAbd Allah. *Al-Maṣābīḥ fī ithbāt al-imāma* [*Master of the Age: An Islamic Treatise on the Necessity of the Imamate*], translated by Paul Walker. London: Tauris, 2007.

al-Maqqarī, *Analectes sur l'histoire et la littérature des arabes d'Espagne* [*Nafḥ al-ṭīb min ghuṣn al-Andalus al-raṭīb*], edited by R. Dozy, G. Dugat, L. Krehl, and W. Wright. 2 vols. Reprint edition. London: Oriental Press, 1967. First published in 1855–61 by Brill.

———. *Azhār al-riyāḍ fī akhbār ʿiyāḍ*. 2 vols. Cairo: Bayt al-Maghrib, 1940.

———. *The History of the Mohammedan Dynasties of Spain* [*Nafḥ al-ṭīb min ghuṣn al-Andalus al-raṭīb*], edited by Pascuel de Gayangos. London: Oriental Translation Fund of Great Britain and Ireland, 1840.

al-Maqrīzī, Tāqī al-Dīn Abu'l-ʿAbbas Aḥmad. *Description Historique et Topographique de l'Égypte*, translated by U. Bouriant and P. Casanova. Mémoires publiés par les membres de la Mission archéologique française au Caire, 17. Paris: Leroux, 1900.

———. *Ittiʿāẓ al-ḥunafā' bi-akhbār al-a'imma al-Fāṭimiyyīn al-khulafā'* [Lessons for the seekers of the truth on the history of

Fatimid Imams and caliphs]. Vol. 1 edited by Jamāl al-Dīn al-Shayyāl and vols. 2 and 3 edited by Muḥammad Ḥilmī Muḥammad Aḥmad. Cairo: Dār al-fikr al-ʿArabī, 1967.
——. *Al-Mawāʿiẓ wa-l-iʿtibār bi dhikr al-khiṭaṭ wa-l-āthār* [Exhortations and instructions on the districts and antiquities]. Bulaq: Dār al-ṭibāʿah al-Miṣrīyah, 1853.
——. *Al-Mawāʿiẓ wa-l-iʿtibār bi dhikr al-khiṭaṭ wa-l-āthār* [Exhortations and instructions on the districts and antiquities], edited by Ayman Fu'ād Sayyid, 5 vols. London: Mu'assasat al-furqān l-il-turāth al-Islāmī, 2002–3.
al-Muqaddasī, Shams al-Dīn Abū ʿAbdallāh Muḥammad. *Aḥsan al-taqāsīm fī maʿrifat al-aqālīm* [*The Best Divisions for Knowledge of the Regions*], translated by Basil Collins. Reading, UK: Garnet, 2000.
——. *Description of Syria, Including Palestine*. London: Palestine Pilgrim's Text Society, 1885.
——. *Aḥsan al-taqāsīm* [Description de l'Occident musulman au IVe–Xe siècle], translated by Charles Pellat. Algiers: Carbonel, 1950.
al-Muqaffaʿ, Sāwīrus. *Taʾrīkh baṭārikat al-kanīsa al-Miṣriyya* [*The History of the Patriarchs of the Egyptian Church*], edited and translated by Aziz Suryal Atiya. 4 vols. Cairo: Société d'Archéologie Copte, 1948–74.
al-Musabbiḥī. *Al-Juzʾ al-arbaʿūn min akhbār Miṣr*. Cairo: al-Maʿhad al-ʿilmī al-Faransī lil-āthār al-sharqīyah, 1978.
Ibn Muyassar. *Akhbār Miṣr*. Cairo: Institut français d'archéologie orientale, 1981.
Nasir-i Khusraw. *Book of Travels* [*Safarnama*], translated by W. M. Thackston. Albany, NY: Bibliotheque Persica, 1986.
al-Nuʿmān, al-Qāḍī Abū Ḥanīfa b. Muḥammad. *Asās al-taʾwīl* [The foundation of allegorical interpretation], edited by ʿArif Ṭāmir. Beirut: Dār al-thaqāfa, 1966.
——. *Daʿāʾim al-Islām* [Pillars of Islam], edited by ʿA. al-Fyzee. Cairo: Dār al-ma ʿārif, 1951–60.
——. *Founding the Fatimid State: The Rise of an Early Islamic Empire: An Annotated English Translation of al-Qāḍī al-Nuʿmān's Iftitāḥ al-daʿwa wa ibtidāʾ al-dawla* [Commencement of the mission and establishment of the state], translated by Hamid Haji. London: Tauris in association with the Institute of Ismaili Studies, 2006.
——. *The Pillars of Islam: Daʿāʾim al-Islām of al-Qāḍī al-Nuʿmān*, edited by Ismail Kurban Husein Poonawala. 2 vols. *Vol. 1: ʿIbādāt: Acts of Devotion and Religious Observances*. Oxford: Oxford University Press, 2002–4.
——. *The Pillars of Islam: Daʿāʾim al-Islām of al-Qāḍī al-Nuʿmān*, edited by Ismail Kurban Husein Poonawala. 2 vols. *Vol. 2: Laws Pertaining to Human Intercourse*. Oxford: Oxford University Press, 2007.
——. *Taʾwīl al-daʿāʾim* [The allegorical interpretation of the pillars], edited by M. Ḥasan al-Aʿẓamī. Cairo: Dār al-. maʿārif, 1967.
——. *Taʾwīl al-daʿāʾim* [The allegorical interpretation of the pillars], 3 vols. Beirut: Dār al-aḍwāʾ, 1995.
al-Nubāhī, Ibn al-Ḥasan. *Histoire des juges d'Andalousie intitulée kitab al-Markaba al-ʿUlya*, edited by E. Lévi-Provençal. Cairo: Scribe Egyptien, 1948.
al-Qalqashandī, Aḥmad ibn ʿAlī. *Kitāb ṣubḥ al-aʿshā fī ṣināʿat al-inshā*. 2 vols. Cairo: al-Hayʾa al-Miṣrīyah al-ʿāmma li-l-kitāb, 2006.
al-Sabi, Hilal. *Rusūm dār al-khilāfah* [*The Rules and Regulations of the Abbasid Court*], translated by Elie A. Salm. Beirut: American University of Beirut, 1977.
al-Shābushtī, ʿAlī ibn Muḥammad Abū al-Ḥasan. *Al-Diyārāt: The Shabushti's Book of Monasteries*, edited by Gurgis Awwad. Piscataway, NJ: Gorgias Press, 2008.
al-Shayzarī, ʿAbd al-Raḥmān ibn Naṣr, *The Book of the Islamic Market Inspector* [*Nihāyat al-rutba fī talab al-ḥisba*], translated by R. P. Buckley. Oxford: Oxford University Press, 1999.
al-Sijistānī, Isḥāq ibn Aḥmad Abū Yaʿqūb. *Kashf al-maḥjūb*, edited by Henry Corbin. Tehran: Institut franco-iranien, 1949.
al-Ṭabarī, Sulaymān ibn Jarīr, *The History of al-Ṭabarī* [*Taʾrīkh*]. *Vol. 23: Al-Manṣūr and al-Mahdī*, translated by Hugh Kennedy. Albany, NY: State University of New York Press, 1990.
Yaḥyā ibn Saʿīd al-Anṭākī. *Taʾrīkh* [*Histoire de Yahya-ibn-Saʿīd d'Antioche*], translated by I. Kratchkovsky and A. Vasiliev. *Patrologia Orientalis* 18 (1924): 699–833.
——. *Taʾrīkh* [*Histoire de Yahya-ibn-Saʿīd d'Antioche*], translated by I. Kratchkovsky and A. Vasiliev. *Patrologia Orientalis* 23 (1932): 347–520.
——. *Taʾrīkh* [*Histoire de Yahya-ibn-Saʿīd d'Antioche*], translated by I. Kratchkovsky, F. Micheau, and G. Troupeau. *Patrologia Orientalis* 47 (1997): 373–559.

MODERN SOURCES

Abel, Louis Félix-Marie and Louis-Hugues Vincent. *Jerusalem nouvelle: Fascicule 1 et 2, Aelia capitolina, le Saint-Sepulcre et le Mont des oliviers*. Paris: Librairie Victor Lecoffre, 1926.
Abu-Izzeddin, Nejla M. *The Druzes: A New Study of Their History, Faith, and Society*. Leiden: Brill, 1984.
Abu-Lughod, Janet L. *Cairo: 1001 Years of the City Victorious*. Princeton Studies on the Near East. Princeton, NJ: Princeton University Press, 1971.
Ackerman-Lieberman, Phillip. "The Muḥammadan Stipulations: Dhimmī Versions of the Pact of ʿUmar." In *Jews, Christians, and Muslims in Medieval and Early Modern Times*, 197–206. Leiden: Brill, 2014.
Aguadé, Jorge. "Abu Rakwa." In *Actas del IV Coloquio hispano-tunecino*, 9–27. Madrid: Palma de Mallorca, 1983.
Ahsan, M. M. *Social Life under the Abbasids, 170–289 AH, 786–902 AD*. Arab Background Series. London: Longman, 1979.
Akhtar, Ali Humayun. *Philosophers, Sufis, and Caliphs: Politics and Authority from Cordoba to Cairo and Baghdad*. Cambridge: Cambridge University Press, 2017.
Alexandrin, Elizabeth. "Prophetic Ascent and the Initiatory Ascent in Qāḍī al-Nuʿmān's Asās al-Taʾwīl." In *The Prophet's Ascension: Cross-Cultural Encounters with Islamic Miʿrāj Tales*, edited by Christiane Gruber and Frederick Colby, 157–71. Bloomington: Indiana University Press, 2010.
Allouche, Adel. "The Establishment of Four Chief Judgeships in Fatimid Egypt." *Journal of the American Oriental Society* 105 (1985): 317–20.

Almagro, Antonio. "The Dwellings of Madīnat al-Zahrā': A Methodological Approach." In *Revisiting Al-Andalus: Perspectives on the Material Culture of Islamic Iberia and Beyond*, edited by Glaire D. Anderson and Mariam Rosser-Owen, 1–26. Leiden: Brill, 2007.

AlSayyad, Nezar. *Cairo: Histories of a City*. Cambridge, MA: Belknap Press, 2011.

AlSayyad, Nezar, Nasser Rabbat, and Irene Bierman, eds. *Making Cairo Medieval*. Lanham, MD: Lexington Books, 2005.

Amedroz, H. F. *The Eclipse of the Abbasid Caliphate: Original Chronicles of the Fourth Islamic Century*. 7 vols. Oxford: Basil Blackwell, 1920.

Amir-Moezzi, *The Spirituality of Shi'i Islam: Beliefs and Practices*. London: Tauris, 2011.

Anderson, Glaire D. "Islamic Spaces and Diplomacy in Constantinople (Tenth to Thirteenth Centuries CE)." *Medieval Encounters* 15, no. 1 (January 1, 2009): 86–113.

——. *The Islamic Villa in Early Medieval Iberia: Architecture and Court Culture in Umayyad Cordoba*. Burlington, VT: Ashgate, 2013.

Anderson, Glaire, Corisande Fenwick, and Mariam Rosser-Owen, eds. *The Aghlabids and Their Neighbours: Art and Material Culture in 9th-Century North Africa*. Leiden: Brill, 2017.

Anderson, Glaire, and Jennifer Pruitt. "The Three Caliphates, a Comparative Approach." In *A Companion to Islamic Art and Architecture*, edited by Finbarr Barry Flood and Gülru Necipoğlu, 223–49. Blackwell Companions to Art History. Hoboken, NJ: Wiley, 2017.

Anderson, Glaire D., and Mariam Rosser-Owen, eds. *Revisiting al-Andalus: Perspectives on the Material Culture of Islamic Iberia and Beyond*. The Medieval and Early Modern Iberian World 34. Leiden: Brill, 2007.

Anglade, Elise. *Catalogues des boiseries de la section islamique, Musée du Louvre*. Paris: Ministère de la culture et de la communication, Editions de la Réunion des musées nationaux, 1988.

Arberry, Arthur John, ed. *The Koran Interpreted: A Translation*. New York: Simon and Schuster, 1996.

Assaad, S. A. *The Reign of al-Hakim bi-Amr Allah (386/996–411/1021): A Political Study*. Beirut: The Arab Institute for Research and Publishing, 1974.

Atiya, Aziz. "Abū al-Makārim." *The Coptic Encyclopedia*, edited by Aziz Atiya. New York: Macmillan, 1991.

——. *A History of Eastern Christianity*. Notre Dame, IN: University of Notre Dame Press, 1968.

——. "Ḳibṭ." In *Encyclopaedia of Islam, Second Edition*. Accessed online Apri 12, 2019. http://dx.doi.org.ezproxy.library.wisc.edu/10.1163/1573-3912_islam_SIM_4358

Auld, Sylvia. "The Minbar of al-Aqsa: Form and Function." In *Image and Meaning in Islamic Art*, edited by Robert Hillenbrand, 42–60. London: Altajir Trust, 2005.

Auth, Susan H. "Significance of Egyptian, Classical and Christian Themes in Coptic Art." In *Coptic Studies on the Threshold of a New Millennium: Proceedings of the Seventh International Congress of Coptic Studies, Leiden, August 27–September 2, 2000*, edited by Mat Immerzeel and Jacques van der Vliet, 1141–58. Leuven: Peeters, 2004.

Avner, Rita. "The Dome of the Rock in Light of the Development of Concentric Martyria in Jerusalem: Architecture and Architectural Iconography." *Muqarnas* 27 (2010): 31–49.

Avni, Gideon, and Jon Seligman. "New Excavations at the Church of the Holy Sepulchre Compound." In *One Land, Many Cultures: Archaeological Studies in Honor of Stanislao Loffreda OFM*, edited by G. Bottini, G. Claudio, L. Di Segni, and L. Chrupcala, 153–62. Jerusalem: Franciscan Printing Press, 2003.

Bacharach, Jere. *Fustat Finds: Beads, Coins, Medical Instruments, Textiles, and Other Artifacts from the Awad Collection*. Cairo: American University in Cairo Press, 2002.

——. *Islamic History through Coins: An Analysis and Catalogue of Tenth-Century Ikhshidid Coinage*. Cairo: American University in Cairo Press, 2006.

Badawy, Alexander. *Coptic Art and Archaeology: The Art of the Christian Egyptians from the Late Antique to the Middle Ages*. Cambridge, MA: MIT Press, 1978.

Baer, Eva. "Fatimid Art at the Crossroads: A Turning Point in the Artistic Concepts of Islam?" In *L'Égypte fatimide: Son art et son histoire. Actes du colloque organisé à Paris les 28, 29 et 30 mai 1998*, edited by Marianne Barrucand, 385–94. Paris: Presses de l'Université de Paris–Sorbonne, 1999.

Balard, Michel. "Notes sur le commerce entre l'Italie et l'Égypte sous les Fatimides." In *L'Égypte fatimide: Son art et son histoire. Actes du colloque organisé à Paris les 28, 29 et 30 mai 1998*, edited by Marianne Barrucand, 627–33. Paris: Presses de l'Université de Paris–Sorbonne, 1999.

Balog, Paul. "Monnaies islamiques rares fatimites et ayoubites." *BIE* 36 (1953–54): 327–45.

Bar-Asher, Meir. *Scripture and Exegesis in Early Imāmī Shiism*. Leiden: Brill, 1999.

Bareket, Elinoar. *Fustat on the Nile: The Jewish Elite in Medieval Egypt*. Leiden: Brill, 1999.

Barrucand, Marianne. "Les chapiteaux de remploi de la mosquée al-Azhar et l'émergence d'un type de chapiteau médiévale en Égypte." In *L'Égypte fatimide: Son art et son histoire. Actes du colloque organisé à Paris les 28, 29 et 30 mai 1998*. Paris: Presses de l'Université de Paris–Sorbonne, 1999.

——, ed. *L'Égypte fatimide: Son art et son histoire. Actes du colloque organisé à Paris les 28, 29 et 30 mai 1998*. Paris: Presses de l'Université de Paris–Sorbonne, 1999.

——. "Sabra al-Mansuriyya and Her Neighbors during the First Half of the Eleventh Century: Investigations into Stucco Decoration." *Muqarnas* 26 (2009): 349–76.

——. *Trésors fatimides du Caire: Exposition présenté a l'Institut du monde arabe du 28 avril au 30 août 1998*. Paris: Institut du monde arabe, 1998.

al-Bāshā, Ḥasan Maḥmūd Ḥasan. "Tabaq min al-khazaf bi-ism Ghabn mawla al-Ḥākim bi-Amr Allah," *Bulletin of the Faculty of the Arts, Cairo University* 18 (1965): 71–85.

Beckwith, J. *Coptic Sculpture 300–1300*. London: Tiranti, 1963.

Behrens-Abouseif, Doris. "The Facade of the Aqmar Mosque in the Context of Fatimid

Ceremonial." *Muqarnas* 9 (1992): 29–38.
——. *Islamic Architecture in Cairo: An Introduction. Vol. 3: Studies in Islamic Art and Architecture.* Leiden: Brill, 1989.
——. "Locations of Non-Muslim Quarters in Medieval Cairo." *Annales islamologiques* 22 (1986): 117–32.
——. *The Minarets of Cairo: Islamic Architecture from the Arab Conquest to the End of the Ottoman Empire.* London: Tauris, 2010.
Bennison, Amira. *The Great Caliphs: The Golden Age of the ʿAbbasid Caliphs.* New Haven: Yale University Press, 2010.
Bennison, Amira K., and Alison L. Gascoigne. *Cities in the Pre-Modern Islamic World: The Urban Impact of State, Society and Religion.* SOAS/Routledge Studies on the Middle East 6. London: Routledge, 2007.
Berchem, Max van. "La chaire de la mosquée d'Hébron et la martyrion de la tête de Husain à Ascalon." In *Festschrift Eduard Sachau,* 298–310. Berlin: Reimer, 1915.
——. *Matériaux pour un corpus inscriptionum arabicarum. Vol. 1: Égypte.* Cairo: Institut français d'archéologie orientale, 1894–1903.
——. *Matériaux pour un corpus inscriptionum arabicarum. Vol. 2: Syrie du Sud.* Cairo: Institut français d'archéologie orientale, 1920–27.
——. "Une mosquée du temps des Fatimites au Caire: Notice sur le Gâmi' el Goyûshi'." *Mémoires de l'Institut Egyptien* II (1889): 605–19.
——. "Notes d'archéologie arabe: Monuments et inscriptions Fatimites," *Journal Asiatique* 18 (1891): 411–95; 18 (1892): 47–86; and 19 (1892): 377–407.
Bianquis, Thierry. "ʿAbd al-Gani ibn Saʿid, un savant sunnite au service des Fatimides." Paper presented at the Actes du XXIXe Congrès international des orientalistes, Paris, 1975.
——. "Autonomous Egypt from Ibn Ṭūlūn to Kāfūr, 868–969." In *The Cambridge History of Egypt: Islamic Egypt, 640–1517,* edited by Hugh Kennedy, 86–119. Cambridge: Cambridge University Press, 1998.
——. "Une crise frumentaire dans l'Égypte fatimide." *Journal of the Economic and Social History of the Orient* 23, no. 1/2 (1980): 67–101.
——. *Damas et la Syrie sous la domination fatimide (359–486/969–1076).* 2 vols. Damascus: Institut français de Damas, 1986–89.
——. "L'espace politique des Fatimides." In *L'Égypte fatimide: Son art et son histoire. Actes du colloque organisé à Paris les 28, 29 et 30 mai 1998,* edited by Marianne Barrucand, 21–29. Paris: Presses de l'Université de Paris–Sorbonne, 1999.
——. "Al-Ḥākim bi Amr Allāh ou la folie de l'unité chez un souverain fatimide." *Les Africains* 11 (1978): 107–33.
——. "La prise de pouvoir par les Fatimides en Égypte." *Annales islamologiques* 11 (1972): 49–108.
——. "Al-Ẓāhir li-Iʿzāz Dīn Allāh." *Encylopaedia of Islam, Second Edition.* Accessed online April 12, 2019. http://dx.doi.org.ezproxy.library.wisc.edu/10.1163/1573-3912_islam_SIM_8080
Biddle, Martin. *The Tomb of Christ.* Stroud, UK: Sutton, 1999.
Bierman, Irene. "Art and Architecture in the Medieval Period." In *The Cambridge History of Egypt: Islamic Egypt, 640–1517,* edited by Hugh Kennedy, 339–74. Cambridge: Cambridge University Press, 1998.
——. "The Art of the Public Text: Medieval Islamic Rule." In *World Art: Themes of Unity in Diversity,* edited by Irving Lavin, 283–90. Acts of the XXVIth International Congress of the History of Art. University Park: Pennsylvania State University Press, 1989.
——. "Arts and Politics: The Impact of Fatimid Uses of Ṭirāz Fabrics." PhD, University of Chicago, 1980.
——. "Inscribing the City: Fatimid Cairo." In *Islamische textilkunst des mittelalters: Aktuelle probleme,* edited by Muḥammad ʿAbbās Muḥammad Sālim, 105–14. Riggisberg: Abegg-Stiftung, 1997.
——. *Writing Signs: The Fatimid Public Text.* Berkeley: University of California Press, 1998.
Blair, Sheila. "Floriated Kufic and the Fatimids." In *L'Égypte fatimide: Son art et son histoire. Actes du colloque organisé à Paris les 28, 29 et 30 mai 1998,* edited by Marianne Barrucand. Paris: Presses de l'Université de Paris–Sorbonne, 1999.
——. "What Is the Date of the Dome of the Rock?" In *Bayt al-Maqdis: ʿAbd al-Malik's Jerusalem, Part One,* edited by Julian Raby and Jeremy Johns, 59–88. Oxford: Oxford University Press, 1992.
Blair, Sheila, and Jonathan Bloom, eds. *God Is the Light of the Heavens and the Earth: Light in Islamic Art and Culture.* New Haven: Yale University Press, 2015.
——. "The Mirage of Islamic Art: Reflections on the Study of an Unwieldy Field," *Art Bulletin* 85 (March, 2003): 152–84.
Bloom, Jonathan. *Arts of the City Victorious.* New Haven: Yale University Press, 2007.
——. "The Blue Koran: An Early Fatimid Kufic Manuscript from the Maghrib." In *Les manuscrits des moyen-orient: essais de codicologie et paléographie,* edited by François Déroche, 95–99. Istanbul: Institut francais d'études anatoliennes d'Istanbul et Bibliotheque nationale, 1989.
——. "Book Review: Writing Signs: The Fatimid Public Text. Fatimid Art at the Victoria and Albert Museum." *Journal of the American Oriental Society* 120, no. 2 (2000): 271–73.
——. "Ceremonial and Sacred Space in Early Fatimid Cairo." In *Cities in the Pre-Modern Islamic World: The Urban Impact of Religion, State and Society,* edited by Amira Bennison, 96–114. London: Routledge, 2007.
——. "The Early Fatimid Blue Koran Manuscript," *Graeco-Arabica* 4 (1991): 171–77.
——. "Evanescent Meaning: The Place of Shiʿism in Fatimid Mosques." In *People of the Prophet's House: Artistic and Ritual Expressions of Shiʿi Islam,* 63–71. London: Azimuth, 2015.
——. "The Fatimids (909–1171): Their Ideology and Their Art." In *Islamische Textilkunst des Mittelalters: Aktuelle Probleme,* edited by Muḥammad ʿAbbās Muḥammad Sālim, 15–26. Riggisberg: Abegg-Stiftung, 1997.
——. "Five Fatimid Minarets in Upper Egypt." *Journal of the Society of Architectural Historians* 43 (1984): 162–67.
——. "Jerusalem in Medieval Islamic Literature." In *City of the Great King: Jerusalem from*

David to the Present, edited by Nitza Rosovsky, 205–17. Cambridge, MA: Harvard University Press 1996.
——. "The Introduction of Muqarnas into Egypt." *Muqarnas* 5 (1988): 21–28.
——. "Meaning in Early Fatimid Architecture: Islamic Art in North Africa and Egypt in the Fourth Century AH (Tenth Century AD)." PhD, Harvard University, 1980.
——. *Minaret, Symbol of Islam.* Oxford: Oxford University Press, 1989.
——. *The Minaret.* Edinburgh: Edinburgh University Press, 2013.
——. "The Mosque of al-Ḥākim in Cairo." *Muqarnas* 1 (1983): 15–36.
——. "The Mosque of the Qarafa in Cairo." *Muqarnas* 4 (1987): 7–20.
——. "Nasir Khusraw's Description of Jerusalem." In *No Tapping around Philology: A Festschrift in Honor of Wheeler McIntosh Thackston Jr.'s 70th Birthday*, edited by Korangy Alireza and Daniel J. Sheffield, 395–406. Wiesbaden: Harrassowitz Verlag, 2014.
——. "The Origins of Fatimid Art." *Muqarnas* 3 (1985): 30–38.
——. "Walled Cities in Islamic North Africa and Egypt with Particular Reference to the Fatimids (909–1171)" In *City Walls: The Urban Enceinte in Global Perspective*, edited by James D. Tracy, 219–46. Cambridge: Cambridge University Press, 2000.
Bolman, Elizabeth S., ed. *The Red Monastery Church: Beauty and Asceticism in Upper Egypt.* New Haven: Yale University Press, 2016.
Bolman, Elizabeth S. and Patrick Godeau. *Monastic Visions: Wall Paintings in the Monastery of St. Antony at the Red Sea.* New Haven: Yale University Press, 2002.
Brett, Michael. *The Fatimid Empire.* The Edinburgh History of the Islamic Empires. Edinburgh: Edinburgh University Press, 2017.
——. "Al-Karāza al-Marqusīya: The Coptic Church in the Fatimid Period." In *Egypt and Syria in the Fatimid, Ayyubid and Mamluk Eras*, edited by U. Vermeulen and J. van Steenbergen, 33–60. Leuven: Peeters, 2005.
——. "Population and Conversion to Islam in Egypt." In *Egypt and Syria in the Fatimid, Ayyubid and Mamluk Eras*, edited by U. Vermeulen and J. van Steenbergen, 1–32. Leuven: Peeters, 2005.
——. *The Rise of the Fatimids: The World of the Mediterranean and the Middle East in the Fourth Century of the Hijra, Tenth Century CE.* Leiden: Brill, 2001.
Bryer, David. "The Origins of the Druze Religion." *Der Islam* 52 and 53 (1976): 47–84; 239–64 and 5–27.
Burgoyne, Michael Hamilton. *Mamluk Jerusalem: An Architectural Study.* Blackhurst Hill, Essex: Scorpion Publishing, 1987.
Buschhausen, Helmut. "The Coptic Art of the Fatimids." In *L'Égypte fatimide: Son art et son histoire. Actes du colloque organisé à Paris les 28, 29 et 30 mai 1998*, edited by Marianne Barrucand, 549–68. Paris: Presses de l'Université de Paris–Sorbonne, 1999.
Butler, Alfred J. (Alfred Joshua). *The Ancient Coptic Churches of Egypt.* Oxford: Clarendon Press, 1970.
——. *The Arab Conquest of Egypt, and the Last Thirty Years of the Roman Dominion.* Oxford: Clarendon Press, 1978.
——. *Babylon of Egypt: A Study in the History of Old Cairo.* Oxford: Clarendon Press, 1914.
Cahen, Cl. "Buwayhids or Būyids." In *Encyclopaedia of Islam, Second Edition.* Accessed online April 15, 2019. http://dx.doi.org.ezproxy.library.wisc.edu/10.1163/1573-3912_islam_SIM_1569
Cahen, Cl., M. Talbi, R. Mantran, A. K. S Lambton, and A. S. Bazmee Ansari. "Ḥisba." In *Encyclopaedia of Islam, Second Edition.* Accessed online April 12, 2019. http://dx.doi.org.ezproxy.library.wisc.edu/10.1163/1573-3912_islam_COM_0293
Caiger-Smith, Alan. *Lustre Pottery: Technique, Tradition, and Innovation in Islam and the Western World.* London: Faber and Faber, 1985.
Canard, Marius. "Le cérémonial Fatimite et le cérémonial Byzantin." *Byzantion* 21 (1951): 355–420.
——. "La destruction de l'Église de la Résurrection par le calife Hakim et l'histoire de la descente du feu sacré." *Byzance* 35 (1955): 16–43.
——. "Djarrāḥids." In *Encyclopaedia of Islam, Second Edition.* Accessed online April 12, 2019. http://dx.doi.org.ezproxy.library.wisc.edu/10.1163/1573-3912_islam_SIM_2013
——. "Al-Hākim Bi-Amr Allāh" in *Encylopaedia of Islam, Second Edition.* Accessed online April 12, 2019. http://dx.doi.org.ezproxy.library.wisc.edu/10.1163/1573-3912_islam_SIM_2637
——. "L'impérialisme des Fatimides et leur propagande." *Annales de l'Institut d'études orientales* 6 (1942–47): 156–93.
Cannuyer, Christian. "L'intérêt pour l'Égypte pharaonique à l'époque fatimide étude sur l'Abrégé des Merveilles (*Mukhtaṣar al-'ajā'ib*)." In *L'Égypte fatimide: Son art et son histoire. Actes du colloque organisé à Paris les 28, 29 et 30 mai 1998*, edited by Marianne Barrucand, 483–96. Paris: Presses de l'Université de Paris–Sorbonne, 1999.
Capilla, Calvo, S. "El programa epigráfico de la Mezquita de Córdoba en el siglo X: Un alegato en favor de la doctrina mālikí." *Qurtuba* 5 (2000): 17–26.
——. "Justicia, misericordia y cristianismo: Una relectura de las inscriptions coránicas de la Mezquita de Córdoba en el siglo X." *Al-Qanṭara: Revista de estudios árabes* 31, no. 1 (2010): 149–87.
Capuani, Massimo. *Coptic Art and Monuments through Two Millenia.* Collegeville, MN: Liturgical Press, 2002.
Carboni, Stefano. "Glass Production in the Fatimid Lands and Beyond." In *L'Égypte fatimide: Son art et son histoire. Actes du colloque organisé à Paris les 28, 29 et 30 mai 1998*, edited by Marianne Barrucand, 403–18. Paris: Presses de l'Université de Paris–Sorbonne, 1999.
Chalmeta, P. "Al-Manṣūr." In *Encyclopaedia of Islam, Second Edition.* Accessed online April 12, 2019. http://dx.doi.org.ezproxy.library.wisc.edu/10.1163/1573-3912_islam_SIM_4936
Christie, A. H. "Fatimid Wood Carvings in the Victoria and Albert Museum." *Burlington Magazine for Connoisseurs* 46, no. 265 (1925): 184–85; 187.

Clarke, P. B. "The Ismailis: A Study of Community." *British Journal of Sociology* 27, no. 4 (1976): 484–94.

Cobb, Paul. "Book Review: Ritual, Politics and the City in Fatimid Cairo." *Journal of Near Eastern Studies* 57, no. 1 (1998): 58–59.

Cohen, Mark R. "In the Court of Yaʿqub ibn Killis: A Fragment from the Cairo Genizah." *Jewish Quarterly Review* 80, nos. 3–4 (1990): 283–314.

——. *Under Crescent and Cross: The Jews in the Middle Ages.* Princeton, NJ: Princeton University Press, 2008.

——. *The Voice of the Poor in the Middle Ages: An Anthology of Documents from the Cairo Geniza.* Princeton, NJ: Princeton University Press, 2013.

Cohen, Mark R., and A. L. Udovitch. *Jews among Arabs: Contacts and Boundaries.* Princeton, NJ: Darwin Press, 1989.

Colby, Frederick. "The Early Imami Shiʿi Narratives and Contestation over Intimate Colloquey Scenes in Muḥammad's Miʿrāj." In *The Prophet's Ascension: Cross-Cultural Encounters with Islamic Miʿrāj Tales*, edited by Christiane Gruber and Frederick Colby, 141–56. Bloomington: Indiana University Press, 2010.

Colloque international sur l'histoire du Caire, 27 mars–5 avril 1969. Cairo: Ministry of Culture of the Arab Republic of Egypt General Egyptian Book Organization, 1972.

Combe, Etienne, Jean Sauvaget, and Gaston Wiet. *Répertoire chronologique d'épigraphie arabe.* Cairo: Institut français d'archéologie orientale, 1931.

Constable, Olivia Remie. "Muslim Merchants in Andalusi International Trade." In *The Legacy of Muslim Spain*, edited by Salma Khadra Jayyusi and Manuela Marin, 759–76. Leiden: Brill, 1994.

Contadini, Anna. *Fatimid Art at the Victoria and Albert Museum.* London: V&A Publications, 1998.

——. "Fatimid Ivories within a Mediterranean Context." *Journal of the David Collection* 2 (2004): 227–47.

Cook, Michael. *Commanding Right and Forbidding Wrong in Islamic Thought.* Cambridge: Cambridge University Press, 2000.

Cooperson, Michael. "Baghdad in Rhetoric and Narrative." *Muqarnas* 13 (1996): 99–113.

Corbin, H. *Trilogie Ismaélienne.* Tehran: Department of Iranology, Institut Franco-Iranien, 1961.

Cortese, Delia. *Arabic Ismaili Manuscripts: The Zahid ʿAli Collection in the Library of the Institute of Ismaili Studies.* London: Tauris in association with the Institute of Ismaili Studies, 2003.

——. *Ismaili and Other Arabic Manuscripts: A Descriptive Catalogue of Manuscripts in the Library of the Institute of Ismaili Studies.* London: Tauris, 2000.

——. "Voices of the Silent Majority: The Transmission of Sunnī Learning in Fāṭimī Egypt." In *Jerusalem Studies in Arabic and Islam*, 345–65. Jerusalem: Magnes Press, 2012.

Cortese, Delia, and Simonetta Calderini. *Women and the Fatimids in the World of Islam.* Edinburgh: Edinburgh University Press, 2006.

Cott, Perry Blythe. *Siculo-Arabic Ivories.* Princeton, NJ: Princeton University Press, 1939.

Coüasnon, Charles. *The Church of the Holy Sepulchre in Jerusalem.* London: Oxford University Press for the British Academy, 1974.

Creswell, K. A. C. *Early Islamic Architecture: Umayyads, Early ʿAbbasids, and Tulunids.* Oxford: Clarendon Press, 1932–40.

——. *Early Muslim Architecture.* 2 vols. Oxford: Clarendon Press, 1969.

——. "The Great Salients of the Mosque of al-Hakim at Cairo," *Journal of the Royal Asiatic Society of Great Britain and Ireland* (1923): 573–84.

——. *The Muslim Architecture of Egypt.* Oxford: Clarendon Press, 1952.

Crone, Patricia. *God's Rule Government and Islam: Six Centuries of Medieval Islamic Political Thought.* New York: Columbia University Press, 2004.

Ćurčić, S. "Some Palatine Aspects of the Cappella Palatina in Palermo." *Dumbarton Oaks Papers* 41 (1987): 125–44.

Cutler, Anthony. "The Parallel Universes of Arab and Byzantine Art (with Special Reference to the Fatimid Era)." In *L'Égypte fatimide: Son art et son histoire. Actes du colloque organisé à Paris les 28, 29 et 30 mai 1998*, edited by Marianne Barrucand, 635–48. Paris: Presses de l'Université de Paris–Sorbonne, 1999.

Dadoyan, S. B. *The Fatimid Armenians: Cultural and Political Interaction in the Near East.* Leiden: Brill, 1997.

Daftary, Farhad. *Intellectual Traditions in Islam.* London: Tauris in association with the Institute of Ismaili Studies, 2000.

——. "The Ismaili Daʿwa outside the Fatimid Dawla." In *L'Égypte fatimide: Son art et son histoire. Actes du colloque organisé à Paris les 28, 29 et 30 mai 1998*, edited by Marianne Barrucand, 29–44. Paris: Presses de l'Université de Paris–Sorbonne, 1999.

——. *Ismaili Literature: A Bibliography of Sources and Studies.* London: Tauris in association with the Institute of Ismaili Studies, 2004.

——. *Ismailis in Medieval Muslim Societies.* Ismaili Heritage Series 12. London: Tauris in association with the Institute of Ismaili Studies, 2005.

——. *The Ismāʿīlīs: Their History and Doctrines.* Cambridge: Cambridge University Press, 1990.

——. *Mediaeval Ismaʿili History and Thought.* Cambridge: Cambridge University Press, 1996.

——. *A Short History of the Ismailis: Traditions of a Muslim Community.* Islamic Surveys. Edinburgh: Edinburgh University Press, 1998.

Daftary, Farhad, and Shainool Jiwa, eds. *The Fatimid Caliphate: Diversity of Traditions.* Ismaili Heritage Series 14. London: Tauris in association with the Institute of Ismaili Studies, 2018.

Davis, Stephen J. *The Early Coptic Papacy: The Egyptian Church and Its Leadership in Late Antiquity.* Cairo: American University in Cairo Press, 2004.

Denoix, Sylvie. *Décrire le Caire Fusṭāṭ-Miṣr d'après Ibn Duqmāq et Maqrīzī: L'histoire d'une partie de la ville du Caire d'après deux historiens égyptiens des XIVe–XVe siècles.* Etudes urbaines 3. Cairo: Institut français d'archéologie orientale, 1992.

Dessus-Lamare, A. "Le mushaf de la Mosquée de Cordoue et son mobilier mécanique," *Journal Asiatique* 23 (1938): 552–75.

Dodd, Erica Cruikshank. *The Frescoes of Mar Musa al-Habashi.* Toronto: Pontifical

Institute of Mediaeval Studies, 2001.
Dodd, Erica Cruikshank, and Shereen Khairallah. *The Image of the Word: A Study of Quranic Verses in Islamic Architecture.* Beirut: American University of Beirut, 1981.
Dodds, Jerilynn. *Architecture and Ideology in Early Medieval Spain.* University Park: Pennsylvania State University Press, 1990.
——. "The Great Mosque of Córdoba." In *Al-Andalus: The Art of Islamic Spain*, 11–25. New York: The Metropolitan Museum of Art, 1992.
——. "Islam, Christianity, and the Problem of Religious Art." In *Late Antique and Medieval Art of the Mediterranean World*, edited by Eva R. Hoffman, 350–66. Malden, MA: Blackwell, 2007.
Dodds, Jerrilynn Denise, María Rosa Menocal, and Abigail Balbale. *The Arts of Intimacy: Christians, Jews, and Muslims in the Making of Castilian Culture.* New Haven: Yale University Press, 2008.
Dridi, Audrey. "Christians of Fustat in the First Three Centuries of Islam: The Making of a New Society." In *A Cosmopolitan City: Muslims, Christians, and Jews in Old Cairo*, edited by Tanya Treptow and Tasha Vorderstrasse, 33–40. Chicago: Oriental Institute, 2015.
Durak, Koray. "Through an Eastern Window: Muslims in Constantinople and Constantinople in Early Islamic Sources." In *From Byzantium to Istanbul: 8000 Years of a Capital, June 5–September 4, 2010, Sabancı University, Sakıp Sabancı Museum, Istanbul*, 102–11. Istanbul: Sakıp Sabancı Museum, 2010.
Ecker, Heather. "The Great Mosque of Cordoba in the Twelfth and Thirteenth Centuries." *Muqarnas* 20 (2003): 113–41.
Ecker, Heather. *Caliphs and Kings: The Art and Influence of Islamic Spain.* Washington, DC: Arthur M. Sackler Gallery, 2004.
Ehrenkreutz, A. S. "Kāfūr." In *Encyclopaedia of Islam, Second Edition.* Accessed online April 12, 2019. http://dx.doi.org.ezproxy.library.wisc.edu/10.1163/1573-3912_islam_SIM_3781
Elad, Amikam. *Medieval Jerusalem and Islamic Worship: Holy Places, Ceremonies, Pilgrimage.* Leiden: Brill, 1995.
Eliav, Yaron Z. "The Temple Mount in Jewish and Early Christian Traditions: A New Look." In *Jerusalem: Idea and Reality*, edited by Tamar Mayer and Suleiman Mourad, 47–66. London: Routledge, 2008.
Elisséeff, N. "Ḥimṣ." In *Encyclopaedia of Islam, Second Edition.* Accessed online April 8, 2019. http://dx.doi.org.ezproxy.library.wisc.edu/10.1163/1573-3912_islam_COM_0289
Ess, Josef van. *Chiliastische Erwartungen und die Versuchung der Göttlichkeit: Der Kalif al-Hakim (386–411 H.).* Heidelberg: Carl Winter, 1977.
Ettinghausen, Richard. "The 'Bevelled Style' in the Post-Samarra Period." In *Archaeologica Orientalia in Memoriam Ernst Herzfeld*, edited by G. C. Miles, 72–83. Locust Valley, NY: Augustin, 1952.
——. "Early Realism in Islamic Art." In *Studi orientalistici in onore di Giorgio Levi della Vida*, 259–62. Rome: Roma Istituto per l'Oriente, 1956.
——. "Painting in the Fatimid Period: A Reconstruction." *Ars Islamica* 9 (1942): 112–24.
Ettinghausen, Richard, Oleg Grabar, and Marilyn Jenkins-Madina. *Islamic Art and Architecture, 650–1250.* New Haven: Yale University Press, 2001.
Evelyn-White, Hugh. *The Monasteries of the Wadi 'n Natrun.* 3 vols. New York: Arno Press, 1973.
Feliciano, Maria Judith. "Review of Arts of Intimacy." *Speculum* 85, no. 4 (2010): 395.
Fierro, Maribel. *'Abd al-Rahman III: The First Cordoban Caliph.* Oxford: Oneworld, 2005.
——. "Madinat al-Zahara', el paraíso y los Fatimíes." *Al-Qanṭara* 25, no. 2 (2004): 299–327.
——. "The Mobile Minbar in Cordoba: How the Umayyads of al-Andalus Claimed the Inheritance of the Prophet." *Jerusalem Studies in Arabic and Islam* 33 (2007): 149–68.
——. "Plants, Mary the Copt, Abraham, Donkeys and Knowledge: Again on Bāṭinism during the Umayyad Caliphate in al-Andalus." In *Differenz und Dynamik im Islam: Festschrift fur Heinz Halm*, 125–44. Würzberg: Ergon, 2012.
——. "La politica religiosa de 'Abd al-Raḥmān III." *Al-Qanṭara* 25, no. 1 (2004): 119–56.
Flood, Finbarr Barry. "Between Cult and Culture: Bamiyan, Islamic Iconoclasm, and the Museum." *Art Bulletin* 84, no. 4 (2002): 641–59.
——. "From the Prophet to Postmodernism? New World Orders and the End of Islamic Art." In *Making Art History*, edited by E. Mansfield, 31–53. London: Routledge, 2007.
——. *The Great Mosque of Damascus: Studies on the Makings of an Umayyad Visual Culture.* Leiden: Brill, 2001.
——. "Idol Breaking as Image Making in the Islamic State." *Religion and Society: Advances in Research* 7 (2016): 116–38.
——. "The Medieval Trophy as an Art Historical Trope: Coptic and Byzantine 'Altars' in Islamic Contexts." *Muqarnas* 18 (2001): 41–72.
——. *Objects of Translation: Material Culture and Medieval "Hindu-Muslim" Encounter.* Princeton, NJ: Princeton University Press, 2009.
——."Umayyad Survivals and Mamluk Revivals: Qalawunid Architecture and the Great Mosque of Damascus." *Muqarnas* 14 (1997): 57–79.
Flury, Samuel. *Die Ornamente der Ḥākim und der Azhar Moschee.* Heidelburg: Carl Winter, 1912.
Forsyth, John. "The Byzantine-Arab Chronicle (938–1034) of Yahya b. Sa'id al-Antaki." 2 vols. PhD, University of Michigan, 1977.
Frantz-Murphy, G. "A New Interpretation of the Economic History of Medieval Egypt: The Role of the Textile Industry 254-567/868–1171." *Journal of the Economic and Social History of the Orient* 24, no. 3 (1981): 274–97.
Frenkel, Yehoshua. "The Ketubba (Marriage Document) as a Source for the Study of the Economic History of the Fatimid Period." In *Egypt and Syria in the Fatimid, Ayyubid and Mamluk Era*, 33–48. Leuven: Peeters, 2001.
Freund, W. H. C. *The Rise of the Monophysite Movement: Chapters in the History of the Church in the Fifth and Sixth Centuries.* Cambridge: Cambridge University Press, 1972.

Friedmann, Yohanan. "Dhimma." In *Encyclopaedia of Islam, Third Edition*. Accessed online April 12, 2019. http://dx.doi.org.ezproxy.library.wisc.edu/10.1163/1573-3912_ei3_COM_26005

———. *Tolerance and Coercion in Islam: Interfaith Relations in the Muslim Tradition*. Cambridge: Cambridge University Press, 2006.

Fyzee, A. A. A. *The Book of Faith from the Da'ā'im al-Islām (Pillars of Islam) of al-Qāḍī al-Nu'mān b. Muḥammad al-Tamīmī*. Bombay: Nachiketa Publications, 1974.

———. *A Compendium of Fatimid Law*. Simla, India: Indian Institute of Advanced Study, 1969.

Gabra, Gawdat. *The Churches of Egypt: From the Journey of the Holy Family to the Present Day*. Cairo: American University in Cairo Press, 2007.

———, ed. *Coptic Civilization: Two Thousand Years of Christianity in Egypt*. Cairo: American University in Cairo Press, 2014.

Gabra, Gawdat, and Marianne Eaton-Krauss. *The Treasures of Coptic Art in the Coptic Museum and Churches of Old Cairo*. Cairo: American University in Cairo Press, 2006.

Gabra, Gawdat, William Lyster, Cornelis Hulsman, Stephen J. Davis, and Norbert Schiller, eds. *Be Thou There: The Holy Family's Journey in Egypt*. Cairo: American University in Cairo Press, 2001.

Gabra, Gawdat, and Tim Vivian. *Coptic Monasteries: Egypt's Monastic Art and Architecture*. Cairo: American University in Cairo Press, 2002.

Gabriele, Matthew. *An Empire of Memory: The Legend of Charlemagne, the Franks, and Jerusalem before the First Crusade*. Oxford: Oxford University Press, 2013.

Gabrieli, F., and U. Scerrato. *Gli Arabi in Italia: Cultura, contatti e tradizioni*. Milan: Libri Scheiwiller, 1979.

García-Arenal, Mercedes. *Messianism and Puritanical Reform: Mahdīs of the Muslim West*. The Medieval and Early Modern Iberian World 29. Leiden: Brill, 2006.

Garen, Sally. "Santa María de Melque and Church Construction under Muslim Rule." *Journal of the Society of Architectural Historians* 51, no. 3 (1992): 288–305.

Gayraud, Roland-Pierre. "Iṣṭabl 'Antar (Fostat) 1990: Raport de fouilles." *Annales Islamologiques* 27 (1993): 225–32.

———. "La nécropole des Fatimides à Fostat." *Dossiers d'archéologie* 9 (1998): 34–41.

———. "La Qarāfa al-Kubrā, dernière demeure des Fatimides." In *L'Égypte fatimide: Son art et son histoire. Actes du colloque organisé à Paris les 28, 29 et 30 mai 1998*, edited by Marianne Barrucand, 443–64. Paris: Presses de l'Université de Paris–Sorbonne, 1999.

Ghalib, Mustafa. *Islamic Art in Egypt, 969–1517: An Exhibition*. Cairo: Wizārat al-thaqāfah, 1969.

———. *Majmua'at rasā'il al-Kirmānī*. Beirut: Mu'assasah al-jāmi'īyah, 1987.

Gil, Moshe. *Documents of the Jewish Pious Foundations from the Cairo Geniza*. Publications of the Diaspora Research Institute 12. Leiden: Brill, 1976.

———. *A History of Palestine, 634–1099*. Cambridge: Cambridge University Press, 1992.

Glidden, H. W., and D. Thompson. "Ṭirāz Fabics in the Byzantine Collection, Dumbarton Oaks. Part One: Ṭirāz from Egypt." *Bulletin of the Asia Institute* 2 (1988): 123–33.

Goitein, Shelomo Dov. "The Exchange Rate of Gold and Silver Money in Fāṭimid and Ayyūbid Times: A Preliminary Study of the Relevant Geniza Material." *Journal of the Economic and Social History of the Orient* 8 (1965): 1–46.

———. *Jews and Arabs: Their Contacts through the Ages*. New York: Schocken Books, 1964.

———. *Letters of Medieval Jewish Traders*. Princeton, NJ: Princeton University Press, 1973.

———. "The Main Industries of the Mediterranean Area as Reflected in the Record of the Cairo Geniza." *Journal of the Economic and Social History of the Orient* 4 (1961): 168–97.

———. *A Mediterranean Society: The Jewish Communities of the Arab World as Portrayed in the Documents of the Cairo Geniza*, 6 vols. Reprint edition. Berkeley: University of California Press, 1999. First published in 1967.

———. "Petitions to Fatimid Caliphs from the Cairo Geniza." *Jewish Quarterly Review* 45 (1954): 30–38.

———. *Studies in Islamic History and Institutions*. Leiden: Brill, 1966.

———. "Urban Housing in Fāṭimid and Ayyūbid Times (as Illustrated by the Cairo Geniza Documents)." *Studia Islamica* 47 (1978): 5–23.

Goitein, S.D., and O. Grabar. "al-Ḳuds." In *Encyclopaedia of Islam, Second Edition*. Accessed online April 8, 2019.http://dx.doi.org.ezproxy.library.wisc.edu/10.1163/1573-3912_islam_COM_0535

Grabar, Oleg. *The Dome of the Rock*. Cambridge, MA: Belknap Press, 2006.

———. *The Formation of Islamic Art*. Revised and enlarged edition. New Haven: Yale University Press, 1987.

———. "Imperial and Urban Art in Islam: The Subject-Matter of Fatimid Art." In *Colloque international sur l'histoire du Caire, 27 mars–5 avril 1969*, 173–90. Cairo: Ministry of Culture of the Arab Republic of Egypt, 1972.

———, ed. *Muqarnas*. Vol. 8: K. A. C. Creswell and His Legacies (1991).

———. "Notes sur le mihrab de la Grande Mosquée de Cordoue." In *Le Mihrab*, edited by Alexandre Papadopoulo, 115–22. Leiden: Brill, 1990.

———. *The Shape of the Holy: Early Islamic Jerusalem*. Princeton, NJ: Princeton University Press, 1996.

———. "The Shared Culture of Objects." In *Byzantine Court Culture from 829 to 1204*, edited by Henry Maguire, 115–30. Washington, DC: Dumbarton Oaks, 1997.

Graham, William A. "Light in the Qur'an and Early Islamic Exegesis." In *God Is the Light of the Heavens and the Earth: Light in Islamic Art and Culture*, edited by Sheila Blair and Jonathan Bloom, 43–60. New Haven: Yale University Press, 2015.

Griffith, Sidney. *The Church in the Shadow of the Mosque: Christians and Muslims in the World of Islam*. Princeton, NJ: Princeton University Press, 2010.

———. "The Kitāb Miṣbāḥ al-'Aql of Severus Ibn al-Muqaffa': A Profile of the Christian Creed in Arabic in Tenth

Century Egypt." *Medieval Encounters* 2, no. 1 (1996): 15–42.

Grohman, Adolf. "The Origin and Development of Floriated Kufic." *Ars Orientalis* 2 (1957): 183–214.

Grossmann, Peter, and Gawdat Gabra. "Christian Architecture in Egypt." In *Coptic Civilization: Two Thousand Years of Christianity in Egypt*, edited by Gawdat Gabra, 177–93. Cairo: American University in Cairo Press, 2014.

Grube, E. J. *Cobalt and Lustre: The First Centuries of Islamic Pottery, The Nasser D. Khalili Collection of Islamic Art*. Oxford: Oxford University Press, 1994.

——. "A Drawing of Wrestlers in the Cairo Museum of Islamic Art." *Quaderni di studi arabi* 3 (1985): 89–106.

——. *Islamic Pottery of the Eighth to the Fifteenth Centuries in the Keir Collection*. London: Faber and Faber, 1976.

——. "Fatimid or Not Fatimid? That Is the Question: Some Notes on Two Dishes in the Treasury of San Marco in Venice." In *Facts and Artefacts in the Islamic World: Festschrift for Jens Kroger on His 65th Birthday*, edited by Annette Hagedorn, 13–19. Leiden: Brill, 2007.

——. "Fostat Fragments." In *Islamic Painting and the Arts of the Book*, edited by B. W. Robinson, 23–66. London: Faber and Faber, 1976.

——. *Further Studies in Islamic Painting*. London: Pindar Press, 2003.

——. "Realism or Formalism: Notes on Some Fatimid Lustre-Painted Ceramic Vessels." In *Studi in onore di Francesco Gabrieli nel suo ottantesimo compleanno*, 423–32. Rome: Università di Roma, 1985.

——. *Studies in Islamic Painting*. London: Pindar Press, 1995.

——. "Studies in the Survival and Continuity of Pre-Muslim Traditions in Egyptian-Islamic Art." *Journal of the American Research Center in Egypt* 1 (1962): 75–102.

——. "Three Miniatures from Fustat in The Metropolitan Museum of Art in New York." *Ars Orientalis* 5 (1963): 89–95.

Goldhizer, J., C. van Arendock, and A. S. Triton. "Ahl al-Bayt." In *Encyclopaedia of Islam*, Second Edition. Accessed online April 9, 2019. http://dx.doi.org.ezproxy.library.wisc.edu/10.1163/1573-3912_islam_SIM_0378

Gruber, Christiane J., and Frederick Stephen Colby, eds. *The Prophet's Ascension: Cross-Cultural Encounters with the Islamic Mi'rāj Tales*. Bloomington: Indiana University Press, 2010.

Guidetti, Mattia. *In the Shadow of the Church: The Building of Mosques in Early Medieval Syria*. Arts and Archaeology of the Islamic World 8. Leiden: Brill, 2017.

Haase, Claus-Peter. "Some Aspects of Fatimid Calligraphy on Textiles." In *L'Égypte fatimide: Son art et son histoire. Actes du colloque organisé à Paris les 28, 29 et 30 mai 1998*, edited by Marianne Barrucand, 403–18. Paris: Presses de l'Université de Paris–Sorbonne, 1999.

Ḥabīb, Ra'ūf. *The Coptic Museum: A General Guide*. Cairo: General Organization for Government Printing Offices, 1967.

Halm, Heinz. "Le destin de la princess Sitt al-Mulk." In *L'Égypte fatimide: Son art et son histoire. Actes du colloque organisé à Paris les 28, 29 et 30 mai 1998*, edited by Marianne Barrucand, 69–72. Paris: Presses de l'Université de Paris–Sorbonne, 1999.

——. *The Empire of the Mahdi: The Rise of the Fatimids*. Leiden: Brill, 1996.

——. *The Fatimids and Their Traditions of Learning*. London: Tauris, 1997.

——. "The Isma'ili Oath of Allegiance ('ahd) and the 'Sessions of Wisdom' (majālis al-ḥikma) in Fatimid Times." In *Mediaeval Isma'ili History and Thought*, 91–116. Cambridge: Cambridge University Press, 1996.

——. *Die Kalifen von Kairo: Die Fāṭimiden in Ägypten, 973–1074*. Munich: Verlag C. H. Beck, 2003.

——. "Nachtrichten zu Bauten der Aglabiden und Fatimiden in Libyen und Tunesien." *Die Welt des Orients* 23 (1992): 129–57.

——. *Das Reich des Mahdi: Der Aufstieg der Fatimiden*. Munich: Beck, 1991.

——. "Der Treuhänder Gottes: Die Edikte des Kalifen al-Ḥākim." *Der Islam* 63 (1986): 11–72.

Hamdani, Abbas. "Urban Violence at Baghdad in the Rivalry between the Abbasid and Fatimid Caliphates." In *Ismaili and Fatimid Studies in Honor of Paul E. Walker*, 197–219. Chicago: Middle East Documentation Center, 2010.

Hamdani, Sumaiya. *Between Revolution and State: The Path to Fatimid Statehood*. London: Tauris, 2006.

Hamilton, R. W. *The Structural History of the Aqsa Mosque*. Oxford: Oxford University Press, 1949.

Hampikian, Nairy, and Monique Cyran. "Recent Discoveries Concerning the Fatimid Palaces Uncovered during the Conservation Works on Parts of Al-Ṣāliḥiyya Complex." In *L'Égypte fatimide: Son art et son histoire*, edited by Marianne Barrucand, 639–63. Paris: Presses de l'Université de Paris–Sorbonne, 1999.

Hanne, Eric. *Putting the Caliph in His Place: Power, Authority and the Late Abbasid Caliphate*. Madison, NJ: Fairleigh Dickinson University Press, 2007.

Harmanşah, Ömür. "ISIS, Heritage, and the Spectacles of Destruction in the Global Media." *Near Eastern Archaeology* 78, no. 3 (2015): 170–77.

Hasson, Isaac. "Muslim Literature in Praise of Jerusalem: Faḍā'il Bayt al-Maqdis." In *The Jerusalem Cathedra*, edited by Lee Levine, 3 vols., 1:168–84. Jerusalem: Yad Izhak Ben-Zvi Institute, 1981.

Hasson, Izhak. "The Muslim View of Jerusalem—The Qur'ān and Ḥadīth." In *The History of Jerusalem: The Early Muslim Period 683–1099*, edited by Joshua Prawer and Haggai Ben-Shammai, 349–85. New York: New York University Press, 1996.

Hawary, H., H. Rached, and G. Wiet. *Catalogue général du musée arabe du Caire: Stèles funéraires*. Cairo: l'Institut français d'archéologie orientale, 1932.

Heijer, Johannes den. "Considérations sur les communautés chrétiennes en Égypte fatimide: L'état et l'église sous le vizirat de Badr al-Jamālī (1074–1094)." In *L'Égypte fatimide: Son art et son histoire. Actes du colloque organisé à Paris les 28, 29 et 30 mai 1998*, edited by Marianne Barrucand, 569–78. Paris: Presses de l'Université de Paris–Sorbonne, 1999.

——. "Coptic Historiography in the Fāṭimid, Ayyūbid and Early Mamlūk Periods." *Medieval Encounters* 2, no. 1 (1996): 67–98.

——. *Mawhub ibn Mansur ibn Mufarrig et l'historiographie copto-arabe: Étude sur la composition de l'histoire des patriarches d'Alexandrie*. Corpus Scriptorum Christianorum Orientalium 513. Leuven: Peeters, 1989.

——. "Relations between Copts and Syrians in the Light of Recent Discoveries at Dayr as-Suryān." In *Coptic Studies on the Threshold of a New Millenium: Proceedings of the Seventh International Congress of Coptic Studies, Leiden, August 27–September 2, 2000*, 923–38. Leuven: Peeters, 2004.

Heijer, Johannes den, Yaacov Lev, and Mark Swanson. "The Fatimid Empire and Its Population." *Medieval Encounters* 21, nos. 4–5 (2015): 323–44.

——. "Non-Muslim Communities in Fatimid Egypt (10th–12th centuries CE)." *Medieval Encounters* 21, nos. 4–5 (2015): 319–21.

Herz Bey, Max. *Catalogue of the National Museum of Arab Art*, edited by Stanley Lane-Poole. London: Bernard Quaritch, 1896.

Hijri, Zulfikar, and Farhad Daftary. *The Ismailis: An Illustrated History*. London: Azimuth Editions in association with the Institute of Ismaili Studies, 2008.

Hillenbrand, Carole. *The Crusades: Islamic Perspectives*. Edinburgh: Edinburgh University Press, 1999.

Hillenbrand, Robert. "The Ayyubid Aqsa: Decorative Aspects." In *Ayyubid Jerusalem 1187–1250: An Architectural and Archaeological Study*, edited by Mahmoud Hawari, 301–26. Oxford: Archaeopress, 2007.

——. *Islamic Architecture: Form, Function, and Meaning*. New York: Columbia University Press, 1994.

——. "Medieval Córdoba as a Cultural Centre." In *The Legacy of Muslim Spain*, 1:112–35. Leiden: Brill, 1994.

——. "'The Ornament of the World': Medieval Córdoba as a Cultural Centre." In *Islam in the West: Critical Concepts in Islamic Studies. Volume II: Religion and Culture*, edited by David Westerlund and Ingvar Svanberg, 313–37. London: Routledge, 2011.

Hodgson, M. G. S., M. C. Şehabeddin Tekindağ, and M. Tayyib Gökbilgin. "Durūz" in *Encyclopaedia of Islam, Second Edition*. Accessed online May 17, 2019. http://dx.doi.org.ezproxy.library.wisc.edu/10.1163/1573-3912_islam_COM_0198

Hoffman, Eva. "Between East and West: The Wall Paintings of Samarra and the Construction of Abbasid Princely Culture." *Muqarnas* 25 (2008): 107–32.

——. "A Fatimid Book Cover: Framing and Re-Framing Cultural Identity in the Medieval Mediterranean World." In *L'Égypte fatimide: Son art et son histoire. Actes du colloque organisé à Paris les 28, 29 et 30 mai 1998*, edited by Marianne Barrucand, 403–18. Paris: Presses de l'Université de Paris–Sorbonne, 1999.

——, ed. *Late Antique and Medieval Art of the Mediterranean World*. Malden, MA: Blackwell, 2007.

——. "Pathways of Portability: Islamic and Christian Interchange from the Tenth to Twelfth Century." *Art History* 24, no. 1 (February 2001): 17–50.

——. "Translating Image and Text in the Medieval Mediterranean World between the Tenth and Thirteenth Centuries." In *Medieval Encounters* 18 nos. 4–5 (2012): 584–623.

Hunt, Lucy-Anne. *Byzantium, Eastern Christendom and Islam: Art at the Crossroads of the Medieval Mediterranean*. London: Pindar Press, 1998.

——. "Churches of Old Cairo and Mosques of al-Qāhira: A Case of Christian-Muslim Interchange." In *Byzantium, Eastern Christendom and Islam: Art at the Crossroads of the Medieval Mediterranean*, vol. 1, edited by Lucy-Anne Hunt, 319–42. London: Pindar Press, 1998.

——. "Stuccowork at the Monastery of the Syrians in the Wādī Naṭrūn: Iraqi-Egyptian Artistic Contact in the ʿAbbasid Period." In *Christians at the Heart of Islamic Rule: Church Life and Scholarship in ʿAbbasid Iraq*, edited by David Thomas, 93–127. Leiden: Brill, 2003.

Huntington, Samuel. *The Clash of Civilizations?: The Debate*. New York: Foreign Affairs, 1996.

Husayn, M. K. *Ṭaʾifat al-durūz*. Cairo: Dār al-Maʿārif, 1962.

Ivanow, W. *Ismaili Tradition Concerning the Rise of the Fatimids*. Oxford: Oxford University Press, 1942.

——. "The Organization of the Fatimid Propaganda." *Journal of the Bombay Branch of the Royal Asiatic Society* 15 (1939): 1–35.

Jacoby, David. "Bishop Gunther of Bamberg, Byzantium and Christian Pilgrimage to the Holy Land in the Eleventh Century." In *Zwischen Polis, Provinz und Peripherie: Beitriige zur Byzantinischen Geschichte und Kultur*, edited by Lars Hoffmann. Wiesbaden: Harrassowitz Verlag, 2005.

Jarrar, Sabri. "Al-Maqrizi's Reinvention of Egyptian Historiography through Architectural History." In *The Cairo Heritage: Essays in Honor of Laila Ali Ibrahim*, 31–54. Cairo: The American University in Cairo Press, 2000.

Jenkins, Marilyn. "Early Medieval Islamic Pottery: The Eleventh Century Reconsidered." *Muqarnas* 9 (1992): 56–66.

——. "An Eleventh-Century Woodcarving from a Cairo Nunnery." In *Islamic Art in The Metropolitan Museum of Art*, edited by Richard Ettinghausen, 227–40. New York: The Metropolitan Museum of Art, 1972.

——. "Fatimid Decorative Arts: The Picture the Sources Paint." In *L'Égypte fatimide: Son art et son histoire. Actes du colloque organisé à Paris les 28, 29 et 30 mai 1998*, edited by Marianne Barrucand, 421–27. Paris: Presses de l'Université de Paris–Sorbonne, 1999.

——. "Muslim: An Early Fatimid Ceramist." *The Metropolitan Museum of Art Bulletin* 26, no. 9 (1968): 359–69.

——. "Saʿd: Content and Context." In *Content and Context of Visual Arts in the Islamic World*, edited by Priscilla P. Soucek. University Park: Pennsylvania State University Press, 1988.

——. "Western Islamic Influences on Fatimid Egyptian Iconography." *Kunst des Orients* (1965): 91–107.

Jirjis, Majdi. *The Emergence of the Modern Coptic Papacy: The Egyptian Church and Its Leadership from the Ottoman Period to the Present. Vol. 3: Popes of Egypt.*

Cairo: American University in Cairo Press, 2011.
Jiwa, Shainool. "The Baghdad Manifesto (402/1011): A Re-Examination of Fatimid-Abbasid Rivalry." Accessed online April 13, 2019. https://iis.ac.uk/academic-article/baghdad-manifesto-40-1011-re-examination-fatimid-abbasid-rivalry-0
——. *The Fatimids: 1. The Rise of a Muslim Empire.* World of Islam. London: Tauris in association with the Institute of Ismaili Studies, 2018.
Johns, Jeremy. *Arabic Administration in Norman Sicily: The Royal Diwan.* Cambridge: Cambridge University Press, 2002.
——. "Archaeology and the History of Early Islam: The First Seventy Years." *Journal of the Economic and Social History of the Orient* 46 (2003): 411–36.
——. "A Tale of Two Ceilings: The Capella Palatina in Palermo and the Mouchroutas in Constantinople." In *Art, Trade, and Culture in the Islamic World and Beyond,* edited by Alison Ohta, J. M. Rogers, and Rosalind Wade Haddon, 58–73. London: Gingko Library, 2016.
Kaplony, Andreas. *The Ḥaram of Jerusalem, 324–1099: Temple, Friday Mosque, Area of Spiritual Power.* Stuttgart: Steiner, 2002.
——. "Manifestations of Private Piety: Muslims, Christians, and Jews in Fatimid Jerusalem." In *Governing the Holy City,* edited by J. Pahlitsch and Lorenz Korn. Wiesbaden: Reichert, 2004.
Kennedy, Hugh. "Egypt as a Province in the Islamic Caliphate, 641–868." In *The Cambridge History of Egypt, I: Islamic Egypt 640–1517,* edited by Carl Petry. Cambridge: Cambridge University Press, 2008.
——. "The Late Abbasid Pattern." In *The New Cambridge History of Islam. Volume 1: The Formation of the Islamic World, Sixth to Eleventh Centuries,* edited by C. F. Robinson, 360–93. Cambridge: Cambridge University Press, 2010.
Khemir, S. "The Palace of Sitt al-Mulk and Fāṭimid Imagery." PhD, School of Oriental and African Studies (University of London), 1990.
Khoury, Nuha. "The Meaning of the Great Mosque of Cordoba in the Tenth Century." *Muqarnas* 13 (1996): 80–98.
Khs-Burmester, O. H. E. *A Guide to the Ancient Coptic Churches of Cairo.* Giza: Société d'archaeologie copte, 1955.
Kister, M. J. "'You Shall Only Set Out for Three Mosques': A Study of an Early Tradition." *Le Muséon* 82 (1969): 173–96.
——. *Rāḥat al-ʿaql,* edited by M. Kamil Hussein and M. Mustafa Hilmy. Cairo: Dar al-Fiqr, 1953.
Koerner, J. "The Icon as Iconoclash." In *Iconoclash: Behind the Image. Wars in Science, Religion, and Art,* 164–213. Cambridge, MA: MIT Press, 2002.
Kraemer, Joel. "A Jewish Cult of the Saints in Fāṭimid Egypt." In *L'Égypte fatimide: Son art et son histoire. Actes du colloque organisé à Paris les 28, 29 et 30 mai 1998,* edited by Marianne Barrucand, 579–601. Paris: Presses de l'Université de Paris–Sorbonne, 1999.
Kubiak, Wladyslaw. *Al-Fusṭāṭ: Its Foundation and Early Urban Development.* Cairo: American University in Cairo Press, 1987.
Kubiak, Wladyslaw, and George Scanlon. "Fusṭāṭ Expedition: Preliminary Report, 1966." *Journal of the American Research Center in Egypt* 10 (1973): 11–25.
——. "Fusṭāṭ Expedition: Preliminary Report, 1971: Part I." *Journal of the American Research Center in Egypt* 16 (1979): 103–24.
——. "Fusṭāṭ Expedition: Preliminary Report, 1971: Part II." *Journal of the American Research Center in Egypt* 27 (1980): 77–96.
Kühnel, E., and L. Bellinger. *Catalogue of Dated Tiraz Fabrics: Umayyad, ʿAbbasid, Fatimid.* Washington, DC: National Publishing Company, 1952.
Lamm, C. J. "Fatimid Woodwork, Its Style and Chronology." *Bulletin de l'Institut d'Égypte* 18 (1935): 59–91.
Lane-Poole, Stanley. *The Art of the Saracens in Egypt.* Reprint edition. Lahore: Al-Biruni, 1976. First published in 1888 by Librairie Byblos.
——. *Cairo: Sketches of Its History, Monuments and Social Life.* New York: Arno Press, 1892.
——. *A History of Egypt in the Middle Ages.* London: Methuen, 1925.
Lassner, Jacob. *The Shaping of Abbasid Rule.* Princeton, NJ: Princeton University Press, 1980.
Leisten, Thomas. *Architektur für Tote: Bestattung in architektonischem Kontext in den Kernländern der islamischen Welt zwischen 3./9. und 6./12.* Jahrhundert. Berlin: Reimer, 1998.
——. "Dynastic Tomb or Private Mausolea: Observations on the Concept of Funerary Structures of the Fāṭimid and ʿAbbāsid Caliphs." In *L'Égypte fatimide: Son art et son histoire. Actes du colloque organisé à Paris les 28, 29 et 30 mai 1998,* edited by Marianne Barrucand, 465–79. Paris: Presses de l'Université de Paris–Sorbonne, 1999.
——. *Excavation of Samarra.* Mainz am Rhein: Von Zabern, 2003.
Leroy, Jules. *Les manuscrits coptes et coptes-arabes illustrés.* Paris: Geuthner, 1974.
——. *Les peintures des couvents du Désert d'Esna.* Cairo: Institut français d'archéologie orientale, 1975.
Lester, Ayala, Yael D. Arnon, and Rachel Polak. "The Fatimid Hoard from Caesarea: A Preliminary Report." In *L'Égypte fatimide: Son art et son histoire. Actes du colloque organisé à Paris les 28, 29 et 30 mai 1998,* edited by Marianne Barrucand. Paris: Presses de l'Université de Paris–Sorbonne, 1999.
Le Strange, G. *Palestine under the Moslems.* London: Alexander P. Watt, 1890.
Lev, Yaacov. "Aspects of the Egyptian Society in the Fatimid Period." In *Egypt and Syria in the Fatimid, Ayyubid, and Mamluk Eras,* 1–32. Leuven: Peeters, 2001.
——. "Coptic Rebellions and the Islamization of Medieval Egypt (8th–10th Century): Medieval and Modern Perceptions." *Jerusalem Studies in Arabic and Islam* 39 (2012): 303–44.
——. "The Fatimid Caliphs, the Copts, and the Coptic Church." *Medieval Encounters* 21, nos. 4–5 (2015): 390–410.
——. "The Fāṭimid Imposition of Ismāʿīlism on Egypt (358–86/969–96)." *Zeitschrift der Deutschen Morgenländischen Gesellschaft* 138, no. 2 (1988): 313–25.
——. "The Fatimid Princess Sitt

al-Mulk." *Journal of Semitic Studies* 32 (1987): 237–49.

——. "The Faṭimid Vizier Yaʿqub Ibn Killis and the Beginning of the Fatimid Administration in Egypt." *Der Islam* 58, no. 2 (1981): 237–49.

——. "From Revolutionary Violence to State Violence: The Fāṭimids (297–567/909–1171)." In *Public Violence in Islamic Societies: Power, Discipline, and the Construction of the Public Sphere, 7th–19th Centuries CE*, edited by Christian Lange and Maribel Fierro, 67–86. Edinburgh: Edinburgh University Press, 2009.

——. "Persecutions and Conversion to Islam in Eleventh Century Egypt." *Asian and African Studies* 22 (1988): 73–91.

——. *State and Society in Fatimid Egypt*. Arab History and Civilization, Studies and Texts. Leiden: Brill, 1991.

——. "Wāsiṭa." In *Encyclopaedia of Islam, Second Edition*. Accessed online April 12, 2019. http://dx.doi.org.ezproxy.library.wisc.edu/10.1163/1573-3912_islam_SIM_7887

Lévi-Provençal, E. *Inscriptions arabes d'Espagne*. Leiden: Brill, 1931.

Levy-Rubin, Milka. *Non-Muslims in the Early Islamic Empire*. Cambridge, UK: Cambridge University Press, 2011.

Lewis, Bernard. "The Roots of Muslim Rage." *Atlantic* (September 1990): 47–60.

Lézine, Alexandre. *Architecture de l'Ifriqiya: Recherches sur les monuments aghlabides*. Paris: Klincksieck, 1966.

——. *Mahdiya: Recherches d'archéologie islamique*. Paris: Klincksieck, 1965.

Madelung, Wilfred. "Abū Yaʿqūb al-Sijistānī and the Seven Faculties of the Intellect." In *Mediaeval Ismaʿili History and Thought*, edited by Farhad Daftary, 85–90. Cambridge: Cambridge University Press, 1996.

——. "The Fatimids and the Qarmaṭīs of Baḥrayn." In *Mediaeval Ismaʿili History and Thought*, edited by Farhad Daftary, 21–74. Cambridge: Cambridge University Press, 1996.

Mahfoudh, Faouzi. "La grande mosquée de Mahdiya et son influence sur l'architecture médiévale Ifriqiyenne." In *L'Égypte fatimide: Son art et son histoire. Actes du colloque organisé à Paris les 28, 29 et 30 mai 1998*, edited by Marianne Barrucand, 127–40. Paris: Presses de l'Université de Paris–Sorbonne, 1999.

Makdisi, George. *History and Politics in Eleventh Century Baghdad*. Aldershot, UK: Variorum, 1990.

——. *Ibn ʿAqīl et la résurgence de l'Islam traditionaliste au XIe siècle*. Damas: Institut français de Damas, 1963.

Mann, Jacob. *The Jews in Egypt and in Palestine under the Fatimid Caliphs*. New York: Ktav Publishing, 1970.

Mann, Vivian B., Thomas F. Glick, and Jerrilynn D. Dodds. *Convivencia: Jews, Muslims, and Christians in Medieval Spain*. New York: Braziller in association with the Jewish Museum, 1992.

Mansouri, Mohammed-Taher. "Juifs et Chrétiens dans le Maghreb fatimide (909–969)." In *L'Égypte fatimide: Son art et son histoire. Actes du colloque organisé à Paris les 28, 29 et 30 mai 1998*, edited by Marianne Barrucand, 603–11. Paris: Presses de l'Université de Paris–Sorbonne, 1999.

Manzano Moreno, E. "The Iberian Peninsula and North Africa." In *The New Cambridge History of Islam. Volume 1: The Formation of the Islamic World: Sixth to Eleventh Centuries*, edited by C. F. Robinson, 581–621. Cambridge: Cambridge University Press. 2010.

Marçais, Georges. *Architecture musulmane d'occident*. Paris: Arts et metiers graphiques, 1954.

Marçais, G., and Lucien Golvin. *La grande mosquée de Sfax*. Tunis: Institut national d'archeologie et arts, 1960.

Marzouk, M. A. "The Earliest Fatimid Textile (Tiraz al-Mansuriya)." *Bulletin of the Faculty of Arts, Alexandria University* 11 (1957), 37–56.

Mazot, Sibylle. "L'architecture d'influence nord-africaine a Palerme." In *L'Égypte fatimide: Son art et son histoire. Actes du colloque organisé à Paris les 28, 29 et 30 mai 1998*, edited by Marianne Barrucand, 665–79. Paris: Presses de l'Université de Paris–Sorbonne, 1999.

Medieval Encounters 21, nos. 4–5: Non-Muslim Communities in Fatimid Egypt (10th–12th centuries) (2015).

Meinecke-Berg, Viktoria. "Fatimid Painting: On Tradition and Style. The Workshop of Muslim." In *L'Égypte fatimide: Son art et son histoire. Actes du colloque organisé à Paris les 28, 29 et 30 mai 1998*, edited by Marianne Barrucand, 349–58. Paris: Presses de l'Université de Paris–Sorbonne, 1999.

Melikian-Chirvani, Assadullah Souren, and Hirmer Verlag, eds. *The World of the Fatimids*. Toronto: Aga Khan Museum in association with the Institute of Ismaili Studies and Hirmer Verlag, 2018.

Menocal, María Rosa. *The Ornament of the World: How Muslims, Jews, and Christians Created a Culture of Tolerance in Medieval Spain*. Boston: Little, Brown, 2002.

Meri, Josef W. *The Cult of Saints among Muslims and Jews in Medieval Syria*. Oxford: Oxford University Press, 2002.

Micheau, F. "Baghdad in the Abbasid Era: A Cosmopolitan and Multi-Confessional Capital." In *The City in the Islamic World Handbuch der Orientalistik: Erste Abteilung, Nahe und der Mittlere Osten*, edited by R. Holod, S. K. Jayyusi, A. Petruccioli, and A. Raymond, 221–45. Leiden: Brill, 2008.

Mikhail, Maged S. A. *From Byzantine to Islamic Egypt: Religion, Identity and Politics after the Arab Conquest*. London: Tauris, 2016.

Miles, George Carpenter. *Fāṭimid Coins in the Collections of the University Museum, Philadelphia, and the American Numismatic Society*. New York: American Numismatic Society, 1951.

Milstein, Rachel. "Hebrew Book Illumination in the Fatimid Era." In *Late Antique and Medieval Art of the Mediterranean World*, edited by Eva Rose F. Hoffman. Blackwell Anthologies in Art History 5. Malden, MA: Blackwell, 2007.

Milwright, Marcus. *The Dome of the Rock and Its Umayyad Inscriptions*. Edinburgh: Edinburgh University Press, 2016.

Monneret de Villard, Ugo. *La necropoli musulmana di Aswan*. Cairo: Institut français d'archéologie orientale, 1930.

Morelon, Régis. "Un aspect de l'astronomie sous les

Fatimides: L'importance d'Ibn al-Haytham dans l'histoire de l'astronomie arabe." In *L'Égypte fatimide: Son art et son histoire. Actes du colloque organisé à Paris les 28, 29 et 30 mai 1998*, edited by Marianne Barrucand, 519–26. Paris: Presses de l'Université de Paris–Sorbonne, 1999.

Morris, Colin. *The Sepulchre of Christ and the Medieval West from the Beginning to 1600*. Oxford: Oxford University Press, 2005.

Mostafa, Heba. "The Early Mosque Revisited: Introduction of the Minbar and the Maqsura." *Muqarnas* 33 (2016): 1–16.

Mottahedeh, Roy. *Loyalty and Leadership in an Early Islamic Society*. London: Tauris, 2001.

Mourad, Suleiman. "A Note on the Origin of Faḍā'il Bayt al-Maqdis Compilations." *Al-Abhath* 44 (1996): 31–38.

———. "The Symbolism of Jerusalem in Early Islam." In *Jerusalem: Idea and Reality*, edited by Tamar Mayer and Suleiman Mourad, 86–102. London: Routledge, 2008.

Mouton, Jean-Michel. "La présence chrétienne au Sinaï à l'époque fatimide." In *L'Égypte fatimide: Son art et son histoire. Actes du colloque organisé à Paris les 28, 29 et 30 mai 1998*, edited by Marianne Barrucand, 613–24. Paris: Presses de l'Université de Paris–Sorbonne, 1999.

Mujir al-Din. *Histoire de Jérusalem et d'Hebron*, translated by Henry Sauvaire. Paris: Laroux, 1876.

Mulder, Stephennie. "The Mausoleum of Imam al-Shafi'i." *Muqarnas* 23 (2006): 14–46.

———. "Seeing the Light: Enacting the Divine at Three Medieval Syrian Shrines." In *Envisioning Islamic Architecture: Essays Honoring Renata Holod*, edited by David Roxburgh, 89–109. Leiden: Brill, 2014.

———. *The Shrines of the 'Alids in Medieval Syria: Sunnis, Shi'is and the Architecture of Coexistence*. Edinburgh: Edinburgh University Press, 2014.

Nanji, Azim. "Nāṣir-i Khusraw." In *Encyclopaedia of Islam, Second Edition*. Accessed online April 12, 2019. http://dx.doi.org.ezproxy.library.wisc.edu/10.1163/1573-3912_islam_SIM_5827

———. "Portraits of Self and Others: Isma'ili Perspectives on the History of Religions." In *Mediaeval Isma'ili History and Thought*, edited by Farhad Daftary, 153–60. Cambridge: Cambridge University Press, 1996.

Necipoğlu, Gülru. "The Dome of the Rock as Palimpsest: 'Abd al-Malik's Grand Narrative and Sultan Süleyman's Glosses." *Muqarnas* 25 (2008): 17–105.

———. *The Topkapı Scroll: Geometry and Ornament in Islamic Architecture: Topkapı Palace Museum Library MS H. 1956*. Sketchbooks and Albums. Santa Monica, CA: Getty Center for the History of Art and the Humanities, 1995.

Nicol, Norman D. *A Corpus of Fatimid Coins*. Trieste: Bernardi, 2006.

Nieuwenhuyse, Stijn van. "The Uprising of Abū Rakwa and the Bedouins against the Fāṭimids." In *Les lieux de culte en Orient: Jacques Thiry in honorem*, 245–64. Brussels: Bruxelles centre d'histoire des religions, 2003.

Nirenberg, David. *Communities of Violence: Persecution of Minorities in the Middle Ages*. Princeton, NJ: Princeton University Press, 2015.

Northedge, A. *The Historical Topography of Samarra*. London: British School of Archaeology in Iraq, 2005.

Obeid, Anis. *The Druze and Their Faith in Tawhid*. Syracuse, NY: Syracuse University Press, 2006.

O'Kane, Bernard, ed. *Creswell Photographs Re-Examined: New Perspectives on Islamic Architecture*. Cairo: American University in Cairo Press, 2009.

———. "The Egyptian Art of Tiraz in Fatimid Times." In *The World of the Fatimids*, edited by Assadullah Souren Melikian-Chirvani, 178–89. Toronto: Aga Khan Museum in association with the Institute of Ismaili Studies and Hirmer, 2018.

———. "Monumental Calligraphy in Fatimid Egypt." In *The World of the Fatimids*, edited by Assadullah Souren Melikian-Chirvani, 142–59. Toronto: Aga Khan Museum in association with the Institute of Ismaili Studies and Hirmer, 2018.

———. *The Mosques of Egypt*. Cairo: American University in Cairo Press, 2016.

———. *The Treasures of Islamic Art in the Museums of Cairo*. Cairo: American University in Cairo Press, 2006.

———. "The Ziyada of the Mosque of al-Hakim and the Development of the Ziyada in Islamic Architecture." In *L'Égypte fatimide: Son art et son histoire*, edited by Marianne Barrucand, 141–58. Paris: Presses de l'Université de Paris–Sorbonne, 1999.

O'Leary, De Lacy. *A Short History of the Fatimid Khalifate*. London: Kegan Paul, Trench, Trübner, 1923.

117th Pope and Patriarch of Alexandria and the See of St. Mark. *The Biography of Saint Samaan the Shoemaker "the Tanner" Mattaos; Bishop and Abbot of the Syrian Monastery*. Cairo: Church of Saint Samaan the Tanner in Mokattam, 1994.

Ousterhout, Robert. "Rebuilding the Temple: Constantine Monomachus and the Holy Sepulchre." *Journal of the Society of Architectural Historians* 48, no. 1 (March 1989): 66–78.

Pauty, Edmond. *Bois sculptés d'églises coptes (époque fatimide)*. Cairo: Institut français d'archéologie orientale, 1930.

———. *Catalogue général du Musée arabe du Caire: Les bois sculptés jusqu'à l'époque Ayyoubide*. Cairo: Institut français d'archéologie orientale, 1931.

———. *Les palais et les maisons d'époque musulmane au Caire*. Cairo: Institut français d'archéologie orientale, 1933.

Perlman, M. "Ghiyār." In *Encyclopaedia of Islam, Second Edition*. Accessed online April 10, 2019. http://dx.doi.org.ezproxy.library.wisc.edu/10.1163/1573-3912_islam_SIM_2503

Peters, F. E. *Jerusalem: The Holy City in the Eyes of Chroniclers, Visitors, Pilgrims, and Prophets from the Days of Abraham to the Beginnings of Modern Times*. Princeton, NJ: Princeton University Press, 1985.

Philon, H. *Early Islamic Ceramics, Benaki Museum Athens, Ninth to Late Twelfth Centuries*. London: Islamic Art Publications, 1980.

Poonawala, Ismail. "Ismā'īlī Ta'wīl of the Qur'ān." In *Approaches to the History of the*

Interpretation of the Qur'an, 199–222. Oxford: Clarendon Press, 1988.

——. "Al-Qāḍī al-Nu'mān and Isma'ili Jurisprudence." In *Mediaeval Isma'ili History and Thought*, edited by Farhad Daftary, 117–45. Cambridge: Cambridge University Press, 1996.

Prawer, Joshua, and Haggai Ben-Shammai, eds. *The History of Jerusalem: The Early Muslim Period, 638–1099*. New York: New York University Press, 1996.

Pruitt, Jennifer. "Fatimid Architectural Patronage and Changing Sectarian Identities (969–1021)." PhD, Harvard University, 2009.

——. "The Fatimid Holy City: Destroying and Building Jerusalem in the Eleventh Century." *The Medieval Globe*, 2017, 35–56.

——. "Method in Madness: Recontextualizing the Destruction of Churches in the Fatimid Era." *Muqarnas* 30 (2013): 119–39.

——. "The Miracle of Muqattam: Moving a Mountain to Build a Church in Fatimid Egypt." In *Sacred Precincts: The Religious Architecture of Non-Muslim Communities across the Islamic World*, edited by Mohammad Gharipour, 277–90. Leiden: Brill, 2014.

Puente, Cristina de la. "La caracterización de Almanzor: Entre la epopeya y la historia." In *Estudios onomástico-biográficos de al-Andalus*, 8:367–402. Madrid: Consejo superior de investigaciones científicas, Departamento de estudios arabes, 1988.

Rabbat, Nasser. "'Ajīb and Gharīb: Artistic Perception in Medieval Arabic Sources." *Medieval History Journal* 9, no. 1 (2006): 99–113.

——. "Architects and Artists in Mamluk Society: The Perspective of the Sources." *Journal of Architectural Education* 52, no. 1 (1998): 30–37.

——. "Al-Azhar Mosque: An Architectural Chronicle of Cairo's History." *Muqarnas* 13 (1996): 45–67.

——. "The Dome of the Rock Revisited: Some Remarks on al-Wasiti's Accounts." *Muqarnas* 10 (1993): 67–75.

——. "The Meaning of the Umayyad Dome of the Rock." *Muqarnas* 6 (1989): 12–21.

——. "The Medieval Link: Maqrizi's Khitat and Modern Narratives of Cairo." In *Making Cairo Medieval*, edited by Irene Bierman, Nasser Rabbat, and Nezar al-Sayyad, 29–57. Lanham, MD: Lexington Books, 2005.

——. "Ṭirāz." In *Encyclopaedia of Islam, Second Edition*. Accessed online April 13, 2019. http://dx.doi.org.ezproxy.library.wisc.edu/10.1163/1573-3912_islam_COM_1228

Raby, Julian, and Jeremy Johns, eds. *Bayt al Maqdis: 'Abd al-Malik's Jerusalem*. Oxford: Oxford University Press, 1992.

Rāghib, Yūsuf. "La Mosquée d'al-Qarāfa et Jonathan M. Bloom." *Arabica* 41 (1994): 419–21.

——. "Sur deux monuments funéraires d'al-Qarāfa al-Kubrā'." *Annales islamiques* 12 (1978): 67–83.

——. "Sur un groupe de mausolées du cimitère du Caire." *Revue des études islamiques* 40 (1972): 189–95.

——. "Un oratoire fatimide au sommet du Muqaṭṭam." *Studia islamica* 65 (1987): 51–67.

Ravaisse, Paul. "Essai sur l'histoire et sur la topographie du Caire d'après Makrizi." In *Memoirs de la mission archéologique française au Caire* 1 (1889): 409–79.

——. "Essai sur l'histoire et sur la topographie du Caire d'après Makrizi." In *Memoirs de la mission archéologique française au Caire* 3 (1890): 1–114.

Raymond, André. *Cairo*. Cambridge, MA: Harvard University Press, 2001.

——, ed. *The Glory of Cairo*. Cairo: American University in Cairo Press, 2000.

Reinert, Stephen. "The Muslim Presence in Constantinople, 9th–15th Centuries." In *Studies on the Internal Diaspora of the Byzantine Empire*, 125–50. Washington, DC: Dumbarton Oaks, 1998.

Richards, D. S. "Fragments of a Slave Dealer's Day-Book from Fusṭāṭ." In *Documents de l'Islam médiéval: Nouvelles perspectives de recherche*, 89–96. Cairo: Institut français d'archéologie orientale, 1991.

Robinson, B. W. *Islamic Art in the Keir Collection*. London: Faber and Faber, 1988.

Robinson, Chase F. *A Medieval Islamic City Reconsidered: An Interdisciplinary Approach to Samarra*. Oxford: Oxford University Press, 2001.

Robinson, Cynthia."The Arts of Intimacy: Christians, Jews, and Muslims in the Making of Castilian Culture." *Art Bulletin* 91, no. 3 (September 2009): 369–73.

——. "Power, Light, Intra-Confessional Discontent, and the Almoravids." In *Envisioning Islamic Art and Architecture: Essays in Honor of Renata Holod*, edited by David J. Roxburgh, 22–45. Leiden: Brill, 2014.

——. "Qurtuba: Some Critical Considerations of the Caliphate of Cordoba and the Myth of Convivencia." In *Reflections on Qurtuba in the 21st Century*, 111–32. Madrid: Casa árabe, 2013.

——. "Talking Religion, Comparatively Speaking: Throwing Some Light on the Multi-Confessional Landscape of Late Medieval Iberia." *La corónica* 1 (2012): 263–97.

Rosen-Ayalon, M. *The Early Islamic Monuments of al-Ḥaram al-Sharīf: An Iconographic Study*. Jerusalem: Institute of Archaeology at the Hebrew University of Jerusalem, 1989.

——. "An Early Source on the Construction of the Dome of the Chain on the Temple Mount." *Cathedra* 11 (1979): 184–85.

Roxburgh, David. *Writing the Word of God: Calligraphy and the Qur'an*. Houston: Museum of Fine Arts, Houston, 2007.

Rubsenson, Samuel. "Translating the Tradition: Some Remarks on the Arabization of the Patristic Heritage in Egypt." *Medieval Encounters* 2, no. 1 (1996): 4–14.

Ruggles, D. Fairchild. "The Eye of Sovereignty: Poetry and Vision in the Alhambra's Lindaraja Mirador." *Gesta* 2 (1997): 180–89.

——. *Gardens, Landscape, and Vision in the Palaces of Islamic Spain*. University Park: Pennsylvania State University Press, 2000.

——. "The Stratigraphy of Forgetting: The Great Mosque of Cordoba and Its Contested Legacy." In *Contested Cultural Heritage: Religion, Nationalism, Erasure, and Exclusion in a Global World*, edited by

H. Silverman. New York: Springer, 2011.

Runciman, S. "The Byzantine 'Protectorate' in the Holy Land." *Byzantion* 18 (1948): 207–15.

Russel, Dorothea. "Are There Any Remains of the Fatimid Palaces of Cairo?" *Journal of the American Research Center in Egypt* 3 (1964): 115–21.

Rustow, Marina. *Heresy and the Politics of Community: The Jews of the Fatimid Caliphate.* Ithaca, NY: Cornell University Press, 2014.

Saba, Matt. "Abbasid Lusterware and the Aesthetics of ʿAjab." *Muqarnas* 29 (2012): 187–212.

——. "A Restricted Gaze: The Ornament of the Main Caliphal Palace of Samarra." *Muqarnas* 32 (2015): 155–96.

Sacy, Silvestre de. *Exposé de la religion des Druzes.* Reprint edition. Cambridge: Cambridge University Press, 2013. First published in 1838.

Safran, Janina M. *Defining Boundaries in al-Andalus: Muslims, Christians, and Jews in Islamic Iberia.* Ithaca, NY: Cornell University Press, 2015.

——. *The Second Umayyad Caliphate: The Articulation of Caliphal Legitimacy in al-Andalus.* Cambridge, MA: Harvard University Center for Middle Eastern Studies, 2001.

Salām Shāfiʿī, Maḥmūd. *Ahl al-dhimma fī Miṣr fī l-ʿaṣr al-Fāṭimī al-awwal.* Cairo: np, 1995.

Saleh, Marlis. "Church Building, Repair, and Destruction in Fatimid Egypt." In *Ismaili and Fatimid Studies in Honor of Paul E. Walker*, 177–96. Chicago: Middle East Documentation Center, 2010.

——. "Government Intervention in the Coptic Church in Egypt during the Fatimid Period." *Muslim World* 91, nos. 3–4 (2001): 381–97.

——. "Government Relations with the Coptic Community in Egypt during the Fatimid Period (358–567 AH/969–1171 CE)." PhD, University of Chicago, 1995.

Samir, Khalil. "The Role of Christians in the Fāṭimid Government Services of Egypt to the Reign of al-Ḥāfiẓ." *Medieval Encounters* 2, no. 3 (1996): 177–92.

Sanders, Paula. "Bohra Architecture and the Restoration of Fatimid Culture." In *L'Égypte fatimide: Son art et son histoire*, edited by Marianne Barrucand, 159–65. Paris: Presses de l'Université de Paris–Sorbonne, 1999.

——. "The Court Ceremonial of the Fatimid Caliphate in Egypt." PhD, Princeton University, 1984.

——. *Creating Medieval Cairo: Empire, Religion, and Architectural Preservation in Nineteenth-Century Egypt.* Cairo: American University in Cairo Press, 2008.

——. "The Fatimid State, 969–1171." In *The Cambridge History of Egypt. Vol. 1: Islamic Egypt, 640–1517.* Cambridge: Cambridge University Press, 1998.

——. *Ritual, Politics, and the City in Fatimid Cairo.* Albany, NY: State University of New York Press, 1994.

——. "Robes and Honor in Fatimid Egypt." In *Robes and Honor: The Medieval World of Investiture*, edited by Stewart Gordon. The New Middle Ages. New York: Palgrave, 2001.

Sayyid, Ayman Fuʾād. *La capitale de l'Égypte jusquà l'époque fatimide: Al-Qāhira et al-Fusṭaṭ. Essai de réconstitution topographique.* Stuttgart: Steiner, 1998.

——. *Al-Dawlah al-Fāṭimīyah fī Miṣr.* Cairo: Al-Dār al-Miṣrīya al-Lubnānīya, 2000.

——. "Le grande palais fatimide au Caire." In *L'Égypte fatimide: Son art et son histoire*, edited by Marianne Barrucand, 117–26. Paris: Presses de l'Université de Paris–Sorbonne, 1999.

Scanlon, George T. "Fatimid under Glazed Painted Wares: A Chronological Readjustment." In *A Way Prepared Essays on Islamic Culture in Honor of Richard Bayly Winder*, edited by F. Kazemi and R. D. McChesmey. New York: New York University Press, 1988.

——. *Fusṭāṭ Expedition Final Report. Vol. 1: Catalogue of Filters.* Winona Lake, IN: Eisenbrauns, 1986.

——. *Fusṭāṭ Expedition: Preliminary Report: Back to Fustat-A 1973.* Cairo: Institut français d'archéologie orientale, 1981.

——. *Fustat Expedition: Preliminary Report, 1965. Part I.* Cairo: American Research Center in Egypt, 1966.

——. "Fusṭāṭ Expedition: Preliminary Report, 1968. Part I." *Journal of the American Research Center in Egypt* 11 (1974): 81–91.

——. "Fusṭāṭ Expedition: Preliminary Report, 1968. Part II." *Journal of the American Research Center in Egypt* 13 (1976): 69–89.

——. "Fusṭāṭ Expedition: Preliminary Report, 1972. Part I." *Journal of the American Research Center in Egypt* 28 (1981): 57–84.

——. "Fusṭāṭ Expedition: Preliminary Report, 1972. Part II." *Journal of the American Research Center in Egypt* 19 (1982): 119–29.

——. "Fusṭāṭ Expedition: Preliminary Report, 1978." *Journal of the American Research Center in Egypt* 21 (1984): 1–138.

——. "Fustat Fatimid Sgraffiato: Less than Lustre." In *L'Égypte fatimide: Son art et son histoire. Actes du colloque organisé à Paris les 28, 29 et 30 mai 1998*, edited by Marianne Barrucand, 265–283. Paris: Presses de l'Université de Paris–Sorbonne, 1999.

Seipel, Wilfried. *Schatze der kalifen: Islamische kunst zur fatimidenzeit.* Vienna: Kunsthistorisches Museum, 1998.

Serjeant, R. B. *Islamic Textiles: Material for a History up to the Mongol Conquest.* Beirut: Librairie du Liban, 1972.

Shafer, Ann. "Sacred Geometries: The Dynamics of 'Islamic' Ornament in Jewish and Coptic Old Cairo." In *Sacred Precincts: The Religious Architecture of Non-Muslim Communities across the Islamic World*, edited by Mohammad Gharipour, 158–77. Leiden: Brill, 2014.

Shalem, Avinoam. *Islam Christianized: Islamic Portable Objects in the Medieval Church Treasuries of the Latin West.* Frankfurt am Main: Peter Lang, 1996.

——. *Oliphant: Islamic Objects in Historical Context.* Leiden: Brill, 2004.

——. "The Rock-Crystal Lionhead in the Badisches Landesmuseum in Kalsruhe." In *L'Égypte fatimide: Son art et son histoire. Actes du colloque organisé à Paris les 28, 29 et 30 mai 1998*, edited by Marianne Barrucand, 359–66. Paris: Presses de l'Université de Paris–Sorbonne, 1999.

Shalev-Hurvitz, Vered. *Holy Sites Encircled: The Early Byzantine Concentric Churches of Jerusalem.* Oxford: Oxford University Press, 2015.

Sharon, Moshe. *Corpus Inscriptionum Arabicarum Palaestinae*, 6 vols. Leiden: Brill, 1997–2017.

Sheehan, Peter. *Babylon of Egypt: The Archaeology of Old Cairo and the Origins of the City*. Cairo: American University in Cairo Press, 2010.

Shehab, Behia. "Fatimid Kūfī Epigraphy on the Gates of Cairo: Between Royal Patronage and Civil Utility." In *Calligraphy and Islamic Architecture in the Muslim World*, edited by Mohammad Gharipour and Irvin Cemal Schick, 275–89. Edinburgh: Edinburgh University Press, 2013.

Shenoda, Maryann M. "Displacing Dhimmī, Maintaining Hope: Unthinkable Coptic Representations of Fatimid Egypt." *International Journal of Middle Eastern Studies* 39 (2007): 587–606.

——. "Re-Envisioning Persecution: Imagining a Converted World." *Medieval Encounters* 21, nos. 4–5 (November 2015): 411–30.

Shepard, Jonathan. "Holy Land, Lost Lands, Realpolitik: Imperial Byzantine Thinking about Syria and Palestine in the Later 10th and 11th Centuries." *Al-Qanṭara* 33, no. 2 (2012): 505–45.

Simaika Pasha, Marcus, and ʿAbd al-Masiḥ Effendi. *Catalogue of the Coptic and Arabic Manuscripts in the Coptic Museum, the Principal Churches of Cairo and Alexandria and the Monasteries of Egypt*. Cairo: Government Press, 1939.

Singer, Lynette. *The Minbar of Saladin*. New York: Thames and Hudson, 2008.

Sirry, Munʿim. "The Public Role of the Dhimmīs during ʿAbbāsid Times." *Bulletin of the School of Oriental and African Studies* 74 (2011): 187–204.

Smet, D. de. "Éléments chrétiens dans l'ismaélisme yemenite sous les derniers Fatimides: Le problème de la gnose ṭayyibite." In *L'Égypte fatimide: Son art et son histoire. Actes du colloque organisé à Paris les 28, 29 et 30 mai 1998*, edited by Marianne Barrucand, 45–54. Paris: Presses de l'Université de Paris–Sorbonne, 1999.

——. "Les interdictions alimentaires du calife fatimide al-Ḥākim: Marques de folie ou announce d'un règne messianique." *Egypt and Syria in the Fatimid, Ayyubid and Mamluk Eras*, proceedings of the 1st, 2nd and 3rd International Colloquium organized at the Katholieke Universiteit Leuven in May 1992, 1993 and 1994, edited by J. Steenberger, U. Vermeulen, and D. de Smet, 139–62. Leuven: Peeters, 1995.

Smoor, P. "The Master of the Century: Fāṭimid Poets in Cairo." In *Egypt and Syria in the Fatimid, Ayyubid and Mamluk Eras, Egypt and Syria in the Fatimid, Ayyubid and Mamluk Eras*, proceedings of the 1st, 2nd and 3rd International Colloquium organized at the Katholieke Universiteit Leuven in May 1992, 1993 and 1994, edited by J. Steenberger, U. Vermeulen, and D. de Smet, 53–70. Leuven: Peeters, 1995.

Soifer, Maya. "Beyond Convivencia: Critical Reflections on the Historiography of Interfaith Relations in Christian Spain." *Journal of Medieval Iberian Studies* 1, no. 1 (January 1, 2009): 19–35.

Sokoly, Jochen. "Between Life and Death: The Funerary Context of Tiraz Textiles." In *Islamische Textilkunst des Mittelalters: Aktuelle Probleme*, edited by Muḥammad ʿAbbās Muḥammad Sālim, 71–78. Riggisberg: Abegg-Stiftun, 1997.

——. "Textiles and Identity." In *A Companion to Islamic Art and Architecture*, edited by Finbarr Barry Flood and Gülru Necipoğlu, 223–49. Blackwell Companions to Art History. Hoboken, NJ: Wiley, 2017.

——. "Ṭirāz Textiles from Egypt: Production, Administration and Uses of Ṭirāz Textiles from Egypt under the Umayyad, ʿAbbāsid and Fāṭimid dynasties." PhD, University of Oxford, 2001.

Soucek, Priscilla. "Byzantium and the Islamic East." In *The Glory of Byzantium: Art and Culture of the Middle Byzantine Era, AD 843–1261*, edited by Helen C. Evans, 402–33. New York: The Metropolitan Museum of Art, 1997.

Stern, S. M. *Fatimid Decrees: Original Documents from the Fatimid Chancery*. London: Faber and Faber, 1964.

——. "Heterodox Ismāʿīlism at the Time of al-Muʿizz." *Bulletin of the School of Oriental and African Studies* 17 (1955): 10–33.

——."Recherches sur la mosquée Aqsa et ses mosaiques." *Ars Orientalis* 5 (1963): 27–47.

——. *Studies in Early Ismāʿīlism*. Max Schloessinger Memorial Series. Jerusalem: Magnes Press, 1983.

Stillman, Norman A. "The Non-Muslim Communities: The Jewish Community." In *The Cambridge History of Egypt. Vol. 1: Islamic Egypt, 640–1517*, edited by Hugh Kennedy, 198–210. Cambridge: Cambridge University Press, 1998.

Suleman, Fahmida. "Glorifying the Imamate: Architecture and Ritual in the Shiʿi Shrines of Syria." In *People of the Prophet's House: Artistic and Ritual Expressions of Shiʿi Islam*, 54–62. London: Azimuth, 2015.

——. "The Lion, the Hare and Lustre Ware: Studies in the Iconography of Lustre Ceramics from Fatimid Egypt (969–1171 CE)." PhD, University of Oxford, 2003.

——, ed. *People of the Prophet's House: Artistic and Ritual Expressions of Shiʿi Islam*. London: Azimuth, 2015.

——, ed. *Word of God, Art of Man: the Qur'an and Its Creative Expressions: Selected Proceedings from the International Colloquium, London, 18–21 October 2003*. Oxford: Oxford University Press in association with the Institute of Ismaili Studies, 2007.

Swanson, Mark N. *The Coptic Papacy in Islamic Egypt (641–1517)*. Cairo: American University in Cairo Press, 2010.

Swelim, Tarek. *Ibn Tulun: His Lost City and Great Mosque*. Cairo: American University in Cairo Press, 2015.

Tabbaa, Yasser. "The Resurgence of the Baghdad Caliphate." In *A Companion to Islamic Art and Architecture*, edited by Finbarr Barry Flood and Gülru Necipoğlu. Blackwell Companions to Art History. Hoboken, NJ: Wiley, 2017.

——. "The Transformation of Arabic Writing: Part 2, the Public Text." *Ars Orientalis* 24 (1994): 119–47.

——. *The Transformation of Islamic Art during the Sunni Revival*. Seattle: University of Washington Press, 2001.

Talbot, Alice-Mary. "Byzantine Pilgrimage to the Holy Land from the Eighth to the Fifteenth Century." In *The Sabaite*

Heritage in the Orthodox Church from the Fifth Century to the Present, edited by J. Patrich, 97–110. Leuven: Peeters, 2001.

Talbi, Mohamed. "Al-Mahdiyya." In *Encyclopaedia of Islam*, Second Edition. Accessed online April 6, 2019. http://dx.doi.org/10.1163/1573-3912_islam_COM_0621

Taylor, Christopher. *In the Vicinity of the Righteous: Ziyāra and the Veneration of Muslim Saints in Late Medieval Egypt*. Leiden: Brill, 1999.

———. "Reevaluating the Shi'i Role in the Development of Monumental Islamic Funerary Architecture: The Case of Egypt." *Muqarnas* 9 (1992): 1–10.

Thomas, Thelma. "The Arts of Christian Communities in the Medieval Middle East." In *Byzantium: Faith and Power (1261–1557)*, edited by Helen C. Evans, 415–48. New York: The Metropolitan Museum of Art; New Haven: Yale University Press, 2004.

———. "Christians in the Islamic East." In *The Glory of Byzantium: Art and Culture of the Middle Byzantine Era, AD 843–1261*, 365–71. New York: The Metropolitan Museum of Art, 1997.

Triano, Antonio Vallejo. "Madīnat al-Zahrā': Transformation of a Caliphal City." In *Revisiting al-Andalus: Perspectives on the Material Culture of Islamic Iberia and Beyond*, edited by Glaire D. Anderson and Mariam Rosser-Owen, 1–26. Leiden: Brill, 2007.

———. "Madīnat al-Zahrā': The Triumph of the Islamic State." In *Al-Andalus: The Art of Islamic Spain*, 27–40. New York: The Metropolitan Museum of Art, 1992.

Tritton, A. S. *The Caliphs and Their Non-Muslim Subjects: A Critical Study of the Covenant of 'Umar*. Oxford: Oxford University Press, 1930.

Tronzo, William. *The Cultures of His Kingdom: Roger II and the Cappella Palatina in Palermo*. Princeton, NJ: Princeton University Press, 1997.

Tudela, Benjamin of. *Itinerary of Benjamin Tudela: Travels in the Middle Ages*. Malibu, CA: J. Simon, 1983.

Tyre, William of. *A History of Deeds Done beyond the Sea*, edited by Emily Babcock and August Krey. 2 vols. New York: Columbia University Press, 1943.

Udovitch, Abraham. "Fatimid Cairo: Crossroads of World Trade—From Spain to India." In *L'Égypte fatimide: Son art et son histoire. Actes du colloque organisé à Paris les 28, 29 et 30 mai 1998*, edited by Marianne Barrucand, 681–91. Paris: Presses de l'Université de Paris–Sorbonne, 1999.

Vatikiotis, P. "Al-Hakim bi Amr Allah: The God-King Idea Realised." *Islamic Culture* 29 (1958): 1–8.

———. *The Fatimid Theory of State*. Lahore: Orientalia Publishers, 1957.

Velji, Jamel. *An Apocalyptic History of the Early Fatimid Empire*. Edinburgh: Edinburgh University Press, 2016.

Virani, Shafique N. *The Ismailis in the Middle Ages: A History of Survival, A Search for Salvation*. Oxford: Oxford University Press, 2007.

Vorderstrasse, Tasha, and Tanya Treptow, eds. *A Cosmopolitan City: Muslims, Christians, and Jews in Old Cairo*. Chicago: Oriental Institute, 2015.

Walker, Alicia. *The Emperor and the World: Exotic Elements and the Imaging of Middle Byzantine Imperial Power, Ninth to Thirteenth Centuries CE*. Cambridge: Cambridge University Press, 2012.

———. "Pseudo-Arabic 'Inscriptions' and the Pilgrim's Path at Hosios Loukas." In *Viewing Inscriptions in the Late Antique and Medieval World*, 99–123. New York: Cambridge University Press, 2015.

Walker, Paul. *Abū Ya'qūb al-Sijistānī: Intellectual Missionary*. London: Tauris in association with the Institute of Ismaili Studies, 1996.

———. "Al-'Azīz bi-Llāh." In *Encyclopaedia of Islam, Third Edition*. Accessed online April 12, 2019. http://dx.doi.org.ezproxy.library.wisc.edu/10.1163/1573-3912_ei3_COM_22695

———. *Caliph of Cairo: Al-Hakim bi-Amr Allah, 996–1021*. Cairo: American University in Cairo Press, 2009.

———. "The 'Crusade' of John Tzimisces in the Light of New Arabic Evidence." In *Fatimid History and Ismaili Doctrine*, 302–27. Burlington, VT: Ashgate Variorium, 2008.

———. *Early Philosophical Shiism: The Ismaili Neoplatonism of Abu Ya'qub al-Sijistani*. Cambridge Studies in Islamic Civilization. Cambridge: Cambridge University Press, 2008.

———. *Exploring an Islamic Empire: Fatimid History and Its Sources*. London: Tauris, 2002.

———. *Fatimid History and Ismaili Doctrine*. Burlington, VT: Ashgate Variorium, 2008.

———. "Fatimid Institutions of Learning." *Journal of the American Research Center in Egypt* 34 (1997): 179–200.

———. "Al-Ḥākim and the *Dhimmīs*." *Medieval Encounters* 21 (2015): 345–63.

———. *Ḥamīd al-Dīn al-Kirmānī: Ismaili Thought in the Age of al-Ḥākim*. London: Tauris, 1999.

———. "The Identity of One of the Ismaili Da'is Sent by the Fatimids to Ibn Hafsun." *Al-Qantara: Revista de estudios árabes* 21, no. 2 (2000): 387–88.

———. "Islamic Ritual Preaching (Khuṭbas) in a Contested Arena: Shī'īs and Sunnīs, Fatimids and Abbasids." *Anuario de estudios medievales* 42, no. 1 (2012): 119–40.

———. "The Ismaili Da'wa in the Reign of the Fatimid Caliph al-Ḥākim." *Journal of the American Research Center in Egypt* 30 (1993): 160–82.

———. "The Ismā'īlī Da'wa and the Fāṭimid Caliphate," in *The Cambridge History of Egypt. Vol. 1: Islamic Egypt, 640–1517*, 120–50. Cambridge: Cambridge University Press, 1998.

———. "Al-Maqrīzī and the Fatimids." *Mamlūk Studies Review* 7, no. 2 (2003): 83–97.

———. *Orations of the Fatimid Caliphs: Festival Sermons of the Ismaili Imams: An Edition of the Arabic Texts and English Translation of Fatimid Khuṭbas*. Ismaili Texts and Translations Series 10. London: Tauris in association with the Institute of Ismaili Studies, 2009.

———. "In Praise of al-Hakim: Greek Elements in Ismaili Writings on the Imamate." *Mélanges de l'Université Saint-Joseph* 57 (2004): 367–92.

———. *The Wellsprings of Wisdom: A Study of Abū Ya'qūb*

al-Sijistānī's Kitāb al-Yanābī'. Salt Lake City: University of Utah Press, 1994.

Ward, Seth. *The Caliphate in the West: An Islamic Political Institution in the Iberian Peninsula*. Oxford: Clarendon Press, 1993.

——. *Dhimmīs and Others: Jews and Christians and the World of Classical Islam*. Winona Lake, IN: Eisenbraus, 1997.

——. "Taqī al-Dīn al-Subqī: On Construction, Continuance, and Repairs of Churches and Synagogues in Islamic Law." In *Studies in Islamic and Judaic Traditions II: Papers Presented at the Institute for Islamic-Jewish Studies, Center for Judaic Studies*, edited by William Brinner and Stephen Ricks, 169–88. Atlanta: Scholars Press, 1989.

Warner, Nicholas. *The Monuments of Historic Cairo: A Map and Descriptive Catalogue*. Cairo: American University in Cairo Press, 2005.

Watenpaugh, Heghnar Z. "Resonance and Circulation: The Category 'Islamic Art and Architecture.'" In *A Companion to Islamic Art and Architecture*, edited by Finbarr Barry Flood and Gülru Necipoğlu, 1223–1244. Hoboken, NJ: Wiley, 2017.

Watson, Oliver. *Ceramics from Islamic Lands*. London: Thames and Hudson, 2004.

Weigert, G. "A Note on the Muḥtasib and Ahl al-Dhimma." *Der Islam* 75 (1998): 331–37.

Wensinck, A. J., and C. E. Bosworth. "Makka." In *Encyclopaedia of Islam, Second Edition*. Accessed online April 12, 2019. http://dx.doi.org.ezproxy.library.wisc.edu/10.1163/1573-3912_islam_COM_0638

White, Hugh G. Evelyn. *The Monasteries of the Wadi Natrun*, 3 vols. New York: The Metropolitan Museum of Art, 1926–1933.

Wiet, G. "Une nouvelle inscription fatimide au Caire." *Journal Asiatique* 249 (1961): 13–20.

Wiet, G., and L. Hautecoeur. *Les mosqueés du Caire*. 2 vols. Paris: Leroux, 1932.

Wilfong, Terry. "The Non-Muslim Communities: Christian Communities." In *The Cambridge History of Egypt: Islamic Egypt, 640–1517*. Cambridge: Cambridge University Press, 1998.

Williams, Caroline. "The Cult of 'Alid Saints in the Fatimid Monuments of Cairo. Part I: The Mosque of al-Aqmar." *Muqarnas* 1 (1983): 37–52.

——. "The Cult of 'Alid Saints in the Fatimid Monuments of Cairo. Part II: The Mausolea." *Muqarnas* 3 (1985): 39–60.

Yalman, Suzan. "'Ala al-Din Kayqubad Illuminated: A Rum Seljuq Sultan as Cosmic Ruler." *Muqarnas* 29 (2012): 151–86.

Yavuz, Yildirim. "The Restoration Project of the Masjid al-Aqsa by Mimar Kemalettin." *Muqarnas* 13 (1996): 149–64.

PHOTO CREDITS

Drawn by Ahmed Abdelazim: 1.1, 1.25; Drawn by Saeed Arida courtesy of Aga Khan Documentation Center at MIT: 1.11, 1.14, 1.19, 4.13; © Ashmolean Museum, University of Oxford: 1.18, 3.1, 3.2, 3.3, 3.7, 3.17, 3.18, 5.2, 5.3, 5.11; Author Photo: 1.7, 1.8, 1.10, 1.13, 1.15, 1.16, 1.20, 1.21, 1.22, 1.26, 1.27, 1.28, 1.29, 1.30, 2.2, 2.3, 2.6, 2.7, 2.8, 3.5, 3.8, 3.9, 3.10, 3.11, 3.12, 3.13, 3.14, 3.15, 3.19, 4.1, 4.2, 4.5, 4.6, 4.8, 4.10, 4.14, 5.1, 5.4, 5.5, 5.6, 5.7, 5.8, 5.9, 5.10, 5.12, 5.13, 5.14, 5.16, 5.17; © Bardo Museum: 1.4; Brandmeister [Public domain], via Wikimedia Commons: 4.11; Photo by Walter Denny: 1.6; The Coptic Museum, Cairo: 2.2; dbimages/Alamy Stock Photo: 4.4; Photo by Ángel M. Felicísimo/CC-BY-SAA: 1.9; Courtesy of the Getty's Open Content Program: 2.1; Russell Harris/Alamy Stock Photo: 3.4; Heritage Image Partnership Ltd/Alamy Stock Photo: 1.17; Museum of Islamic Art, Cairo: 1.26, 1.27, 1.28, 1.29, 1.30, 2.5, 4.8; Photo by Pernille Klemp © The David Collection, Copenhagen: 1.24; Drawn by Bill Nelson: 0.1, 1.12; Photo by Bernard O'Kane: 3.6, 4.7; PHGCOM [Public domain], via Wikimedia Commons: 3.16; Andrew Shiva/CC BY-SA 4.0: 5.15; Marek Szarejko/CC BY-SA 2.0, via Wikimedia Commons: 1.3; The Metropolitan Museum of Art: 1.5, 4.9; © Smithsonian Institution, Washington, D.C.: 1.31; Talmoryair [Public domain], from Wikimedia Commons: 4.12; © Victoria & Albert Museum: 2.4; Photo by Caroline Williams: 1.23.

INDEX

Page numbers in italics indicate illustrations. Names starting with "al-" are alphabetized by the subsequent part of the name.

Abbasid caliphate: Abu Rakwa and, 120; beveled and ornamental style of, 40, *41*, 51, 103; Buyids and, 115, 156; Carolingians and, 107, 173n38; Christians and, 58, 175n89; Companions of the Prophet Muhammad, cursing of, 156, 171n72; compared to Fatimid caliphate, 5, 116–17, 156; in decline, 6, 122; defeat of Umayyad caliphate (750), 134; "false Imams" of, 115; al-Hakim's increasing popularity in, 123–24; Hanafism of, 161n16; Jerusalem (731–973) and, 134–36, 143, 151; luster bowl, 18, *18*; al-Mahdi declaring rival caliphate to, 15; minaret as part of mosques in, 16, 23, 102; origins of, 161n16; palace of, 37, 51; visual expressions of legitimacy, 3, 4, 23. *See also* Baghdad; Samarra

ʿAbd al-Malik, 136, 140

ʿAbd al-Rahman III (r. 929–61), 4, 6, 20–22, 102, 161n9, 161n16; Abu Rakwa claiming to be heir to, 90

Abraham (Coptic patriarch r. 975–78), 66

Abraham's ascent narratives, 178n78

Abu Bakr, 90, 96

Abu al-Futuh, 97

Abu al-Makarim Saʿdallah Jirjis ibn Masʿud, 57–59, 175n9

Abu al-Qasim Husaini, 142

Abu Rakwa revolt (1004–7), 71, 90–92, 96, 120, 123, 155, 171nn75–76

Abu Salih, 111–13, 174nn57–58

Aghlabids, 15, 102, 162n8

al-Akhram, 127, 129

Aleppo (Syria), 6, 44, 67, 178n85

Alexandria (Egypt), 49, 91, 103, 163n35

Alexandrin, Elizabeth, 149, 178n76, 178n78

ʿAli (cousin and son-in-law of the Prophet Muhammad), 4, 8, 15, 81, 84, 90, 93, 161n16, 162n16

ʿAli al-Asadi, 123

ʿAlids, 26–27, 84, 93, 97, 102, 124

ʿAli ibn ʿAbd al-Rahman, 142

Almoravids and Almohads, 158

Amir-Moezzi, 178n79

Anba Abraham (Coptic patriarch), 59

Anba Ephraim (Syrian patriarch), 62

al-Andalus, 14, 21, 36, 37, 38, 90, 161n16

Aqsa Mosque (Jerusalem), *126*, *128*, *133*, 133–49, *135*, *138*, 176n34; archways, *138–39*, 140–42; compared to Church of the Holy Sepulcher, 148; Fatimid design of concentric circles in, 143, 147, 148–49; fire (1967), 179n12; inscriptions, 142–43, 149; *isrāʾ* (night journey) and *miʿrāj* (ascension) of Muhammad associated with, 139–42, 144, 146–49, 178n76; *maqṣūra*, *138–39*, *139*, 140–43, *142–43*, 145, 146–49, 177n57; mosaics, 140–43, 148, 178n79; roundels, use of, 142–43, 145, 147–48, 178n72, 178n75; sanctification of, 127–28; trompe l'oeil effect, 143, 147; al-Zahir's renovation, 140–49, *141*

Arculf (late seventh-century bishop), 106–7, *108*

al-Ashmunayn, destruction of church in, 112

astronomy and observatory, 69, 105, 170n59

ʿAysha (Muhammad's wife), 90

Ayyubids, 164n74, 165n79

al-ʿAziz Bi'llah (r. 975–96), 27–28; Cairo and, 45, 69; Christian churches and their destruction under, 47, 66, 67, 106; Christians' relationship with, 47, 58, 59, 64–65, 67, 69, 110, 111, 153; compared to al-Hakim, 69, 90, 123, 154; construction of Mosque of al-Hakim begun under, 30–32, 73; death of, 70; expansion goals of, 44; Fatimid palace and, 37; Jerusalem and, 133; Melkite Christian wife of, 50, 110; monuments built under, 44; Muqattam miracle and, 62

Babylon (Egypt), 49, 163n35

Badr al-Jamali, *98*, 99

Baghdad, 6, 15, 19, 23, 123, 156, 163n22; as Abbasid capital, 87, 125, 134

Baghdad Manifesto (1011), 124

Banu Qurra, 90–91, 96, 171n79

Banu Tayy, 177n43

Barjawan, 71, 169n5

Basil II (Byzantine emperor r. 976–1025), 97

bāṭin vs. *ẓāhir*: Druze views on, 129; Fatimid palace in terms of, 42–45; Fatimid vs. Sunni views on, 5–6, 114; al-Hakim's realignment from *bāṭin* to *ẓāhir*, 95, 116–17, 124, 155–56; interpretative flexibility of *bāṭin* beliefs, 50; Ismaili-specific views on, 14, 102, 154; jihad over interpretations of, 21; al-Kirmani on, 114–15; minarets of the Mosque of al-Hakim, interpretation of, 81–83

Baybars II (Mamluk ruler r. 1309–10), 99

Behrens-Abouseif, Doris, 170n43

Ben Ezra Synagogue (Cairo), 49, 162n26

Berbers, 15, 27, 91, 122, 129, 171n79, 173n40

Bible citation: Isaiah 1:3, 61; Matthew 17:20, 59

Bierman, Irene, 44, 81–82, 102, 161n10, 162n18, 164n54, 170nn38–39, 170n41, 172n13

Bimin (monk), 131

Bloom, Jonathan, 28, 81, 102, 162n16, 163n22, 163n39, 164n66, 169n3, 170n54, 172n8, 172n13

Bohra Ismaili, 33, *34*

al-Buraq (sacred steed of Muhammad), 146, 147

Butler, Alfred, 63, 65

Buyids, 6, 115, 117, 124, 154, 156

Byzantine empire, 4, 21, 27, 48, 67; closing Mosque of Constantinople, 111; Fatimid peace treaties with, 122, 136, 150, 178n85; Fatimids engaged in campaigns against, 71, 96, 109, 117; protection of Church of the Holy Sepulcher in Jerusalem, 106; relations with Fatimids at time of destruction of Church of the Holy Sepulcher, 111; restoration of Church of the Holy Sepulcher by, 139–40, 150, 178n81

Cairo: as capital, 1, 3, 10, 13–14, 24, 27, 45, 87, 105, 125, 153, 154, 156; as center of learning under al-Hakim, 87, 92, 105, 154; city gates, 20, 26; destruction by al-Hakim, 11; differentiated from al-Qahira, 161n2; al-Hakim's attachment to, 69, 71–72, 92, 103; map of, *25*; origin as army camp, 24, 164n55; Saffron Tombs (*turbat al-za'farān*), 27, 36, 44; societal hierarchy in relationship to knowledge of, 44; walls of, 99; al-Zahir and, 133. *See also* Fatimid palace (al-Qahira); Fustat-Misr; Mosque of al-Hakim; *and other specific monuments*
call to prayer, 16, 24, 29, 96, 114, 120, 162, 169n3
Charlemagne (r. 742–814), 107, 173n38, 173n50
Christian churches and monuments, 7, 10, 47–67; Christian funding for upkeep of monuments in Jerusalem, 108; church restoration, 48, 58, 66–67; Ibn Raga's construction of church dedicated to St. Michael, 88; monasteries, 55–58, 88; monuments in Fatimid Egypt, 55–59; Muqattam miracle, 59–66, *62*; Muslim resistance to and obstacles to church restoration and construction, 10, 65–66, 88–89, 154, 171n70; reconstruction or building under al-Hakim, 88–89, 92, 131; shared artistic forms with Fatimid Egypt, 51–55; sources on, 7, 9; woodwork, *52–53*, 53; al-Zahir's restoration of Christian Jerusalem, 150–51. *See also* Church of the Holy Sepulcher; destruction of Christian churches and monuments; *specific churches, monasteries, and shrines*
Christians: Arabicization of, 65; al-'Aziz's relationship with, 47, 58, 59, 64–65, 67, 69, 110, 153; celebrations by, 56, 109, 119; conversion to Islam, 113, 131; corruption in church practices, 111, 173n52, 174n54; Fatimid tolerance of, 10, 24, 47, 48, 51, 64–65, 71; al-Hakim's relationship with, 3, 88–90, 119, 125, 131, 154, 172–73n34; in Jerusalem, 108–9; al-Mu'izz's relationship with, 58–59, 67, 69, 153; relations among Muslims, Jews, and Christians, 4, 7, 51, 56, 64, 162n26; return to faith of those who had converted to Islam, 131; violence against, 108–9. *See also* Byzantine empire; Coptic Christianity; *dhimmīs*; Pact of 'Umar
Church of al-'Adhra' (Wadi al-Natrun monastic complex), decorative stucco from, 51, *51*
Church of Saint Barbara (Cairo), wooden screen, *52–53*, 53
Church of Saint George (Madaba, Jordan), mosaic from, 106, *108*
Church of Saint Mennas (al-Hamra), 112
Church of Saint Mercurius (Monastery of Abu Sayfayn), 59, *60*, 62–64
Church of Saint Theodore, 112
Church of the Holy Sepulcher (Jerusalem): aedicula and dome, 106, *107*; Arculf's schematic of, 106–7, *108*; centrality in struggle for dominance in Jerusalem of Islam vs. Christianity, 109; Charlemagne and, 173n38, 173n50; compared to Aqsa Mosque, 148; destruction of, 1, 11, 69, 96–97, 106–13, 120, 123, 151, 154, 155, 172n34, 173n47, 174n53; ivory of three Marys at tomb of Christ, 106, *107*; medieval nomenclature of "the Garbage Heap" for, 110, 173n49; mob violence damaging (966), 109; mosaic depictions of, 106, *108*; mosque constructed on top of section of, 173n44; Muslim reaction to destruction of, 110; pilgrimages to, 109, 119, 178n81; protection under treaty with Byzantine empire, 106; ramifications of destruction of, 1, 151, 158; al-Zahir allowing Byzantine restoration of, 127, 136–37, 139–40, 150–51, 177n37, 178n81
Companions of the Prophet Muhammad, curses on: Abbasid and Baghdad mosques displaying, 156, 171n72; Abu Rakwa using to rally revolt against al-Hakim, 90, 171n78; al-Hakim ordering inscriptions, 70, 89–92, 154, 171n71; al-Hakim ordering removal of curses, 96, 120, 155
concentric circle designs, use of, 81–82, 84, 93, 143
Constantine VIII (Byzantine emperor r. 1025–28), 150
Constantine IX Monomachos (Byzantine emperor r. 1042–55), 150
Constantinople mosque, 111, 150
Cook, Michael, 116–17
Coptic Christianity: celebrations, 56; destruction of Church of the Holy Sepulcher and, 110, 111; Fatimids and, 9, 48–50, 58; luster ceramic bowl, *46*, *54*; Monophysite belief system, 48, 110, 173n51; in al-Qahira, 24
Cordoba: Great Mosque of, 21–23, *22–23*, 102, 121–22, *121–22*, 177n51; Madinat al-Zahra', 20, *21*, 162n21, 164n57; as Umayyad capital, 87, 125. *See also* Umayyads (Cordoba)
Council of Chalcedon (451), 48, 111, 173n51
Creswell, K. A. C.: on Aqsa Mosque, *141*, 178n63; on Mausoleum of Badr al-Jamali, 169n22; on minarets of Mosque of al-Hakim, 73, *74*, 169n23, 169n30; on Mosque of al-Azhar, 29–30, 164n67; on Mosque of al-Hakim, 33, *33*; on Mosque of al-Lu'lu'a ("the Pearl"), 130, *130*; on al-Qahira, 163n39; on Qarafa cemetery ruins, 172n7; on renovation of minarets of Mosque of al-Hakim, 99; on staircases and space between minaret and bastion, 100
Crone, Patricia, 5, 161n8
Crusades, 1, 4, 11, 40, 157–58
Damascus: Abbasids moving capital to Baghdad from, 134; under Fatimid control, 109; minarets of mosque of, 73, 81
dār al-'ilm (house of knowledge) established by al-Hakim, 86–87, 92, 95, 96, 101, 103, 105, 120, 154, 155, 170n59
da'wa. *See* Ismaili Shi'ism
den Heijer, Johannes, 56
destruction of Christian churches and monuments: under al-Hakim, 10–11, 89, 96, 101, 105–13, 112–13, 117, 123, 125, 131, 155, 171n70; under al-Mansur, 121–22; under al-Mu'izz and al-'Aziz, 67, 106; under al-Mutawakkil, 175n89; under al-Zahir, 150. *See also* Church of the Holy Sepulcher
dhimmīs: al-Hakim's treatment of, 70, 87–89, 95, 118–20, 127, 131, 155, 171n73, 172–73n34; *muḥtasibs* (Islamic market inspectors), role of, 118–19, 155, 175n79; al-Mu'izz and al-'Aziz's tolerance of, 47–51, 64–65, 67, 69, 110, 153; as "People of the Book," 7, 48; restrictions and dress codes imposed on, 56, 90, 117–19, 131; al-Zahir's treatment of, 132. *See also* Christians; interfaith relations among Muslims, Jews, and Christians; Jews
Dome of Gabriel (Jerusalem), 147
Dome of the Prophet (Jerusalem), 147, *147*
Dome of the Rock (Jerusalem), *128*, *132*, 133–36, *137*, 140–41, 144–47, *146*, *148*, 173n36, 176n34, 177n41, 177n56, 178n70
Druze: contemporary configuration of, 175n5; five-pointed star adopted by, 93; al-Hakim's divinity and, 69–70, 127, 128; rise of, 11, 128–31, 156; al-Zahir's attempts to counter heresy of, 127, 132, 140, 149
Durzan (mother of al-'Aziz), 44, 130

Fadl ibn Salih, 66–67, 91
Fahd ibn Ibrahim, 71, 88
Fakhr al-Mulk, 115, 124

Fatima (daughter of Muhammad), 4, 20, 81
Fatimid caliphate: architectural sources for, 3, 7–9, 162n25; caliph's role, 5; ceremonies, importance of, 32, 37, 121, 164n71; dynasty as descendants from Muhammad, 84–86; economy of, 91, 164n50; as golden age, 1, 47, 51, 64–65, 156, 157; history, 3–6; Imam's role and presence, 5–6, 14, 18–20, 23, 27, 44, 86, 115–16, 153, 161n17, 163n26; al-Kirmani on, 114; Maghreb period, 14–23; map of, *2*; origins of, 14; rival caliphates, 4–6, 115; as Seveners, 161n17; turmoil at end of al-Hakim's reign, 128–29; visual expressions of legitimacy, 3, 4, 23, 151, 157. *See also* Ismaili Shi'ism; *specific rulers*
Fatimid palace (al-Mahdiyya), 13, 16–19
Fatimid palace (al-Mansuriyya), 19–20
Fatimid palace (al-Qahira), 9, 36–45; administration outside walls of, 44; carved wooden beams, 38, *38–40*, 53, 165n86; construction of, 44, 45, 165n76; demise of, 165n79; eastern and western sections, 37, 162n14; Hugh of Caesaria describing, 40–42; *majālis al-ḥikma* (Sessions of Wisdom) at, 42, 83, 103, 128, 153, 174n61; Nasir-i Khusraw's description of, 37–38, 165n84; poets celebrating importance of, 13, 42; restorations under al-Mustansir, 37; societal hierarchy in relationship to, 44, 45; walls and gates, 37–38; watchmen and other workers at, 37, 40–41
Flood, Finbarr, 158
Flury, Samuel, 172n8
Fulcher, Geoffrey, 40–41
Fustat-Misr, 8, 24–32; anti-Sunni messages from al-Hakim in, 154; Ben Ezra Synagogue, 49, 162n26; burning of (1020), 69, 129; ceremonial merging with al-Qahira, 121; Christian churches in, 56; Christians in, 49, 55, 88; al-Hakim's rule of, 103; intermingling of religions in, 58, 95; Jews in, 49; map of, *25*; ritual processions in, 32, 121. *See also* Mosque of 'Amr; Mosque of Ibn Tulun

Geniza documents, 49, 88, 162n26, 179n6
al-Ghazali, 119–20
Goitein, Shelomo Dov, 179n6
Grabar, Oleg, 147, 176nn26–27, 176n30, 177n41, 177n49
Great Palace. *See* Fatimid palace (al-Qahira)
grilled windows, *83*, 83–84, *85*

al-Hafiz (Fatimid Imam-caliph r. 1130–49), 29
al-Hakam II (Andalusi Umayyad caliph r. 961–76), 21, 161n16, 175n88
al-Hakim bi-Amr Allah (Fatimid Imam-caliph r. 996–1021): architectural program of early years of, 70–72, 92, 154; architectural program of final years of, 127, 156; architectural program of middle years of, 95, 113, 120–25, 155; born in Cairo (985), 69, 71; childhood name of al-Mansur, 70–71; Christian mother of, 50, 110; Christians, relationship with, 3, 88–90, 119, 125, 131, 154, 172–73n34; as "Commander of the Faithful," 117; compared to al-Mansur (ruler of al-Andalus r. 978–1002), 122; compared to al-Mu'izz and al-'Aziz, 69, 90, 123, 154; death/disappearance of (1021), 132, 149, 176n18; divinity of, 69–70, 127, 128, 129, 149; endowments of, 102–3, 105, 117, 120, 125, 155; extent of kingdom of, 103, 123; final years of (1017–21), 127–28; glorified use of his name, 84, 149, 170n46; ideological propaganda program and popularity of, 113, 115–16, 123, 175n91; known as "mad" Egyptian caliph, 1, 3, 10, 69, 110, 121, 154, 158; medieval scholars' opinions on reign of, 176n17; middle years of (1007–13), 96–97; most notable events associated with, 69, 92, 121, 154; patronage of, 70, 87, 96, 105, 117, 125; religious changes during his reign, 95–96, 101, 102, 115–16, 119, 120, 124–25, 128, 131, 154–56, 174n61, 176n15; violence and cruelty of, 69, 71, 169n9. *See also dār al-'ilm*; destruction of Christian churches and monuments; minarets of Mosque of al-Hakim; Mosque of al-Hakim; Mosque of al-Maqs; Mosque of Rashida
Halm, Heinz, 170n59
Hamdanids, 6
Hamilton, Robert, 135, 177n46
Hanafism, 161n16
Hanging Church (al-Mu'allaqa) (Cairo), 59, *60*, 61, 62
Haram al-Sharif (Jerusalem), 127–28, *128*, 133–40, *146*, 150–51; Nasir-i Khusraw's description of, 144–45. *See also* Aqsa Mosque; Dome of the Rock
Harun al-Rashid (Abbasid caliph r. 786–809), 107, 173n38
al-Hasan ibn Bishr al-Dimashqi, 66
Hasanids, 24
Helena (Byzantine empress r. 325–30), 106
Herz, Max, 100
Hilal al-Sabi', 109, 172n34
ḥisba manuals, 118–20
The History of the Patriarchs of the Egyptian Church (multiple authors), 9, 56–58, 60, 63, 66, 110–11, 113, 131, 132, 172n34, 173n45
Holy Sepulcher. *See* Church of the Holy Sepulcher
Hugh of Caesaria, 40–41, 162n1
Husayn (grandson of Muhammad), 4
Husaynids, 24

Ibn al-Athir, 66
Ibn al-Haytham, 105
Ibn Aybak, 164n68
Ibn Duqmaq, 28
Ibn Hani', 20
Ibn Hayyan, 122
Ibn 'Idhari, 13, 17–18, 19, 121–22
Ibn Ilyas (cousin of al-Hakim), 129, 132, 149, 156
Ibn al-Jarrah, 96–97
Ibn Khallikan, 176n17
Ibn Killis, 164n68
Ibn al-Qalanisi, 110
Ibn Raga's conversion to Christianity, 88, 113
Ibn Taghribirdi, 176n17
ibn Yunis, 'Ali ibn 'Abd al-Rahman, 105
Idrisids, 6
Ikhshidids, 24, 27, 58, 136, 173n40, 177n40
image destruction: al-Hakim as "image breaker," 158, 179n11; Muslims using to provoke destruction of churches, 123; Protestant Reformation and, 179n11
Institute of Ismaili Studies, 8–9, 174n62
interfaith relations among Muslims, Jews, and Christians, 4, 7, 51, 56, 64, 162n26; apogee in tenth to thirteenth centuries, 1, 179n6; comparing premodern with modern Islam's position, 179n7; in Crusades period, 157–58, 179n6; mingling of shared art forms between Islam and Christianity and between Islam and Judaism, 51, 57–58. *See also dhimmīs*
international trade, 5, 26, 49, 162n26, 164n50
Iraq. *See* Abbasid caliphate
'Isa ibn Nasturus, 48, 67
Isma'il b. Ja'far al-Sadiq, 4
Ismaili Shi'ism of Fatimids: Baghdad Manifesto against, 124; calling themselves "People of Truth," 6; *da'wa* (mission) and *dā'īs* (missionaries), 5–6, 14, 43, 45, 81, 86, 113, 115, 128, 129, 155, 170n50, 174n61; Druze and, 129; early schism in, 162n6; Ismailization efforts of al-Hakim, 90, 92, 93; *isrā'* and *mi'rāj* story's interpretation by, 149; meaning of Fatimid architecture for, 9, 14, 42–45, 81–83, 153, 154, 159; Nasir-i Khusraw's conversion to, 165n80; oath of secrecy required in, 43; in al-Qahira, 29; relationship with and differences from Sunni

Ismaili Shi'ism of Fatimids, *continued*: majority, 1, 4–6, 8, 24, 28–29, 50, 67, 175n95; revelation of hidden truths, 43–44, 82, 83; sources on, 7–8; symbolism of, 1, 10, 42, 70, 81–84, 93, 170n35, 178n75; *ta'wīl* (allegorical interpretation) in, 5, 43, 81–82, 86, 93, 97, 101, 114, 124, 154; turmoil at end of al-Hakim's reign, 128–29. *See also bāṭin* vs. *ẓāhir*; Fatimid caliphate
al-Istakhri, 124

Jarrahid revolt (1010), 71, 96–97, 102, 172n13
Jawhar (Fatimid general), 23–29, 36–37, 50–51, 58, 96, 103, 163n39
Jerusalem: Abbasid control of (751–973), 107, 134–36; Charlemagne and Carolingian investment in, 107, 173n38; Crusades and, 157; destruction as defining act of identity of, 179n12; earthquake damage in, 134, 135, 150; under Fatimid control, 3, 4, 106, 136–40, 144–45, 151; al-Hakim allowing church reconstruction, 131; ideological reasons for al-Zahir's choosing to restore, 127, 132, 140, 149, 156, 158; Ikhshidids and, 136; Islamic ascension story and change in meaning of city to Fatimids, 140, 176n27; Jarrahid revolt threatening Fatimid power in, 97; minarets of mosque of, 73, 81; Muslim grassroots efforts to restore and embellish the city, 134–36, 151; Nasir-i Khusraw's description of, 37, 165n80; as pilgrimage destination, 109, 119, 144, 145, 177n56, 178n81; al-Qadi al-Nu'man on praying in mosque of, 81; religious strife in tenth century in, 108–9; Umayyads and, 134, 136, 139, 143; al-Zahir's restoration of, 11, 127, 133–34, 136–44, 150–51, 156–57. *See also* Aqsa Mosque; Church of the Holy Sepulcher; Dome of the Rock; Haram al-Sharif
Jews: conversion to Islam, 113; Copts and, 9; distinctive clothing, required to wear, 90, 119, 171n73; Fatimids and, 24, 48, 49–50; first and second temple in Jerusalem, 139, 179n12; Geniza documents and, 49, 88, 162n26; al-Hakim's treatment of, 3, 90; in Jerusalem, 108; Karaites, 49–50; Muslim-Christian alliance at expense of, 65; Rabbanites, 49–50; relations among Muslims, Jews, and Christians, 4, 7, 51, 56, 64, 158, 162n26; al-Zahir's treatment of, 132. *See also dhimmīs*
jizya (tax paid by non-Muslims), 7, 48
John I Tzimiskes (Byzantine emperor r. 969–76), 109

Kafur, 24, 173n40
Karaites, 49–50
Khamarawaih ibn Ahmad ibn Tulun, 57–58
Kharijites, 15, 16, 23, 102, 163n21
al-Kindi: *Khiṭaṭ Miṣr* (Districts of Egypt), 57
al-Kirmani, 9, 113–20, 123–25, 128–29, 155, 175n91; *Lights to Illuminate the Proof of the Imamate*, 115
Koerner, Joseph, 179n11
Kufic script, 35, *35*, 75, *76*, 77, 82, 100, *100*, 103, 136, 169n25, 169n29
Kutubiyya Mosque (Marrakech), 163n27

light, significance of, 29, 83–84, 93, 124, 154, 170nn40–41, 177n53; Gothic use of light metaphor, 170n44
luster ceramics, 18, *18*, *46*, 53–55, *54–55*

Madaba (Jordan) mosaic, 106, *108*
Maghreb, 9; Fatimid cities in, 14–23; Fatimid rule over, 3, 15, 23; al-Hakim's rule of, 103; Umayyad in rivalry for allegiance of, 6. *See also* al-Mahdiyya; al-Mansuriyya
al-Mahdi (Abbasid caliph r. 775–85), 134, 135, 140, 148, 176n36
al-Mahdi (Fatimid Imam-caliph r. 909–34), 4, 15, 27
al-Mahdiyya (Tunisia), 9, 14, 15, 23, 162n11; as Fatimid capital, 19; Great Mosque of, 16, *17*, 73; map of, *16*; marble relief with musician and seated ruler, 18, *18*, 38; sacred royal city separate from urban areas in, 16–19, 163n48
Malik ibn Sa'id al-Fariqi, 103, 174n61
Maliki Sunnism, 15, 23, 161n16
Mamluks, 8, 24, 99, 158, 164n74
al-Ma'mun (Abbasid caliph r. 813–33), 135–36, 170n59, 177n37
al-Mansur (Abbasid caliph r. 754–75), 134–35, 176n30
al-Mansur (Fatimid Imam-caliph r. 946–53), 19, 23, 27
al-Mansur (ruler of al-Andalus r. 978–1002), 121–23, 175n88
al-Mansur Abu 'Ali. *See* al-Hakim bi-Amr Allah
al-Mansuriyya (Egypt), 26–27
al-Mansuriyya (Tunisia), 9, 14, 19–20, 23–24, 29, 44, 162n21, 170n38
al-Maqqari, 122
al-Maqrizi, Taqi al-Din Ahmad b. 'Ali: on Cairo as seat of Fatimid caliphate, 27; on Christians and construction of churches, 56–58, 88–89, 171n70; on Church of the Holy Sepulcher, 109; on *dār al-'ilm* (house of knowledge) construction, 87; on Fatimid palace hierarchy, 43–44; on al-Hakim providing religious objects to Cairo's mosques, 105; on al-Hakim's endowments, 103; on al-Hakim's relationship with his subjects, 71; on al-Mansuriyya's fortifications, 26; on Mecca kaaba decoration, 148; on Monastery of al-Qusayr's destruction, 112; on Monastery of Saint John the Baptist, 174n58; on Mosque of al-Hakim, 32, 73, 97, 164–65n74; on Mosque of al-Lu'lu'a, 130; on Rashida mosque, 72; as source, 7, 8, 113, 165n76; on al-Zahir, 132–33
Marilhat, Prosper: *Ruins of the Mosque of al-Hakim*, 33, *33*
Mawhub ibn Mansur, 56
Mazyadids, 6
Mecca: counter-caliph to al-Hakim in, 71, 97; Fatimid control of, 4, 26–27, 163nn45–46; al-Hakim's rule of, 103; Jarrahid revolt threatening Fatimid power in, 97, 102; kaaba in, 13, 148; minarets of mosque of, 73, 81; Nasir-i Khusraw's description of, 37, 165n80; pilgrimage to, 27, 86, 97; al-Qadi al-Nu'man on praying in mosque of, 81; Umayyads and, 6
Medina: Fatamid control of, 4, 26, 103; Jarrahid revolt threatening Fatimid power in, 102; minarets of mosque of, 73, 81; al-Nu'man on praying in mosque of, 81
Melkite Christians, 9, 48–50, 57, 67, 89, 110, 111
memory devices, 82, 86, 125, 149, 178n74
Michael of Tinnis, 9, 56–57, 58, 59, 63–65, 71, 88, 110–11, 112, 174n54
minarets: Cordoban Umayyad use of, 21, *22*, 23, 162n16; meaning of term "minaret," 169n3; mosques with multiple minarets, 73, 81; style from ninth-century Baghdad, 102; in tenth century, Fatimids vs. Abbasids, 16, 23, 164n63
minarets of Mosque of al-Hakim, 10, 33, 93; covering of (bastions), 1, 11, 69, *94*, 95, 96, 97–102, *98*, 115–16, 120, 124, 130, 154, 155, 172n13; description of, 73–80, 169n23; grilled windows, *83*, 83–84, 170n43; height of, 162n16; inclusion of al-Hakim's name in, 113; inscriptions, 75, *76*, 77, 80, 81, 84, 100, *100*, 101, 155, 169n25, 170n45; meaning of choosing preservation instead of destruction of, 124–25; northern bastion, *98*, 99; northern minaret, 75, *75–76*, *83*; oratory of western minaret, *68*, 77, 80, *80*, 93, 124, 156, 169n30, 171n83; restoration in medieval period, 164n74; scholarly interpretation of, 81–86; western bastion, *98*, 99–100, *100*; western minaret, *74*, 77, *77–80*, *98*
minbars, 20–21, 23, 105, 179n12

Monastery of Khandaq (Cairo), 58
Monastery of al-Qusayr (Cairo), 57, 111–12, 131, 175n9
Monastery of Saint John the Baptist, 112, 174n58
mosaics: Aqsa Mosque, 140–43, 148, 177n49; Church of the Holy Sepulcher depicted in, 106, *108*; Great Mosque of Cordoba, 21, 177n51; Haram al-Sharif gateway, 144, 145; Mecca kaaba, 148; Monastery of al-Qusayr's depictions of Virgin Mary, 112; similarities between Haram al-Sharif and the Holy Sepulcher, 177n50
Mosque of ʿAmr (Cairo), 24, 30, 89, 92, 105, 119, 121
Mosque of al-Aqmar (Cairo), 29, 84, *85*, 87, 130, 165n78, 178n80
Mosque of al-Azhar (Cairo), 9, *12*, *30–31*; compared to Mosque of al-Hakim, 35; construction of, 29–32, 44, 45, 101, 164n61, 164n68; endowment of, 96, 103, 120, 155; minaret and, 162n16; naming of, 19–20, 29; wooden doors donated by al-Hakim, 103–5, *104*
Mosque of Constantinople, 111, 150
Mosque of Cordoba. *See* Cordoba
Mosque of al-Hakim (Cairo), 9, 10, *33–35*, 103–5; Bohra restoration (1980), 33, *34*, 164n74; built as al-Anwar mosque, 29, 32, 72–73, 92; compared to Mosque of al-Azhar and Mosque of Ibn Tulun, 35; concentric circle designs, use of, 81–82, 84, 93; connection to Fatimid palace, 32; construction and completion of, 32–35, 44, 45, 72, 73–86, 92–93, 105, 154; drawings of (by Creswell), *74–75*, *77*; floriated Kufic script, 35, *35*, 75, *76*, 77, 82, 100, *100*, 103, 169n25, 169n29; al-Hakim praying at, 121; inscriptions, *35*, 35–36, 73, 75, *76*, 80, 81, 82, 84–85, *100*, 101, 124, 172n8; minbar, 105; name of, 32; plan of, *34*, 35; portals, 73, 93; post-Fatimid developments, 33; stone towers, 70; al-Zahir and, 133. *See also* minarets of Mosque of al-Hakim
Mosque of Ibn Tulun (Cairo), 24, 29, 30, *35*, 35–36, 51, 100, 103, 105, 119
Mosque of al-Luʾluʾa ("the Pearl," Cairo), 129–30, *130*, 156
Mosque of al-Mahdiyya (Tunisia), 16, *17*, 73
Mosque of al-Maqs (Cairo), 169n14; endowment of, 96, 101, 103, 106, 120, 155, 172n24; al-Hakim's choice of location outside of al-Qahira, 72, 87, 92, 154
Mosque of Qarawiyyin (Fez, Morocco), 21
Mosque of Qayrawan (Tunisia), 16, *17*, 99, *99*, 102, 124
Mosque of Rashida (Cairo): built on site containing graves of Christians and Jews, 88, 105, 154; endowment of, 96, 101, 103, 106, 120, 155; al-Hakim praying at, 121; al-Hakim's choice of location outside of al-Qahira, 72, 87, 92, 154; initial mud brick structure and subsequent reconstruction in stone, 72, 106, 124; lamps decorated with animals in, 172n24
Mosque of Sfax (Tunisia), 99, *99*, 102, 124
Mosque of Sousse (Tunisia), 102
Mosque of Tunis (Tunisia), 102
Muʿawiya ibn Abi Sufyan, 90
Muhammad (prophet): Druze considering al-Hakim as superseding, 129; Fatimid caliphs as successors to, 4, 80; *isrāʾ* (night journey) and *miʿrāj* (ascension), 139–42, 144, 146–49, 177n56, 178n70; Mosque of al-Aqmar facade including name of, 84; Mosque of al-Hakim celebrating family of, 84; staff of, 32
muḥtasib. *See ḥisba* manuals
al-Muʿizz li-Din Allah (Fatimid Imam-caliph r. 953–75), 23–28, 44, 58–67; Cairo and, 45; Christian churches and their destruction under, 47, 66, 67, 92, 106; Christians' relationship with, 58–59, 67, 69, 153; compared to al-Hakim, 69, 90, 123, 154; gold dinar from reign of, *82*; Great Palace and, 36; house of wisdom (*dār al-ḥikma*) as distinguished from house of knowledge (*dār al-ʿilm*) and, 165n93; Jerusalem and, 133; monuments built under, 44; Muqattam miracle and fictitious conversion to Christianity, 63, 65, 173n45; Yaʿqub ibn Killis as vizier under, 48
Mulder, Stephennie, 158
al-Muqaddasi, 19, 26, 108, 135, 163n22, 176n34
Muqattam Hills (Cairo), 26, 62, *130*, 175n9; al-Hakim and, 69, 105, 129, 132, 156; Mosque of al-Luʾluʾa, 129–30, *130*, 156; observatory constructed in, 105
Muqattam miracle, 59–66, *62*, 173n45
Musa (Jewish friend of Yaʿqub ibn Killis), 59–61
al-Musabbihi, 87, 103, 164n68, 169n15, 169n19, 177n45
muṣallā (open-air prayer space), 28, 30, 32, 93, 164n57
Muslims: on al-Hakim's policies toward Christians, 89, 110, 131; on al-Muʿizz policies toward Christians, 65–66; relations among Muslims, Jews, and Christians, 4, 7, 51, 56, 64, 162n26. *See also* call to prayer; Ismaili Shiʿism; Sunnis
al-Mustansir (Fatimid Imam-caliph r. 1036–94), 37, 144, 157
al-Mutawakkil (Abbasid caliph r. 847–61), 166n2, 171n74, 175n89

Nahya Monastery (Giza), 58–59, 112
Nasir-i Khusraw: on Cairo's pre-capital status, 164n55; conversion to Ismailism, 165n80, 177n54; on Fatimid palace, 7, 37–38, 45; on Jerusalem's Aqsa Mosque, 177n49, 177n53; on Jerusalem's Haram al-Sharif, 136, 140, 144–45, 146; on reconstruction of Church of the Holy Sepulcher, 178n88
Necipoğlu, Gülru, 176n27
Nestorians, 67, 168n58, 173n53
Nikephoros I (patriarch), 150
Nikephoros II Phokas (Byzantine emperor r. 963–69), 109
al-Nuʿman, al-Qadi, 14, 28, 43, 51, 82, 162n4, 162n16, 171n2, 174n61; *Asās al-taʾwīl* (The foundation of allegorical interpretation), 149; *The Pillars of Islam*, 51, 81, 114; *Taʾwīl al-daʿāʾim* (The allegorical interpretation of the pillars), 81, 114

Pact of ʿUmar, 48, 89, 117–18, 155, 174n74
Palestine: Fatimid architecture in, 7; Fatimid control in peril in, 140; Fatimid desire to conquer, 27; Jarrahids in power over, 97. *See also* Jerusalem
pilgrimages: Christian pilgrimages to Church of the Holy Sepulcher, 109, 119, 178n81; to Fatimid palace and al-Qahira, 42, 80, 81, 84, 153, 170n54; hajj to Mecca, 27, 86, 97; to Imam's palace, 20; Jerusalem as destination, 144, 145, 176n30; minarets of Mosque of al-Hakim, significance for, 81, 170n54; safe travel assured for, 24
Pyxis of al-Mughira, 18, *19*

al-Qadir (Abbasid caliph r. 991–1031), 124
al-Qahira: ceremonial merging with Fustat-Misr, 121; *dār al-ʿilm* (house of knowledge) established in, 86–87; establishment of, 23–27; first coin minted with name of, 163–64n49; al-Hakim's rule of, 103; hierarchy of monuments within, 44; map of, *25*, *36*; al-Maqrizi as source on, 8; meaning of name, 27, 163–64n49; open-air prayer space (*muṣallā*), 28, 30, 32, 164n57; as palace-city, 28–45; as pilgrimage destination, 81, 84, 170n54; restricted access to, 28; usage compared to "Cairo," 161n2. *See also* Fatimid palace (al-Qahira)
al-Qaʾim (Fatimid Imam-caliph r. 935–46), 19, 27
Qalqashandi, 164n68
Qarafa cemetery (Cairo), 44, 129, 130, 156
Qarafa Mosque (Cairo), 130, 165n102
Qarmatians, 26, 27, 162n6, 177n43

Qayrawan (Tunisia): Abu Rakwa settling in, 90; Aghlabids in, 15; Great Mosque of Qayrawan, 16, *17*, 99, *99*, 102, 124
Qirwash ibn Muqallad, 123–24
Qur'anic verses, 5, 6; 2:256, 132; 5:55, 82; 9:18, 84–86; 9:107, 102; 11:73, 84; 17:1, 141, 147, 178n66; 24:26–28, 101, 116; 24:27, 172n16; 24:35, 83; 62:9, 101–2. *See also specific mosques for inscriptions*

Rabbanites, 49–50
Rabbat, Nasser, 162n16, 164n57, 164n63
Ravaisse, Paul, 165n76
religious identity: changes under al-Hakim, 95–96, 101, 102, 115–16, 119, 120, 124–25, 128, 131, 154–56, 174n61, 176n15; complexity of, 4, 7, 111, 156, 158; relationship with architectural space, 1, 3, 153–55, 161n5; in rivalry among caliphates, 6–7. *See also bāṭin* vs. *ẓāhir*; *dhimmīs*; Ismaili Shi'ism; Sunnis
Romanos III Argyros (Byzantine emperor r. 1028–34), 136, 150
al-Ruknu al-Deen Baybars al-Jashankir, 164n74

Sabra al-Mansuriyya, 19
Salamiyya (Syria), 14–15
Saleh, Marlis, 173n45, 176n17
Samaan the Tanner, 61
Samarra, 20, 23, 40, 51, 134, 162n21, 163n22. *See also* Abbasid caliphate
Sanders, Paula, 28, 32, 81, 102, 121, 163n48, 164n71, 170n50, 170n60, 172n13
Santiago de Compostela (Spain), destruction of Christian shrine of, 121–23
Sawirus ibn al-Muqaffa', 56, 59, 61, 65
Sevener Shi'ism, 161n17
al-Shabushti: *Al-Dīyārāt* (The monasteries), 57
sharī'a (Islamic law), 5, 24, 43, 51, 56, 114, 117–19, 129, 155
al-Shayzari, 119
Shepard, Jonathan, 178n81
Shi'ism, sects of, 6–7. *See also* Abbasid caliphate; Buyids; Fatimid caliphate; Ismaili Shi'ism
al-Sijistani, 43, 45, 82, 170n39, 171n6
Sitt al-Mulk (r. 1021–23), 50, 70, 130, 132, 150
Slav Mukhtar, 87
Spain. *See* al-Andalus; Umayyads (Cordoba)
Sufis, 136
Suleymaniye Mosque (Istanbul), 178n72
Sunni Revival, transformation of writing in, 170n37
Sunnis, 3; anti-Fatimid views of, 1, 4–6, 8, 24, 28–29, 50, 67, 175n95; conversion efforts of Fatimids to make Sunnis join Shi'ism, 113, 115–16, 123, 175n91; al-Hakim's anti-Sunni policies, 92, 96, 120, 154, 175n82; al-Hakim's covering of minarets as part of rapprochement with, 1, 96, 102, 115–16, 124–25, 155; madrasas, 170n55; Maliki, 15, 23, 161n16. *See also* Abbasid caliphate; Abu Rakwa revolt; al-Andalus; Companions of the Prophet Muhammad
Syria: Fatimid architecture in, 7; Fatimids fighting for control of, 4, 27, 177n43; al-Hakim's rule of military districts of, 103. *See also* Byzantine empire; Damascus

Tabbaa, Yasser, 170n37
Tulunids, 58, 136, 177n40
Tunisia: Aghlabids in, 15; Fatimid architecture in, 7, 14, 26, 153; al-Mahdi in, 15. *See also* al-Mahdiyya; al-Mansuriyya
Twelver Shi'ism, 6, 117, 124, 161n8, 178n79

'Umar ibn Khattab (r. 633–44), 117–19
Umayyads (Cordoba): Abassid forms and, 163n22; Abu Rakwa and, 90–91, 96, 120; campaigns against Christians, 122; coins using "Imam" title for ruler, 163n26; compared to Fatimid caliphate, 116–17; cursing of Imams by, 179n1; declaration of caliphate (929), 20; decline in power of, 90; "false Imams" of, 115; Holy War against Fatimids, 15, 20–21; Malikism and, 161n16; al-Mansur (r. 978–1002), 121–23; minarets, 21, *22*, 23, 162n16; origins of, 4; Pyxis of al-Mughira, 18, *19*; visual expressions of legitimacy, 3, 4, 23
Umayyads (Damascus): Abassid defeat of (750), 134; Jerusalem and, 134, 136, 139, 143
Umm al-Rasas (Jordan), mosaic from, 106
Uqaylids, 6
urbanism of al-Hakim, 10, 69–70, 154, 170n60; compared to other caliphates, 153; Ismailization efforts of al-Hakim, 90, 92; middle years of al-Hakim and, 95, 117, 120–25; Muslim resistance to and obstacles to church restoration and construction, 10, 65–66, 88–89, 154, 171n70. *See also* Cairo; Fustat-Misr; Mosque of al-Maqs; Mosque of Rashida; al-Qahira
'Uthman's Qur'an, 23, 171n83

van Berchem, Max, 100, 173n44
vizier's role, 42, 48, 59, 67, 73, 169n19

Walker, Paul, 113, 115, 165n93, 174n61, 175n91
walled cities, 15–16, 26, 28, 45, 99, 163n39
William of Tyre, 13, 42, 45, 109–10, 113, 173n52
Williams, Caroline, 178n80
women: *dhimmī* women, dress requirements for, 119; al-Hakim's restrictions on, 3, 72, 101, 116, 175n79; mosque-tomb complexes of Fatimid women, 44; in societal hierarchy, 44
woodwork: carved wooden beams (Fatimid palace), 38, *38–40*, 53, 165n86; church screen (Church of Saint Barbara), *52–53*, 53; wooden doors (Mosque of al-Azhar), 103–5, *104*

Yahya al-Antaki: on Abu Rakwa's revolt, 91, 171n78; on Church of the Holy Sepulcher destruction, 110, 173–74n53; on Church of the Holy Sepulcher restoration, 150; on conversion of Christians and Jews to Islam, 113; emigration of, 176n12; on Fatimid Egypt, 57; on Fatimid relations with Byzantine empire, 67; on al-Hakim's ideological propaganda, 123; on al-Hakim's justice, 88–89; on al-Hakim's permission for Christian church reconstruction, 131; on al-Hakim's religious reversals, 171n71, 176n15; on al-Hakim's sanity, 69, 154; on al-Hakim's treatment of Sunnis, 175n82; al-Zahir's reign not covered by, 133
Ya'qub ibn Killis, 48, 59–61, 66, 73
Yemen, 3, 6–7

Zacharius (patriarch), 88
ẓāhir. *See bāṭin* vs. *ẓāhir*
al-Zahir (Fatimid Imam-caliph r. 1021–36): compared to al-Hakim, 132; ideological reasons for choosing to restore Jerusalem, 127, 132, 140, 149, 156, 158; peace treaty with Byzantines, 111, 136, 150; reopening of Mosque of Constantinople and, 174n55; restoration of Christian Jerusalem and, 150–51; restoration of Jerusalem and, 127, 133–34, 136–44, 156–57; as successor of al-Hakim, 127, 129. *See also* Church of the Holy Sepulcher
Zaydis, 6–7